ANCIENT INDO-EUROPEAN DIALECTS

ANCIENT INDO-EUROPEAN DIALECTS

Proceedings of the
Conference on Indo-European Linguistics
Held at the University of California, Los Angeles
April 25-27, 1963

Edited by

HENRIK BIRNBAUM *and* JAAN PUHVEL

UNIVERSITY OF CALIFORNIA PRESS

Berkeley and Los Angeles

1966

UNIVERSITY OF CALIFORNIA PRESS
BERKELEY AND LOS ANGELES, CALIFORNIA

CAMBRIDGE UNIVERSITY PRESS
LONDON, ENGLAND

© 1966 BY THE REGENTS OF THE UNIVERSITY OF CALIFORNIA

LIBRARY OF CONGRESS CATALOG CARD NUMBER: 65–28528

PREFACE

In a broad sense, the conference here recorded in print constitutes a sequel to the Conference on Indo-European Linguistics held at the University of Texas in May, 1959, under the chairmanship and subsequent editorship (*Evidence for Laryngeals*) of Werner Winter. The idea of perpetuating and regularizing such close-knit and centripetal meetings of American Indo-Europeanists was born in informal conversations at the Ninth International Congress of Linguists in August, 1962, possibly as a reaction to the bewildering diaspora of endeavors and the lack (or incongeniality) of focus at that mass reunion.

In the administrative frame of the Center for Research in Languages and Linguistics, and with the direct support of the Chancellor of the University of California, Los Angeles, the preparations began in November, 1962, and culminated in meetings on the UCLA campus on Thursday, April 25 (papers by Hoenigswald, Lehmann, Watkins, Beeler, Polomé, Cowgill), and Friday morning, April 26 (Hamp, Emeneau, Senn), and at the University of California Conference Center at Lake Arrowhead in the San Bernardino Mountains on Friday night (Birnbaum) and Saturday morning, April 27 (Collinder, Winter, Lane, Puhvel). In addition to the visitors and local participants who presented papers, the conference was attended by five members of the faculty of the U.S. Army Language School at Monterey, California (M. Beliakoff, S. Kaminski, M. Marku, A. Potop, M. Stude), and by numerous linguistic scholars of the University of California. A number of these (J. Erickson, M. Han, H. Hoijer, W. Welmers, T. Wilbur, D. Worth, G. Worth) participated in the residential part of the conference at Lake Arrowhead. Numerous family members of the participants, from near and far, stayed at the Arrowhead Center to enjoy the mountain setting enhanced by a late-season snowfall.

The topic of the conference was chosen with a view to utilizing to best advantage the unique and varied competences of the participants. Each author was asked to treat the area that best suited his particular specialization in the field of Indo-European languages. It was decided to concentrate on delimitation of subgroups as such, as a necessary first step, rather than attacking at the same time such vast overall dialect issues as the *satəm* question or the ideas of certain authors regarding "Southern" or "European" dialect groupings. Further reflections on the nature of the general topic and on possible future treatments are found at the end of the final paper in this volume.

The discussions accompanying each contribution were recorded; the authors were subsequently provided with the materials pertaining to their papers and asked to ready the latter for print in the light of comments and hindsights. All works published here are such end products, except for those of M. S. Beeler, who did not submit a revised version, and B. Collinder, whose paper is a summary of an oral presentation somewhat apart from the main topic.

In editing, we have striven for a reasonable degree of external stylistic uniformity, yet without attempting to cramp the individual propensities of the contributors in regard to such matters as the type of references, quotations, and footnotes. Sometimes current minor variations in symbolizing Indo-European forms have likewise been allowed to stand (e. g., *ŭ* beside ə, *k′* beside *k̂*, when preferred by the authors). No general index has been thought necessary, since most papers are relatively self-contained in their respective areas. Only well-known abbreviations current in Indo-European linguistics have been consistently employed; self-evident partial, or locally explained abbreviations have generally been left to the discretion of the authors.

The copy of these proceedings has profited from helpful comments kindly supplied by Professor Yakov Malkiel of the University of California, Berkeley. We also acknowledge with gratitude a generous publication subsidy from the Ford Foundation Grant for International Training and Comparative Studies, administered by the Institute of International and Foreign Studies at UCLA.

In presenting the results of these deliberations to the scholarly world at large, we hope to have taken another step toward organized regular self-expression for Indo-European studies in America. May the line drawn from Austin in 1959 to Los Angeles in 1963 extend to other seats of learning in years to come!

H. B., J. P.

CONTENTS

CRITERIA FOR THE SUBGROUPING OF LANGUAGES
Henry M. Hoenigswald 1

THE GROUPING OF THE GERMANIC LANGUAGES
Winfred P. Lehmann 13

ITALO-CELTIC REVISITED
Calvert Watkins 29

THE INTERRELATIONSHIPS WITHIN ITALIC
Madison S. Beeler 51

THE POSITION OF ILLYRIAN AND VENETIC
Edgar G. Polomé 59

ANCIENT GREEK DIALECTOLOGY IN THE LIGHT OF MYCENAEAN
Warren C. Cowgill 77

THE POSITION OF ALBANIAN
Eric P. Hamp 97

THE DIALECTS OF OLD INDO-ARYAN
M. B. Emeneau 123

THE RELATIONSHIPS OF BALTIC AND SLAVIC
Alfred Senn 139

THE DIALECTS OF COMMON SLAVIC
Henrik Birnbaum 153

DISTANT LINGUISTIC AFFINITY
Björn Collinder 199

TRACES OF EARLY DIALECTAL DIVERSITY IN OLD ARMENIAN
Werner Winter 201

Criteria for the Subgrouping of Languages

Henry M. Hoenigswald
UNIVERSITY OF PENNSYLVANIA

Since the problem of subclassification is the problem of the family tree itself it is not surprising that it should have been extensively discussed in the literature, both general and Indo-Europeanist.[1] As the remainder of this conference is devoted to the specific Indo-European aspects, I prefer to treat, under the assigned heading of "Criteria for the Subgrouping of Languages," just that: the criteria to be followed in the establishment of linguistic subclassifications in general. I accept it as part of the assignment that subgrouping in the genealogic sense (as distinct from isoglossic overlapping in a graded area) is considered feasible, or rather that our interest is concentrated on particular families—of which Indo-European (IE) may or may not be one—for which the family tree is a realistic model.

It is not quite possible to divorce this, of all problems, from its history. Among the facts to be remembered is that the idea of the tree is much older than its reasoned use, inasmuch as it comes right down to us from the Tower of Babel as well as from the Greek conception that some nations are offshoots (by way of that conspicuous Greek institution, colonization) of other nations and that such past history can be recognized through a study of "similarities" in speech. In both these powerful traditions we have the motif of descent and differentiation; with the Greeks, specifically, differentiation by subsequent bifurcations. A. Borst's *Turmbau von Babel* gives an indication of the ramifications of the theology of dispersal. They deserve mention because of the extent to which they have set our minds in the direction of seeing something natural, even inevitable, in a table of descent by lines, nodes, and resultant strings. This conception was revitalized by an influence that could not help exerting itself very concretely in view of the close profes-

[1] Thanks are due to the Center for Advanced Study in the Behavioral Sciences at Stanford for facilitating work on this paper. J. Greenberg, *Essays in Linguistics* 48 (Chicago, 1957); M. Haas, *Lg.* 39.56 (1963), and many others imply that the question is customarily neglected. It is true that it is easier to prove relationship than subrelationship. But the criteria of subgrouping have constituted one of the most frequently discussed topics in comparative linguistics from the middle of the last century to this day.

sional association between nineteenth-century linguists and classical (and Germanist) text critics. I am here thinking particularly of that other pattern of lines, nodes, and strings: the stemma descending from its archetype.[2] Here, then, is one of the examples of apparent continuity of a concept reaching from so-called prescientific to scientific linguistics. It is well to remember that it is precisely such examples that pose the severest problems, as special care must be taken to recognize the different implications with which different periods will endow one and the same term.

Porzig[3] has ably described how the controversy about the "dialects" of Indo-European grew imperceptibly out of a situation characterized by self-evidence at the top—the family as a whole being well set off against other families; self-evidence near the bottom—the major subfamilies, such as Germanic and Greek, being equally well defined; and a major problem in between.[4] Within an area such as Romance, which more nearly approximates graded character, the lower boundary of the problem zone is fuzzy. Hall's notable and in many ways successful attempt to illustrate the workings of the Comparative Method and the family-tree concept with Romance material is conspicuously silent on one fundamental step, namely that whereby a given language is placed at a given node in the tree.[5] It may be said that the very coherence of the analysis offered there justifies the arrangement of the nodes. We shall begin by explaining how this is possible.

By way of an introduction let us consider two given (i.e., nonreconstructed) languages, A and B, which are recognized as related but about whose position in time, relative or absolute, we need claim no knowledge. If the Comparative Method is applied to all corresponding morphs, a reconstructed ancestor "language," X, is obtained in the sense that the phonemic changes (phoneme replacements) that occur between X and A and between X and B can be stated.[6] When this is done, we need to distinguish between two kinds of possible finding: (*a*) that both the historical phonologies, X > A and X > B, contain merger processes; or, (*b*), that one, say, X > A, contains no merger process, in which case we say that X collapses with A or is (phonemically) "like" A.[7] In tabular form,

---

[2] Cf. fn. 13 and *Anthropological Linguistics* 5.1.1–11 (1963).

[3] *Die Gliederung des indogermanischen Sprachgebiets* 17–52 (Heidelberg, 1954).

[4] See also Greenberg, *loc. cit.*

[5] *Lg.* 26.6–27 (1950); *Readings in Linguistics* 303–314 (Washington, 1957).

[6] My *Language Change and Linguistic Reconstruction* 144–150 (Chicago, 1960), and F. Householder, *IJAL* 28.79 (1962).

[7] This is entirely different from saying that the phonemic systems are identical.

(a)

	B
A	X

(b)

	B
A	A

where it is clear that the corresponding tree diagrams are

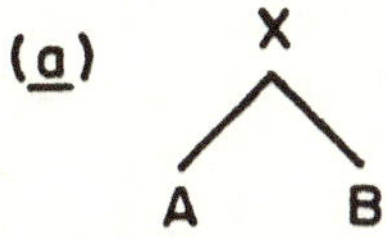

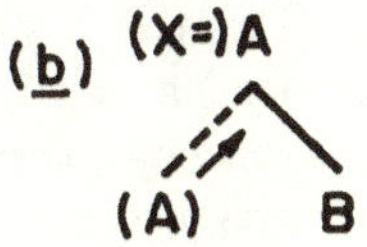

In other words, if the reconstructed ancestor of two languages is found to collapse with one of the two, this is necessarily the ancestor of the other. Descent is a special instance of relationship. It can be shown that questions such as whether Middle Persian is in truth the later stage of Old Persian, or whether Latin is the true ancestor of a given Romance language, are commonly argued on just these grounds (at least on the phonological side).

For a discussion of subgrouping, three or more languages are required. That three languages, A, B, and C, may form six different trees can be seen from the following classification of possible ancestors for all the 3(3–1)/2 = 3 language pairs.

1) We may find that the reconstructions made from two pairs—say A/B and A/C—are "alike," while the third reconstruction (B/C) is "different"; and that neither reconstruction is "like" A, B, or C. Labeling the first ancestor X, the second Y, we have

	B	C
A	X	X
B		Y

and hence,[8]

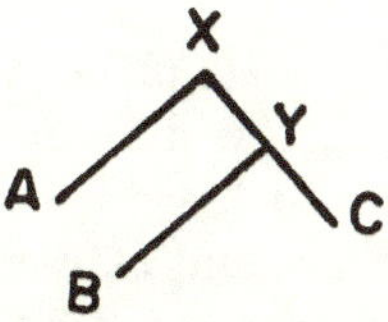

[8] The lengths of the limbs and limb sections (i.e., absolute time as well as the proportions among stretches of time) do not matter here (Greenberg's formulation, *loc. cit.*, may mislead some readers). All that matters is the configuration of the nodes with regard to each other. For this reason we keep varying the height of A, B, C, and Y in our diagrams.

None of the three given languages is an ancestor (or earlier stage). B and C form a subgroup (with regard to which A is "unaffiliated"). As a corollary, the ancestor of X/Y must be like X itself. Middle High German, Modern Greek, and Ancient Doric Greek are in the position of A, B, and C respectively. Here differentiation is greatest, and historical accident (i.e., the historical accident that an ancestor should exist in recorded form) at a minimum. The other five cases may be considered as special instances of the same, with collapsings.

2) All three reconstructed ancestors are alike, so that Y = X; but this X is different from A, B, and C:

	B	C
A	X	X
B		X

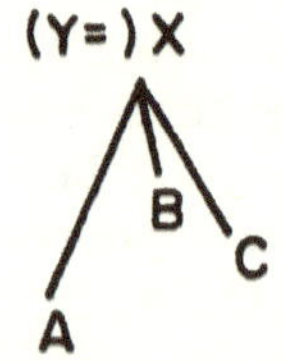

None of the given languages is an ancestor. There are no subgroups. The ancestors collapse into one another; there is a triple breakup instead of two bifurcations. Examples abound—at least such examples as are posited for the purpose of clinging to the tree model at all cost.

3) The reconstructed remote ancestor and the reconstructed subancestor differ, as in 1, but the remote ancestor is found to collapse with the unaffiliated language (X = A):

	B	C
A	A	A
B		Y

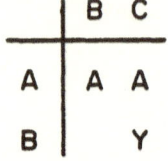

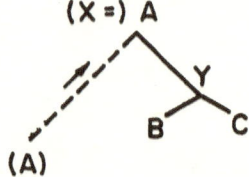

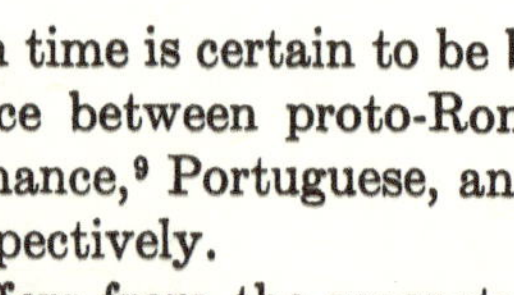

A is the ancestor of Y, B, and C. Its place in time is certain to be before B and C. Latin (disregarding the difference between proto-Romance and the literary language), proto-Ibero-Romance,[9] Portuguese, and Old Spanish are examples of A, Y, B, and C, respectively.

4) The reconstructed remote ancestor differs from the reconstructed subancestor, as in 1 and in 3, but the subancestor turns out to be like one of the members of the subgroup (Y = B):

---

[9] The validity of such constructs is accepted for the sake of the argument.

	B	C
A	X	X
B		B

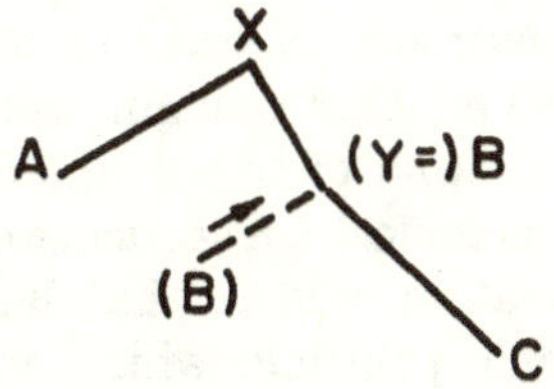

B is an older stage of C, and thus must antedate C.[10] Vedic Sanskrit, Latin (see above), and Spanish are in that position.

5) The reconstructed remote ancestor differs from the reconstructed subancestor, as in 1, 3, and 4, but the former is found to collapse with the unaffiliated language (X = A, as in 3) and the latter, with one of the members of the subgroup (Y = B, as in 4):

	B	C
A	A	A
B		B

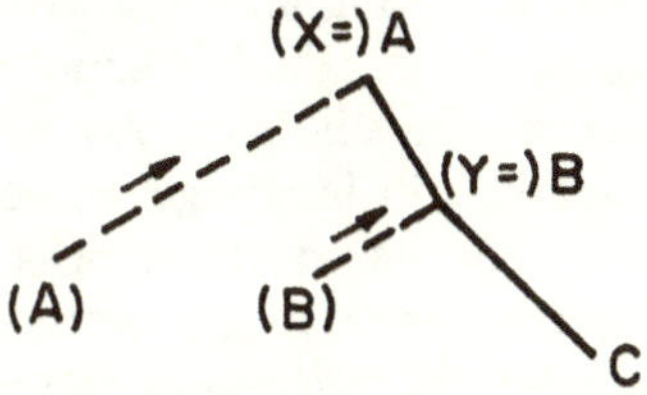

B is an older stage of C; A is an older stage of B and of C.

6) The reconstructed remote ancestor is like the reconstructed subancestor, as in 2, and also like one of the three given languages (see 3); Y = X = A):

	B	C
A	A	A
B		A

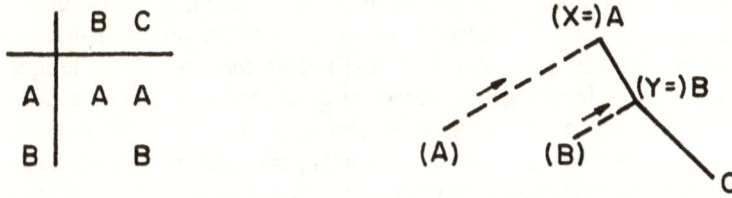

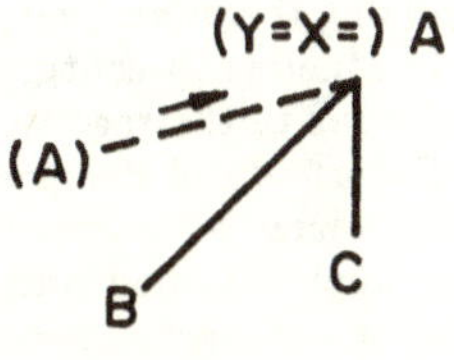

Latin, Sardinian, and Old Spanish may represent A, B, and C.

The preceding treatment, which can of course be extended to more than three languages, shows us what subrelationship is a special[11] instance of. Just as certain particular configurations among pairwise

[10] Where only one line of descent from a language is available, that language is often called an older stage, rather than an ancestor, of its descendants, although of course there is no consistency.

[11] Or rather, the most general.

reconstructions lead to a definition of the notion of descent—*b*, 3, 4, 5, 6—so another configuration (namely 1, as contrasted with 2) gives rise to the kind of tree diagram that depicts a subgrouping with all its real chronological consequences. Furthermore, we have here a partial demonstration, and to that limited extent a formal derivation, of Brugmann's principle which centers on the concept of a body of shared "innovations" (rather than on the degree of resemblance—a term that seems to be ineradicable from the literature).[12] The limitation in question consists in the fact that the classical "comparative" method which underlies our pairwise reconstructions applies to sound change only, whereas linguistic innovations are of course by no means all phonological.[13] Yet it is not an arbitrary limitation, since the Comparative Method has the very special property of furnishing us, in and of itself, with a clear separation between antecedent and replacement, hence, if you will, between retention and innovation of a sort. After all, the essence of the Comparative Method is simply to say that if (in our morph-to-morph translations) a phoneme /x/ or a distinctive feature /x/ of language A corresponds, in language B, sometimes to /y/ and sometimes to /z/, without correlated differences in the surrounding environment, the ancestor is like B, and A is the innovator; whereas, with such correlated environmental differences, the innovating language is B.

---

[12] I. Dyen, *Lg.* 29.577–590 (1953); C. D. Chrétien, *IJAL* 29.66–68 (1963), points out that priority should perhaps be accorded to Berthold Delbrück.

[13] The scholarly practice which the Brugmann-Delbrück principle summarizes was already part of the tools of the profession, being essentially that followed by August Schleicher who died in the late 1860's. Its sources, in turn, are many, but chief among them (and very active in Schleicher's own life history) is the influence of early nineteenth-century textual criticism with its reliance on the exclusively shared error in the reconstruction of the ramifications from a manuscript archetype. Delbrück and Brugmann were primarily trying to formulate their experience with Schleicher's Comparative Method, in which what was in fact handled were not so much retained and innovated features in the structure as retained and eliminated contrasts between forms. Making the necessary allowance for the difference in terminology, the claim was not that the "innovations" must be essential in the sense that they set one subgroup apart in typological complexion any more than the manuscript philologist will claim that the occurrence of certain copying errors in a given strain of codices essentially reveals the traditions or the outlook of the copyists. Quite the contrary, the value of a manuscript error lies precisely in its presumably mechanical, unspecific nature and in its lack of any relationship with relevant history. Its real function is to give away, by random accident, an otherwise irretrievable state of affairs. Just for that reason the theorists of text criticism like to point out that errors are not to be counted (although they must be weighed to guard against the probability of the same error arising twice independently). One shared error, if nontrivial in nature, may be sufficient to establish a manuscript family, at least in theory.

We can see what a so-called shared innovation is, and what it is not. Its prototype is the phonological merger in its precious irreversibility (e.g., the merger into /x/ of language A in the first alternative, above). Although Brugmann speaks of lexical and grammatical innovation as well, the argument comes back, again and again, to the safe grounds of sound change. Clearly, "innovation" in this sense is not at all the same thing as a "new feature." In fact, a merger which is not compensated again in some Martinetian shift must lead to a structural impoverishment rather than to an increase. Those IE languages (like Slavic or Iranian) in which voiced aspirates and nonaspirates fall together (*dh*, *d* > '*d*') "innovate," if not jointly, at least identically; and they do so precisely by giving up a feature, namely aspiration. This, perhaps, is relevant to C. Watkins' remarks on "negative innovation."[14]

Apropos of the IE word for the number "five", Watkins thinks it naïve to believe that the Latin *qu* and the archaic Celtic *q* are "same" in any simple, definable sense, the Latin *qu* being one structure point out of four, the Celtic *q* being one out of three, owing to the absence of a voiceless labial stop in Celtic.[15] This is, of course, absolutely right, and it is important that the point should have been made at last. It is also true, however, that once we rescue the Delbrück-Brugmann formula from its wrong implications, all is well. What makes the two assimilations of *p* > k^w (before another k^w in the word) identical "innovations" is the circumstance that an IE *p* merges with the same IE k^w in both Latin and Celtic, regardless of the systemic—or even only the phonetic—nature of the replacing phones and phonemes on each side.[16]

A Brugmannian innovation is thus both weaker and stronger than an innovated structure in the nontechnical sense.[17] Why it is weaker is easy to see. It is stronger precisely in being neutral, and in being statable in terms of unstructured yes-or-no items which remain invariant under any kind of systemic interpretation or notation that one might want to apply. No reasonable controversy can very well alter the fact that Latin *quīnque* 'five' and *quis* 'who' (with an old k^w) begin alike. In spite of their elemental character—or rather, just because their genuinely elemental

[14] See p. 31.

[15] See p. 34.

[16] This is not saying that this makes Italo-Celtic all right. It only means that this particular sound change is not so easily dismissed. Its Achilles's heel is elsewhere: the sequence $k^w \ldots k^w$ had existed in the ancestor only in reduplicated formations. Aside from these, the Celtic-Italic sound change is therefore not a true, homonymy-producing, irreversible merger, but only an exchange of features within a neutralized sector. See also note 27.

[17] See note 13.

character is frankly conceded—Brugmann's innovations are not open to the charge of atomism. This charge would be justified if illegitimate use were made of them—if, for instance, we were asked to list and count them, and then match these lists against lists representing other competing groupings of languages in some kind of test of strength. This would indeed immediately place us at the mercy of particular structural interpretations and particular notations, many of which are bound to have been chosen over different but equivalent notations by criteria that are not necessarily relevant. Everybody may well be agreed that the Verner mergers of the accentually conditioned instances of *p*, *t*, *k'*, k^w with *bh*, *dh*, *g'h*, g^wh in Germanic are not four innovations but one, as would have appeared from an appropriately chosen descriptive formulation in the first place. But this is only a ludicrously extreme case. The very countability of change events is a consistent notion only so long as uniqueness is claimed for one particular phonemic or componential statement of the two stages involved. To be sure, long itemized lists, often made to look impressive by judicious use of a favorable notation, are not lacking in the writings on subclassification problems, but they are acts of desperation. The milder tendency to accumulate evidence found in Brugmann and others is mainly a necessary hedge against accidental, independent duplication of innovations in separate daughter languages. Brugmannian innovations are not for counting—the question, in principle, is whether they are at all present or entirely absent in a given set of descendant languages. Of course, this amounts to saying that if languages A and B share an authentic "innovation" as against language C, then there can be none linking C and B against A. Where this nevertheless happens, as it frequently does, it indicates the inadequacy of the family tree as a device to depict a language relationship.

It is not always realized how very different lexical evidence is in this respect. Where A and B agree on some dictionary item (i.e., on a morph, or morph sequence, with phonemes that correspond), it may be ascribed to a common source, that is, if borrowing can be excluded, to the common ancestor. Where they disagree, however, the mere information implicit in the matching will never tell us which is the innovator: A, or B, or both. Thus, *equa* and *caballa* are pitted against each other in the Romance languages, and if means are available to prove that *caballa* is the innovation, they have nothing to do with the Comparative Method.[18] If the true analogies were preserved in extending that method to the lexicon, the existence of the various mutually translatable words for

[18] M. G. Bartoli, *Introduzione alla neolinguistica* 6 (Geneva, 1925), disregarding all geographic implications.

'mare' could only tell us that the ancestor had a morpheme for 'mare'. The morph or morphs that made it up are no more retrievable by mere matching, in the absence of material consensus among the daughter languages, than is, say, the exact phonetic nature of the Proto-Indo-European voiced aspirates. In instances such as this we often appeal to the greater plausibility of one phonetic development over another (e.g., [bʻ] > [β], rather than [β] > [bʻ]), but we also know that in so doing we cannot be safe from arbitrariness or at least from typological (areal) presuppositions. Just so, Greenberg says apropos of semantic change (p. 53): "It is often difficult to know what is retention and what is innovation, for a semantic change that takes place in one direction can often just as easily occur in reverse fashion. A term for 'day' often becomes 'sun', but likewise a term that means 'sun' frequently comes to mean 'day'." In fact it matters little whether the particular question before the house happens to have the form, "Which of the two morphs for a given meaning (morpheme) is old, which is new?" or the form, "Which of two meanings for a given morph is old, which new?" In glaring contrast to sound change, we find that there is always one variable too many: if the tree is known (from recorded history, or because there is a successful phonology-based reconstruction), we can say that a morph that occurs in one member of a subgroup is an innovation as against a competitor shared by another member of the subgroup with an unaffiliated language. On the other hand, after a morph is known to have supplanted another, all the languages sharing the innovation, as well as some showing a third morph (a further innovation) instead, form a subgroup. By itself, then, this does not accomplish much. (It is, incidentally, necessary to remember that the phenomenon of morph replacement is made to play a quite different role in the context of glottochronology.[19])

If morphological and semantic change is all but disqualified as a potential source of criteria for subgroupings through some kind of "comparative" method, it is luckily amenable (along with sound change) to internal reconstruction. Such reconstruction utilizes concepts like productivity and isolation (of forms in paradigms, of meanings in semantic fields, and the like). What this sort of reasoning can contribute to questions of subgrouping is well known to Indo-Europeanists through the work of Benveniste, Thieme, and Szemerényi, and perhaps best of all through Sturtevant's much-quoted argument (whether its implications be accepted or not) concerning the 'Indo-Hittite' constructs containing sentence connectives and enclitic pronouns.[20] Note that although con-

---

[19] Dyen, *IJAL* 28.153–161 (1962), and the earlier work quoted there.
[20] *Lg.* 15.11–19 (1939).

frontation (of Hittite with Indo-European) is involved here, the procedure is internal (with subsequent confirmation from the other partner) rather than technically 'comparative.' Or again, when Benveniste reconstructs, by internal reasoning, the earlier presence of the verb for 'sowing' in Indo-Iranian (or in the prehistory of Indo-Iranian), this identifies the historical Indo-Iranian languages as having innovated, in this one respect, rather than retained a state of affairs. In this particular instance this may be no great revelation; but as Szemerényi has just reminded us, more and more similar instances have come to light.[21] It is true that in the lexical field the mere obsolescence of morphs in certain environments, with divergent (rather than identical) replacements in a given set of daughter languages, is not sufficient evidence for subgrouping, since one and the same factor in the extralinguistic setting may well bring about the same result repeatedly and independently. Yet it is a frequent fallacy to classify "mere" obsolescence as something akin to retention (apparently because the word suggests something old rather than something new).[22] Obviously it is as much of an innovation as is addition. Thus also the role of irregularity, or a "highly irregular alternation," when shared by a set of daughter languages, is more complex than Greenberg makes it,[23] because it is twofold: while it is true that such an irregularity is a retention when contrasted with later leveling by analogic change, it is an innovation with regard to the stage which preceded it and which can sometimes be recovered either by internal reconstruction or by other means.

Every comparative linguist knows that the principal difficulties in subgrouping are of two kinds. It may happen that his rules (some of which we have just discussed) are smoothly applicable but turn out to lead to results that are wrong or improbable in the light of some information which is by good fortune available. He may for instance set up a subgroup on the strength of an innovation which, to be sure, is common to a set of sister languages but may be shown in some independent way to have occurred separately in each, perhaps at different times. In reality the languages are coördinate descendants (pattern 2 above). Actually, however, this kind of error is likely to show up under his second category where it will contribute to the trouble without necessarily being amenable to any kind of solution. This second category consists of course of the classics of the wave theory and of the subsequent writings on the subject. It consists of instances in which our rules furnish us with a subgrouping only so long as certain features in the lan-

---

[21] *Innsbrucker Beiträge zur Kulturwissenschaft, Sonderheft* 15 (1962), p. 192.
[22] See note 14.
[23] *Op. cit.* 51.

guages are excluded. If these features are, on the contrary, included, and others excluded, a different and contradictory subgrouping results. If the elimination of few and otherwise weak features will support a particular subgrouping, this subgrouping is accepted; if the battle is about equal the difficulty is considered insoluble. This has led to voluminous and sometimes highly sophisticated discussion both of data and of principles, and to a general questioning both of our criteria for the purpose of recovering plausible histories and of the plausibility of supposed history itself. We need no special illustrations of this all-pervasive problem.[24]

On the whole that discussion has not been productive of better procedures. A great deal has of course been said about the probability with which certain innovations can occur independently and thus give the mistaken impression that they occurred in the ancestor. There is a conviction that some changes are "trivial" per se—this is particularly often said of sound changes, and we are asked to distinguish striking, out-of-the way sound changes (perhaps changes subject to an unusually whimsical conditioning) from run-of-the-mill ones. Those whose belief in universals is tempered by a respect for area typologies are only a little better off in this respect, since sister languages are very frequently also areal neighbors and might, inasmuch as they are subject to the same typological straitjacket, be just as well at the mercy of universals of change. Still, the excentrical or isolated location of a given sister language should certainly be taken into account when the alleged triviality of a change is weighed: what is "trivial" for the next language need not even be natural for the language in question. It should also be clear that typological pressure is better understood in terms of a resulting structure than in terms of the particular changes whereby that structure is reached (or maintained!); vowel length was abolished both in Sardinian and in the other Romance languages, but the means of abolishing it were different, and the event as a whole must therefore not be placed in the ancestor period; it remains correctly reconstructable. The relevant question therefore is a difficult one: how many different means were available to separate daughter languages for attaining the parallel structural goal?[25]

Sometimes the sources of delusion or frustration are quite specific. Those who think that Mycenaean is to be subgrouped with Arcado-Cyprian[26] at first relied on "similarities," some of which have turned out

---

[24] W. Porzig, *Gliederung* passim.
[25] "Drift" no doubt belongs here.
[26] (-Ionic-Attic.)

to be retentions (very much to be expected in view of the absolute chronology). In the phonological field one of the last strongholds is the change from *ti* to *si*, where Doric, Boeotian, Thessalian, and Pamphylian have retained *ti*. Granting for the moment that the minor factual contradictions and exceptions that complicate the picture are cleared up, this does indeed look like a shared innovation. But how important is it? The overwhelming majority of examples involves instances of *ti* after a vowel or after *n*—that is, in positions where original *si* no longer occurred, so that the critical area is just about reduced to where the sequences *nti* and *ntsi* collapse into *nsi*.[27] The fluctuation of phones in neutralized position may still be an important phenomenon to study, especially in linguistic geography, but when it comes to sizing up the chances against secondary parallel development it is hardly in a class with the truly incisive irreversible merger processes. Quite a few of Porzig's attempts to establish a relative chronology among (shared) phonological innovations suffer from the same difficulty. He presents as self-evident the view that the change from *sr* to *str* in Slavic must be later than the change from *k'* to *s*, because *k'r* likewise goes to *str*;[28] but there is nothing wrong with, or even implausible in, positing a period in which *str* (from *str*, *sr*) and *k'r* were in contrast, and a subsequent change of *k'* merging (1) with *s* where *s* occurs and (2) with its automatic substitute, *st*, before *r* where *s* does not occur. Porzig's general chronology may still be right, but not just for the reason given.

Scholars have always come to a point where the factors of early borrowing among the members of a family[29] and of the isoglossically graded area obtrude themselves. Apparently this must be looked upon as a matter of either known or suspected historical fact. Where there is no sudden, relatively neat separation among daughter communities, the difference between borrowed and inherited material is blurred, and the area in which one change takes place overlaps with the area in which another change takes place. This is beyond the topic of subgrouping as a technical task, although of course the points of contact and conflict are many.[31]

(Participants in the discussion following the conference presentation of the first version of this paper: Hamp, Lehmann, Watkins, Emeneau.)

[27] W. Cowgill points out that this is not entirely negligible since it leads to the homonymy of *légonsi* 'they say' (from *-nti*) and 'to those who say' (from *-ntsi*). See also note 16.

[28] P. 78.

[29] On the effects of intrafamily borrowing, see three paragraphs above, and Dyen's review of Greenberg's *Essays* in *Lg*. 35.549–550 (1959).

[30] Attempts at subgrouping through generative grammar (or generative phonology) in the work of Halle, Klima, Kiparsky, Matthews, Saporta, Schramm, and Stockwell may be fruitful.

The Grouping of the Germanic Languages

Winfred P. Lehmann
UNIVERSITY OF TEXAS

1. *The problem in Germanic*

Determining the dialects immediately after the Proto-Germanic period, especially distinguishing the post-Germanic linguistic situation from the distribution of Germanic dialects at the time of our earliest records, has been one of the chief concerns in recent Germanic study. The widely used handbooks, Streitberg's *Urgermanische Grammatik* (1896), Hirt's *Handbuch des Urgermanischen* 1 (1931), Prokosch's *A Comparative Germanic Grammar* (1939), and those that are chiefly derivative, posit three subgroups: North, East, and West Germanic.

Yet this classification is largely based on the distribution we find several centuries after the beginning of the Christian era. Because our linguistic information on the Germanic dialects is late, and because even the accounts in classical authors—Caesar, Tacitus, Jordanes, and others—were produced long after the Proto-Germanic period, we cannot avoid dealing with the subsequent alignments when we attempt to determine the earliest grouping of the Germanic languages. Most of the recent publications have therefore concentrated on the interrelationships of the Germanic dialects in the first centuries A.D. notably the West Germanic dialects. For Streitberg, West Germanic consisted of two subgroups, English-Frisian, developing to English and Frisian, and German (for Prokosch, German and Dutch), developing into Low German and High German, which in turn developed into Low Franconian and Low German proper (Old Saxon), Middle German and Upper German. The recent publications have attempted to clarify the earlier situation from which these subgroups emerged, in great part as a result of political and cultural movements of the first six centuries A.D. This earlier situation, for which our best evidence is from classical authors and from archaeology, not from linguistic data, must in turn be analyzed for the alignment that is the topic of this paper. In the larger context of Indo-European studies, a review of the Germanic situation may have its greatest interest in illustrating problems that arise when the materials of a well-documented language group date from a time that by a millennium or more is later than the division of the protolanguage into subgroups.

2. *Brief survey of proposed classification*

The threefold division and its background are well treated in the volume of the *Geschichte der indogermanischen Sprachwissenschaft* devoted to *Germanisch*, which was undertaken by Streitberg and brought out after his death by Michels. (The history of this important survey illustrates problems faced in arriving at contemporary views in a leisurely subject like historical linguistics. Already in press in Strassburg in 1918, the work was moved, with its publisher, at the end of the war, to remain unprinted until after Streitberg's death in 1925; the first part, in which our problem is surveyed, appeared in 1927—but when bound with the second part its title page carries the misleading date 1936.)

The early work on the problem shows considerable divergence of classification. Rask, *Undersøgelse* . . . (1818), following Adelung, set up two groups in the "Gothic" family: a Northern or Scandinavian, and a "Germanic," to which (Moeso-)Gothic belonged. On the other hand, Grimm, *Deutsche Grammatik* (1819), proposed four subgroups of tribes: (1) the Goths and related tribes; (2) the Lombards, Bavarians, Burgundians, Alemannians, and Franks; (3) the Saxons, Westfalians, Frisians, and Angles; and (4) the northern group. Grimm saw these not as totally disparate tribes, but as groups merging through transitions with one another. In the third edition of his grammar (1840) he maintained this alignment, speaking, however, of languages rather than of tribes as being connected in various degrees and accordingly forming a continuous set of dialects, almost in accordance with the subsequent views of Schmidt (see Streitberg, Michels, Jellinek, pp. 9–10).

The broad acceptance of the tripartite classification is often credited to Müllenhoff, *Deutsche Altertumskunde*, but may be primarily attributable to Schleicher, who, in his book *Die deutsche Sprache* (1860), stated that Germanic had undergone a tripartite division into Gothic, Deutsch (West Germanic), and Northern. Oddly, the generally tremendous influence of Scherer on Germanic studies here lacked its usual impact, for his proposed bipartite division, in *Zur Geschichte der deutschen Sprache* (1868), into East Germanic (Gothic and Northern) and West Germanic failed to be incorporated in our handbooks. Yet his criterion was linguistic, one subsequently used somewhat differently by Krause, *Handbuch des Gotischen* (1953): the maintenance of final *s* in East Germanic but not in West Germanic. Nevertheless, the view of Schleicher, in which the subsequent distribution figured largely, is that still generally proposed today, as in the sixteenth edition of Braune's *Gotische Grammatik* by Ebbinghaus (1961).

Like Scherer, Schmidt found little following for his conclusion, stated in *Zur Geschichte des indogermanischen Vokalismus* (1875), that the northern dialect was both East and West Germanic, forming a transition from Gothic to Anglo-Saxon, just as Anglo-Saxon and Frisian in turn provide a transition from the North to Old Saxon.

The assumptions underlying these classifications are obvious, from the view of Grimm that linguistic divisions paralleled tribal ones, through the Schleicherian tree to the Schmidtian alignment based on the wave theory. They must also be noted for subsequent classifications. For although recent Germanists have attempted to base their classifications on linguistic evidence, it is obvious that they have found it difficult to exclude cultural alignments from linguistic classification. Using cultural criteria is particularly attractive, for they are provided us at a time when we have no texts. In this way Tacitus' designations reflecting cultic and other cultural practices—Ingvaeones (the North Sea area), Istvaeones (the Weser-Rhine area), Erminones (the Elbe area)—have been used even by dialect geographers. Though we should prefer designations drawn from linguistic analysis, we are also aware that dialect divisions conform to cultural alignments, and that it is excessively puristic to exclude any reflection of cultural groupings from dialect classifications.

Although we may question the introduction of Tacitus' names, the recent tremendous volume of publication on the early Germanic dialects has clarified our classification. Here only a small selection of the bibliography can be listed; for a fuller list, especially of reviews, even the special monographs are inadequate, and one must make use of the standard bibliographies, such as the *Linguistic Bibliography*. The recent interest has had two primary aims: questioning the time-honored tripartite classification, and determining more precisely the interrelationships within the West Germanic dialects. The earlier publications dealing with these two problems are well summarized by Karstien, *Historische deutsche Grammatik* I (1939); the most recent survey has appeared in *Sravnitel'naja grammatika germanskix jazykov* 1 (1962), though this apparently went to press earlier than Žirmunskij's article on the early dialects in *Voprosy germanskogo jazykoznanija* (1961). Two useful surveys were published in this country, by Springer (1941) and Philippson (1954).

Among the important preliminary articles is Wrede's (1924), in which he proposed that Gothic influenced Old High German, especially Bavarian, a view reminding one of Rask's. The largest, full-scale study is Maurer's *Nordgermanen und Alemannen* (1952^3), which somewhat surprisingly proposed an interrelationship between North Germanic and Alemannic. After much debate, a great deal of it in reviews of Maurer, the most plausible conclusions are presented in two sober treatments by Schwarz: of the linguistic situation in *Goten, Nordgermanen,*

Angelsachsen (1951), and of the tribal alignments in *Germanische Stammeskunde* (1956).

It now seems difficult to avoid the view that we should posit two subgroups after Proto-Germanic, one consisting of the North and East Germanic dialects, which I propose to call Northeast, the other of the West Germanic group. This is essentially the view of Schwarz, 1956 (p. 39), who summarizes the situation by drawing up two charts, one to illustrate the dialect situation after Proto-Germanic, around 200 B.C., the other to illustrate the subsequent realignments, around A.D. 200:

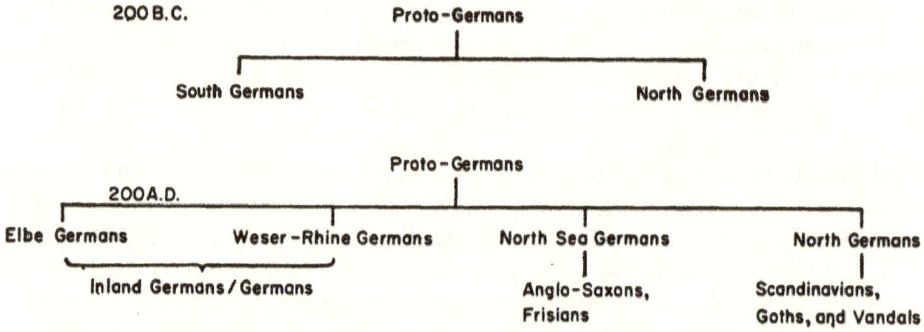

Evidence for this view, also that of Žirmunskij, is taken primarily from innovations common either to Northeast or to West Germanic. The chief such evidence is given below, followed by a presentation of the material that led to various differing positions. The innovations cited permit us to draw the significant isoglosses in the post-Germanic period.

3. *Material on which classification is based*

3.1 *Innovations in the Northeast Germanic group*

3.1.1. The most striking innovation common to Gothic and the Nordic languages is the development of a stop in geminate *j* and *w* clusters. Examples are, for *-jj-*: Goth. *twaddje*, ON *tueggia* vs. OHG *zweiio* 'of two'; for *-ww-*, Goth. *triggwa*, ON *tryggva*, OHG *triuwa* 'troth'. (Kuhn has contested the assumption that this is a common innovation, citing like Noreen the sixth-century Næsbjærg bracteate inscription *niuwila* [not **nig(g)wila*] and the Karstad form *baijoR* [not **bag(g)joR*] [1944 and 1955–1956]. Noreen's contention is based on the assumption that every NGmc. *-jj- -ww-* developed a stop. We hold however that the stop arose only in reflexes of laryngeal plus *y*, *w*, a combination not capable of reconstruction in these words, cf. Goth. *niujis*, ON *nýr*; the etymon of *baijoR* is unclear.)

3.1.2. A second innovation is the development of an *-īn-* suffix in

Gothic and the Nordic languages in the present participle feminine in contrast with WGmc. *-jō-* and PIE *-ī-*; cf. Goth. *nimandei(n)*, ON *nemande* vs. OHG *nemantiu* 'taking'.

3.1.3. A third innovation is the development of a productive inchoative class marked by a *-na-* suffix; cf. Goth. *fullnan*, ON *fullna* 'become full'.

3.1.4. By contrast the West Germanic dialects have introduced an innovation in the second singular preterit indicative, an *-i* ending with the plural vocalism, while the *-t* ending was preserved in Gothic and the Nordic dialects, and in the West Germanic preterit presents; cf. OHG *nāmi*, OS *nāmi* vs. Goth. *namt*, ON *namt*; OE *bude*, OS *budi*, OHG *buti* vs. Goth. *-baust*, ON *bautt*.

3.1.5. As a further innovation the West Germanic dialects have developed the contract verbs illustrated by OHG *gān* 'go', *stān* 'stand', *tuon* 'do', which are totally lacking in Gothic and the Nordic dialects.

Since Northeast Germanic and West Germanic are dialect groupings, there is no reason for reconstructing Proto-Northeast Germanic or Proto-West Germanic. When reconstructed forms from the period between Proto-Germanic and the attested dialects seem useful, they can better be labeled pre-Old English, pre-Old Saxon and so on.

3.2 *Common innovations in the North and West Germanic dialects*

The assumption of two subgroups after Proto-Germanic receives further support when we examine in detail the innovations common to West Germanic and the Scandinavian dialects.

3.2.1. As in ON *lāta* and OHG *lāzzan*, PGmc. *ē* may seem to have been lowered in these dialects, distinguishing them sharply from Gothic, cf. Goth. *lētan*. Yet *ē* is also attested in Old Frisian, cf. *lēta*, and in Anglian, cf. *forlētes*. Bennett (1950) has clarified this situation, suggesting that PGmc. *ē* was lowered in a central innovating area which did not reach to Gothic on the one hand or to Frisian and Anglian on the other. The change is therefore relatively late. Moreover, it attests continuing contacts between the various Germanic groups, among them contacts over the North Sea between the continental and the northern dialects. On the basis of this conclusion, we can readily account for the other features shared by the North and West Germanic dialects. We interpret them as innovations, the results of late changes spread through portions of the northern and the West Germanic area.

3.2.2. A second such innovation is the change of PGmc. *z* to *r*; cf. ON *meire*, OE *māra*, OHG *mēro*, but Goth. *maiza* 'more'.

3.2.3. A third is the production of a new demonstrative by the addition of *-se* to the demonstrative stem: ON *þesse*, OE *þes*, OHG *dese* 'this'.

3.2.4. A fourth shared characteristic is the marking of many class-seven strong preterits by $\bar{e}^2$, in contrast with reduplication in Gothic; cf. ON *hēt*, OE *hēt*, OHG *hiaz*, but Goth. *haihait*. The history of the development of this *ē*, and the status of reduplication, are two of the most complex grammatical problems in the Germanic languages, but here we are concerned merely with the difference between Gothic and the other dialects.

The Scandinavian languages also share lexical items with the coastal West Germanic languages. These suggest a division of the West Germanic dialects near the sea—Old English, Old Franconian, Old Saxon—from those inland, and have led to the designation North Sea Germanic as opposed to Inland Germanic.

3.2.5. The shared lexical innovations are primarily agricultural and geographical terms. An excellent example is ME *bule*, EFris. *bulle*, MDu. *bolle*, *MLG bulle*, ON *boli* as opposed to OE *stēor*, OFranc. *stier*, OS *stior* 'bull,' and Goth. *stiur*, ON *stjōrr* (preserved primarily in names); for it is an innovation based on a nickname, possibly 'the bellower', more likely the animal whose special function was breeding, cf. Gk. *φαλλός*, etc. The increasing attestation of the word 'bull' in the northern dialects, plus the maintenance of *Stier* with the meaning 'bull' in Old High German, and in the Nordic dialects but with a different meaning, supports the conclusion that 'bull' is a late innovation. For other lexical items, see Foerste, pp. 10–13.

3.2.6. A grammatical isogloss is provided by the third singular present of 'be'. (Foerste, p. 10). Unlike OHG *ist*, Goth. *ist*, this lacks final *-t*, presumably by analogy with the endingless preterit presents; cf. ON *es*, OE *is*, OFr. *is*, OFris. *is*, OS *is* (beside *ist*). The assumption of remodeling by analogy with preterit presents is supported by the second singular, which like the second singular of preterit presents, cf. OE *scealt*, *const*, etc., came to end in *-t*, e.g., ON *est*, OS *bist*, OE *bist*, with *bis* attested once (Sievers, Brunner, §427. Anm. 5 and 7). (Other influences may also have contributed to the development of these forms, e.g., *-st* from false division when the second singular pronoun followed [Sievers, Brunner, §356, 201.6], and the third singular with *-t* as a sandhi form [Schönfeld §124]). Whatever the causes, the occurrence of a third singular form without *-t* in the three coastal dialects of West Germanic and in Scandinavian gives evidence of interrelations between these dialects subsequent to the earliest dialect division of Proto-Germanic.

3.2.7. Further innovations permit us to follow subsequent alignments, such as that of North Sea Germanic as a whole, and subsequently its split into two groups, one west, one east of the Weser.

Features of the numeral system are particularly characteristic for North Sea Germanic, e.g., OE *nigon*, OFris. *niugun*, Du. *negen*, OS *nigun*, as opposed to Goth. *niun*, OHG *niun*, ON *níu*. See Frings (1960), Foerste, pp. 17–20, for others.

As a mark of the subsequent alignment we may note that in the western group the distinction between the dative and accusative of the first and second person pronouns was lost, e.g., OE *mē* vs. OHG *mir, mih*, OE *ðē* vs. OHG *dir, dih* (Foerste, pp. 15–16). The single form was probably introduced from the plural pattern, cf. OE *ūs* and *ēow*. On the other hand, the distinction between dative and accusative became more prominent in Inland Germanic, for it was introduced in the plural as well, cf. OHG *uns, unsih*; *iu, iuwih*. The Inland Germanic distinction is also attested in eastern North Sea Germanic, including Anglian, with *ūs, ūsih*; *ēow, ēowic* (Sievers, Brunner, §332. Anm. 4). Lexical characteristics as well support the assumption of an east-west subdivision (Foerste, pp. 14–15) and indicate that the boundaries within the Germanic area shifted, as we should expect from dialect investigations today, with shifts in cultural and political preëminence.

3.2.8. Because of this lack of unity among the various later dialects, the phenomenon of umlaut has seemed puzzling. For umlaut, the fronting of stressed back vowels before *i ī j*, is a characteristic feature of late Germanic, common for all dialects except Gothic (this in spite of van Coetsem, p. 39). Yet we know that it was carried through independently in Old Norse, Old English, Old High German to Middle High German, as well as in the other dialects.

The establishment of umlaut is instructive of other Germanic innovations, although there were probably separate front allophones of the back vowels already in late Proto-Germanic (Antonsen). While common to the various dialects, the separate allophones were established as phonemes only after the dialects had become distinct from one another. Common changes may in this way reflect similar structural patterns (see also Rajevskij). We do not need to assume for them subsequent transmission in accordance with a wave theory nor a communion of common development. Rather they are in accord with observations on "drift." The phenomena labeled umlaut indicate relatively late structural similarity throughout the Proto-Germanic area.

3.3 *Lexicostatistical studies*

A lexical study of the Germanic dialects by Arndt supports remarkably the absolute dates for the Proto-Germanic period—to the beginning of our era—but suggests that the North and West Germanic dialects maintained lexical unity until several centuries later. This lexical unity was subsequently disrupted in accordance with our assumption of distinct subgroups for Scandinavian, North Sea Germanic, and Inland

Germanic. Yet variations between conclusions based on phonological-morphological criteria, and on lexical evidence, reflect the possibility of greater effect of continued contact on the vocabulary than on the grammar. Arndt's findings indicate that we must assume continued contacts between the various Germanic dialects, not a clean break at any given time, except possibly for Gothic versus the dialects other than Old High German. It is highly interesting in view of their suggested subsequent contacts that Arndt's figures show greater lexical unity of Gothic with Old High German than with any other dialect.

3.4 *Common innovations in the West Germanic dialects*

In addition to the innovations they share with the Nordic dialects, the West Germanic dialects contain joint changes. On the basis of these we must view them as one dialect group.

3.4.1. The most notable such innovation is the West Germanic consonant gemination. Before resonants, especially [j], various consonants were affected; cf. Goth. *satjan*, ON *setja*, but OE *settan*, OS *settian*, OHG *setzen*; Goth. *snutrs*, ON *snotr*, but OE *snottor*, OS *snottar*, OHG *snottar* 'wise'.

Borrowings from Latin also underwent this change, e.g., OE *pytt*, OHG *phuzzi* from Lat. *puteus* 'well'. We conclude therefore that the change was relatively late, and that its results were spread when the West Germanic dialects were contiguous.

3.4.2. A second change is that of PGmc. /ngw/ to /ng/; cf. Goth. *siggwan*, ON *syngua*, but OE *singan*, OS *singan*, OHG *singan*. Like the previous change, this involves the Germanic system of phonotactics.

3.4.3. By a third change, PGmc. *ð* > WGmc. *d*; cf. Goth. *fadar*, ON *faðer* but OE *fæder*, OS *fadar*, OHG *fater*.

3.4.4. As a further distinguishing characteristic, Proto-Germanic final *z* was lost; cf. Goth. *dags*, ON *dagr* vs. *dæg*, OS *dag*, OHG *tac*. Krause, pp. 41–46, using the Runic *dagaR*, distinguishes on the basis of this varied treatment three groups of dialects: the *dagaz*, or North Germanic, the *dags*, or East Germanic, the *dag*, or West Germanic. This classification is based on data from the later dialects, and therefore reflects their development at a time relatively far from Proto-Germanic. While useful, it should not be equated with a statement of the initial division of Proto-Germanic.

For other innovations, see Hammerich (1955). Since the enumerated innovations are common to all the non-Northeast dialects, we posit a West Germanic dialect community as a grouping which includes the various dialects referred to as Ingvaeonic, Istvaeonic, and Erminonic, or as North Sea Germanic, Weser Germanic, and Elbe Germanic.

3.5 *Common features in Gothic and Old High German*

In 1924 Wrede proposed that Gothic was closely associated with Old High German, especially Bavarian, citing the following evidence.

3.5.1. In contrast with OE *hē*, *hine*, the Gothic third person pronoun is *is*, *ina*, the Old High German, *er*, *ina*. Yet these forms are not restricted to Gothic and Old High German; *is* is attested in Old Swedish runic materials, cf. Krause §177n.

3.5.2. With Bavarian *es*, *enk* 'you', Gothic maintained dual forms in the pronoun, e.g., *jut**, *igqis*. Yet duals are found in other dialects as well; cf. Springer.

3.5.3. Wrede also pointed to the retention of nasals before voiceless spirants in Gothic and Old High German, and to the retention of distinct third person plural forms in the verb. Both of these features are characteristic retentions, with innovations in other dialects. Of no greater validity for assuming a close association between Gothic and Old High German is the common feature in the third singular and second and third plural present of verbs; in these forms Gothic and Old High German show reflexes of Germanic voiced fricatives; cf. OHG *biutit*, Goth. *biudiþ*—also Mk. 16.7 *gibid-uh*—vs. OE *beodeþ*, OFris. *biadeth* 'offers' 3rd sg. pres.; cf. Karstien, pp. 16–17. This distribution exemplifies two possible distributions of PIE *t*. In some verbs, as in Skt. *bhávati*, the root was accented, and accordingly by Verner's law PIE $t >$ PGmc. ð; in others, as in Skt. *tudáti*, the stem vowel was accented, and accordingly PIE $t >$ PGmc. *þ*, the form generalized in Old English and Old Frisian. Generalizations of the same form in Gothic and Old High German do not require assumptions of mutual influence.

There are also parallels in vocabulary which allow us to suggest contacts between Gothic- and Old High German-speakers after the introduction of Christianity. The Old Bavarian *pherinctac* 'Friday' like Goth. *paraskaiwe* derives from Gk. παρασκευή 'preparation day'; similarly OHG *sambaztag*, Goth. *sabbatodags* 'Saturday' derive from Gk. σάββατον. Moreover, the usual word for 'baptize' is *fulwian* in Old English, but Goth. *daupjan*, OHG *touffan*. From such agreement in vocabulary we assume influence of Gothic on Old High German in the fifth and sixth centuries, rather than early interrelationship. Such influences may also account for other similarities, such as the preposition Goth. *hindar*, OHG *hintar* vs. OS *aftar*, OE *be-æftan* 'after'.

3.6 *Innovations common to Old English and Old Frisian*

Old English and Old Frisian share a considerable number of innovations, especially in vowels with primary stress.

3.6.1. PGmc. *a* was fronted to *æ* in closed syllables, except before nasals; OE *dæg*, OFris. *dei* vs. OHG *tag* 'day'.

3.6.2. PGmc. *ay* > *ā*, which later was fronted in Old Frisian; OE *āgon*, OFris. *āgun* > *ēgun* vs. OHG *eigun* 'they have'.

3.6.3. PGmc. *a*, *ǣ*, *i*, *u* were modified before nasals, especially before nasal and voiceless fricatives: PGmc. *a ǣ* (*ē*[1]) before nasals > *o ō*; OE *mon*, OFris. *mon* vs. OHG *man* 'man'; OE *mōna*, OFris. *mōne* vs. OHG *māno* 'moon'.

3.6.4. PGmc. *an* before voiceless fricatives > *ō*, also under weak stress; OE *ōðer*, OFris. *ōther*, cf. OHG *ander* 'other'; OE *oraþ* < **oranþ-*, cf. Goth. *uz-anan* 'breathe out', ON *ǫnd* 'breath', with *-aþ* < *-ōþ* in early Old English.

3.6.5. PGmc. *i* and *u* before *nf*, *nþ*, *ns*, were lengthened with loss of the nasal; OE *fīf*, OFris. *fīf* vs. OHG *finf* 'five'.

3.6.6. The three persons in the plural of the present indicative have the same ending, e.g., OE *bindaþ*, OFris. *bindath* vs. OHG *binten*, *bintet*, *bintant*. The ending is from PGmc. *-anþ*, in which the nasal was lost before voiceless fricative, with subsequent reduction in length of the *ō* under weak stress.

3.6.7. The negative *ne* was contracted with following verbs, especially auxiliaries; cf. OE *nāt*, OFris. *nēt* 'I don't know'; see Levin.

Examination of these developments indicates that they are the result of diffusion through a contiguous dialect area. For, as in OFris. *dei* and *ēgun*, the changes are not completely parallel throughout the area. Moreover, some of them spread to Saxon as well, such as the loss of nasals before fricatives and the reduction of present plural forms to one. We must therefore assume an early period of relatively close association between speakers of (pre-)Old English and (pre-)Old Frisian, possibly preceded by a period of association with Saxon, with subsequent disruption; see Hammerich (1939).

3.7 *The shifting linguistic situation in North Germany*

The Germanic area that may illustrate most clearly the shifting influences of neighboring dialects is northern Germany. In brief we may characterize it by saying that it originally shared many characteristics with Old English, Old Frisian, Old Franconian, but gradually fell under the cultural domination of the south, taking over innovations from Old High German (Inland Germanic). We can determine the conflicting influences even in the small number of materials from Old Saxon times. Literary documents, the *Heliand* and *Genesis*, already incorporate southern features, whereas the homely materials remain in the North Sea tradition. Characteristics that Old Saxon shares with the North Sea dialects are as follows.

3.7.1. Nasals are lost before voiceless fricatives with lengthening of preceding vowels; OS *fīf* vs. OHG *finf* 'five'.

3.7.2. Only one form is used in the plural of the present indicative; OS *bindath*, OE *bindaþ*, vs. OHG *binten, bintet, bintant.*

3.7.3. The dative singular of the first and second personal pronoun is taken from the accusative (but cf. 3.2.7. above);

OS d.a. *mi*,	cf. OE *mē*,	vs.	OHG *mir, mih*
OS d.a. *iu*,	cf. OE *ēow*,	vs.	OHG *iu, iuwih*

3.7.4. A different stem is used in the third singular personal pronoun; OS *hē*, cf. OE *hē*, vs. OHG *er.*

The conflicting influences of the neighboring dialect areas may also be seen in the two Old Saxon forms *niman* and *neman* 'take', cf. OE *niman*, OHG *neman*; OS *giban* and *geban* 'give', cf. OE *gifan*, OHG *geban.*

Differing forms in the medieval period indicate clearly the shifting influence. In Old Saxon, for example, we find oblique forms of the third person pronoun used in reflexive patterns, in contrast with OHG *sih*, but in Middle Low German these patterns use *sik*. Further, in Old Saxon we find the innovation *bium*, parallel with OE *biom, beom*, vs. OHG *bin* 'I am', but in Middle Low German we find *bin*. Located between two focal areas, the northern German speech was modified in keeping with each, when the focal area in question was dominant.

Old Franconian similarly reflects a succession of influences. It is basically a Franconian overlay on North Sea Germanic speech, with many North Sea characteristics maintained (Schönfeld, pp. xxix–xxxii), some of which are not common to Frisian. Without attempting to indicate the background of Old Franconian in detail, we may use it like Old Saxon to illustrate the difficulty of determining precisely the late Proto-Germanic situation in an area which was subsequently exposed to various cultural alignments.

4. *Further complexities in the late Germanic situation*

The deeper understanding of language achieved from study of contemporary dialects has enabled us to clarify the late Germanic linguistic situation. Through migrations, as that of Germanic speakers to Britain, or to Iceland, or to the east beyond the Elbe and Saale rivers, distinct dialects developed. To the extent that intercommunication was preserved, however, innovations were transmitted from dialect to dialect; relatively compact dialect groups arose, such as Old High German—composed of Alemannic, Bavarian, Lombard—or Old English—composed of Anglian, Kentish, West Saxon—or even less compact groups, such as the complex making up Old English, Old Frisian, Old Franconian, and for a time Old Saxon. When these areas were so large that intercommunication outside them was infrequent, and also when political and social conditions hindered communication, distinct subdialects developed, some of which, such as Vandal, vanished with their speakers.

One further feature of linguistic change permits us to account for similarities between Germanic dialects that have been interpreted as a result of common innovations: similar, but independent, developments in languages of similar structure. Such developments require even more delicate manipulation than do those such as umlaut, which reflect allophonic alignments of an earlier period.

In south Germany, especially in Alemannic areas, *n* was lost before voiceless fricatives with compensatory lengthening of the preceding vowels, a development parallel to that in the northern area: Alem. *ūs*, cf. OE *ūs*, OS *ūs*. The territory between maintained the nasals, as in NHG *uns*. By a clumsy, prestructural theory it may be suggested that the similar treatment in the north and south points to an interrelationship; yet the phenomenon of similar independent development is relatively common, not distinctive enough to support an assumption of mutual influence (cf. Fourquet, p. 3). The situation is worth noting as an indication of the importance of understanding possible changes in language and the causes of them. Since linguistic changes are not unique, we no longer assume close interrelationship, or an earlier protolanguage wherever parallel developments are attested in two dialects.

Moreover, the numerous correspondences in vocabulary between Alemannic and North Germanic presented by Kolb (1957) and discussed in an important review by Senn (1958) are largely relics of the earlier situation.

5. *Grouping of the Germanic dialects in accordance with contemporary linguistic theory*

The complexities of the Germanic grouping can accordingly be interpreted on the basis of findings of dialect geography. The very aim of attempting linguistic groupings may lead to overclassification, especially when simplification is introduced for pedagogical purposes. Since our handbooks were largely produced by neogrammarians, it has been fashionable to whip them for overly rigid grouping. Yet Streitberg (1936, p. 10) can quote with apparent approval Grimm's comments of 1840:

The Gothic language is closely related to High German, though it maintains at the same time a certain connection with the northern languages. High German,

Low German, Netherlandic, Anglo-Saxon are mutually tied closely together, but in such a way that Saxon, Anglo-Saxon, and English in addition show notable contact with the northern languages. High German and Low German once were connected through Franconian; some faint traces of this connection can still be observed today in Netherlandic. Frisian forms a bridge between Danish and Saxon. . . .

Grimm's remarks differ only in emphasis from Wrede's statement of 1924 which led to the tremendous attention of the subsequent decades to grouping:

I view the entire Germanic language area as a large continuous complex extending from the southeast to the northwest, whose individual members were of every conceivable irregularity and were shifted and displaced again and again in the course of centuries. The vanished Gothic forms the beginning; the Gothicized West Germanic of the later German adjoins it; thereupon follows the purer West Germanic of North Germany, which since the days of the *Heliand* poet has been increasingly Germanized; this German impact is lacking in Anglo-Saxon, which was isolated by the sea; this however in turn reaches over to the East Germanic Nordic. And in this way the Germanic languages have always been in movement, always in unrest and mutual influence. . .

(See Streitberg [1936, p. 178].)

It may be important to note the change in emphasis, the greater insistence on difficulties resulting from attempts to classify social phenomena. Without some classification our handbooks would lack form. Yet even the more flexible classifications we propose are made in the realization that they reflect our needs to manage the data rather than to produce rigid pigeonholes.

Our evidence leads us to posit a fairly uniform Proto-Germanic, so uniform that all our data share similar results of the first consonant shift. In the course of time Proto-Germanic split into northeast and (south)-west groups. This initial dialect division was soon modified by subsequent interrelationships. For understanding of the later situation we must admit considerable contact among the various Germanic areas, often by sea. Details of these contacts may in part be reconstructed from tenuous linguistic evidence, more fully from poetic recollections, as in *Beowulf*, from classical writers, and from archaeological discoveries. These assure us that the Germanic peoples maintained a mobility that fostered the spread of cultural features, including linguistic items. A tremendous expenditure of effort in the last four decades has led to improved understanding of the changing Germanic groupings. The more flexible classification that has resulted may also be instructive for other Indo-European dialect areas.

Bibliography

Antonsen, E. H. "Germanic umlaut anew," *Lg.* 37.215–230. 1961.

Arndt, W. W. "The Performance of Glottochronology in Germanic," *Lg.* 35.180–192. 1959.

Bennett, W. H. "The Germanic Development of Indo-European ē," *Lg.* 26.232–235. 1950.

———. "A West Norse-Frisian-Kentish Parallel," *IALR* 1.71–80. 1953.

Braune, W. *Gotische Grammatik.* 16th ed. by E. A. Ebbinghaus. Tübingen, 1961.

Coetsem, Fr. van. *Das System der starken Verba und die Periodisierung im älteren Germanischen.* Amsterdam, 1956.

Cordes, G. "Zur Frage der altsächsischen Mundarten," *ZfMa.* 24.1–51, 65–78. 1956.

DeCamp, D. "The Genesis of the Old English Dialects; A New Hypothesis," *Lg.* 34.232–244. 1958.

Foerste, W. "Die Herausbildung des Niederdeutschen," *Festschrift für Ludwig Wolff.* 9–27. Neumünster, 1962.

Fourquet, J. *L'ordre des éléments de la phrase en germanique ancien. Publ. de la Faculté des Lettres de l'Université de Strasbourg.* 86. Paris, 1938.

Frings, Th. *Grundlegung einer Geschichte der deutschen Sprache.* Halle, 1948 (1957).

———. "Ingwäonisches in den Bezeichnungen der Zehnerzahlen," *Fryske Studzjes. Festschrift für J. H. Brouwer.* 7–39. Assen, 1960.

Grimm, J. *Deutsche Grammatik,* I–IV. Zweite Ausgabe, neuer vermehrter Abdruck. 1870–1898.

Haeringen, C. B. van. *Netherlandic language research.* Leiden, 1960².

Hammerich, L. L. "Über das Frisische," *Mélanges linguistiques offerts à Holger Pedersen.* 351–358. Copenhagen, 1939.

———. "Die germanische und die hochdeutsche Lautverschiebung," *PBB (T)* 77.1–29, 165–203. 1955.

Hirt, H. *Handbuch des Urgermanischen* I–III. Heidelberg, 1931–1934.

Höfler, O. "Die hochdeutsche Lautverschiebung und ihre Gegenstücke bei Goten, Vandalen und Burgundern," *AÖAW* 93.294–318. 1956.

Karstien, C. *Historische deutsche Grammatik.* I. Heidelberg, 1939.

Kolb. E. *Alemannisch-nordgermanisches Wortgut.* Frauenfeld, 1957.

Krause, W. *Handbuch des Gotischen.* Munich, 1953.

Kuhn, H. Rev. of F. Maurer, *Nordgermanen und Alemannen. AfdA.* 63.5–13. 1944.

———. "Zur Gliederung der germanischen Sprachen," *ZDA* 86.1–47. 1955–1956.

Levin, S. K. "An Anglo-Frisian Morphological Correspondence," *Orbis* 9.73–78. 1960.

Maurer, F. *Nordgermanen und Alemannen.* Studien zur germanischen und frühdeutschen Sprachgeschichte, Stammes- und Volkskunde.³ Bern, 1952.

Müllenhoff, K. *Deutsche Altertumskunde.* 1–5. Berlin, 1890–1920.

Philippson, E. A. Rev. of E. Schwarz, *Goten, Nordgermanen, Angelsachsen. JEGP* 52.242–249. 1951.

———. "Neuere Forschungen zum Westgermanenproblem und zur Ausgliederung der germanischen Stämme," *Symposium* 8.18–32. 1954.

Prokosch, E. *A Comparative Germanic Grammar.* Philadelphia, 1939.
Rajevskij, M. V. "Razvitije odnotipnyx fonem v rodstvennyx jazykax kak problema sopostavitel'noj fonologii," *Problemy morfologičeskogo stroja germanskix jazykov.* 116–121, V. I. Jarceva, ed. Moscow, 1963.
Rask, *Undersøgelse om det gamle Nordiske eller Islandske Sprogs Oprindelse.* Copenhagen, 1818.
Rooth, E. "Zur altsächsischen Sprachgeschichte," *NdMitt* 13.32–49. 1957.
Scherer, W. *Zur Geschichte der deutschen Sprache.* Berlin, 1868.
Schleicher, A. *Die deutsche Sprache.* Stuttgart, 1860.
Schmidt, W. *Zur Geschichte des indogermanischen Vokalismus.* Weimar, 1871–1875.
Schönfeld, M. *Historische Grammatica van het Nederlands,*[6] by A. van Loey. Zutphen, 1960.
Schwarz, E. *Goten, Nordgermanen, Augelsachsen.* Studien zur Ausgliederung der germanischen Sprachen. Bern, 1951.
———. *Germanische Stammeskunde.* Heidelberg, 1956.
Senn, A. Rev. of E. Kolb, *Alemannisch-nordgermanisches Wortgut. JEGP* 59.298–302. 1958.
Sievers, E., and K. Brunner. *Altenglische Grammatik.* Halle, 1942 (1951).
Springer, O. "German and West Germanic," *GR* 16.3–20. 1941.
Sravnitel'naja grammatika germanskix jazykov. 1. M. M. Guxman, ed. Moscow, 1962.
Streitberg, W. *Urgermanische Grammatik.* Heidelberg, 1896.
———, V. Michels, and M. H. Jellinek. *Germanisch. Die Erforschung der indogermanischen Sprachen.* Berlin/Leipzig, 1936.
Wolff, L. "Die Stellung des Altsächsischen," *ZdA* 71.129–154. 1934.
Wrede, Fr. "Ingwäonisch und Westgermanisch," *ZfdMa* 19.270–283.
Žirmunskij, V. "O plemennyx dialektax drevnix germancev," *Voprosy germanskogo jazykoznanija.* Moscow, 1961.

(Participants in the discussion following the conference presentation of the first version of this paper: Collinder, Polomé, Lane, Winter, Cowgill, Hamp, Birnbaum.)

Italo-Celtic Revisited

Calvert Watkins
HARVARD UNIVERSITY

The notion of Italo-Celtic unity was born in 1861, in a study by C. Lottner, *Kuhns Beiträge* 2.309 ff. It grew and flourished over three-quarters of a century, primarily under the patronage of the greatest Indo-Europeanist of the age, Antoine Meillet. And it was buried in 1929 by C. Marstrander in a "diskusjon" in *NTS* 3.241–259. Since then it has been resurrected and buried again, more than once.[1] Its ghost evidently lives on; otherwise we may assume it would not have been deemed worthy of figuring among the topics for this conference.

From their very beginnings, Indo-European studies have been faced with a problem. We have the several attested languages; the number and precision of the similarities among these languages are such that they cannot be due to chance. It is this "one fact"[2] that indicates the hypothesis of a common origin. The immediate question is, then, how we are to envisage the historical passage from this common original to the divergent attested languages—"wie es eigentlich gewesen."

The first answer was Schleicher's *Stammbaum* (of 1861), which was followed shortly—though never completely replaced—by Schmidt's *Wellen* of 1872. Both of these theories are an attempt to answer the question, What are the relationships of the attested Indo-European

---

[1] Compare the following, which is only a partial listing: G. Devoto, *Silloge linguistica Ascoli* 200–240 (Torino, 1929); G. Bonfante, *I dialetti indoeuropei* (Naples, 1931); F. Ribezzo, *Rivista indo-greco-italica* 16.27–40 (1932); A. Meillet, *Esquisse d'une histoire de la langue latine*[3], chap. 3 (Paris, 1933); J. Vendryes, *La position linguistique du celtique* (Rhys lecture, *Proceedings of the British Academy* 23 [1937]); J. Whatmough, *Foundations of Roman Italy* 116 (London, 1937); T. Bolelli, *Annali della Scuola Normale Superiore di Pisa*, Ser. 2, 9.97–120 (1940); Whatmough, *HSCP* 55.19–20 (1944); M. Dillon, *AJP* 64.124–134 (1944); Devoto, *Gli antichi italici*[2] 44–47 (Firenze, 1951); E. Pulgram, *Studies presented to Joshua Whatmough* 246–247 (*The Hague*, 1957); Pulgram, *The Tongues of Italy* 229–230 (Cambridge, Mass., 1958). For a broader view of the positions of Italic and Celtic in Indo-European, cf. H. Krahe, *Sprache und Vorzeit* (Heidelberg, 1954); W. Porzig *Die Gliederung des idg. Sprachgebiets* 93–151 (Heidelberg, 1954); V. V. Ivanov, *Vopr. jaz.* 1956.111–121.

[2] To use the expression of O. Szemerényi, *Trends and tasks in comparative philology* 7 (London, 1962).

languages among themselves? Can they be arranged in subgroups? Schmidt's hypothesis had the great merit of introducing a geographical frame to the earlier rather disembodied notions of linguistic subgroups, and the subsequent development of dialectology has reinforced this manner of envisaging the relations of the Indo-European languages. In particular the contribution of dialectology has been the isogloss, the linguistic feature shared between two languages that are, were, or may be presumed to have been, in contact. The isogloss is the expression for what has long been and continues to be[3] the primary criterion for linguistic subgrouping: the common innovation.

The common innovation is so firmly anchored in traditional linguistic thinking that to question its utility smacks of lèse majesté. But one may be permitted to suggest that it is overemphasized. For to consider common innovations alone in subgrouping, and to ignore common retentions, is possible only if we consider language as a mechanical sum of linguistic features, some of which "change" and some of which do not—the atomistic view of the neogrammarians. It is inconsistent with the concept of language as a structured system, and of linguistic history as a succession of systems. At any given stage of a given language, retentions and innovations are part of the same synchronic structure. If two languages agree in maintaining the productivity of a given structural feature, rather than replacing it by something else, we may well have in this retention a primary dialectal datum. It is precisely this notion of the importance of common retentions as evidence for Italo-Celtic unity which Meillet maintained, in the addendum to the second edition of his *Esquisse d'une histoire de la langue latine*, "Chronologie des langues européennes." His remarks have been interpreted as a quasi renunciation of the notion of Italo-Celtic unity (Bolelli, *op. cit.* 106), but this is incorrect; in the third edition, the addendum was incorporated into the body of the text, but the notion of an Italo-Celtic unity was maintained. Meillet saw that the agreement of Italic and Celtic alone in *retaining* the subjunctive in *-ā-*,[4] or of the passive in *-r* (shared with other languages), is a primary datum; the importance of this point for historical linguistic methodology cannot be overlooked.

I would add another point. Lists of innovations very nearly always contain only "positive" features: particular shapes of morphemes, such

---

[3] Cf. H. M. Hoenigswald, *Language change and linguistic reconstruction* 151 (Chicago, 1960).

[4] "Le procédé a un aspect profondement indo-européen," *Les dialectes indo-européens*², avant-propos, p. 3. His view is confirmed by that of N. Trubetzkoy and E. Benveniste (see *BSL* 47.11–20 [1951]); I cannot agree with the dissenting views of G. S. Lane, *Lg*. 38. 245–253 (1962).

as the Italic and Celtic gen. *-ī*, superl. *-samo-*, deverbative suffix *-ti* + *ō/n-*, and so forth. But what we may call "negative" innovations are equally important. We must always ask ourselves, what has the given language restricted or eliminated? Celtic and Italic agree remarkably in having severely limited the productivity of deverbative nouns of the type *τεμ-* → *τομός/τομή*, while retaining enough isolated examples to show that this morphophonemic derivational pattern once existed in these languages. The innovation of the suffix *-ti* + *ō/n-*, and its fortune as deverbative formation, is in a certain sense only a consequence of the primary innovation of eliminating deverbative nouns in *CeC-* → *CoCo/ā-*. The history of the suffix *-tiō/n-* is complex in Italic and Celtic, and not nearly so parallel in the two groups as the outward form would appear: we have also *-iō/n-* in archaic forms like Lat. *ūsucapiō*, and OIr. *Ériu* 'Ireland', *íriu* 'land'; and the functional opposition *-tiō* : *-tu-* in Latin (continuing IE *-ti-* : *-tu-*) appears unknown in Celtic. The implementations of the suffix in Latin and in Celtic are not parallel; while *-tiō* is the principal deverbative suffix in Latin, *-tiu* is relatively infrequent in Celtic. If the structural contexts are not comparable, then an isolated identity such as *-tiō* : *-tiu* is not significant. In Latin, we know that *-tiō* replaced *-iō* in many cases, cf. *paciō* (Festus) → *pactiō*, which also weakens the comparison. Considering that *-tiō/n-* has affinities also in Armenian (H. Pedersen, *KZ* 38.220 [1905]), it is best to leave it out of the Italo-Celtic question and consider only the negative innovation as significant.

There is a third historical "component" of any language which must be considered in any question of dialectal relations with other languages: "divergence," or what is shared with no language of the family. On the face of it, this seems obvious. But in fact, in most of the literature on linguistic subgrouping, all the attention is given to the similarities between languages, and little or none to the differences. The two must be balanced against each other; the probative force of a few striking "common innovations" of a pair of languages is considerably weakened if they can be set against a large number of structurally significant divergences between the two. It is the neglect of this aspect of the problem, more than any other single factor, which in my opinion vitiates the concept of an Italo-Celtic unity.

In the question of subgrouping, as in any other linguistic problem, we must consider the total structure of the languages under investigation. In particular, it is of the greatest importance *where* in the system any of these features—shared retentions, shared innovations, and divergences—are. To use the generative model, which may be profitably applied to dialectal problems, we may ask, How early is the rule? Relative depth in the structure is an index of relative antiquity.[5] The subgrouping question is partly one of relative chronology. If the features shared by two languages—and here I would include both retentions and innovations—are older, and more deeply imbedded in their structures than are the divergences between them, then we may speak of a "unity." But this "unity," e.g., Indo-Iranian, is primarily terminological; there is no question of a "single common language," though in "real" terms we might speak of a definable dialect area. The term "unity" as thus used simply expresses certain chronological relations between shared features and divergences. As Benveniste has stated (*Origines de la formation des noms en indo-européen* 2 [Paris, 1935]), "La fixation d'une chronologie devra être la préoccupation dominante des comparatistes."[6]

Italic and Celtic are closely related. This is universally admitted by Indo-Europeanists, and will be taken for granted here. This fact, determined simply by inspection, is one necessary condition for making the hypothesis of an Italo-Celtic unity. The other necessary condition is that Italic and Celtic may themselves be reduced to the unities of Common Italic and Common Celtic. Common Celtic would appear to present no difficulty;[7] for Meillet, Common Italic was equally evident. But more recent scholarship, particularly in Italy, has cast considerable doubt on the unity of Italic. Since for other reasons, which will appear, I reject the notion of Italo-Celtic unity, and since the Italic question is dealt with elsewhere at this conference, I shall ignore it, and simply consider Meillet's position as given.

With all these methodological preliminaries as a background, I propose first to examine once again the evidence adduced by Meillet to prove the existence of an Italo-Celtic unity, and to explore certain characteristic features of Common Celtic and Common Italic in order to determine whether in fact they coincide in any profound way.

Meillet has examined the Celtic-Italic isoglosses in two places: *Les dialectes indo-européens*, chap. 3 (Paris, 1908), and *Esquisse d'une histoire de la langue latine*[3], chap. 3 (Paris, 1933). The earlier work gives a straight list of what is common to Celtic and Italic alone. The later version gives

[5] See L. Bloomfield, "Menomini morphophonemics," *TCLP* 8.105–115 (1939); M. Halle, "Phonology in a generative grammar," *Word* 18.54–72 (1962); Halle, "On the role of simplicity in linguistic descriptions," in *Structure of language and its mathematical aspects. Proceedings of Symposia in Applied Mathematics* 12. 89–94 (1961).

[6] It is gratifying to be able to equate this expression with the synchronic concept of the ordered rule, classically stated by Bloomfield in his "Menomini morphophonemics" only three years after the publication of Benveniste's *Origines*.

[7] As E. P. Hamp has shown, *Lochlann* 1.211 (1958), the "isogloss" between P-Celtic and Q-Celtic is structurally trivial.

in many ways a more interesting, though less clear list. As well as strictly Italo-Celtic features, it includes features that are shared with Indo-Iranian, and present "marginal" or peripheral conservations, as well as certain items of the lexicon which are common to "North-Western" Indo-European languages. We shall follow, in general, the earlier list, considering only what is peculiar to Celtic and Italic; linguistic features reflecting either peripheral conservations or a certain Western Indo-European linguistic community do not in themselves prove a specific Italo-Celtic unity, nor do they necessarily imply one. Meillet's list has been discussed and commented on many times; most relevant works are noted in note 1 above. I do not intend to repeat what has been said in detail, but only to add a few additional comments to each item, in order better to evaluate it.

The first two items on Meillet's list are the only common phonetic features: the assimilation $p \ldots k^w > k^w \ldots k^w$, and the treatment °*r*, °*l* > *ar al*, differing from that of *r̥*, *l̥* > Lat. *or*, *ol*, Celt. *ri*, *li*.[8] The second of these may now be eliminated as a specific "Italo-Celtic" feature, after J. Kuryłowicz, *L'apophonie en indo-européen* 166 ff. (Wrocław, 1956); we have the characteristic development of an antevocalic zero-grade *TaR-o-* in all the "Southern" Indo-European languages, Celtic, Italic, Greek, and Armenian. The concept of the latter as a dialect area in Indo-European, though it in no way implies a common language, deserves further exploration; I would like to have seen it—and similar larger dialectal groupings—figure among the topics treated at this conference.

As for the assimilation $p \ldots k^w > k^w \ldots k^w$, it is well to remember that it affects only three lexical items, Lat. *quīnque*, *coquō*, *quercus*; and that, as pointed out by Hoenigswald, there were no inherited roots of the shape $k^w \ldots k^w$. The case of *quercus* is peculiar. Meillet states that the name of the Hercynian forest Ἑρκύνια indicates only that the change $p \ldots k^w > k^w \ldots k^w$ is posterior to that of *k^wu* to *ku*: the resultant **perkūn-* (cf. Lith. *Perkūnas*) was then free to lose its *p* in Celtic, as regularly.[9] But *quercus* indicates that in Latin, $p \ldots k^w > k^w \ldots k^w$ is *prior* to $k^wu > ku$. The relative lateness of the latter change is indicated by Umbrian *pufe* and Oscan *puf* : Lat. *ne-cubi* (*ubi*), which show $k^w > p$ also before *u*. The simplest explanation for the variance between Celtic

[8] W. Cowgill has suggested (*per litteras*) that "the occasional change of *-ow-* to *-aw-* in words like W *naw*, Lat. *cavus*" might be considered a shared phonologic innovation of Italic and Celtic. But I would reject this in view of the irregularity and unpredictability of the change in both languages, and the simple fact that the lexical items affected do not correspond: W *naw* but Lat. *nouem*.

[9] On certain problems of this group of cognates, see the brilliant article of V. V. Ivanov, "K etimologii baltijskogo i slavjanskogo nazvanij boga groma," *Vopr. slav. jaz.* 101–111 (1958).

and Italic is to assume that the assimilation is independent in each. The contexts of this assimilation in the two groups are actually not parallel. In Latin we have the substitution of k^w for *p*, with both continuing to exist in the inventory: the consonantal "square" remains unaffected. But Celtic shows a different picture, precisely because of the "loss" of Indo-European *p*: the consonantal "square" was replaced by a "triangle" opposing *t*, *k*, k^w/p.[10] It seems equally plausible to suggest that Celtic φ from *p* simply fell together with the new structure point k^w/p in the environment we describe in Indo-European terms as *p* . . . k^w, yielding dialectally k^w . . . k^w or *p* . . . *p*. This is rather similar to merging with *k* before *s* and *t*; *k* in this position represents the neutralization of the opposition k^w/p : *k*, hence we can simply set up $\varphi > k^w/p$ here as well.

Besides the three Latin lexemes mentioned, there is a fourth that shows a divergent assimilation: *prope*. The collocation *prope* : *proximus* indicates an internal reconstruction **prok*^{w}*-*, as Ernout and Meillet point out. They suggest that the reverse assimilation *prok*^{w}*-* > *prop-* should be attributed to the Latin nontolerance of initial $k^w r$-; but we have ample evidence that this cluster was tolerated in Goidelic Celtic, cf. R. Thurneysen, *A grammar of Old Irish* 137 (Dublin, 1946), abbr. *OIGr. Proximus* indicates that the assimilation must be more recent—or synchronically a later rule—than the neutralization of k^w and *k* before *s*; we have here also divergent systems, since Latin preserves *ps* distinct whereas Celtic merges *ps* with *ks* and $k^w s$. In either event we have a chronological problem which can be most easily resolved by assuming that the assimilation is independent in Italic and in Celtic.

One final form which deserves to figure in the literature is the following. In Old Irish, in combinations of digits and tens (such as the numerals 11–19 and 21–29), the tens follow in the genitive. The form that functions as genitive of *deich n-* 'ten' (**dekm̥*) is disyllabic *dëac*, archaic *déec: di rainn deac* 'twelve parts'. This form *deac* (*c* = /g/) cannot be related to *deich n-*, or derived from **dekm̥*. The only reasonable derivation is given both by Pedersen (*VKG* 2.133) and Thurneysen (*OIGr.* 247): **dwei-penk*^{w}*-* 'two fives, twice five'. Such a multiplicative counting system is doubtless Common Celtic; we have possible traces in Middle and Modern Welsh *deunaw* 'eighteen', literally 'twice nine', or Breton *triouec'h* 'eighteen', literally 'thrice six', as well as in the well-known vigesimal units. The preservation of the sequence *p* . . . k^w in the word for 'five', when the second member of a compound (**dwei-penk*^{w}*-* > *deac*), may be taken as the final piece of evidence for the independence of the assimilation *p* . . . k^w > k^w . . . k^w in Celtic and Italic.

[10] Hamp, *loc. cit.*: k^w/p realized as k^w in Goidelic, *p* in Brittonic.

These two are the phonological developments presumed to be shared by Italic and Celtic; both must be rejected. When we set beside them the enormous differences between the two in the earliest reconstructible stages of the phonological system of each, it is difficult to imagine a unity any later than Late Indo-European itself. This situation contrasts notably with that of Baltic and Slavic, where in general a rather simple set of phonological rules operating fairly late—"palatalizations" of the velars, metatheses, monophthongizations, and so on—will generate Common Slavic forms from those of Common Baltic. For "Italo-Celtic," on the other hand, we would have to account for the unvoicing and spirantization of the "aspirates" in Italic, and their voicing and merger with the voiced unaspirated stops in Celtic; the maintenance of a consonantal square in Italic (the Oscan and Umbrian elimination of the labiovelars is surely late, as is that of Greek), and the peculiar form of the development of a triangular system in Celtic, intimately bound up with the "loss" of Indo-European *p*; the Italic preservation intact of the five-vowel system with a correlation of length, beside the Celtic rearrangement of the long vowels and diphthongs (*ē* > *ī*, *ei* > *ē*) and elimination of *ō* (> *ā* or *ū*). The sheer inefficiency of generating these two systems from anything except Indo-European itself is enough to justify rejecting an intermediate Italo-Celtic unity.

The last item in Meillet's list is a small set of lexemes common to Celtic and Italic alone: some eight items, increased by three in the *Esquisse*. It should be pointed out immediately that Meillet himself was able to give a far longer list of inherited lexemes occurring uniquely in Greek and Armenian—some twenty-five items—without for that postulating a Greco-Armenian unity.[11] As is well known in Indo-European studies (and is deserving of wider recognition among American linguists), simple and unstructured lexical correspondences are the weakest possible evidence for genetic classification or subgrouping.[12]

Not all the Italo-Celtic lexemes adduced by Meillet are exact cognates, e.g., *īmus* : *ísel*, *pectus* : *ucht*, *terra* : *tír*, *ille* / *ollo-*, *ul-trā* : *t-all*. Of those that are, the only ones of structural significance (because they are part of a system!) are the preverbs and prepositions *dē* : *dí-*, *co(m)-* : *co(m)-*, and the latter, as Cowgill points out, must be also connected with Germanic *ga-*. To these I would also add *re(d)-* : *fri(th)-* < *wr̥t*[13] (: Lat. *uertō*). These three preverbal forms testify to the close relationship of Italic and Celtic; their evidence is similar to that of Lat. *ad* : OIr. *ad-* : Goth. *at*, showing somewhat wider affinities. But they can in no

---

[11] *Esquisse d'une grammaire comparée de l'arménien classique*^{2} (Vienna, 1936).

[12] Cf. K. V. Teeter, *Proc. IX Int. Cong. of Ling.* 771–777 (The Hague, 1964).

[13] Cf. Hamp, *Bull. of the Board of Celt. Stud.* 15.124–125 (1953).

sense be taken as indicating a unity; we need only juxtapose the total system of preverbs and prepositions in the two language groups to see that they neither "recover" each other, nor "complete" each other.[14] To look from the Celtic side, there is no Latin or Italic cognate of *ar* 'before' (incl. *ir-* : περὶ), *aith-* (semantically = *re(d)-*), *co* 'to', *do* 'to', *íar* 'after', *ni-* 'down', *oc* 'at', *oss-* 'up, off', *tar* 'across', *to-* 'to', *tret* 'hrough'. From the Latin side, there is no Celtic cognate of *ab, ante, apud, circum, ob, per, prae*. Certain of these could perhaps be reduced, for example, *tar* : *trāns* as ultimate cognates; but such equations could be balanced by, for instance, the absence of *s-* in Ir. *fo, for* < **upo, *upor* : *sub, super*. Anyone who takes the trouble to set up for himself the *system* of preverbs and/or prepositions in the two languages, even in rigorously excluding late developments in each, will be convinced that in no way can the two be reduced to a unity.

The composite suffix *-tiō/n-*, item seven on Meillet's first list, has already been discussed above. In the later list, Meillet points also to the suffix *-tū-t-*, which is found principally in Italic, Celtic, and Germanic. Such forms doubtless are evidence for early contact among the three groups, but they are clearly distinct; *-tūt-* is masculine in Celtic, but feminine in Latin.

The sixth item on Meillet's list is the superlative suffix **-samo-* (**-s°mo-*): the type *maximus* (*maxumus*), Osc. *nessimas* 'proximae', OIr. *nessam*, W *nesaf* 'nearest'. In such forms as these, it is clear that the suffixes are identical. But it is important to note that the identity between the two is valid only for the athematic adjectives: **mag-samo-*, etc. For the thematic type we have different forms: Lat. **-is-samo-* > *-issimus*, or **-(r)o-samo-* > *-errimus* (type *miserrimus*), but Celt. **-isamo-* (OW *hinhaf*, OIr. *sinem* 'oldest' < **senisamo-* to **seno-*, cf. Gaul. Οὐξισάμη). Add to this the fact that Umbrian shows no *-s-* in *nuvime* 'newest' (IIa 26). The two (*-isamo-* and *-samo-*) are not the same; they could be derived from the same form only by ignoring the *-is-* of Lat. *-is-simo-*, and by assuming that the Celtic form has been generalized from the suffixation of *-samo-* to *i*-stem adjectives, like Lat. *ācerrimus* **ācri-samo-*. But considering the numerical preponderance of *o*-stem adjectives in Celtic, together with the fact that the adjective is one place where the thematic nominal type is most ancient in Indo-European, an influence of *i*-stem adjectives in Celtic is not readily admissible. We

[14] In this way I would answer the point—in itself methodologically significant and worth retaining—of the late J. Vendryes, who stated (*Revue celtique* 42.380 [1925]): "Le résultat de la comparaison n'est pas que les langues italiques et celtiques se recouvrent, mais que sur presque chaque point de leur structure elles se complètent."

must regard the two groups, Italic and Celtic, as closely similar, in that they alone share the *-s-*; but the formation cannot be completely reduced to a unity.

The difference of the total system in each group of the superlative, and of the comparison adjective in general, also speaks strongly against a unity. In Celtic, *-samo-* is the unique superlative formation, whereas in Latin we have forms such as *īmus, summus, infimus, optimus, ultimus,* with suffixes **-mo-, *-amo-, *-tamo-*, all of which have other well-known Indo-European affinities. In Celtic the only comparable forms are found in the ordinals in *-am-*(+ *-eto-*), e.g., Gaul. *sextametos, decametos,* OIr. *sechtmad, dechmad,* cf. Lat. *septimus, decimus,* Skt. *saptamá-, daśamá-*. The relation of these to the superlative formations deserves fuller exploration.

We may add to all this the fact that the Celtic comparison of the adjective includes a fourth term, the equative ('as good as'). The formation is of obscure origin and different in the two branches of Celtic, but the category itself is surely old. Thurneysen (*OIGr.* 237) conjectures that the two are related: MW *-het* < **-iset* . . . , with the **-t-* appearing in Ir. *-ith(ir)*. But it is difficult to account for the suffixation of *-ir*; the final palatalized *-r'* of *móir* 'as great as' (*mór* 'great'), *lir* 'as many as' (*il* 'many') is not easily segmented out. On the other hand, the Brittonic *-het* can be analyzed as **is* + *eto-*, with a suffix curiously paralleling the superlative **-is* + *amo-*; just as *-amo-* is an ordinal suffix in *septimus, saptamá-*, so *-eto-* is an ordinal suffix in Ir. *cóiced* 'fifth'. The productive Irish ordinal suffix *-mad*, which ultimately prevails throughout (Mod. Ir. *cúigmhadh* /ku:g'u:/, etc.), simply combines the two, **-am(o)* + *eto-*.

There are notable syntactic differences as well: in Celtic the equative, comparative, and superlative are uninflected forms and are syntactically construed only as predicate nominatives. In the original version of the present paper, I suggested that this obligatory predicate nominative construction represented a notable archaism; I have since discovered that this view was anticipated by Meillet in an article in the *Mélanges J. Loth* 122–125 (Paris, 1927). The question merits a fresh examination, which I believe would uphold the essential correctness of Meillet's and my view; but it cannot be attempted here. We have, in any event, simply on the immediate evidence of the data, a rather deep divergence between Italic and Celtic.

Meillet's third item is the genitive singular of *o*-stems in *-ī*, which belongs to the plane of nominal declension. Between the publication of Meillet's first and second lists came Wackernagel's comparison of the Indo-Iranian type *mithunī-kṛ-* 'to pair', Av. *dāityō-aēsmi buyå* 'may you become *dāityō-aēsma-* ('with religiously suitable firewood')',[15] which provided an attestation of a similar formation outside of Italic and Celtic. This equation has recently been denied, in a long study by A. Bloch in *KZ* 76.182–242 (1959–1960), which would perhaps throw the morpheme *-ī* back into the sphere of Italic and Celtic once more. The formation is, however, also attested in the Illyrian Messapic. The peculiarity of its implementation in Messapic, gen. sg. *-ī* to *yo*-stems (nom. sg. *-es*) but gen. sg. *-aī* to *o*-stems (nom. sg. *-as*), would militate against its having been borrowed from Italic on the soil of Italy, particularly since the nearest adjacent Italic languages do not themselves show a genitive in *-ī* (Oscan *-eis* < *i*-stems).

The integration into the paradigm of the *o*- and *yo*-stems of a form in *-ī* in the function of a genitive singular may be a common "Southwestern" feature of Italic, Celtic, and Messapic. But we know that a single dialectal group in Indo-European may show divergent forms of the *o*-stem genitive, as in OPruss. *deiwas* (< **-oso*) : Lith. *diẽvo* (< abl. **-ōd*). The closest dialect to Latin within Italic, Faliscan, shows a gen. sg. *-osio* in the earliest texts (*eko kaisiosio*, Vetter 245); [16] the same form is in my opinion preserved in the Latin pronominal genitives of the type *eiiu-s*, *quoiiu-s* (*cuius*), as well as in OIr. *a* (leniting) 'his', MW *eidd-aw* < **esyo*. Under these circumstances it would appear that the implementation of *-ī* was not entirely parallel, nor equally general, in Italic and Celtic; we may note that in older Latin the genitive of *yo*-stems was *-ī* (which perhaps agrees with Skt. *-ī* to both *-a-* and *-ya-*), whereas OIr. *-i* requires **-iī* (*-iyī*) to *yo*-stems.

The great variation among the Indo-European languages in the form of the *o*-stem genitives would indicate that there simply was no Indo-European form; this is supported by the identity of nom. *-aš* and gen. *-aš* in Hittite, and by the absence of a genitive case in Luvian, where the relational *-ašša/i-* functionally parallels the Old Latin type *erīlis fīlius*, or Old Russian *knjažĭ dvorŭ*.[17] This would suggest that the genitive singular of *o*-stems is one place in the system where we should expect innovations to occur. It is not surprising that Italic and Celtic should settle on a morpheme *-ī* which clearly existed in Indo-European somewhere in the penumbra between an inflexional and a derivational form (I find it hard to separate the "feminine" *-ī*). But considering that Italic also tried out *-osyo*, and that *-ī* recurs as genitive singular also in Mes-

[15] *Mélanges Saussure* 125–152 (Paris, 1908).

[16] Cf. J. Safarewicz, *Eos* 47.101–105 (1954), who defends the "prisca latinitas" of *Metioeo Fufetioeo* in Ennius (*Ann.* 126).

[17] I hope to examine elsewhere the formal and particularly syntactic evidence for the late and secondary character of the genitive in general in Indo-European.

sapic, we must conclude that the community of -ī in Italic and Celtic is attributable to early contact, rather than to an original unity.

Meillet's fourth item is the deponent and passive desinences characterized by -*r*(-), e.g., OIr. -*berar* 'fertur', Umbr. *ferar* 'feratur' (but OIr. -*berthar* 'feratur', with -*t*-). With the discovery of Tocharian and Hittite it became clear to Meillet and others that these endings represented the conservation of very archaic forms, which had been replaced in varying fashions in other Indo-European languages. For Meillet this was a classic case of "marginal" preservation: "Il s'agit donc d'un type ancien conservé dans les langues périphériques mais éliminé dans la partie centrale du domaine." (*Esquisse*[3] 24.) To explain the *r* endings as "marginal" implies that they are ab initio incompatible with the desinential system reconstructed on the basis of Greek and Indo-Iranian. But this view is by no means necessarily correct. In a brief but suggestive article,[18] Kuryłowicz has sketched how we may derive both the systems of Greek and Indo-Iranian on the one hand, and those of Italic, Celtic, and Hittite on the other, from the *same* original system. While some of the data remain to be accounted for, and while certain of Kuryłowicz's morphological transformations are not altogether satisfactory, I am convinced that he has pointed out the right direction for future productive research on the problem.

For the specific relation of the Italic and Celtic forms, it is sufficient to reproduce Kuryłowicz's remarks (*loc. cit.*, 134): 'It is scarcely necessary to observe that the mediopassive endings have been transformed independently in Keltic and in Italic.' To attempt to survey the whole development of the desinential system in each language group would involve a separate study, indeed a monograph; no such survey can be contemplated here. I point out that in view of the disparity in the other and more fundamental persons of the paradigm, the identity of the 1st sg. Lat. ind. *sequor*, subj. *sequar* : OIr. ind. -*moiniur*,[19] subj. -*menar*, is far more likely to reflect parallel and independent development than to be a common inheritance. It should further be noted that in Irish as in other Indo-European languages the most archaic forms of the indicative, reflecting earlier "injunctive" forms, are found in the Old Irish imperative (outside the 2nd sg. ind.), rather than in the Old Irish indicative.[20]

---

[18] Hibernica. III. The deponential (mediopassive) endings, *Biul. Polsk. Tow. Jęz.* 20.131–136 (1961).

[19] Ir. *sechur*, cited by Meillet, *Esquisse*[3] 23, as an exact cognate of *sequor*, does not exist. Since it is a weak *i*-verb in the earliest Irish, we should expect in any case 1st sg. *se(*i*)*chiur*.

[20] For the demonstration, see pp. 41–49 of my study, "Preliminaries to a historical and comparative analysis of the syntax of the Old Irish verb," *Celtica* 6.1–49 (1963). The same has been arrived at independently by W. Meid, in his (un-

For this reason it is a priori more likely that the earliest Celtic mediopassive personal endings of which we have sure information are 1st sg. *-ur*, 2nd sg. *-the*, 3rd sg. *-eth*, 1st pl. *-emmar*, 3rd pl. *-etar* (*OIGr*. 373). The 2nd pl. is, in classical Old Irish, identical with the active form *-id*(*-ith*), and Meillet regards this as significant, recalling the secondary origin of Lat. *-minī* (and archaic ipv. *-minō*). But as D. A. Binchy has pointed out privately, in archaic Old Irish texts we have good evidence for the 2nd pl. ipv. *fomna(i)s* 'beware!' to *fo-moinethar*,[21] hence an old ending *-ais*. One is tempted to compare Gk. -(ε)σθε, though that has been taken as secondary.

Before passing on to Meillet's fifth item and the last in my ordering, namely the mood and tense signs *-ā-*, *-s-*, and *-b-*, it is important to add a brief note on the participles and the formation of the feminine. In his celebrated article, "Essai de chronologie des langues indo-européennes," *BSL* 32.1–28 (1931), Meillet presented a number of arguments for the late character of the feminine gender. His theory has been much discussed, but this is clearly not the place to review the whole issue; I would only call attention to one point. Meillet notes the absence of a feminine in Latin *i*-stem adjectives (type *fortis*), regarding it as ancient, and notes that Celtic agrees (type *maith* 'good'). He further calls attention to the absence of a feminine in the Latin participles, and the type *ferēns* is also singled out as an archaic survival in *Esquisse*[8] 19. Whatever view one may take of the Latin forms—a **bher(e)ntī* would yield *ferēns* in Latin, cf. Skt. *naptī́* : *neptis* and *mēns* < **mentis*—it should be made clear that Celtic shows unmistakable traces of distinct masculine and feminine participial forms. These are all the more probative for the fact that the participle as a deverbative grammatical category was given up in the Celtic languages at a relatively early date. We need only point to OIr. *carae* m. 'friend' < **karant-s* (: *caraid* 'loves'), and *birit* f. 'sow' < **bher(e)ntī* (: *berid* 'bears') or m. *cano*, gen. *canat* 'poet of the fourth degree' beside f. *canait* 'Sängerin', both from the verbal root *can-* 'sing'.[22] The feminines in **-(e)ntī* must be old, on the evidence of the equation *Brigit* (an ancient Irish pagan goddess, cf. Cormac's Glossary §150) : Vedic *bṛhatī́* 'the exalted one' (recurring as a divine epithet, e.g., of Uṣas). The sole counterexamples one might cite are the adjective *tee*, *té* (n. pl. *teit*) 'hot' < **tep-ent-*, which has the same form for all genders,

published) *Habilitationsschrift*; cf. his articles in *ZCP* 29.155–179 (1962), *Orbis* 10.434–438 (1961).

[21] Cf. *ZCP* 11.97 §56 (Audacht Moraind, version B), and see the RIA Dictionary s.v. *fo-moinethar*.

[22] For a fuller collection and analysis, see Vendryes, *Corolla Linguistica* (Festschrift Sommer) 229–234 (Wiesbaden, 1955); J. Pokorny, *Münch. Stud. zur Sprachwiss.* 15.5 ff. (1959).

or the feminine gender of *doe* (acc. sg. *doit*) 'upper arm'. But there is no indication that *doe* was ever a participle, and since *tee* is the only adjective stem in **-nt-*, its inflexion would naturally tend to be assimilated to that of other consonantal stem adjectives, which do not differentiate the feminine.

We may conclude with the examination of the verbal system proper. Meillet's evidence for Italo-Celtic inheritances includes the subjunctives in *-ā-* and in *-s-* (archaic *aduenat, faxō*) and in the future in *-b-*. In his final statement on Italo-Celtic (*Esquisse*[3]), Meillet no longer maintained the equation of the Latin *b*-future with the Old Irish *f*-future; it is not mentioned. Rather, as he clearly states (p. 30), the *b*-future is a purely Latin development, built on the imperfect in *-bā-*, which is confined to Italic. In rejecting the equation *-b-* : *-f-* Meillet followed Thurneysen (cf. *OIGr.* 398), and in this view he was eminently justified. "Les rapprochements valent seulement dans la mesure ou ils sont soumis à des règles strictes";[23] Old Irish *-f-* cannot be derived from IE **bh*, hence this equation, however tempting,[24] must be abandoned once and for all. The Irish *f*-future remains an enigma, but it has no connections with Italic, and any explanation for it must come from within Celtic, specifically Goidelic.

The Old Irish subjunctive in *-s-*, preserved residually in Early Welsh, is not a Common Celtic subjunctive in *-s-*; it is a Common Celtic aorist indicative in *-s-*. I have demonstrated this at some length in my *Indo-European origins of the Celtic verb. I. The sigmatic aorist* (Dublin, 1962), and the argumentation need not be reiterated here. The distribution of the *s*-subjunctive in Celtic, and its athematic character, preclude comparison with the sporadic Latin type *faxō*. I do not wish to go into the complex question of the origin of this type in Latin, which demands another monograph. Suffice it to say that the coexistence of a subjunctive in *-s-* and a subjunctive in *-ā-* in Celtic and Latin (where the "subjunctive" in *-s-* appears as a future) is not common patrimony; it is a historical accident.

The archaic character of the subjunctive in *-ā-*, as well as its original optative function, have been discussed above. It is one of the few forms that do testify to the early close relation of Italic and Celtic. But this should not conceal from us the fact that the implementation of this modal morpheme *-ā-* in the two systems is not the same. In Celtic, *-ā-* was originally suffixed to all verbs, strong as well as weak; in the weak *i*-verbs the type *do-lugi* 'forgives, remits' < **log-yo/ī-* ("iterative-causative" to **legh-*) with subj. (2nd pl.) *do-logaid* < **log-ā-* is surely more ancient

[23] Meillet, *La méthode comparative en linguistique historique* 41 (Oslo, 1925).
[24] Cf. A. Sommerfelt, *MSL* 22.230–233 (1921).

than the corresponding Latin type *mon-e-ā-s*. Similarly, in Celtic but not Italic, the weak verbs in stem vowel *-ā-* also form a subjunctive in *-ā-*, with the result that indicative and subjunctive are identical; we have a very old vowel-dropping rule, *-ā-* + *-ā-* > *-ā-*. For Common Celtic we can posit two forms alone on the modal plane: an "optative" in *-ā-*, and a "desiderative" with reduplication and a suffix *-s-* (OIr. *s*-future),[25] which was confined to nonderived ("strong") verbs. The relation of these to each other in Common Celtic is unclear, but we do know that they could not have originally complemented each other in the omnibus function of a "subjunctive." While the form in *-ā-* recurs in Italic, that with reduplication and *-s-* has a correspondent only in the Indo-Iranian desiderative.

The total picture of the modal category in Italic is entirely different. Beside the old optative in *-ā-*, Latin shows the old optative in *-yē/ī-* (*siēs/sīmus, edim, uelim*). In Latin it was doubtless more productive at an earlier period, since it was incorporated into the innovated perfect subjunctive **-is-ī-* (*fēcerim*). But for this optative formation we have no analogue in Celtic whatsoever. The imperfect subjunctive in **-sē-* is common to Latin and the Italic dialects (*essēs, fusíd*); no comparable form exists in Celtic. The morpheme *-sē-* is perhaps an Italic creation, but it was not made up out of whole cloth. We may assume the *-s-* of *-sē-* is the same as that followed by *-e/o-* in *faxō*, which leaves us with a mark *-ē-*.

This *-ē-* recurs elsewhere in Latin as a modal or tense morpheme: in the future of primary verbs (*ferēs, faciēs*), which was doubtless earlier a mood, and in the present subjunctive of *ā*-verbs (*laudem, -ēs*). The manuals separate these two, and derive neither from an original *-ē-*; the future is equated with Greek and Vedic long-vowel subjunctive, *ferēs* : φέρῃς : *bharās*(*i*), and the subjunctive is derived from an athematic optative suffix, **laudā-yē-m*. There are serious difficulties with both these explanations. The long vowel subjunctive shows apophony *ē/ō* in the paradigm, repeating the distribution of *e/o*. It is very difficult to explain why Latin should have generalized *-ē-* in all the persons, including the first singular; the form replaced by subj. *-am* was *-em* (archaic *sinem, faciem*), probably to differentiate the form from the impf. subj. *-em*, and not a putative *-ō* identical with the indicative. The optative morpheme was apophonic *-yē/ī-*, and it is equally difficult to explain why in the putative type *-ā-yē-* Latin should have generalized the full grade *-yē-* throughout the paradigm (*laudēmus, -ētis, -ent*), when the undeniable trend in the language was to generalize the weak grade *-ī-*, as in *edim*,

[25] Unless the *s*-future is a late reduplicated form of the *s*-subjunctive, which is perhaps less likely.

uelim.[26] For these reasons I prefer to take both formations at face value; they show an Italic modal morpheme *-ē-*. It is this *-ē-* which was suffixed to *-s-* in the Italic period, to form the new modal suffix *-sē-*. It is worth noting that beside the modal signs *-ā-*, *-ē-*, *-sē-*, we have one form in Latin showing that a parallel *-sā-* was formed: the adverb *dumtaxat* < *dum . . . tag-sā-t* 'until it touch' (the earlier 'tmesis' is preserved in *CIL* 1².582).[27] The modal sign *-ē-* is ancient in Italic; but no trace of it is found in Celtic. It is tempting to relate the Latin modal system with *-ā-* and *-ē-* to the Balto-Slavic infinitive and preterit stems in *-ā-* and *-ē-* (Lith. extended pret. *-ėjo-*), which C. S. Stang derives from aorists.[28] But this is put forth simply as a hypothesis.

In the total system of the finite verb in Latin, we have a fundamental opposition of infectum and perfectum, a present, past, and future of each in the indicative, and a present-future and past in the subjunctive—ten functional structure points in all. Leaving aside the present of infectum and perfectum (i.e., the perfect), which show characteristic retentions of a variety of Indo-European types, the forms present the following configuration:

	Indicative		*Subjunctive*	
	Infectum	*Perfectum*	*Infectum*	*Perfectum*
fut.	*-be-*, *-ē-*, *-(s)e-*	*-is-e-*		
pres.			*-ā-*, *-ē-*, *-ī-*	*-is-ī-*
past	*-bā-*	*-is-ā-*	*-sē-*	*-is-sē-*

Of all the rich variety of forms here, one and one alone is also found in Celtic: *-ā-*. This organization of the verbal system is Common Italic, but it bears little or no resemblance to that of Common Celtic, which looks far more like the organization of the verbal system of Common Greek.[29]

Under these circumstances of both formal and functional disparity, we are led to the unavoidable conclusion that Italo-Celtic unity is a myth. The only common language from which both Italic and Celtic can be

[26] The tendency to generalize the weak grade in cases of paradigmatic apophony is itself a noteworthy common feature of Celtic and Italic, as is the morphophonemic suppression of the reduplicating syllable in the composition of verb and preverb.

[27] The formal identity of this **-sā-* with the **-sā-* underlying the Brittonic subjunctive is a coincidence. Cf. my *Indo-European origins of the Celtic verb* 145–156.

[28] *Das slavische und baltische Verbum* 188 ff. (Oslo, 1942).

[29] Cf. *IE origins of the Celtic verb* 107–110.

derived is Indo-European itself; the only single grammar that could account for each would be the grammar of Indo-European. For this reason I must reject the final part of Meillet's statement (*Esquisse*[3] 27) that "les colons qui ont porté en Occident les parlers sur lesquels reposent l'italique et le celtique avaient sensiblement la même langue." The dictum itself, however, is worthy of retention; if we delete the last five words, we have an elegant linguistic statement of the nature of the historical transmission of common languages. Meillet himself stated in 1925 that "la période de communauté italo-celtique rend peu de services";[30] as in other aspects of both historical and descriptive linguistics, want of utility is prima facie evidence of want of verisimilitude.

Meillet has spoken at several places of an "Indo-European nation," an "Italo-Celtic nation," and an "Italic nation." The precise value of the term *nation* as used by Meillet is uncertain; he himself saw clearly that Indo-European society was tribal and familiar, and "ne comportait pas dǝ pouvoir central" (*La méthode comparative* 19). In fact, it is difficult to imagine what an "Italo-Celtic nation" would consist of, and what would justify the use of the term except the hypothesis of a single language. Ireland was Irish-speaking for millennia before anybody could be accused of "bringing starvation to the whole Irish nation." The very concept of "nation" was foreign to Celtic-speaking cultures down almost to the present day, and the Celts never developed the notion of a polity such as is familiar from Greek and Roman tradition. As for the Romans, the development of a nation is a process that took place in historical times, and certainly on the soil of Italy itself. The picture to be gathered from extralinguistic data of the migrations of "Italic" speakers into Italy would seem to preclude any consideration of an "Italic nation" and, a fortiori, an "Italo-Celtic nation."[31]

In ancient Ireland as depicted in the Irish Law Tracts, which furnish the clearest and most direct picture of what Indo-European tribal society must have been like,[32] the highest social unit was the *túath*, an amorphous collection of joint families (Ir. *fine*) "ruled" by a 'petty-king' (Ir. *rí*). Any putative larger social entity (such as would seem to be required by Meillet's "nation") was in ancient Ireland purely a personal relation (generally one of obligation) between the 'petty-king' and an 'over-king' (Ir. *ruiri* < *ro* + *rí*), who might himself be under a personal obligation to a 'king of over-kings' (Ir. *rí ruirech*). But the 'over-king' had no rights of "government" or administration or levy over the *túath* of the *rí*, nor did the 'king of over-kings' over the *túath* of the 'over-king'.

[30] *La méthode comparative* 17.

[31] See especially Pulgram, *The Tongues of Italy* 229n.

[32] I must acknowledge my profound indebtedness to D. A. Binchy's stimulating Harvard lectures on the Institutions of the Insular Celts.

The 'king of over-kings' was, in Ireland, the king of a province (e.g., Ulster, Connacht); but the "province" was purely a geographical area of Ireland, not a political unit, as is shown by its Irish name *coiced*, lit. 'fifth'.

That for some Italic speakers the highest social unit was likewise at one time the **toutā* may be inferred from Osc. *touto* 'populus', Umbr. *tota* 'civitas'. But this is a general feature of Western Indo-European languages, as shown by Goth. *þiuda* and especially *þiudans* 'king' (with Gmc. *-*ono*-). The 'king' is literally 'he in whom the *þiuda* is realized';[33] it is the king who personally represents, symbolizes, the tribe, both in its relations with the outside world (other tribes) and with the supernatural.

The linguistic expression in Indo-European for this relation is the suffix *-*no*- (or its dialectal replacement, as in Germanic): Goth. *þiuda* → *þiudans*.[34] The same process is found in Slavic: Serbo-Croatian *žúpa* 'territorial or administrative unit' → *žùpân* 'ruler of a *župa*, he who represents the *župa*'.[35] For Celtic, following a brilliant suggestion of Binchy, we may compare the name of a powerful Northern British tribe *Brigantes* → **brigantīnos* 'he who represents the Brigantes',[36] the etymon of MW *brëenhin* 'king' which ousted the older *rhi* < **rēg-s*. Finally the formation recurs, as is well known, in Lat. *tribūnus* (with lengthened stem vowel before secondary suffix) 'he who represents, who *is* the *tribus*'.

The word *tribus* is worthy of further consideration. It is found also in Umbrian, always in asyndetic conjunction with *tota*-; it is applied by the Iguvini to themselves, as in, for example, III 24–25 *tutape(r) iiuvina trefiper iiuvina* 'pro civitate Iguvina, pro tribu Iguvina' (Vetter), as well as to the hostile inhabitants of Tadinum, twenty kilometers away, as in, for example, VIb 53–54 *pis est totar tarsinater trifor tarsinater* 'quisquis est

---

[33] To utilize Benveniste's analysis of the parallel suffix *-*to*-, *Noms d'agent et noms d'action en indo-européen* 167–168 (Paris, 1948).

[34] First pointed out by F. de Saussure; see the *Cours*, Pt. V, chap. 4; and cf. R. Godel, *Les sources manuscrites du Cours* 111 (Geneva, 1957). For a full treatment see Meid, *Beitr. zur Namenforschung* 8.72–108, 113–126 (1957).

[35] Slav. *župan* is evidently in ablaut with the title OCz. *hpan*, Pol. *pan*, v. Vasmer, *Russ. etym. Wb.* s.v. *župa*, *župan*, *pan*. But the connection of Skt. *gopā́*- seems farfetched. It should be noted that the Slavic title *župan* was sociopolitically significant enough in prehistoric times to be borrowed into Turkic; it is attested in the form ΖΩΑΠΑΝ, ΖΟΑΠΑΝ in the ninth-century Proto-Bulgar inscription of the Treasure of Nagy-Szent-Milkós, before our earliest documentation in Slavic itself. See O. Pritsak, *Die bulgarische Fürstenliste und die Sprache der Protobulgaren* (*Ural-Altaische Bibliothek* I) 85–90 (Wiesbaden, 1955).

[36] Binchy would define him rather as 'he who incarnates, *is* the goddess *Brigantī*'. Either interpretation is possible; from the Indo-European point of view the relation was identical, cf. Lith. *Perkúnas* '(the god) who incarnates the sacred oak'.

civitatis Tadinatis, tribus Tadinatis'. According to Whatmough,[37] such passages "imply a territorial division into tribes (*trifu*) as well as the larger unit of the city (*tota*)." It is difficult, however, to account for the consistent singular *trifu*, if the *tota* were the larger unit and comprised a number of *trifu*. The difficulty becomes even clearer if we transpose the passage to Rome: *pro civitate Romana* parallels *tutaper iiuvina*, but a *pro tribu Romana* would not make sense. Furthermore, in III 23–25 we would seem to have an ascending order: *fratrusper atiieries, ahtisper eikvasatis, tutape(r) iiuvina, trefiper iiuvina* 'pro fratribus Atiediis, pro actis (= *vītīs*) collegialibus (?),[38] pro civitate Iguvina, pro — Iguvina'. Umbrian *trifu* in these passages makes far better sense if we translate it as *populus*, or better as Irish *túath*; it is the highest Umbrian sociopolitical (as well as geographical) unit. Whatmough invokes Livy (31.2.6.) *per Umbriam, qua tribum Sapiniam vocant*, as evidence for the tribe being a territorial division of the city. But the passage makes better sense if *tribus* denotes precisely the territory of a petty "kingdom," in short a *túath*. In this respect *trifu* is the semantic replacement of the inherited Italic **toutā*. The latter has been specialized in the strictly local acceptation 'city', as is clear from the locative with postposition VIa 26 *toteme iouine* 'in civitate Iguvina'. In Oscan, however, *touto* retained the meaning of 'populus', and it is surely no accident that no form of *trifu-* is found in Oscan or closely related dialects.

In Latin, it is the existence of the derivative *tribū-nus*, 'he who represents the *tribus*', which demonstrates that the same replacement of the Italic sociopolitical unit **toutā* by *tribus* occurred as in Umbrian. It is this fact that explains the complete absence from native Latin of the Western Indo-European word **teutā*.[39] Now such a replacement of linguistic terms implies that an earlier social institution, the **toutā*, was replaced by a newer social institution, the *tribus*; and commonly such replacements of institutions are brought about by borrowings from, or the imposition of, a dominant foreign culture. The geographical position of this innovation in Italy, in Latin and in Umbrian, would immediately

---

37 *The Foundations of Roman Italy* 200.

38 So, most recently, with some hesitation, A. Ernout, *Le dialecte ombrien* 107, 117 (Paris, 1961), following Vetter for *ahtis*, Buck for *eikvasatis*.

39 The adjective *tōtus* is a dialect borrowing; on its semantic history see now Szemerényi, *Fachtagung für idg. u. allgem. Spr.* (*Innsbrucker Beiträge zur Kulturwissenschaft, Sonderheft* 15 [1962]) 195–198, though his interpretation is not entirely satisfactory. Note, however, that Hitt. *tuzzi-* must be excluded from this group, as shown by Benveniste, *Hittite et indo-européen* 122–124 (Paris, 1962). I still insist that the term is Western Indo-European, despite Pers. *toda*, Sogd. *twōk* 'mass, crowd'; the latter are not sociologically significant.

suggest the neighboring Etruscan as the source, and the Etruscan political dominance in the two areas is well known.[40]

Evidence for the Etruscan connections of *tribus* has been shown by C. O. Thulin;[41] it is apparent in the names of the three oldest *tribūs* of Rome, *Ramnes Luceres Tities*, though their tripartition and the social symbolism they reflect in Roman legend is probably an Indo-European inheritance, as G. Dumézil has convincingly shown.[42]

The Indo-European etymology for *tribus* is given by Walde-Hofmann as *tri-* + *bhū-*, 'vermutlich ursprgl. "Drittel"'; Ernout and Meillet qualify this as a "simple supposition," and the linguistic analysis is all against it. In the first place, in no Indo-European language are ordinals or fractions compounded with the verb **bhū-*, and it is not easy to imagine what the function of such a verb in the compound would be. In the second place, a root form, **-bhus*, with gen. sg. *-bhous* (Umb. *trifor* = Lat. *tribūs*), as the second member of a compound, is otherwise unknown in Italic, or for that matter anywhere else in Indo-European. Forms such as Rig-Vedic *śam-bhú-*, *vi-bhú*, *mayo-bhú-*, are found mostly in nom. and acc. sg. (and never in gen. sg.), and are in origin clearly shortened forms of the corresponding cases of *śam-bhū́-*, *vi-bhū́*, *mayo-bhū́-*. To assert that Italic underwent the same development, purely on the evidence of the single form *tribus*, would be methodologically unjustified. And finally, the real impetus[43] toward the segmentation *tri-bhu-* goes back only to a typical etymology of Varro, *L.L.* 5.55: *ager Romanus primum divisus in partis* tris, *a quo* tribus *appelata Titiensium, Ramnium, Lucerum*, i.e., the three oldest tribes of Rome. That there was an original geographical division in Rome under the Etruscans, into three *tribus*, is perhaps possible, and this situation would lend itself to reinterpretation on another level in terms of a tripartite social ideology. But in Umbrian there is no indication at all of a connection between *trifu* and 'three'; it is always *the* tribus (= populus) Iguvina, Tadina. The specifically three ancient tribes of Rome may be equally well, if not better, taken as purely symbolic legend; the four urban tribes at the time of Servius Tullius (Livy 1.43.13), and the sixteen original rural tribes, are probably closer to the truth.

If a native Italic compound **tri-bhu-* thus appears unlikely in the extreme, then we must reject an Indo-European etymology for *tribus*,

---

[40] For Umbrian, cf. Whatmough, *op. cit.* 206.

[41] *Die Etruscische Disciplin. III. Die Ritualbücher* 48–49 (*Göteborgs Högskolas Årsskrift* 1909.1).

[42] Cf. *Jupiter Mars Quirinus IV*, 113–170 (Paris, 1948); *L'héritage indo-européen à Rome* 184–234 (Paris, 1949); *Rituels indo-européens à Rome* 53 (Paris, 1954).

[43] The Δωριέες τριχάικες (τ 177) is probably mere coincidence.

trifu; a root form **tribhu-* would be impossible in Indo-European (*t* . . . *bh*). On the basis of their geographical distribution in Italy, in the sphere of Etruscan political dominance only, and on the evidence of other associations of *tribus* with Etruscan in Roman tradition, I would suggest that Latin *tribus* and Umbrian *trifu* are both loanwords from Etruscan.[44]

The original "Italic" sociopolitical structure may be conjectured to have been quite similar to that of Ireland: an amorphous collection of *túatha*, each "ruled," or represented by, a 'petty-king' (*rí*). The system was nowhere preserved intact; in Oscan territories the *touto* remained the political unit, but the petty-king was replaced by the administrative and judicial office of the *meddix tuticus* (Osc. *meddíx túvtíks*). In this change we may see the development of a native South Italic form of democracy;[45] but it is well to remember that the *meddix tuticus*, invested with a more modern concept of public authority, doubtless wielded far more administrative rule and power than his Italic ancestor or Celtic congener, the *rí tuaithe*, ever did.

In Umbria and in Rome the old Italic unit of the **toutā* was replaced, under Etruscan influence or direction, by a new geographical administrative unit, the *tribus*. The memory of this organizational innovation was preserved in Roman tradition about the king Servius Tullius: *conditor omnis in civitate discriminis ordinumque* (Livy 1.42.4); *quadrifariam enim urbe divisa regionibus collibusque, qui habitabantur, partes eas tribus appellavit* (1.43.13). In Rome, the foreign origin of *tribus* did not prevent the creation of the term *tribūnus*; though *tribus* is a borrowed word for a borrowed institution, the structural relation between *tribus* and *tribūnus* 'he who represents the *tribus*', is Indo-European both in form and in function.

The *tribūnus* was thus functionally comparable to the Irish *rí* or petty-king. In this position he is the replacement of the earlier *rēx*. The latter term was reapplied to a newer, and far more powerful office of kingship, the (at least partially) Etruscan *rēx*. In function the Roman monarch had little in common with the Indo-European **rēg-s*, or the Irish *rí*; traces of the sacral aspect of his original function are carried over in the office of the *rēx sacrōrum* (*sacrificulus*). It is a curious irony to reflect on the fact that it is primarily to the Etruscans that we owe the preservation in Latin—alone among the Italic languages[46]—of the ancient Indo-European term for 'king'.

The preceding pages, the final portion of this study, will have served

---

[44] Hoenigswald points out that another very probable Etruscan loanword in Latin, *idus*, shares with *tribus* the structural rarity of being a feminine *u*-stem.

[45] Whatmough, *op. cit.* 393–395.

[46] The feminine derivative occurs in Marrucinian, but only as a divine name: (Vetter 218) *regen[ai] peai cerie iouia* 'Reginae Piae Cerriae Iouiae'.

their purpose if they have shown that the considerations of a set of data in Celtic (in our case the institutions of tribe and kingship, together with their linguistic expression) may serve as a productive frame of reference in which to explain a related set of data in Italic. In this manner it may prove useful to consider Italic and Celtic together; but in no sense have we spoken, or should we speak, of an Italo-Celtic unity, either as a language, or as a culture.

The notion of "common languages"—Common Greek, Common Slavic, etc., on the one hand, Indo-Iranian, Balto-Slavic, Italo-Celtic on the other—is probably our most important single inheritance today from Schleicher's *Stammbaum*.[47] The first type we use every day; the second type we use according to the particular group and the given scholar.

The utility of such a notion as Common Greek cannot, I think, honestly be questioned, so long as we understand it to mean the set of linguistic features—both "retentions" and "innovations," or "divergences"—that serves to specify uniquely and set off all attested forms of Greek from (*a*) Indo-European itself, and (*b*) all other Indo-European "common languages." Such a definition is purely operational, and an analytical tool. It makes no specific supposition that there ever existed a community that spoke Common Greek as so defined. For example, certain of the features included in the specification may be incompatible at a given time; the same is true for what we specify as Common Indo-European. On the other hand it in no way excludes the possibility that such a community may have in fact existed; in this sense, the notion of Common Greek is not a fiction. But whether such a community existed or not is, from the point of view of the linguistic definition of Common Greek, irrelevant.

For the second type of "common language," for example, Balto-Slavic, we are in a somewhat different situation. When we posit a Common Slavic and a Common Baltic, defined as above, it would appear that a Common Balto-Slavic is not possible, since Common Baltic is inter alia that which differentiates Baltic from Slavic, and vice versa. But, if Common Baltic and Common Slavic are identical in large part, in respect to the set of features specified, then it may be more efficient to combine them into a single common language. A single grammar can account for both. Indo-Iranian is such a case; though there do exist notable differences between the two groups—not least, perhaps, is the quite extraordinary lack of resemblance between modern Indo-Aryan languages and modern Iranian languages—it is doubtless the intuitive

[47] No matter what we may feel about the *Stammbaum*, let us not forget that it was that model that first demonstrated that Sanskrit was not "Indo-European" itself, but a derivate of Indo-European, like everything else.

recognition of the precision of the identities between Common Indic and Common Iranian which led B. Delbrück in 1880 to retain the subgrouping of Indo-Iranian alone among the Indo-European languages.[48]

For Balto-Slavic one can entertain some doubts. But the identities are there, and the differences between Letto-Lithuanian and Old Prussian are sometimes greater than the differences between Letto-Lithuanian and Common Slavic. Hence we may leave the question of a Common Balto-Slavic open; V. V. Ivanov and V. N. Toporov suggest in fact that the grammar of Slavic is only a development of the grammar of Baltic.[49]

For Italo-Celtic, however, it seems evident that the consideration and comparison of Common Celtic and Common Italic, together with the not inconsiderable difficulties of the latter as a viable notion, would totally exclude any question of a common language. Common Celtic and Common Italic simply do not agree in the vast majority of instances; they cannot be superimposed one on the other. They show certain similarities, indeed. But these may be shared by the one group or the other with Germanic, or Greek, or Tocharian, or Hittite, or, finally, with Indo-Iranian (*marginalità*). We have, in the last analysis, two separate Indo-European language groups in recorded history, and (at least) two separate entities in prehistory, as defined above: Common Celtic and Common Italic.

(Participants in the discussion following the conference presentation of the first version of this paper: Cowgill, Senn, Hoenigswald, Hamp, Emeneau, Birnbaum, Polomé.)

---

[48] *Einleitung in das Sprachstudium* 137.

[49] K postanovke voprosa o drevnejšix otnošenijax baltijskix i slavjanskix jazykov, *IV Meždunar. Sjezd Slavistov. Doklady* (Moscow, 1958), esp. p. 39.

The Interrelationships Within Italic*

Madison S. Beeler
UNIVERSITY OF CALIFORNIA, BERKELEY

In treating a topic such as this, the first question that arises is how to define the term *Italic*, a word that has been used in widely varying senses for many years. When I was a graduate student I was not aware, or not made aware, of any difference of opinion on this question: Italic was a branch of Indo-European which comprised two subgroups; one denominated Latin-Faliscan and the other Oscan-Umbrian, the latter grouping including the so-called minor dialects such as Paelignian, Volscian, and Marrucinian. The time at which I was being introduced to the study of the languages of ancient Italy, however, was not long after a period which saw the appearance of a serious challenge to the doctrine I have just referred to and which had become an established part of the traditional classification of the Indo-European languages. This challenge, foreshadowed by the work of a number of scholars (among whom may be mentioned Alois Walde and Friedrich Müller-Izn), is associated chiefly with the name of the Florentine Indo-Europeanist Giacomo Devoto, who has been followed and supported by several other Italian linguists. Their position is, in brief, that Latin-Faliscan and Oscan-Umbrian owe their similarities to relatively late linguistic convergence, that the differences between the two groups are sharp and of ancient date, that these two groups therefore never constituted a subgroup intermediate between Proto-Indo-European and the attested languages, and that only Oscan-Umbrian (together with the so-called minor dialects mentioned above) properly deserves the appellation "Italic."

This restriction of application of the term is in conflict with extensions that it has received from time to time. It has been suggested more than once, for example, that the sparse relics of an obviously Indo-European language which have come to light in eastern Sicily can be interpreted as exhibiting features that would connect it rather closely with Latin, and so make it, too, "Italic," but the data are so meager, and the opinions of those who have worked with the language so divergent, that any position that has been taken in confronting the problem is not easily

* For reasons beyond the control of the editors, this contribution is published here in its original conference version, with only editorial changes.

assailable. Much the same may be said for attempts to identify an Indo-European language of "Italic" connections (the "Italic" here meant is rather of the Oscan-Umbrian variety) in some of those inscriptions of eastern central Italy called (by Whatmough in *Prae-Italic Dialects*) Southern East Italic. Here, however, there are not only many uncertainties in the transcription of the epigraphic material; it is even far from sure whether the language is Indo-European at all. Since nothing that would command even a limited measure of agreement among qualified students of this obscure language can be said, it will also be omitted from further discussion in this paper.

The situation is, I think I may say, different for another proposed extension of "Italic," an extension first put forward by myself. I refer to the hypothesis that Venetic ought properly to be classified as a member of the group that includes Latin and Faliscan and Oscan-Umbrian. The language of the some three hundred inscriptions from various sites in northeastern Italy was traditionally called "Illyrian," a group labeled "Veneto-Illyrian" or the like was set up, and the relationship with the undoubtedly Illyrian Messapic of the southeastern end of the peninsula was taken to be close. A new theory which appeared in 1950 was that of Hans Krahe, who assigned to Venetic a position within Indo-European separate from that of any other established group or subgroup, although special affinities with Germanic, "Italic," and Illyrian were recognized. The question of the genetic affiliations of this language has been rather widely debated during the past twelve or fourteen years, and a number of positions differing more or less widely from one another are currently defended. I had expected to discuss the problem in the present paper, and to reiterate my conviction that the linguistic facts of Venetic are best accounted for by the theory that the language was more closely related to Latin and Faliscan than it was to any other branch of Indo-European. But after I learned that Professor Polomé was going to recognize the interest this question has aroused by devoting a separate report to it I thought it better to omit further discussion of it here.

The question therefore, that I shall examine in what follows is the character of the relationship among Latin and Faliscan and Oscan-Umbrian; this will be the definition given to "Italic" during the remainder of what I have to say. Now Oscan and Umbrian are each of them languages with a marked individuality, and differ not only in many matters of phonology but also in several areas of morphology. Instances of the former are the widespread correspondence of Umbrian monophthongs to Oscan diphthongs (Umb. *erer* : Osc. *eiseis*, Umb. *muneklu* : Osc. *múiníkú*, Umb. *sve* : Osc. *svai*), Umb. *r* vs. Osc. *s, z* (*-arum*, the ending of the genitive plural of nouns of the first declension, vs. Osc. *-asúm*, *-azum*), and anaptyxis in Oscan (*aragetud* vs. Lat. *argentum*,

Safinim 'Samnium' < **Safniom*), to which there is no systematic Umbrian correspondence. Morphological divergences involve the exclusive Umbrian *-l-* and *-nś-* perfects and the Oscan *-tt-* perfects without counterparts in Umbrian; and the modeling of the dative-ablative plural of consonant stem after the pattern of *i-* stems in Oscan *ligis* < **legifs*, of *u*-stems in Umbrian (*fratrus* < **fratrufs*). But the number of points of agreement between the two languages is overwhelming in its mass, and so far as I know no voice has, in the past hundred years, ever been raised to question the propriety of regarding these languages (and the minor dialects of the Paelignians, Marrucinians, Vestinians, and Volscians) as differentiated forms of a single common ancestor, which is here termed Oscan-Umbrian.

The special question that concerns the position of Faliscan in relation to Latin and to Oscan-Umbrian will be examined later in this paper. The principal issue here may be formulated as follows: Are Latin and Oscan-Umbrian to be classified as offshoots of a hypothetical single language (called Proto-Italic), intermediate in time between Proto-Indo-European and the languages historically attested, and distinct in its phonological and morphological characteristics from both Proto-Indo-European and from the languages we know? Or are Latin and Oscan-Umbrian related to one another as separate branches of Indo-European? Are the undeniable similarities that they and they alone within the Indo-European family exhibit to be attributed to common inheritance from the hypothetical "Proto-Italic," or can they just as well be accounted for by borrowing and convergence within a symbiosis in central Italy which must have endured for hundreds of years? I have in mind such things as the spread of the ablative singular case ending in *-d* from the *o-* stems to nouns of all stem classes, the organization of the system of noun inflection into the five classes and of the system of verb inflection into the four conjugations familiar to us from Latin, the formation of an imperfect tense in *-bhā-* (Oscan *fu-fa-ns*, Lat. *amā-ba-m*), the specialized development of the interrogative-indefinite pronoun (Lat. *quis*, *quid* = Osc. *pis*, *pid*; Lat. *quī*, *quae*, *quod* = Osc. *pui*, *pai*, *púd*; Lat. *quisquis*, *quicquid* = Osc. *pispis*, *pitpit*; Lat. *quī-libet* = Umb. *pis-her*; Lat. *uterque* = Osc. nom. pl. *pútúrús-pid*), the formation of a gerundive in *-nd-* (Lat. *operandam* = Osc. *úpsannam*, Lat. *sacrandae* = Osc. *sakrannas*, Lat. *piandi* = Umb. *pihaner*), the formation of an imperfect subjunctive in *-sē-* (Lat. *foret* and Osc. *fusíd* < **fu-sē-d*, Osc. *herríns* 'caperent' < **her-sē-nd*, Lat. *operārētur* and Paelignian *upsaseter*, both < *opesā-sē-te/or*), the merger of the reflexes of the IE *bh-* and *dh-* as *f-* (Lat. *frātrum* = Umb. *fratrum*, Osc. *fratrum*, IE **bhrāter-*; Lat. *faciat* = Osc. *fakiiad*, Umb. *façia*, cf. Ven. *vha·χ·s·θo*, < IE **dhē-*; Umb. *fust* and Osc. *fust*, both futures 'will be', cf. Lat. *fuit*, < IE **bhū-*; Osc. *feíhúss* 'walls' = Gk.

τεῖχος, < IE **dheiĝh-*; Umb. *feliuf, filiu* 'sucking', cf. Lat. *fīlius*, < IE **dhēy-*), and such a striking similarity as that between Osc. *súm* 'I am' and Lat. *sum*, by contrast with IE **esmi*.

This brief listing of some of the likenesses can be paralleled by another consisting of marked differences. Is there reason to suppose that these differences are of ancient date, or may they be attributed to the periods of separate development subsequent to the breaking up of the posited intermediate unit called "Proto-Italic"? I am referring now to phenomena of the kind that appear in the following examples: the Oscan-Umbrian labialization of the Indo-European labiovelars, cf. Lat. (*con*)-*venit* and Osc. (*kúm*)*bened* < IE **gʷem-*; Lat. *quanta* = Umb. *panta*; Lat. *quattuor* and Osc. *pettiur, petora*; Lat. *vīvus* and Osc. *bivus* < IE **gʷīwo-*; Lat. *neque* and Osc. *nep*; the contrast in the treatment of the "voiced aspirates" which appears in the following sets: Lat. *mediae* and Osc. *mefiaí*, Lat. *līberī* and Osc. *Lúvfreís*, Lat. *rubrōs* and Umb. *rufru*, Lat. *voveō* and Umb. *vufetes* 'votivis' < IE **wogʷh-*; the Latin futures in *-bh-* and *-ē-* (*amābit* and *regēs*) and the Oscan-Umbrian futures in *-s-* (the *fust* cited above, and such forms as Osc. *berest, didest, deiuast*, and Umb. *prupehast, ferest, habiest*); the "regular" Latin perfect marker in *-u-* to which nothing corresponds in Oscan and Umbrian, which in turn display the perfect markers which appear in the following forms: Osc. *duunated* 'donāvit', *prúfatted* 'probāvit', *sakrafír* (< **sakrā-f-ē-r*), Umb. *entelust* 'imposuerit' (fut. pf., cf. *endendis*), Umb. *combifianśiust* 'shall have announced' (< **kom-bheydh-iyā-nki-us-t*); the Oscan-Umbrian infinitive ending *-om* (Osc. *edum* 'to eat', *fatíum* 'to speak', *deíkum* 'to say', Umb. *erom* 'to be', *aferum* 'to perform a lustration'), which contrasts with the Latin ending **-si*.

Most of the evidence bearing on the question formulated above has now been referred to. It is clear that the quantity and nature of this material is such that it may be—and has been—interpreted in quite different ways. Our knowledge of Oscan-Umbrian is severely limited—not in the way that it is for Venetic, for example, but even in the restricted amount of epigraphic material that has survived the two thousand years since the languages ceased to be spoken there is much that is obscure and of uncertain meaning. If the extent of what we know about these ancient tongues were much greater than it is, I suppose it might be easier to be surer of one solution or another to the problem that has been propounded above. The accessions of new inscriptional data, however, remain disappointingly minimal; increased persuasiveness of either hypothesis would, it seems, have to depend on a refinement of historical method and on a much broader base of comparative data than is now accessible. A recent and thorough attempt to reinstate the traditional hypothesis of a Proto-Italic is the Columbia University dissertation of William Diver (1954), written under the direction of André Martinet. One of the arguments developed at length in this as yet unpublished work is the notion that the structures of the vowel systems of Latin on the one hand and of Oscan and Umbrian on the other exhibit an overall likeness, a likeness explained by deriving both systems from a single source. It is also claimed by Diver that the consonant systems of both groups, despite marked differences in detail, agree in the general lines of development, and this agreement is taken as a further argument in favor of a "Proto-Italic." A limited familiarity with the native languages of California which I have acquired of recent years leads me to think that the interpretations placed on the linguistic data of ancient Italy are not the only ones possible. A language I have studied for some time, the Chumish of the Santa Barbara region, has, for example, a six-vowel system and sets of plain and glottalized consonants. I have been much interested to observe that a vowel system of the same structure, even down to the distribution of the allophones, recurs widely throughout the state, an area known for its linguistic diversity, in languages that are contiguous but for which no genetic affinity has ever been demonstrated or even posited. Similarly, the languages of this area are widely characterized by a phonemic contrast between a plain series and a glottalized series, whereas a contrast between a voiced and a voiceless series is extremely rare, if not nonexistent. I find it difficult to account for these facts as the result of chance, and I find it impossible to account for them as due to genetic unity. If they, therefore, must be interpreted as the outcome of convergence through the mechanism of bilingualism within a linguistic area, I see no reason in principle for denying the possibility of such convergence in ancient Italy. Diver's reluctance to accept borrowing of the sort here meant is based partly on archaeology, which is supposed to show little evidence of intercultural contact among the various regions of Italy during the first half of the first millennium B.C. My acquaintance with California archaeology is even more limited than that with California linguistics, but as far as it goes it indicates no greater measure of intercultural contact.

I am convinced, therefore, that similarities between the phonemic systems of contiguous languages do not have to be explained by genetic unity. Much has been made of the similarities in syntactic patterns which have been found to exist between Latin and Oscan-Umbrian; I have elsewhere given my reasons for thinking that such patterns are as subject to diffusion as is phonemic borrowing and as are lexical items. The point is that a very large portion of the likenesses shared by Latin and Oscan-Umbrian may be attributed *either* to borrowing *or* to genetic unity; both hypotheses will continue to have their adherents just so long as our data remain as limited and obscure as they now are, and so long as those data are handled as in the past.

For example: Osc. *pettiur* 'four', Welsh *pedwar* 'id.', and Gothic *fidwor* 'id.' all apparently exhibit in their initial phoneme one and the same innovation in relation to IE k^w. That innovation has been equally interpreted as shared by these three languages and as having developed independently in each. The plausibility of the latter version would seem to be strengthened by the knowledge that the labiovelars appear to have been preserved as such in Mycenaean Greek (their complicated merger with the nonlabialized stops, which appears in later Greek, being then a change that transpired during a period of some five hundred years), and by the divergent development of these consonants within Celtic. Therefore the Oscan-Umbrian labialization may well have been an independent change of the same kind, but the other alternative is not altogether to be ruled out. In the same way the initial stress accent which prehistoric Latin and Oscan-Umbrian both had can be interpreted either as having developed during a period of unity, or as having arisen independently in each language; the similar phenomenon in Germanic must, because of the facts subsumed under Verner's Law, be taken as distinct, and the initial stress of Irish is not shared by Brythonic. In these and similar instances I see no justification for the dogmatic assertion that the "same" innovation is either shared or not shared.

Diver supports himself on archaeological evidence when he sets up an "Italic" speech community in the Italian peninsula which he dates to the middle of the second millennium B.C. A period of some twelve hundred years passes until our knowledge of Latin, Oscan, and Umbrian becomes, in a relative sense, solidly based. The hypothetical Proto-Italic of 1500 B.C. can, in very many respects, have been little differentiated from Proto-Indo-European: on the phonological side, the reflexes of the Indo-European "voiced aspirates" were voiceless (?) fricatives (*bh* and *dh* had in initial position merged into *f*), sonant *r* and *l* appeared as *or* and *ol*, and the Indo-European free accent had been replaced by initial stress; on the morphological side, the ablative singular in *-d* had spread from the *o-* stems to all other stem classes, there had been developed a gerundive in *-nd-* and an imperfect from *-bhā-*, and, as an isolated phenomenon, IE **esmi* had been replaced by **som*. This, when supplemented by a number of lexical items shared by Latin with Oscan-Umbrian and not recurring outside of Italy, and by a small group of similar innovations, is about the sum. All of the features in which the two languages differ are then assumed to have originated during the thousand or so years that elapsed between the middle of the second and the middle of the first millennia B.C. One of the most striking of such features is the complete reshaping of the perfect systems in the two languages. There are scores of perfect forms attested in Oscan and Umbrian, very many of which show roots with Latin cognates; but in only one single verb, so far as I can determine, is the perfect in Latin and in Oscan-Umbrian marked with a cognate morph: Lat. *dedit* = Osc. *deded,* Umb. *dede.* The differences between the two systems have been described above. The question whether such a radical reformation of the verbal structure of a language in two such different fashions can have occurred within the time span of twelve hundred years is unanswerable. As I, however, read the relevant evidence to be gathered from an examination of the histories of the verbal structures of the Germanic and Romance languages over a comparable—or even longer—span of time, the probable answer to that question would seem to be a negative one. But there is no method of predicting the rate of morphological change.

Some words remain to be said about Faliscan. A reëxamination of the total corpus of that language, in the very recent new study by Gabriella Giacomelli (*La Lingua Falisca* [Florence, 1963]), leads me to revise an earlier opinion of mine to the effect that that language constituted, in some sense, the "missing link" between Latin and Oscan-Umbrian. The number of isoglosses shared by Latin and Faliscan (the poorest known of all the languages considered in this paper) is such that the traditional classification of them as constituting a closely knit subgroup must surely be regarded as essentially correct. Yet there are a number of differences (the gentitive singular of *o*-stems in *-osio* is a notable one, and Fal. *ves* = Lat. *vos* is another), and in several of these the Faliscan divergence is strongly similar to or identical with the corresponding feature in Umbrian; the two languages were spoken in contiguous areas. Among these is the early monophthongization of the inherited diphthongs and the presence of medial *-f-* for Indo-European *-bh-* and *-dh-*: the futures *pipafo* and *carefo, loferta* (Lat. *liberta*), *loifirtato* (Lat. *libertatis*), and *efiles* (Lat. *aediles,* < IE **aidh-*); we may also contrast Fal. *fifiked* 'finxit' and *fifiqod* 'finxerunt' with the cognate forms appearing in the Latin glosses and compare them possibly with the Osc. *fifikus*—of uncertain meaning—found in the "Curse of Vibia." That these likenesses may be due to something other than chance is plausible; and if the interpretation of them as the result of influences radiating across the Tiber from Umbrian territory is right, then they would constitute a further example of the kind of convergence that has been referred to above. Faliscan, accordingly, would then be a language of an essentially Latin type which has undergone changes making it, in some parts of its structure, more like the neighboring Umbrian. The same has been said of the Latin of Praeneste, as represented on the famous fibula; the verb form *vhevhaked* resembles the Oscan *fefacid* much more closely than it does the Latin *fēcit*, and the dative ending of *numasioi* is exactly paralled by the Oscan *-úí* and contrasts with the Latin *-ō*.

My conclusion is that the similarities and the differences between Latin and Oscan-Umbrian can be accounted for, though perhaps not equally well, either by the hypothesis of genetic unity or by that of convergence within the linguistic area constituted by the Italian peninsula in prehistoric times. The meagerness of the evidence on the Oscan-Umbrian side makes even more difficult a problem already insoluble in any final sense. If one is, however, to take a position, I may only say that this reëxamination of the evidence does not incline me to modify greatly the attitude expressed in my paper of 1952: that the linguistic differences between the two languages are deep and far-reaching, and that the similarities are not necessarily to be explained by the hypothesis of an intermediate unit. Even Diver (p. 134), the determined defender of the "Proto-Italic" hypothesis, is forced to admit that possibility: "It is probably safe to say that there was more linguistic interaction on the syntactical level than on the phonological or morphological, but it seems unlikely that all similarities can be ascribed to geographical diffusion."

(Participants in the discussion following the conference presentation of this paper: Polomé, Hoenigswald, Collinder, Lehmann, Watkins, Hamp, Cowgill, Emeneau.)

The Position of Illyrian and Venetic

Edgar G. Polomé
UNIVERSITY OF TEXAS

While gathering a rather impressive amount of material on Illyrian for about four decades, Hans Krahe has repeatedly examined the problem of the position of the language whose trace he recognized in widespread onomastic sources, mainly in the Balkan peninsula, but also in Southern Italy. Here, indeed, an important set of inscriptions was available in Messapic, whose "Illyrian" origin is assumed by ancient authors and apparently confirmed by numerous onomastic correspondences with the Balkan material. Furthermore, Krahe restated the view advocated by Carl Pauli and others, that Venetic was also an "Illyrian" dialect, and recognized, with A. von Blumenthal,[1] traces of Illyrian in the "Hyllean" elements of Doric. Though influenced by the wave of "Panillyrism" that swept through the linguistic world in the thirties, he first tried to link up Illyrian closer with Germanic;[2] but after M. S. Beeler had given decisive proof of the fundamental divergences between Messapic and Venetic[3] he had to revise his material and treat the problems of the relations between Germanic and Illyrian, and Germanic and Venetic separately. Although he admitted a closer connection between Venetic and Italic, he then considered Venetic as an autonomous branch of Indo-European;[4] as for Illyrian, pointing to the striking correspondences between Baltic and Illyrian proper names, he confirmed the thesis of the East-Central European origin of this dialect.[5] Studying the oldest layers of European hydronymy in recent years, Krahe practically reverted to J. Pokorny's thesis of a widespread Indo-European substratum in Western Europe,[6] which he calls "Alteuropäisch" and tries to describe in its dialectal features, for example, /f/ vs. /b/ as reflex of PIE/b^h/.[7]

---

1 *Hesych-Studien* 2–10 (Stuttgart, 1930); *IF* 49.169–179 (1931).

2 *IF* 47.321–328 (1929); *Germanen und Indogermanen, Festschrift für Hermann Hirt* 2.565–578 (Heidelberg, 1936).

3 *The Venetic Language* (Berkeley and Los Angeles, 1949), esp. 48–57.

4 "Ein selbständiger Sprachzweig des Indogermanischen" (*Das Venetische. Seine Stellung im Kreise der verwandten Sprachen* 35 [Heidelberg, 1950]).

5 *Sprache und Vorzeit* 111 (Heidelberg, 1954).

6 *Zur Urgeschichte der Kelten und Illyrier* (Halle, 1938).

7 "Indogermanisch und Alteuropäisch," *Saeculum* 8.1–16 (1957); *Vorgeschichtliche Sprachbeziehungen von den baltischen Ostseeländern bis zu den Gebieten um*

From a strictly methodological point of view, it would be necessary to reëxamine the onomastic evidence supplied by Krahe in the light of its cultural background, as far as this is possible with regard to purely archaeological evidence, before deciding whether the etymological connections he suggests are acceptable or not. If, by any chance, some of the views of Pia Laviosa-Zambotti[8] on the penetration of "Mediterranean" elements in Northern Europe were right, we might have to revise our position versus the rather improbable hypotheses of G. Alessio[9] or C. Battisti.[10] Unfortunately, there is no inscriptional evidence whatsoever of the Illyrian dialects spoken in the Balkan Peninsula, since the bronze ring found near Scutari appears to be an early medieval seal ring with a Christian formula in Greek.[11] Therefore, much of the evidence based on the etymological interpretation of purely onomastic data, often occurring at a much later date, remains disputable, and formal comparisons that look quite acceptable may be invalidated upon further examination, e.g., W. Steinhauser's rather appealing connection of the Tyrolian place-name **Umiste* 'Imst' with Skt. *umā́* 'flax'.[12] We know for sure that flax was grown in prehistoric times in the Danubian area, and it has been established that the suffix *-iste* is used to indicate location; but is the similarity in the stem *um-* sufficient to establish a correspondence between an Austrian place name not occurring before the eighth century A.D. (anno 763: *Humiste*) and an Old-Indic word already appearing in the Śatapatha Brāhmaṇa and alternating with a younger rhyme word,

den Nordteil der Adria (Wiesbaden, 1957); *Sprachliche Aufgliederung und Sprachbewegungen in Alteuropa* (Wiesbaden, 1959); *Die Struktur der alteuropäischen Hydronymie* (Wiesbaden, 1963); cf. also J. Untermann, *Die venetischen Personennamen* 178; 183–184; 188–190 (Wiesbaden, 1961).

[8] "I Balcani e l'Italia nella Preistoria," *Origines. Raccolta di scritti in onore di Mons. G. Baserga* (Como, 1954), e.g. 353.

[9] "Un'oasi linguistica preindoeuropea nella regione baltica?," *Studi Etruschi* 19.141–176 (1946/1947).

[10] "Correnti etnico-linguistiche preindoeuropee e periindoeuropee nell'Italia preistorica," *Sostrati e parastrati nell'Italia preistorica* 5–41 (Florence, 1959).

[11] Cf. L. Ognenova, " 'Ilirískijat' nadpis ot severna Albanija," *Studia in honorem Acad. D. Dečev* 333–342 (Sofia, 1958); "Nouvelle interprétation de l'inscription 'illyrienne' d'Albanie," *Bulletin de correspondance hellénique* 83.794–799 (1959).

[12] *Wiener prähistorische Zeitschrift* 19.307 (1932). Krahe has repeatedly restated this etymology, without discussing its validity, merely referring in a footnote (104 n. 266, *Die Sprache der Illyrier. 1. Die Quellen* [Wiesbaden, 1955]) to the quite justified doubts of Karl Finsterwalder about it (cf. "Die historischen Namenschichten des alten Siedlungsraumes von Imst. 1. Der Name Imst und seine Geschichte," *Schlern-Schriften* 110.89–92 (1954); for Finsterwalder, the root **um-* represents the "reduced form" of Gmc. **wem-* 'bubble up' (in O.S. *wemmian* 'hervorsprudeln')!

kṣumā́ 'flax', which makes its non-Indo-European origin probable, so that S. Lévi may be right in deriving the Sanskrit word from Chinese *hu-ma* 'flax'?[13] Much of the evidence adduced to connect Illyrian and Balto-Slavic is equally questionable, as, for example, the river names of Baltic origin, *Týtuva* (tributary of the *Dubisà*) and *Titva* (< *Titwva*, tributary of the *Snov'*, in Byelorussia), which Krahe compares with the Illyrian river name *Titus* and the derived place name *Tituli* (originally, an ethnic name), with reference to a hint by K. Kerényi[14] that it might contain Lat. *titus* 'genius'.[15] Without even questioning the validity of the mythological link between the phallic Roman deity and the Illyrian river name, how can one possibly take the same origin for granted for Baltic river names without any further examination of the Baltic religious context to which they are supposed to refer? Since most of the hydronymic material listed by Krahe as instances of correspondence between Balto-Slavic and Illyrian refers to such common IE stems as **pleu-* 'run, flow', or **ser-* 'flow', W. Porzig[16] adduces only two comparisons as evidence for old connections between the two linguistic groups:

(*a*) *Scordus mons*, *Σκάρδον ὄρος* (Illyria): Lith. *skardùs* 'steep', *skardȳs* 'steep river bank';
(*b*) Macedonian *γράβιον* 'torch, oak wood', N. Gk. (Epirote) *γρᾶβος. εἶδος δρυός*, Umbr. *Grabovio-* (epitheton of the Iguvine gods): Old Pruss. *wosi-grabis* 'spindle tree', Russ. *grab*, *grabína* 'hornbeam'.

In the first instance, it stands to reason that Gmc. **skarð-*, which indicates a breach or opening cut or hewn out in an object, provides as acceptable a clue to the naming of a mountain (cf., e.g., ON *skarð* 'mountain pass'; OE *sceard* 'gap' [applying to the bays and creeks, cut out from the land by the sea]; etc.); moreover, it should be examined, from a strictly geographical point of view, which meaning—'jagged' or 'steep'—applies more readily to the etymon of the assumed further Illyrian derivations from **sko/ard(h)-*, e.g., *Scardōna* (place name and island in Liburnia), or *A-scordus* (river in Macedonia), *Σκαρδα-μύλαι* (place in Laconia), and so on. As for the second example, Porzig himself points out that the Balto-Slavic words refer to different trees; besides, their stem reflects a different gradation-vowel (**grōbh-*, as shown by the Lettish place-name *Gruõbina*, versus **grēbh-*, with further Illyrian

[13] Cf. M. Mayrhofer, *A Concise Etymological Sanskrit Dictionary* 1.108, 292 (1954/1955).
[14] *Glotta* 22.40 (1933).
[15] A comparison based on the meaning *titi sunt columbae agrestes* (Schol. Pers. 1.20) might be more plausible.
[16] *Die Gliederung des indogermanischen Sprachgebiets* 148 (Heidelberg, 1954).

change of *ē to *ā). Even though P. Kretschmer's comparison of the Umbrian epitheton[17] has been accepted by most commentators of the Iguvine tablets, it leaves open the problem of *Mars Gradīvus*[18] and fits only accurately for Jupiter (conceived as a Ζεὺς ἔνδενδρος). It may, accordingly, be preferable to connect Umbr. *Grabovio-* more directly with Gmc. **kraft-* (ON *kraptr* 'power (esp. supernatural power)'; OE *cræft* 'power, strength, skill', etc.), as suggested by G. Dumézil.[19] Anyhow, even the best evidence that Krahe, Porzig and the other linguists claiming a closer relationship between Balto-Slavic and Illyrian can muster, is in no way very impressive. The disputable interpretation of purely onomastic material and the ambiguity of certain assumed common features actually often lead scholars to conflicting conclusions, as when Krahe emphasizes some phonetic and morphological correspondences between Illyrian and Baltic (*u*-vocalism in Illyr. Κακ-ύπ-αρις and Lith. *Kak-upis*, Lett. *Kak̦-upe*; productivity of *-nt-* and *-st-* suffixes; etc.) in order to show a closer connection with the Baltic languages,[20] whereas I. Popović[21] makes use of another selection of lexical and morphological data to infer that the Proto-Illyrians were originally established between the territories of the Proto-Germanic and Proto-Slavic tribes, the latter separating them from the Proto-Balts and the Proto-Thracian ancestors of the Albanese, respectively. It would be too time consuming and tedious to point out all the weaknesses of the material involved; a couple of examples may suffice to illustrate the flaws in both reasonings. The proper names *Scerdis* and *Scerdilaedus*, compared with Lith. *skeřdžius* '(senior) cowherd', are supposed to show a /sk/- initial occurring exclusively in Illyrian and Baltic, versus the initial PIE /k/ of Goth. *hairda* 'herd', OCS *črěda* 'row, herd'; but in assuming this, Krahe overlooks E. Frænkel's comments on the secondary origin of the *s-* in the Lithuanian word[22] and the other possibilities of etymological connections of Illyrian **skerd-*, for example, in regular vowel-alternation with Illyrian **skord-*[23] in *Scordus mons*, or corresponding to Gmc. **skert* : *skart-* (ON *skart* 'show, vain display', MHG *scharz* 'leap', *schërzen* 'jump joyfully, enjoy oneself'). A meaning "der die Herde loslässt"[24] sounds rather unexpected, and if Krahe is right in connecting

[17] *Festschrift für Adalbert Bezzenberger* 89–96 (Göttingen, 1921).

[18] Cf. J. W. Poultney, *The Bronze Tables of Iguvium* 240 (Baltimore, 1959).

[19] *Revue de Philologie* 38.233 (1954). For Dumézil, the further connection with the tree names would point to the particular "strong" type of wood involved!

[20] *Sprache und Vorzeit* 112–114 (Heidelberg, 1924).

[21] "Illyro-Slavica," *AION*, *Sezione linguistica* 1.165–176 (1959).

[22] *s-* from *sérgėti* 'watch over, guard' (cf. *Zeitschrift für slavische Philologie* 20.88 [1943]; *IF* 59.300 [1949].

[23] Cf. A. Mayer, *Die Sprache der alten Illyrier* 2.107 (Vienna, 1959).

[24] Krahe, *Die Sprache der Illyrier* 1.60 (Wiesbaden, 1955).

the second component of *Scerdi-laedus* with Gk. λαιδρός 'bold, impudent', the proposed connection with the Germanic terms certainly makes better sense.

In the case of the inscription *Veselia Felicetas* found on the island of Brattia, Krahe and Popović readily accept Budimir's interpretation of *Felicetas* as a mere translation of the "Illyrian" name *Veselia*, which they connect to OCS *veselъ* 'glad', Lett. *vęsals* 'healthy, unhurt': this apparently neat comparison which Krahe considers "als voreinzelsprachliches Erbe gesichert," is, however, based on the gratuitous assumption that *Veselia* = *Felicetas*, without any consideration for the fact that *duo nomina* may apply to a lady of a Latin (or Latinized) family. Like *Arria Flora* and *Arria Tertulla*, of the same island, she uses the *gentilicium* of her father as first name; she is indeed the daughter of *Viselius Torclesis* (of unknown *praenomen*). *Veselia*, then, is merely a graphic representation of a popular pronunciation of *Viselia*, with [e] < [i], like in *Felicetas*, as J. N. Kalléris has demonstrated it.[25]

The evidence that Krahe adduced to connect Illyrian more closely with Germanic is no better, nor more conclusive. While the etymological connections are apparently valid, the alleged restriction of the reflexes of the stem involved to the two languages is usually not justified, as is true in the comparison of the Illyrian tribal name Ἄβροι with Goth. *abrs* 'strong, violent'. Though the connection of the Gothic adjective with the Old Norse prefix *afar-* 'especially, very' remains disputable, S. Feist's rejection of a relationship with Slavic *obrъ* (name of the Avars > 'giant') may be questioned in view of V. Kiparsky's statement: "Es ist nicht unmöglich, dass slav. **obrъ* und got. *abrs* urverwandt sind (< idg. **obhros*) und das der Avarenname, der in der Gestalt **oborъ* hat übernommen werden müssen, an das einheimische **obrъ* angelehnt worden ist."[26] The Slavic words for 'giant' (Czech *obr*, Slovak *obor*) would then be reflexes of IE **obhro-*.[27] However, Mayer may be right in connecting Goth. *abrs* with ON *afl* 'force' as reflexes of Pre-Gmc. **əp-ró-* : **áp-li-*, in which case Illyrian Ἄβροι has nothing to do with it.[28]

[25] *Les anciens Macédoniens. Étude linguistique et historique* 188–189 (Athens, 1954). Cf. also—with thorough analysis of the related onomastic material—R. Katičić, "Veselia Felicetas," *Beiträge zur Namenforschung* 12.271–279 (1961).

[26] *Gemeinslavische Lehnwörter aus dem Germanischen* 78 (Helsinki, 1934).

[27] Toch. B *epretñe* 'courage', which W. Couvreur connects with Gothic *abrs* in *Archiv Orientální* 18.129 (1950), is, however, a derivative from a Tocharian B adjective *eprete*, consisting of the prefix *e-* and the noun **prete* (: A *prat*), according to W. Winter.

[28] *Die Sprache der alten Illyrier* 2.2; his connection of *Ἄβροι with Lat. *abiēs* 'fir' (*KZ* 66.96–97 [1939]) is, however, questioned by P. Kretschmer in *WZKM* 51.318 (1952).

Similar conclusions are to be drawn in several other instances where Krahe assumes one-to-one correspondences between Germanic and "Illyrian," especially in the case of the Hyllean elements in Doric.[29] Closer examination of Krahe's material actually shows that most of his statements on the position of Illyrian are based on extremely limited and, too often, controversial or unreliable evidence, as in his repeated stress on the term **teutā́* 'tribe, community, people' as indicating a special type of social organization in the Western group comprising the ancestors of the Illyrians, the Celts, the Venetes, the Oscans, the Umbrians, and the Germanic peoples. Though E. Benveniste is probably right in keeping Hitt. *tuzzi-* 'army' out of the picture,[30] O. Szemerényi has duly questioned the assumed restriction of the use of IE **teutā́* to the Western languages by pointing out the Iranian evidence: N. Pers. *toda* 'mass, mob', Sogdian [Christian] *twdy*, [Buddhist] *twδ'k* 'mass, conglomeration'.[31] As for the alleged nonoccurrence of **teutā́* in Latin, which led to far-reaching assumptions of a "democratic revolution" in the North-West-Indo-European world after the departure of the ancestors of the Latino-Falistcans, the convincing recent discussion of the origin of Lat. *tōtus* by G. Bonfante[32] and the constructive further remarks of Szemerényi[33] have made it clear that *tōtus* belongs to the same stem as **teutā́*; the phonetic development **eu* > **ou* > **ō* is presumably ascribable to a suburban dialect, such as Sabine, and the semantic change from *civitas* to 'whole' is a purely Latin phenomenon, to be explained in the sociopolitical context of the all-absorbing *urbs*. Another striking case is that of the Illyrian word for 'trade, market', contained in the place names *Tergeste* 'Trieste', *Tergolape*, in Noricum, as well as *Opitergium* 'Oderzo', in Venezia. It is usually presented as a typical Illyrian-Balto-Slavic isogloss, with reference to OCS *trъgъ*, Russ. *torg*, and Alb. *treg* 'market', which implies that N. Gmc. *torg* 'market' and Finnish *turku* (gen. *turun*) 'market' are loans from Slavic. The problem is actually much more complex: as T. E. Karsten has shown,[34] "eine so

---

[29] Cf. my remarks in *Latomus* 20.143–144 (1961).

[30] *Hittite et indo-européen* 123–124 (Paris, 1962).

[31] *Proceedings of the Seventh International Congress of Linguists* 515 (London, 1956); *Innsbrucker Beiträge zur Kulturwissenschaft, Sonderheft* 15, 195 (1962).

[32] "Lat. tōtus," *Ricerche linguistiche* 4.164–176 (1958).

[33] *Innsbrucker Beiträge zur Kulturwissenschaft, Sonderheft* 15, 195–198 (1962).

[34] "Ist gemeinnord. *Torg* 'Markt' ein slavisches Lehnwort?," *Mélanges de philologie offerts à M. J. J. Mikkola* 32–98 (Helsinki, 1931); Karsten reconstructs a Gmc. prototype **turga-* to a verbal stem **terh-* < IE **derk'-* 'see' (p. 98). The same etymology was proposed independently by B. Hesselman in "Från Marathon till Långheden," *Studier över växtnamn och naturnamn* 189–190 (Stockholm, 1935); the basic idea would be 'to show, display merchandise for perusal by customers'.

frühzeitige skandinavische Anleihe seitens der Slaven ist um so unwahrscheinlicher, als die letzteren selber ihre ältere Handelstermini von den Germanen erhielten." However, trade terms are usually "Wanderwörter," and the problem of **terg-* is, in this respect, rather similar to the still disputed question of the origin of the word *Hansa*; therefore, one can hardly reject the Germanic origin of the Slavic words by mere reference to Illyrian **terg-*, as M. Vasmer or Jan de Vries do.[35] Actually, taking for granted that the word has penetrated into North Germanic and Finnish from Russian, it would be worthwhile to investigate the recent hypothesis of G. J. Ramstedt[36] on the Mongolian origin of Russian *torg*, with the corrective remarks of M. Räsänen.[37] If this proves right, we might have to revise our current views on Illyrian **terg-* and consider it either as one of the occurrences of the Turkic "Wanderwort" or as an altogether different stem (*Tergitio*, in the Pannonian inscription, need not be the Illyrian correspondent of the following Latin word *negotiator*).[38]

Similar facts have been pointed out by H. Kronasser, who recently reëxamined the problem of Illyrian[39] and tried to circumscribe its actual linguistic area in historical times as precisely as possible. His careful analysis led him to the same negative conclusion, that the available

[35] Resp. *Russisches etymologisches Wörterbuch*, vol. 3.123–124 (Heidelberg, 1956), and *Altnordisches etymologisches Wörterbuch* 595 (Leiden, 1960). Formally, no argument can be adduced against such a borrowing (cf. B. Unbegaun, *La langue russe au XVI siècle*. I. *La flexion des noms* 95–96 [Paris, 1935]).

[36] "Finnish *Turku*, Swedish *Torg*, Danish and Norwegian *Torv*, a word from Central Asia," *Neuphilologische Mitteilungen* 50.99–103 (1949). Ramstedt ascribes the word to the silk trade flourishing from A.D. 600 to 1100 between the East and the Baltic Sea along the Volga and across Lake Ladoga; it is derived from Mongol-Turkish *torqa, torgu* 'silk' (> 'merchandise') and has presumably been transmitted by the Old Bolgars. The plausibility of this hypothesis is confirmed by the fact that the name *Turku* of the oldest city in Finland (already mentioned under its Swedish name *Åbo* on an Arabic map from Sicily about A.D. 1100), reflects a Slavic noun *tьrgъ* 'marketplace', originally 'commerce' (B. Collinder). Similarly, Lith. *tur̃gus* 'market(day), market price' was borrowed from Old Russian *tьrgъ* before A.D. 1200; however, as K. Būga showed, Lett. *tìrgus* 'market' is a loanword from another Slavic area (A. Senn; cf. also E. Fraenkel, *Litauisches etymologisches Wörterbuch* 1143 [Heidelberg-Göttingen, 1963]).

[37] "Nochmals Finn. *Turku*, Russ. *Torg*, usw.," *Neuphilologische Mitteilungen* 52.193–194 (1951). Räsänen rather considers an Old-Bolg. **turγu* 'Stehen, Stehenbleiben' as the etymon that was borrowed by the Varangians and transmitted to the Slavic tribes.

[38] Alb. *treg* 'market, marketplace; contract, agreement', remarkably enough, is not taken into consideration by V. Pisani in his study of "Lexikalische Beziehungen des Albanesischen zu den anderen indogermanischen Sprachen," *Jahrbuch für Kleinasiatische Forschung* 3.147–167 (1955) (= *Saggi di linguistica storica* 115–136 [Torino, 1959]).

onomastic data have too often been too rashly interpreted and that even the few glosses explicitly marked as Illyrian need serious reëxamination.[40]

When tackling the problem of Messapic, Kronasser judiciously questions the generally accepted view that the *Iapyges* who settled in southeastern Italy about the eighth century B.C. were definitely "Illyrian" and that the Messapic inscriptions traced back to them reflect an Illyrian dialect.[41] In spite of the considerable attention these inscriptions have received in recent years,[42] their linguistic position still requires clarification. This is essentially because of the nature of the available material:

(a) the bulk of the Messapic inscriptions consists of epitaphs on gravestones or owner's signatures on vases, supplying onomastic data whose interpretation often remains disputable;
(*b*) the votive inscriptions contain a number of Greek divine names whose adaptation to the Messapic phonemic system provides some valuable clues as to its characteristic phonological features;
(*c*) the few longer inscriptions, apparently containing administrative regulations, show some striking parallelism in formulation, but their

[39] "Zum Stand der Illyristik," *Linguistique balkanique* 4.5–23 (1962).

[40] Especially characteristic is the case of ῥινός · ἀχλύς, whose correspondence with Albanian (Geg) *rê*, (Tosk) *re* 'cloud' E. Hamp considers "the most specific and diagnostic that we have in the lexical category" (*Studies presented to Joshua Whatmough* 80 [The Hague, 1957]). As Kronasser convincingly showed (*op. cit.* 8–9), this gloss merely reflects a misinterpretation of Odyssey E 281, where ῥινός indicates that Phaeacia looks like a curved shield looming up from the misty sea (cf. e.g., V. Bérard, *L'Odyssée* 1.156 [Paris, 1947]). Similarly, the interpretation of Δευάδαι as the Illyrian name of the satyrs is based on an emendation of the gloss οἱ σάτοι ὑπ' Ἰλλυριῶν in Hesychius. The usual etymological comparison with Δυάλος is disputable (cf. my note about this Paeonian name of Dionysos in *Latomus* 20.144 [1961]), but the earlier reading of the gloss as σά[ϝ]ιοι might be worth reconsidering with reference to the Macedonian gloss Σαυᾶδαι for *Sileni*, which shows a parallel derivation from the divine name *Sawos (cf. Σάβος · Βακχεία).

[41] The theory that the *Iapyges* are of Illyrian descent goes back to W. Helbig's article "Über die Herkunft der Iapyger," *Hermes* 11.257–290 (1876), and has only recently been seriously questioned by E. Pulgram in *The Tongues of Italy. Prehistory and History* 214–215 (Cambridge, Mass., 1958), and by Kronasser, *loc. cit.*, 20–21.

[42] Cf. Pisani, *Le lingue dell'Italia antica oltre il Latino* 222–236 (Torino, 1953); O. Haas, "Die vier längeren messapischen Inschriften," *Lingua Posnaniensis* 4.64–81 (1953); M. Durante, "Saggi di ermeneutica messapica," *Ricerche linguistiche* 3.155–160 (1954); Krahe, *Die Sprache der Illyrier. 1. Die Quellen* (Wiesbaden, 1955), esp. 12–42; Pisani, "Zu einigen messapischen Inschriften," *Rheinisches Museum für Philologie*, N. F. 100.236–242 (1957); Haas, "Zur messapischen Sprache," *Studia in honorem Acad. D. Dečev* 115–131 (Sofia, 1958); C. de Simone, "Una nuova iscrizione messapica proveniente da Sepino," *IF* 63.253–272 (1958), with a rejoinder by Pisani, *IF* 64.169–171 (1959); O. Parlangèli, *Studi Messapici* (Milano, 1960); and Haas, *Messapische Studien* (Heidelberg, 1962).

interpretation through a strictly etymological approach remains widely unsatisfactory.

Moreover, besides the usual gaps and epigraphical problems characterizing this kind of linguistic material, a large number of Messapic inscriptions lack any type of punctuation, so that the identification of the constituent morphemes is practically left to the discretion of the analyst.[43] As a consequence, most efforts to establish the linguistic position of Messapic within Indo-European rely heavily on the scanty available glosses. As early as 1929, Krahe[44] pointed out some correspondences with Germanic in these glosses, which fitted nicely with his then-prevailing views on the close relationship between Illyrian and Germanic; but apart from βρένδον · ἔλαφον [Hesychius] : dialectal Swedish *brind(e)* 'deer', where apparently only Messapic and Germanic reflect the "theme II" **bhr-en-* with a *-t-* 'enlargement' in the specific meaning of "stag",[45] the other two glosses referred to create some problems:

1) In the comparison βύριον · οἴκημα : OHG *būr* 'dwelling, homestead' the relationship of βύριον (explicitly ascribed to the Messapians only in an emendation to an entry in the *Etymologicum Magnum*) to βαυρία and βᾶρις has not been satisfactorily explained. The assumed monophthongization of *au* to *ā* is not supported by any cogent evidence in the Messapic linguistic material,[46] and a Messapic "ablaut" *au* : *u*[47] would not account for the contrast in quantity with the Germanic vowel.

2) The semantically appealing correspondence between σίπτα · σιώπα.

---

[43] A typical example of subjective isolation of morphemes to serve ad hoc hypotheses is the case of *asstaịẓaḷḷes* appearing as the first line of a dedication, with five out of twelve characters of uncertain reading. This is hesitantly interpreted by F. Ribezzo either as an Illyrian compound of the type *Scerdilaedus* or as two distinct grammatical forms *asstai zalles*, whereas Durante reads *assta izalles* and translates 'good luck remain (with you)', comparing *assta* with Lit. *atstóti* and possibly Lat. *adstare*, and considering *izalles* as the Messapic correspondent of Macedonian ἰζέλα · τύχη ἀγαθή (Hesychius). The existence of a Thracian tribal name *Asta* and the appearance of the name *Assteas* on a crater of circa 350 B.C. suggest the interpretation of *asstaị* as a genitive masculine singular in *-i* instead of *-ihi* to Parlangèli, who then tentatively takes *zalles* as the reflex of **zal-y-os*, a personal name in the masculine singular; but Haas prefers to recognize the dative of the feminine name *dastas* in *[d]asstai*!

[44] "Illyrisch und Germanisch" *IF* 47.321–328 (1929), esp. 326–327.

[45] Cf. my remarks in *Latomus* 20.806–809 (1961).

[46] Cf. Krahe, "Beiträge zur illyrischen Wort- und Namenforschung. 4. Illyr. *Baurea, Burnum*—messap. βαυρία, βύριον," *IF* 47.116–117 (1939). Whether the contrast *au* : *a* in the ancient names of the Calabrian town of Vaste, *Basta* (Pliny) : Βαῦστα (Ptolemy) reflects the same Messapic sound change remains disputable. However, separating βαυρία as 'homestead' from βᾶρις · συνοικία (tentatively compared by Haas, *Messapische Studien* 160, to Latin *forum* with the original meaning of 'palisading') is not more convincing either.

[47] As suggested by Parlangèli, *Studi Messapici* 394.

Μεσσάπιοι [Hesychius] and OHG *gi-swiftōn*·conticescere implies the loss of **w* in the initial cluster **sw-* in Messapic, which obviously conflicts with the treatment of the same cluster in Messapic *veinan* if, according to the prevailing opinion, this word reflects the accusative singular of the third person singular possessive adjective **swei-no-*, with the same *-n-* suffix as in the Germanic possessive, as in Gothic *seins* .[48] In this case, the loss of initial **s-* is parallel to the Albanian treatment of initial IE */sw/ before unstressed vowel in *ve-te* 'self', *ve-të* 'alone'. As the Albanian forms reflect a prototype **swoit-*, Hamp judiciously pointed out that *veinan* showed a three-way correspondence: "The initial matches Albanian; the vocalism is cognate to those found in Albanian, Balto-Slavic and Germanic ... the *-n-* suffix ... is matched in Germanic, and we find further cognates in Baltic." [49]

Even on crucial issues, such as the problem of the reflexes of the so-called IE gutturals, only a few apparently valid results have been reached. The initial formula of the inscription of Vaste (PID II.548), *klohizis*, with its variant *klaohizis* (PID II.474 [Brindisi] and 436 [Carovigno]), is usually analyzed as *kl(a)ohi zis* and translated 'listen, Zeus', by interpreting *kl(a)ohi* as a second person singular imperative corresponding to Skr. *śroṣi*. The appearance of /k/ as a reflex of the late IE palatal */k'/ is then used as an argument to assign Messapic to the *centum* group of languages; but in view of the Baltic forms, Lith. *klausýti*, Lett. *klausīt*, OPruss. *klausīton* 'hear', such evidence is hardly

[48] Cf. Parlangèli, *op. cit.* 380. This interpretation is rejected by Haas ("Zur messapischen Sprache," *Studia in honorem Acad. D. Dečev* 128 [Sofia, 1958]), who postulates a meaning 'law' for *veina-*, of which *vena-* in the formula *venas [de]nθavan* of the inscription of Carovigno (*PID* II.436) would merely be a spelling variant. His translation of *[k]laohi zis venas [de]nθavan* by 'audi, Jupiter, legis pronuntiationem' implies that *denθavan* reflects the accusative of a *nomen actionis* in *-tu-* from the root **g'en-* 'know', parallel to Avestan *zantav-* 'knowledge' (cf. *Lingua Posnaniensis* 4.71 [1953]). Even if the reading of *[de]ṇθavan* appears to be correct in view of *PID* II.371, read by Ribezzo: *klaọ[hi] zi[s] veinas denθavan*, the proposed interpretation of the word remains highly conjectural, especially with regard to the assumed occurrence of the same **g'entu-* in the 'locative' *zenθiborrahe* (allegedly 'im Rathause'), which postulates Messapic /d/ : /z/ as apparently unpredictable alternate reflexes of late IE */g'/ (cf. *Messapische Studien* 188 [Heidelberg, 1962]). Moreover, the preservation of /e/ in *-enθ-* versus /i/ in *inθi* (*ibid.* 168) before *n* + consonant would require some explanation. As for /ei/ : /e/ in *ve(i)na-*, the lack of parallel makes the assumption of a mere spelling variation rather hypothetical, though the current interpretation of *venas* as 'Venus' is hardly satisfactory with regard to the common use of Greek divine names in Messapic and the frequent occurrence of *aprodita*. Anyhow, even if *veina* has to be dropped as an example of initial *v-* from **sw-* in Messapic, the interpretation proposed by Haas (*ibid.* 34, 221) for the doubtful reading *ṿ[e]tai* as 'ipsi' in *PID* II.442 would, if correct, provide an even nicer parallel with Albanian.

[49] *Studies ... Whatmough* 84.

impressive, and it seems equally acceptable to assume depalatalization of late IE */k'/ before /l/ in Messapic, as in Albanian.[50]

Another example of parallel treatment of the late IE palatals in Albanian and Messapic is assumed by Haas, when he rejects Krahe's identification of *daranθao* in the inscriptions of Vaste and Carovigno, and its variant *deranθao* in Brindisi and Valiso, with the place name Taranto,[51] and interprets these forms as reflexes of **g'erontyā* 'council of elders' (= Gk. γερουσία), with /d/ from late IE */g'/ as in Albanian *desha* 'I loved' : Gk. γεύομαι 'I taste', Skt. *jōṣati*—a view Parlangèli finds most acceptable formally as well as semantically.[52]

The other Messapic material adduced in connection with the treatment of the "palatals" is even more conjectural: Pisani postulates the *satəm*-treatment of late IE **g'h* (a) in *hazavaθi*,[53] which he analyses as a verbal form in the third person present indicative, consisting of the prefix *ha-* (corresponding to Lett. *sa-*, Lith. dial. *sà* 'with'), the root *zav-* reflecting late IE **g'hew-* 'pour', hence 'offer (a sacrifice)', plus the thematic vowel *-a-* and the ending *-ti*; and (b) in σελτη,[54] to which he assigns the meaning 'gold' on the flimsy basis of its occurrence on a strip of gold foil and of its formal resemblance to the controversial Thracian ζηλτα on the gold ring of Ezerovo,[55] which Pisani compared with Lith. *žèlts* 'gold' as reflecting late IE **g'helto-*.

The coöccurrence of the proper names *balakrahiahi* and *balasiiri*[*hị*],

---

[50] Cf. S. E. Mann, "The Indo-European consonants in Albanian," *Lg.* 28.33 (1952); Hamp, "OPruss. *Soye* 'rain'," *KZ* 74.128 (1956).

[51] *Messapische Studien* 76.

[52] *Studi Messapici* 291–292.

[53] *Le lingue dell'Italia antica oltre il Latino* 232. Ribezzo, who first published the inscription of Muro in which the form occurs, cuts the continuous text differently and reads *oxxovax noha zavaθi* 'O. noham sacrat', comparing *noha* with Doric (acc. sg.) ναόν 'temple'. Haas, *op. cit.* 52, accepts this and reads the poorly preserved inscription *PID* II.553 similarly as *oxxo*[.] [..] *nohazavaṭ*[*i*]. In his discussion of Ribezzo's views in *Glotta* 30.45 (1943), E. Vetter had, however, considered *ha-* as a 'Präverb mit perfektivierender Bedeutung', also to be found in *hadive* (*PID* II.397), and stated that this made a correction of *hagariti* (*PID* II.493) into *hazavati* possible. Krahe (*Die Sprache der Illyrier* 34 [Wiesbaden, 1955]) ascribed this suggestion to Pisani and called it 'sicher unberechtigt und in der Deutung verfehlt', which in turn provoked a sharp reply by Pisani in *Gnomon* 28.449 (1956).

[54] *Le lingue dell'Italia antica oltre il Latino* 232.

[55] For a survey of the conflicting views on the meaning of the Thracian inscription (including Pisani's interpretation of ζηλτα in *IF* 47.45 [1929], cf. D. Detschew (Dečev), *Die thrakischen Sprachreste* 566–582 (Vienna, 1957). In his posthumously published second edition of "Charakteristik der thrakischen Sprache," *Linguistique balkanique* 2.172, 175 (1960), Dečev interprets ζηλτα as a reflex of a third person singular middle form **k'el-to* of the same type as Gk. ἕδοτο, with the meaning 'buried'.

both in the genitive singular masculine, introduces some further complication into the problem: whether the first element is connected either with Gk. φαλός · λευκός, Skt. *bhálam* 'splendor',[56] or with Skt. *bálam* 'strength'[57] does not make much difference if the second member is **ak'ros* (> Gk. ἄκρος 'topmost', Lat. *ācer* 'sharp, keen')[58] or **k'(ə)r-* (> Gk. καρά, Skt. *śira-* 'head'), but in both instances one of the two names must be borrowed. Pisani preferred to consider the former as Macedonian, as the name Βάλακρος is often attested there,[59] without, however, connecting *siiri-* with "Macedo-Illyrian" Σίρρας,[60] so that the second form would be another example of *satəm*-treatment of the "palatals" in Messapic.

It would be beyond the scope of this paper to reëxamine the whole problem of the "gutturals" in Messapic, where the clitic particle **-k^{w}e* seems to be reflected by *-θi*, whereas **k^{w}os* appears as *kos*, with delabialization of the labiovelar but no lowering of the point of articulation of the vowel. Unfortunately, most of the sound changes postulated in connection with the voiced labiovelars rely on glosses whose Messapic origin is highly disputable, as *sybina*, of which Ennius states: *sybinam appellant Illyri telum uenabuli simile. Sybina* presumably reflects the colloquial Greek form συβίνη of Hellenistic date; σιβύνη and σιγύνη are both occasionally ascribed to Macedonian by scholiasts and lexicographers,[61] but they occur with slight spelling variations all over the Hellenic world. Whether the alternation β : γ reflects two dialectally different treatments of IE /g^{w}h/ in the root **g^{w}hen-* is therefore irrelevant as evidence for the development of labiovelars in Messapic.

It accordingly appears that the interpretation of the Messapic epigraphic material is still too controversial to supply valid evidence as to its precise linguistic position. Though striking correspondences with Albanian have been pointed out by Hamp, it seems at present preferable

---

[56] Gk. φαλακρός 'bald' apparently makes the derivation of Messapic *bala-* from the IE root **bhel-* 'shining, white' obvious, but if *bala-* should mean 'forehead', like Albanian *ballë* and Old Prussian *ballo* (cf. Hamp, *Studies . . . Whatmough* 77–78), the interpretation of the second component of the Messapic name as **k'(ə)r-* 'head' would hardly make sense, and the occurrence of the adjectival **ak'ros* in the second member would also require further explanation.

[57] Cf. Krahe, "Die Behandlung des idg. *ŏ* im Illyrischen," *Studia linguistica in honorem Acad. St. Mladenov* 469 (Sofia, 1957). About Skt. *bálam* 'strength', cf. esp. P. Thieme, *Lg.* 31.445–448 (1955).

[58] Unless an early depalatalization of late IE /k'/ before /r/ is assumed for Messapic as well as for Albanian (cf. Hamp, *op. cit.* 86–87).

[59] Cf. Pisani, *Gnomon* 28.449 (1956).

[60] Cf. Krahe, *Die Sprache der Illyrier* 53 (Wiesbaden, 1955).

[61] For a discussion of the available material and of its various interpretations, cf. Kalléris, *Les anciens Macédoniens* 260–262 (Athens, 1954).

to restate with Parlangèli that "the examination of the relation between Messapic and Albanian is conditioned by two parameters: the degree of kinship between Illyrian and Messapic and the degree of kinship between Illyrian and Albanian"[62]—which makes it a rather hopeless task, since we know Illyrian only through proper names and have no data on earlier developments in Albanian.

Switching over to Venetic, we would expect to be in a better position, as the long debate on its position has led to its growing recognition as an "Italic" dialect. However, in spite of M. Lejeune's endorsement of Beeler's views: "Les seules attaches étroites du vénète nous paraissent être celles qu'il entretient avec latin, falisque et osco-ombrien,"[63] one wonders, upon closer examination of the adduced evidence, whether we are fully entitled to affirm that "all four of these languages are set off from the rest of IE by a number of features peculiar to them. Within "Italic," the great majority of those features shared by Venetic with Latin and Osco-Umbrian are shared by it with both of these languages, although the connections with Latin appear closer. . . ."[64] At any rate, G. B. Pellegrini is reluctant to admit more than a close vicinity between Venetic and Latin, which he considers as "independent dialects" in the West-Indo-European area,[65] and Untermann notes prudently: "Wichtige italische Merkmale sind erst auf italischem Boden entstanden; reicht das, was darüber hinaus das Venetische mit dem Lateinischen oder anderen italischen Sprachen verbindet, zu dem Beweis aus, dass zwischen diesen Sprachen von jeher eine besonders enge Beziehung bestanden hat?" A reëxamination of Beeler's "isoglosses" will enable us to answer this question.

One of the key arguments of this issue is the treatment of voiced aspirates in the languages under consideration, which can be summarized as follows:

	/#-/			/V-V/		
	Venetic	Latin	Osco-Umbrian	Venetic	Latin	Osco-Umbrian
$/b^h/$	?	f-	f-	-b-	-b-	-b-
$/d^h/$	f-	f-	f-	-d-	-d-(-b-)	-f-
$/g^h/$	?	h-	h-	?	-h-	-h-

[62] *Studi Messapici* 14.

[63] *BSL* 49.2.55 (1953). Cf. also Hamp, "Relationship of Venetic within Italic," *AJP* 75.183–186 (1954); Porzig, "Altitalische Sprachgeographie," *Indogermanica. Festschrift für Wolfgang Krause* (Heidelberg, 1960), esp. 172–175.

[64] Beeler, "Venetic and Italic," *Hommages à Max Niedermann* 48 (Brussels, 1956).

[65] *Le iscrizioni venetiche* 271 (Pisa, 1955).

The treatment of initial /dʰ/ is clearly evidenced by *vhaχ.s.θo* [Padova] 'he made', comparable to Lat. *faciō, faxō* (cf. *faxitur* [Titus Livius]), Umbr. *fakust* 'fēcerit', etc.; but in the case of initial /bʰ/, the often alleged example *vhratere.i.* [dat. sg.] '(to the) brother' (= Lat. *frāter*, Skt. *bhrātar-*) is based on a very disputable emendation of the text of *PID* I.6 by F. Sommer[66] and can hardly be considered conclusive; the further evidence adduced to postulate that /bʰ/ became [f] in Venetic in word-initial position rests exclusively on etymological interpretations of proper names like *vhabaitṣa*, whose assumed relationship with Latin *faba* 'bean' is purely conjectural and does not give any clue as to the isolated suffixation in *-a.i.tśa.*[67] Connections like those between the feminine name *Vhrema* and Lat. *fremō* 'rumble, roar' are hardly more than guesses; more significant is the ablaut in *vho.u.go.n.te.i.* [dat. sg.]: *vhugiia*, which makes a comparison with the verbal stem **bheug-* 'run away' of Lat. *fugiō*, Gk. φεύγω [aor. ἔφυγον], and so on, more plausible—the more so as the suffix of the former name may be equated with the present participle ending in *-nt-*.[68] However, if Venetic onomastics show quite a few names with initial *f-*, there are also some examples of initial *b-* where etymologies with IE **bh-* appear to be acceptable, as in *Bo.i.iio.s.* (to a root **bhey-* 'to strike'). These names may, however, be of Celtic or non-Venetic origin, as the boundary between *f-* and *b-* as reflexes of IE **bh-* in onomastic data appears to lie close to the Venetic linguistic area, a fact which accounts for such doublets as Làgole *FVTVS*: *butialos*.[69] On the whole it is therefore possible to admit, nevertheless, the development of PIE /bʰ/ to [f] in initial position in Venetic, but this does not imply a closer relationship with the "Italic" dialects; it merely shows the working of a definite trend, which André Martinet has described for "Italic" on the basis of J. Fourquet's description of the Germanic consonant shift.[70] It seems indeed plausible to assume that Proto-Italic and Proto-Venetic, being in close neighborhood in their original linguistic area, shifted the West-Indo-European triangular

[66] *IF* 42.124 (1924).

[67] If this reading is correct (cf., however, Untermann, *Die venetischen Personennamen* 25–26 [Wiesbaden, 1961], and note 73), it implies a "palatalization" of /t/ + /y/ to an affricate [tˢ]; the name would be a feminine **-ya-* derivative from a masculine name in *-aitos*, for which *v*]*hre.m. a.i.t.o.i.* (if it is the correct reading in *PID* I.121) would provide a parallel (the origin of the formation remains obscure, as Untermann's suggestion [*op. cit.*, 110–111] would have to be backed up by much more conclusive evidence to become acceptable).

[68] It should be noticed, however, that Venetic diverges from Latin in this formation, since the suffix appears as *-ont-*, as in Gothic, Greek, Baltic, and Slavic.

[69] Cf. Untermann, *Die venetischen Personennamen* 190 (Wiesbaden, 1961).

[70] "Some problems of Italic consonantism," *Word* 6.26–41 (1950); revised version in *Economie des changements phonétiques* 332–349 (Bern, 1955).

system of stops $\genfrac{}{}{0pt}{}{d}{d^h}\, t$ to $d\, \genfrac{}{}{0pt}{}{t}{t^h}$ as in Greek; weakening of articulation later changed $[t^h]$ into $[\theta]$, with further labiodentalization to [f] in Italy. As for the medial position, the contrast *-b-* : *-d-* between Latin *līberī* and Venetic *louderobos* is obviously owing to a special development in Latin, and the aberrant *.a.vhro.i.* [dat. sg.] must be a borrowing from Lat. *Afer* .

In the case of $/g^h/$, Latin and Venetic have widely diverged, if my suggestion that *Goltanos* (*PID* I.162) may be connected with the Germanic and Balto-Slavic word for 'gold' proves right.[71] Anyhow, the assumption that initial $/g^h/$ became *h-* in Venetic is hardly acceptable, as the only apparently valid example, the first name *ho.s.θiavos.* [Padova] has a hypercorrect *h-* (perhaps under the influence of Lat. *Hostilius* and the like) and is derived from the Venetic stem *osti-* occurring in names like *ostios* (masc.), *ostina* (fem.), *ostiaros*, *ostiakos*, and so on. As for medial $/g^h/$, *magetlon,* whose meaning and etymology remain quite obscure, cannot be considered cogent evidence for assuming *-g-* as the normal reflex of IE $/g^h/$, parallel to *-b-* and *-d-* as Venetic reflexes of medial $/b^h/$ and $/d^h/$; nor is there the slightest evidence to back up the assumption of *-h-* as the reflex of medial **-gh-* in Venetic, parallel to its treatment elsewhere in Italic. Therefore, apart from the labiodentalization of $[\theta]$ from $[t^h]$ < IE $/d^h/$ in initial position, which is presumably an innovation that originated in Central Italy and spread northward, there is but little conclusive evidence in the treatment of the voiced aspirates to link Venetic very closely with Latin and the other Italic dialects.[72]

The same goes for the change of the diphthong *-eu-* to *-ou-*, which appears in *louderobos* [Este], *louderai* [Pieve di Cadore], as contrasted with preserved *-eu-* in various inscriptions from Làgole, as in *teuta* (: Marruc. *touta*, Osc. *touto*, Umbr. *totam* [acc. sg.], etc.). The latter forms have been ascribed to Gallic influence, but careful study of the onomastic material seems to show that only part of the Venetic territory has taken part in the "Italic" shift of *eu* to *ou*, since it does not occur in Istria. This would account for the coexistence of nouns in *-ou-* (e.g., *houvos* : *Ovia* for **Ovvia* [Piquentum]) and *-eu-* (in]*geugo*[) at Làgole.

Venetic apparently fails to participate in important Italic "phonetic" changes, as, for instance, when it preserves *-tl-* in *magetlon*, whereas

---

71 ΜΝΗΜΗΣ ΧΑΡΙΝ, *Gedenkschrift Paul Kretschmer* 2.91 (Vienna, 1957).

72 In intervocalic position **-dh-* > *-d-* and **-bh-* > *-b-* may be nothing but the loss of "aspiration," without implying the complex development postulated by Martinet: there is *no* evidence that *φ, z, χ* in the Venetic alphabet ever represented fricatives (Lejeune, "Observations sur les inscriptions vénéto-latines," *Studies ... Whatmough* 163 n. 89.

**-tlo-* becomes *-klo-* in Italic (cf. Lat. *-culum*, Osc. *-klúm*, Umbr. *-klu*). As for the sporadic assibilation of /tyV/ to /sV/ at [Làgole] *Volsomnos* vs. [Este] *Voltiiomnos*, it has evidently no connection whatsoever with a similar palatalization process in the Oscan dialect of *Bantia* in Southern Italy.[73]

On the morphological level, only a few forms are attested beyond any reasonable doubt in nominal declension. The use of the ending **-bhos* is often referred to as a key argument in favor of a closer relation between Italic and Venetic, but one thing all scholars have disregarded is the distribution of the **-bhos* ending in Italic. The Venetic evidence for it—*iorobos* (*PID* I.1), *louderobos* (*PID* I.31), *andeticobos* (*PID* I.151)—comprises only forms of the paradigm of the IE *-ŏ-* stems, which is precisely a paradigm in which **-bhos* never occurs in Italic.[74] In Messapic there are a couple of occurrences of *-bas* < **-bhos* in *-ā-* stems, but these can hardly be compared with Lat. *deābus*, *filiābus*, which are younger analogical forms for the purpose of differentiation from the corresponding masculine *diīs*, *filiīs*, with which they are commonly associated.

As for the genitive forms, recent investigations by Untermann[75] have shown that the key example ENONI, in the transcription of the inscription of the lost pail of Canevòi (*PID* I.157), is actually to be read *ENONEI, dative singular of a first name, parallel with ONTEI and APPIOI, the brothers of ENNO, the three of them indicated by the dative plural of the patronymic ANDETICOBOS. The other adduced occurrences of the genitive are equally doubtful:

(*a*) The second names in *PID* I.127 *ituria/makkno.s.* and *PID* I.135 *.u.kona/galkno.s.* are presumably not genitives of *-n-* stems, as this would imply a rather unexpected ablaut *-on-* : *-n-* in the suffix between the dative and the genitive, though the ending *-os* vs. *-es* in Old Latin would eventually not be too surprising, since rural Latin shows forms such as *nominvs* for *nominis*. Both inscriptions are in all probability sets of coupled masculine and feminine last names of husband and wife,

---

[73] *-tś-* in *vhaba.i.tśa* and *iiuva.n.tśa* in Este does not necessarily point to an intermediate stage [ts] from /tyV/, since the former may be misread for *vhaba.i.tn̦ia* and the latter is presumably misspelt with M (= *ś*) for a right-left sequence of *n* + *i*; this is made probable by the fact that, in all its other occurrences, /ty/ is maintained in Southern Venetic. Northern Venetic *metśo* may, however, contain the assumed intermediate state [ts] in the assibilation of prevocalic /ty/, but it can as well stand for **-met(i)sō*, from the same stem as *Metellus* (cf. *Medsillus* : *Messillus* in Aquileia).

[74] Cf. OLat. *prīvicloes*, *castreis*, Osc. *nesimois*, Umbr. *uesclir*.

[75] "Zur venetischen Nominalflexion," *IF* 66.108–118 (1961).

as they also appear in Latin inscriptions on funeral urns; *-os* is accordingly a nominative singular masculine ending.

(*b*) As regards *PID* I.25 *re.i.tii katakna /lo.g.sii* (v.l. *vo.g.sii*) *vhrema.i.stna*, the twice repeated construction with the genitive of the husband's name preceding the name of his wife is rather unexpected on a votive pin, since its only parallel occurrence applies to the name of a deceased person (on an urn); besides, husbands are usually not mentioned by their last name only. The text has therefore been considered "corrupt"; a plausible emendation would be to read *a* instead of *ii*, as it would yield two acceptable Venetic feminine first names, **Reita* and **Logsa*, in association with the patronymics *Katakna* and *Vhremaistna*. At any rate, the inscription can hardly be considered sufficient evidence for assuming the existence of the "Italo-Celtic" *-ī-* genitive of the *-ŏ-* stem in Venetic.

As for the verbal forms, *.a.tra.e..s.t.* (*PID* I.152) remains disputable, though much can be said in favor of Lejeune's comparison with Hitt. *ḫatrāiš*, which implies the meaning *mandauit*.[76] Anyhow, even if one cuts it into an obscure adverb *atra*, plus the third person singular of the present of 'to be', *est*, it yields no material for closer comparison with Italic. As for *doto*, it can hardly be equated with the Skt. active root-aorist *ádāt* on account of its middle ending *-to*; it rather corresponds formally to Ved. *ádita*, Gk. ἔδοτο—third person singular middle of the same root aorist—showing respectively *i* : *o* as reflexes of $*\underset{\circ}{H}_3$, vs. $*eH_3$ in *ádāt*. This would imply that, in contrast to Latin, where $*\underset{\circ}{H}_3$ and $*\underset{\circ}{H}_1$ are reflected by *a* in *datus* : *factus*, Venetic has a different reflex for $*\underset{\circ}{H}_3$, as evidenced by *doto* versus *fagsto* (written *vhaχ.s.θo*).

In *donasto*, again, Venetic differs from Italic, as no such *-s-* preterit occurs there after a denominative stem in *-ā-*, and no parallel can be found there for the use of the middle ending. The latter remark applies to *fagsto* as well, in which the apparent correspondence with Latin *faxō* is rather deceiving. Actually, the Latin form is an *-s-* future, comparable to the Greek type of δείξω, which was reinterpreted as a perfective form, whence its "resultative" connotations; the Venetic form, on the contrary, is a third person singular middle *-s-* aorist with reduced grade of the root, comparable to Gathic Avest. *baxšta*, Skt. *ayukta* (with *-kt-* < **-kṣ-t-*), and so forth.

As for North Venetic *toler* ~ *tuler* (Làgole) ~ *tolar* (Gurina), it has indeed a remarkable third person singular (originally) middle *-r-* ending; yet preservation of this morpheme, as in Umbr. *ferar*, OIr. *canar*, or Hitt. *ešari*, is not necessarily a clue to closer relationship with Italic,

[76] "Hittite *ḫatrāmi* : vénète *atraest*," *BSL* 46.1, 43–47 (1950).

but rather a feature of conservatism in a peripheral language. The vowel alternation *e* ~ *a* before *r* need not point to a different thematic vowel as in OHG *dolēn* : *dolōn*; it may merely be a local dialectal difference in aperture of an unstressed vowel before *r* (*-e-* at Làgole; *-a-* in Gurina).

Accordingly, no cogent argument on the morphological level compels the conclusion that Venetic is an Italic dialect. As for the vocabulary of Venetic, *aisu-* 'god' may well be originally an Etruscan word, as Suetonius stated it and the glosses of Hesychius confirm it; *ekvon* 'horse', interesting as it is for showing the Venetic reflex of PIE /kw/, is too widely spread as a form to give any closer dialectal clue; *-ke* may hardly reflect **-k*^{w}*e* unless we assume delabialization in clitics, but Gk. *καί* and Lyd. *se* have also been compared. As for *loudero-*, the semantic correspondence with Latin *līberī* is striking, to be sure, but this jurisdictional meaning may well be a feature of cultural influence from the Roman world on the Venetic social organization. More reliably interpreted lexical evidence would be necessary to examine the impact of Romanization on the vocabulary, but at least up to now nothing provides definite clues to a widespread exclusive common heritage. Accordingly, the closer kinship between Venetic and Italic cannot be considered as satisfactorily established.

To sum up, in view of the lack of cogency in Krahe's argument favoring closer relations of Illyrian and Venetic with Germanic,[77] it appears impossible in the present state of our knowledge to link Illyrian and Venetic especially closely with any of the languages of the North-West-Indo-European group to which they obviously belong.[78]

(Participants in the discussion following the conference presentation of the first version of this paper: Marku, Senn, Collinder, Birnbaum, Winter, Hamp, Beeler.)

[77] Cf. my remarks in *Revue belge de philologie et d'histoire* 29.313–314 (1951); 32.156 n. 3 (1954); *Latomus* 20.143–145 (1961), and my contribution ("Germanisch und Venetisch") to ΜΝΗΜΗΣ ΧΑΡΙΝ, 2.86–98.

[78] Unfortunately the problem of Venetic could only be sketched too briefly within the scope of this paper; a more exhaustive study of the vocabulary would be required to find out how much is common Italic in the limited lexicon of the language known to us outside the onomastic material; the rather important differences between Venetic and Latin, for instance, in the field of phonotactics, would also deserve further attention, as well as the treatment of the syllabic allophones of the resonants (e.g., does Venetic *voltiio-* actually reflect PIE /wltyo-/ with [l̥]?). Furthermore, a reëxamination of the position of Venetic vs. Illyrian would also be most desirable, though the absence of any reliable nononomastic strictly Illyrian evidence makes it very difficult; as regards onomastic material, the recent work of Untermann provides an excellent basis for further analysis of the Venetic data versus the Illyrian evidence, in the onomastic themes as well as in the derivation processes; the special position of Istria as contact zone would have to be studied with special care in this line of research.

Ancient Greek Dialectology in the Light of Mycenaean*

Warren C. Cowgill

YALE UNIVERSITY

1. In the first half of this century many (probably most) experts believed that there were four principal dialects of Ancient Greek (leaving aside the difficult and little understood Pamphylian): West Greek (including Doric and Northwest Greek), Aeolic (Asiatic Aeolic, Thessalian, Boeotian), Arcado-Cyprian, and Attic-Ionic. It was also believed that the latter three constituted something of a unit (East Greek) against the first, with Arcado-Cyprian intermediate between Aeolic and Attic-Ionic.[1] A substantial minority classed Arcado-Cyprian and Aeolic together as forms of a single dialect ("Achaean" or the like), resulting in a threefold classification: West Greek, Achaean, Attic-Ionic.[2] When features considered typical of one dialect were found in local varieties of another, this was generally taken as evidence for prehistoric tribal migrations and overlayerings; for instance, "Aeolic" dative plurals in -εσσι were taken to indicate an Aeolic substratum in Aetolia, Corinth, and so forth.

2. Closely related to problems of Greek dialectology is the problem of the prehistory of the Homeric epic. From the time of Fick linguists had been agreed that under the Old Ionic component of Homer's language there is an Aeolic layer, implying that Ionians learned to compose epic from Aeolian poets, and no doubt took over much of their subject matter from them as well. But perceptive scholars like Antoine Meillet[3] and Milman Parry[4] had postulated a still earlier "Achaean" layer, reflecting the language of poets of the Mycenaean age; traces of such a layer seemed clearest in the words peculiar to Homer and Arcadian or (especially) Cyprian. But in 1950 Manu Leumann's book *Homerische Wörter* appeared, expressing strong skepticism toward this view; Leumann sug-

* I wish to express here my gratitude to E. L. Bennett and his *Nestor*, which has immeasurably simplified the task of collecting material for this report. That I have nevertheless left many gaps I am painfully aware.

1 So, for example, C. D. Buck, *The Greek dialects*[3] 7–9 (Chicago, 1955).

2 So, for example, O. Hoffmann, *Die griechischen Dialekte* 1.vii (Göttingen, 1891).

3 *Aperçu d'une histoire de la langue grecque*[4] 175 (Paris, 1930).

4 *Harvard Studies in Classical Philology* 43.1–50 (1932).

gested that many of the Homeric words in Arcadian and Cyprian were in fact borrowed by the dialects from the language of epic poetry.

3. No one, it seems, has recently questioned the validity of dialect groups that can be labeled West Greek, Aeolic, Arcado-Cyprian, and Attic-Ionic. Discussions of Greek dialectology in recent years have rather centered on the various possibilities of grouping combinations of these four into larger entities, and on the question of whether Mycenaean constitutes a fifth main group or belongs with one or another of the already established groups. Modern techniques of dialect geography have been used to provide approximate dates for innovations, and the realization that innovations can spread across existing dialect boundaries has led to soberer views of prehistoric migrations. Mycenaean evidence has provided important support for a Mycenaean (Achaean) element in the Homeric language; indeed, the question now is whether an Aeolic component is needed between Achaean and Ionic.

4. Even before the decipherment of Mycenaean the traditional picture was beginning to change. In an article written in 1945 but not published until 1954,[5] Walter Porzig emphasized the agreements between Attic-Ionic and Arcado-Cyprian, suggesting that these were "verschiedenartige Entwicklungen desselben alten Dialekts" (p. 157), which was once spoken in the Peloponnese, Attica, and Boeotia (p. 164). Agreements between Arcado-Cyprian and Aeolic were the result of contact, not of original identity, as Hoffmann thought (p. 163). Aeolic features in the Peloponnese and Crete indicated an Aeolic migration from Thessaly, and it was these Aeolians who created the Mycenaean culture (p. 166).

5. In 1949 Ernst Risch[6] used principles of dialect geography to show that when isoglosses do not agree with tribal boundaries (e.g., the treatment of **-ns*), the most likely inference is that the innovations in question are relatively late, rather than that tribal mixture and overlaying has occurred.

6. When in 1953 Ventris and Chadwick first published the decipherment of Mycenaean,[7] it was immediately clear that the new dialect did not belong with West Greek—cf. most strikingly the development of *ti* to *si* in words like *dososi*[8] 'they will give'. But what was its relationship to the East Greek group? Was it part of an undifferentiated ancestor to all of them? Was it ancestral or closely related to the ancestor of Arcado-

[5] "Sprachgeographische Untersuchungen zu den altgriechischen Dialekten," *IF* 61.147–69.

[6] *Mus. Helv.* 6.9–28.

[7] "Evidence for Greek dialect in the Mycenaean archives," *JHS* 73.84–103.

[8] Mycenaean forms in italics are direct transliterations of the syllabic original; those in Greek letters are phonetic interpretations.

Cyprian, Aeolic, or the two combined? Was it part of a dialect area ancestral to both Arcado-Cyprian and Attic-Ionic to the exclusion of Aeolic?[9] Or was it an aberrant dialect, with no direct or near-direct descendants attested in the first millennium? The answer to these questions was of course intimately tied up with the way the post-Mycenaean dialects were grouped together.

7. In "Evidence," Ventris and Chadwick noted (pp. 101–103) agreements of Mycenaean with Aeolic and Arcado-Cyprian, especially the preposition ἀπύ (vs. Attic-Ionic and West Greek ἀπό) and the development (not universal) of *o* from or next to syllabic resonants, as in *qetoro-* 'four-' *pemo* (beside *pema*) 'seed'. The Mycenaean preposition *posi* recurs in exactly this form nowhere else, but is clearly closer to Arcado-Cyprian πός (which can be derived from it by apocope) than to the forms of any other dialect (Attic-Ionic and Lesbian πρός, Doric and Homeric προτί, Thessalian, Boeotian, West Greek, and Homeric ποτί). In 1953 Ventris and Chadwick accepted the view that Arcado-Cyprian and Aeolic had a common ancestor; they thought Mycenaean should be this ancestor, and, without going into details, suggested that the supposed Aeolisms of Homer were in fact Mycenaean.

8. But the next year appeared Porzig's article mentioned in §4 above, setting forth reasons for grouping Arcado-Cyprian more closely with Attic-Ionic than with Aeolic,[10] and then Risch's even more influential article, "Die Gliederung der griechischen Dialekte in neuer Sicht," *Mus. Helv.* 12.61–76 (1955). Risch tries to set up a relative chronology for the main Greek isoglosses and finds that some of the oldest link Attic-Ionic with Arcado-Cyprian against West Greek and Aeolic. Thus (p. 64) the former have athematic infinitives in -(ε)ναι (type δοϝεναι, δοῦναι), while the latter have -μεν(αι) (type δόμεν, δόμεναι). Attic-Ionic and Arcado-Cyprian agree in having σι from *ti* and σ (rather than ττ or σσ) from **t*(*h*)*y* in words like ἔχονσι, ἔχουσι, and τόσος; the latter phenomenon Risch convincingly explains by a dialectal assibilation of **t*(*h*)*y* prior to the general Greek affrication of stop plus **y* (pp. 66–67), following Pedersen, *Festschrift Wackernagel* 115 (Göttingen, 1923).

9. In fact, Risch finds no early isoglosses separating Attic-Ionic from Arcado-Cyprian or, as far as the evidence goes, Mycenaean. He infers therefore for Mycenaean times a fairly uniform South Greek dialect, of which the isolated Arcadian preserves more features than do the progressive and commercially active cities of Ionia (p. 70).[11]

---

[9] I think no one has called it an ancestor of Attic-Ionic to the exclusion of Arcado-Cyprian.

[10] Cf. also P. Chantraine, *Rev. de phil.* 28.264–265 (1954).

[11] So already *Mus. Helv.* 6.25.

10. As for Aeolic, Risch thinks this was originally closer to West Greek than is generally supposed. In particular, the τι of Boeotian and Thessalian is not borrowed from West Greek, but is native Aeolic; it is rather the Lesbian σι that is a borrowing, from Ionic (p. 71).[12] Indeed, Risch sees no sure example of a difference between Aeolic and West Greek before 1200, and so (*ibid.*) arrives at an original dichotomy between North Greek (Aeolic and West Greek) and South Greek (Attic-Ionic, Arcado-Cyprian, and Mycenaean).

11. Excellent as Risch's study is, there are certain weaknesses, and some of these were pointed out immediately by Ruipérez, *Minos* 3.166–167 (1955). The most important is the treatment of *r̥. Risch had left this isogloss out of account, claiming (p. 72) that the data were too complex to be usable for determining early dialect boundaries. But Ruipérez observes that the development to ορ/ρο had already occurred in Mycenaean—as in *qetoro-* from *k^wetwr̥-*. This agrees with Arcado-Cyprian and Aeolic against Attic-Ionic and West Greek, which have αρ/ρα. Neither treatment can be explained as a later development of the other: cf., for example, Cypr. ἄργυρον and Attic ὀρφανός with original **ar-* and **or-* preserved. The conclusion seems inescapable that already in the second millennium the ancestors of Arcado-Cyprian and Attic-Ionic differed in this feature, and that Mycenaean agreed with Arcado-Cyprian. Ruipérez, it should be noted, does not dispute the essential unity of the ancestors of Arcado-Cyprian and Attic-Ionic; he merely observes that we can recover at least one of the isoglosses running through this area.

12. Ruipérez's other points are less cogent. If he is right in seeing the middle ending -τοι of Arcado-Cyprian and Mycenaean as an archaism against the -ται of most other dialects,[13] then, as he admits, it is possible

[12] Boeotian and Thessalian third plurals in -νθι (e.g., Boeot. καλέονθι, Thes. [Larissa] κατοικείουνθι) support Risch's view. These clearly cannot be borrowed from West Greek, which has only -ντι, and it is hardly thinkable that a WGk. -ντι would have been borrowed by continental Aeolic in time to undergo analogic change to -νθι before the ancestors of Boeotian and Thessalian were effectively split from each other by the very invaders whose presence is presupposed by the putative borrowing. Homeric π(ρ)οτί points in the same direction; cf. Chantraine, *Grammaire homérique* 1^3.511 (Paris, 1957).

[13] *Emerita* 20.8–31 (1952). Cyprian -τοι is attested in *keitoi*, the correct reading in Schwyzer 683.6, on which see now O. Masson, *Les inscriptions chypriotes syllabiques*, no. 11 (Paris, 1961). Note also the 1st sg. *keimai*, Masson 213a. This form favors Ruipérez' view of the chronology of -ται and -τοι, for it is not likely that an original uniform set -μαι -(σ)αι -ται -νται would have been remodeled to a nonuniform -μαι -(σ)οι -τοι -ντοι, even with help from the nonuniform secondary endings -μᾱν -(σ)ο -το -ντο.

(but not likely) that the spread of -ται was post-Mycenaean.[14] Ruipérez thinks that the first millennium contrast between Arcadian (Cyprian evidence on this point is ambiguous) and Attic-Ionic in the treatment of compensatorily lengthened ε and ο must already have existed in the second millennium. But I fail to see why the Arcadian falling together with old η and ω cannot be a post-Mycenaean innovation, not shared by Attic-Ionic. Perhaps I am missing something obvious here; if so, I would welcome enlightenment from my fellow conferees.

13. Meanwhile, Pisani,[15] who believes that Greek is an amalgam of the speech of different groups entering Greece from different directions, proposed that there were originally four such groups: Dorians, Aeolians, Ionians, and Mycenaeans (p. 10). Like Porzig, he assumes a pre-Doric Aeolian invasion of the South: from the mixture of Aeolian and Mycenaean elements come the later Arcadian and Cyprian. To be sure, he does not list any innovations shared by Aeolic and Arcado-Cyprian and lacking in Mycenaean, nor have I come across any certain ones; if Risch is right in taking Myc. *tereja* and *terejae* as coming from τελείει and τελείεεν (see §29), and if, as seems likely to me from the viewpoint of general Indo-European (cf. *Lg.* 35.5 [1959]), Greek contract presents were originally inflected only thematically, then the athematic inflection of contract presents would be such an innovation found in Arcado-Cyprian and Aeolic but lacking (or at least so far unattested) in Mycenaean. Of more value is Pisani's observation that the Arcado-Cyprian words that Leumann had suspected to be loans from Homer and which now turn up in Mycenaean are more likely to be inherited dialect forms (pp. 14–15).

14. Ventris and Chadwick's *Documents in Mycenaean Greek* (1956) lists the same agreements of Mycenaean with Arcado-Cyprian and Aeolic against Attic-Ionic as "Evidence" did: the preposition ἀπύ, and ο from syllabic resonants (p. 74). To this is added the apparent athematic conjugation of *tereja* τελεία 'pays, performs (?)'. With Aeolic, Mycenaean shares adjectives of material in -ειος and -ιος, and patronymic adjectives.

---

[14] But I am beginning to doubt that 1st sg. -μαι alone would have been able to influence analogically 2nd sg. -(σ)οι, 3rd sg. -τοι, and 3rd pl. -ντοι without help from some as yet unconsidered source. Also, on theoretical grounds I would expect a Proto-Indo-European 1st sg. middle *-*A*-*o*-*y* (not *-*A*-*e*-*y*), which as far as I now understand the phonology should give Greek *-(μ)οι, not -μαι. On the other hand, influence of primary -αι by secondary -ο is always possible. It might be then that -ται for expected *-τοι is a feature (whose explanation is still to be found) of Proto-Greek, in which event the agreement of Mycenaean and Arcadian in -τοι would be a significant innovation.

[15] "Die Entzifferung der ägeischen Linear B Schrift und die griechischen Dialekte," *RhM* 98.1–18 (1955).

With Arcado-Cyprian it shares several vocabulary items and (on the testimony of *ote* PY Ta 711) the formation of temporal adverbs in -τε (this also Attic-Ionic). Risch's and Porzig's view (§§4, 10) that the regular Aeolic development of τι was τι leads Ventris and Chadwick to consider the affinities with Arcado-Cyprian and Attic-Ionic more significant than those with Aeolic (p. 75). A more cogent reason for this decision was noted by Chantraine in his review of *Documents*, *Rev. de Phil.* 31.239–246 (1957): of the two Mycenaean-Aeolic agreements listed by Ventris and Chadwick, the patronymic adjectives can be archaisms, and the adjectives of material in -ιος independent innovations (p. 241). In *Grammaire homérique* 1³.578 n. 1 he modifies this last to suggest, with a reference to Schwyzer, *Griech. Gramm.* 1.468 n. 1, that the -ιος adjectives are also a shared inheritance.

15. At the first Mycenaean Colloquium (April, 1956) Risch reported on "la position du dialecte mycénien" (*Etudes mycéniennes* 167–172, 249–258). Although he does not insist that the ancestors of Attic-Ionic and Arcado-Cyprian were absolutely identical in the second millennium ("très proches" [p. 170], "un groupe dialectal sensiblement un" [p. 253], "un groupe dialectal peu différencié" [p. 258]), his report minimizes their differences. He still considers the development of *ṛ unclear, but thinks that the development to ορ/ρο is probably an archaism and hence not decisive for grouping Mycenaean with Arcado-Cyprian (p. 171). Myc. *posi* he thinks is possibly πορσί, metathesized (like Cret. πορτί from προτί) from the *προσί ancestral to Attic-Ionic πρός (*ibid.* and p. 256). 'Απύ seems an archaism (p. 172); in general, where Attic-Ionic and Arcado-Cyprian disagree, Mycenaean agrees with the more archaic. All features shared by Mycenaean with both Arcado-Cyprian and Aeolic seem archaisms, but there are innovations that Mycenaean shares with Attic-Ionic and Arcado-Cyprian (p. 257). Mycenaean agrees with Attic-Ionic against Arcado-Cyprian only in archaisms (p. 258).[16]

16. As was stated above in §11, I do not believe that Risch can be right in considering ορ from *ṛ an archaism, later replaced in some dialects by αρ; at most one can say that the contrast of ορ and αρ is not very important for grouping Greek dialects. Similarly his treatment of *posi* looks rather desperate, and has not generally been accepted. Regarding this word and the pair ἀπύ : ἀπό, it seems likely that Greek inherited both **proti* (cf. Skt. *prati*) and **poti* (cf. Iranian *pati*), both **apo* (cf. Skt. *apa*)

[16] I find a problem here in the idea of post-Mycenaean innovations shared by Arcadian and Cyprian. If we do not allow for parallel drift, presumably anything shared by these two would have to have come into existence before the Dorian conquest of the Peloponnesian coastline, which does not seem to leave very much time for common innovation after the latest Pylian texts.

and **apu* (cf. Schwyzer-Debrunner, *Griech. Gramm.* 2.444). Each dialect has chosen one member of each pair, and it seems reasonable to say that agreement in choice is in itself no reason to group two dialects together,[17] but disagreement is a reason to separate them.[18] Myc. *posi* and *apu* thus show that Mycenaean differed from the ancestor of Attic-Ionic,[19] but only the principle of Occam's razor impels us to see in these prepositions evidence for close relation between Mycenaean and the ancestor of Arcado-Cyprian.

17. In the discussion at the Colloquium following Risch's presentation, Benveniste objected that Risch's scheme required a surprisingly rapid evolution of Attic-Ionic in the centuries immediately following 1200; would it not be more likely that characteristic Attic-Ionic innovations had begun already in Myceanean times? (*Ét. myc.* 263.)

18. At the same Colloquium, Ruipérez (pp. 118–119) and Lejeune (p. 261) suggested that the coexistence at Pylos of *pemo* and (in the work of one scribe) *pema* for **spermn̥* indicated that speakers of dialects ancestral to both Attic-Ionic and Arcado-Cyprian were present at Pylos around 1200.

19. Georgiev, who was also present at the Colloquium, maintained a quite different view,[20] namely that Mycenaean spelling reflects pronunciation fairly accurately (*Ét. myc.* 173–188, especially 175–183). If this were so, Mycenaean would have undergone quite radical sound changes that would make it a separate dead-end branch of Greek, not ancestral or even nearly ancestral to any of the later recorded forms of Greek. But as Risch pointed out (*ibid.* 252), and as most other scholars agree, so aberrant a dialect is much less likely than is a grossly defective writing system.[21]

---

[17] Presumably the changes of any two dialects making the same choice would be fifty-fifty.

[18] I am grateful to I. Dyen for helping me to clarify my thinking on this point, although I am not sure that the view presented here would meet with his approval. That agreement in choice of single features is no reason for grouping together becomes clearer when we consider whether or not it is likely that Mycenaean and Iranian form a subgroup of Indo-European against Attic and Indic.

[19] Unless they coexisted with as yet unattested **porosi* and **apo*; cf. the case of μετά and πεδά, both of which seem inherited, and both of which are possibly attested in Mycenaean.

[20] Proposed also by Merlingen and Lur'je.

[21] Comparison with some contemporary writing systems is illuminating. Hanunoo (a Philippine language) has, as described by H. C. Conklin, *Hanunóo-English Vocabulary* 9–10 (Berkeley, 1953), syllables of the type CV and CVC, but the writing system has only CV, so that syllable-final consonants are regularly left unnoted. Further, the language has separate phonemes *r* and *l*, but the writing does not distinguish them before *a*. F. Lounsbury informs me that Canadian

20. Hugo Mühlestein contributed to the Colloquium a paper emphasizing the agreements of Mycenaean with Aeolic (*Ét. myc.* 93–97). The one exclusively shared innovation he found between the two was a tendency to reduce -*CiV*- and -*CeV*- to -(*C*)*CV*-, as exemplified by Myc. *kuruso* 'golden' for *χρύσιος, *suza* 'fig tree' for συκέα. Aeol. ἄργυρρον 'of silver' (p. 96). To explain the treatments of τι and **ty*, where Mycenaean appears to share a non-Aeolic innovation with Arcado-Cyprian and Attic-Ionic, Mühlestein returned to the old view that Lesbian σι, not Thessalian and Boeotian τι, is the native Aeolic development of τι; and for **ty* he took Thessalian and Lesbian τόσσος, and so on, to reflect the same early assibilation as Mycenaean, Attic-Ionic, and Arcado-Cyprian, but without the specifically Arcado-Cyprian and Attic-Ionic shortening of -σσ- to -σ-. This is ingenious, but fails to account for the -ττ- of Boeotian in forms like ὀπόττα.[22] Mühlestein does not comment on the contrast between Myc. *ote* and Lesb. ὄτα, Boeot. πόκα.

21. In "Achäisch, Jonisch und Mykenisch," *IF* 62.240 (1956), the views of Porzig mentioned above in §4 were discussed and criticized by F. Rodríguez Adrados, who showed that Arcado-Cyprian agreements with Attic-Ionic do not always affect the whole area en bloc, as Porzig had asserted (e.g., Attic-Ionic and Arcadian share ἄν, but Cyprian has κε), while those between Arcado-Cyprian and Aeolic sometimes do (e.g., ξ in aorist and future of ζω-verbs). This suggests for Arcado-Cyprian (of which Adrados believes Mycenaean is an archaic phase) a position between Attic-Ionic and Aeolic. Simlarly the West Greek features of Boeotian and Thessalian rest not so much on late borrowings as on early proximity. Adrados thus arranges the Greek dialects into a chain of five members (p. 245): Doric, Boeotian-Thessalian, Aeolic (i.e., the language of Lesbos and the neighboring coast), Arcado-Cyprian, Attic-Ionic.

22. In 1957 Antonio Tovar, "Nochmals Ionier und Achaeer im Lichte

Eskimos commonly use the Cree syllabary to write Eskimo, resulting in the same neglect of syllable-final consonants; and the Cherokee syllabary, which we know was invented by a Cherokee for writing Cherokee, generally ignores not only length and accent but also *h* and glottal stop everywhere except in syllable initial, so that each sign typically has half a dozen values. In a few instances finer distinctions are indicated. Three of these involve signs distinguishing *di*, *de*, *da* from syllables with *h*-clusters *thi*, *the*, *tha*, which is perhaps of some interest for the special *d*-series of Linear B.

[22] Two possibilities seem open to rescue Mühlestein's view. Either Boeotian -ττ- forms were borrowed from West Greek before the affricate resulting from **ky* and (restored) **ty* had become West Greek -σσ-, Boeotian -ττ-; or, better, **ty* in East Greek first became **ts*, and this then developed like inherited **ts* to give Thessalian and Lesbian -σσ- (like ἐσκεύασσε), Attic-Ionic and Arcadian -σ- (like ἐσκεύασα), but Boeotian -ττ- (like ἐψαφίττατο). Mühlestein's view that **ty* first became **sy* (p. 94) seems highly unlikely.

der Linear-B-Tafeln," ΜΝΗΜΗΣ ΧΑΡΙΝ 2.188–193, noted that Mycenaean caused serious trouble for Kretschmer's view that the Greeks came to Greece in three waves, first Ionians, then Achaeans, and finally Dorians. Accepting this three-wave view and the obvious agreements between Mycenaean and Arcado-Cyprian, Tovar assigned Mycenaean to the second wave, which leads to the paradoxical situation that the earliest attested Greek does not belong to the first wave of invaders. Instead of abandoning or modifying Kretschmer's scheme, Tovar is concerned with showing that a well-characterized Ionic existed already in the second millennium, and so is left with the problem of explaining what the Ionians were doing while their Achaean cousins were ruling the Peloponnese and Crete.

23. By this time Mycenaean studies were well enough established for Mycenaean data to be used in working on problems of Homeric language. In *L'élément achéen dans la langue épique* (Assen, 1957) C. J. Ruijgh defended against Leumann the presence of an Achaean (Mycenaean) layer in the epic language, using as part of his evidence lexical agreements between Mycenaean, Homer, anh Arcado-Cyprian. He put (p. 13) Mycenaean and Arcado-Cyprian together as a separate main dialect of Greek, intermediate between Aeolic and Attic-Ionic—essentially the pre-1950 majority view mentioned in §1.

24. As proof that Achaean was different from Attic-Ionic, Ruijgh used the by-now familiar difference in the treatment of $*\underset{\circ}{r}$. To show that it was different from Aeolic he used its lack of dative plurals in -εσσι (pp. 14–17). To be sure, his rather involved proof that the Aeolic dative plurals in -εσσι existed already before the Dorian expansion has not met with universal acceptance—witness, for example, Szemerényi, *JHS* 79.192 (1959), Nuchelmans, *Mnemosyne* 4:13.158 (1960). I think Ruijgh is probably right in his dating, but only because it is unlikely that features shared by Lesbian and West Aeolic would date from much after the West Greek expansion (the agreement between Boeotian and Thessalian is less cogent, since -εσσι is shared by the intervening Phocian and East Locrian). But I do not think he has succeeded in *proving* that the innovation has to be that old. I agree (along with Wackernagel, Schwyzer, etc.) that the creation of -εσσι seems to require the existence of -οισι in the *o*-stems,[23] and hence must antedate the generalization of -οις in Boeotian and Thessalian. But locative -οισι (replacing -οιϊ, the probable reading of Myc. *-oi*) and instrumental -οις (Myc. *-o*) are both inherited, and Mycenaean still differentiates the two in usage, so that the generalization of -οις in Thessalian and Boeotian may not have occurred until long after the Dorian migrations; indeed, Lesbian -οισι shows that the

[23] This would probably be enough, without positing -αισι in *ā*-stems.

longer form was still flourishing when Aeolian colonists crossed the Aegean, and lasted there down to the relatively late time when the change of **-ns* to -ις made -οισι indispensable to keep dative and accusative apart. It follows that the only secure terminus ante quem for the creation of -εσσι is the point at which effective communication between Asiatic and Western Aeolic ceased. Better proofs that Mycenaean is not ancestral to Aeolic are the treatment of τι and the adverb *ote*.[24]

25. Whatever one may think of the details, the existence of an "Achaean" layer in Homer's language seems by now scarcely disputable. But the attempt of Klaus Strunk to do away with an Aeolic layer altogether, in *Die sogenannten Aeolismen der homerischen Sprache* (1957), is, in my opinion, going too far, and has not convinced many linguists; cf. the criticisms of Hamp, *Glotta* 38.194–198 (1960), and Ruijgh, *Mnemosyne* 4:14.213–215 (1961).

26. In his 1957 review of *Documents* (*Rev. de phil.* 31), Chantraine called attention to the seemingly inconsistent treatment of contract verbs in Mycenaean (p. 240). On the one hand, *toroqejomeno* τροπεόμενος (PY Eq 213.1) is clearly thematic, as in Attic-Ionic; but *tereja* (PY Eb 940.1, *te*[.]*ja* 495.1) seems to belong to an otherwise unknown *τελειάω with athematic inflection, as in Arcado-Cyprian and Aeolic. However, the interpretation of neither form is established beyond doubt (for *tereja* see below §29), and even if we grant that both are correctly understood, thematic inflection of έω-presents is certainly inherited, and athematic inflection of άω-presents may possibly be so (but cf. §13), so that both forms may be archaisms, and Mycenaean would preserve an earlier stage from which Attic-Ionic and Arcado-Cyprian had diverged in opposite directions. In the third printing of the first volume of his *Grammaire homérique*, Chantraine has a new conclusion (pp. 495–513) dating from 1957, in which he presents a good discussion of the prehistoric dialect situation, agreeing substantially with Risch except for not linking Aeolic with West Greek against the other dialects.

27. In 1958 the view that Mycenaean was most closely related to Aeolic (cf. §20) received another champion in Carlo Gallavotti, "Il carattere eolico del greco miceneo," *Rivista di filologia* 86.113–133. Gallavotti bases his case partly on the apparent development of labiovelars to labials before *e* in words like *pereqota*, *opepa* beside *qereqotao*, *oqeqa*, but mainly on an interpretation of ra_2 and ro_2 as ρρα/λλα and ρρο/λλο, with a specifically Aeolic development of prehistoric consonant clusters (pp.

[24] Ruijgh's article of 1958, "Les datifs pluriels dans les dialectes grecs et la position du mycénien," *Mnemosyne* 4:11.97–116, makes some useful observations, but does not sufficiently reckon with the possibility that -οις and -οισι both existed in the Aeolic of the second millennium.

118–128). The development of τι to σι, lacking in Boeotian and Thessalian, he takes to be an innovation of the Mycenaean variety of Aeolic (p. 131).

28. Gallavotti's arguments have not been generally accepted. His view of *ra₂* and *ro₂* is by no means the only possible one, and already at the second Mycenaean Colloquium (Pavia, September, 1958) Chadwick remarked (*Athenaeum* NS 36.303) that Mycenaean words in which *pe* alternated with *qe* regularly contained another *q*. Later Heubeck[25] developed this into a regular sound law for one strain[26] of Mycenaean: *labiovelar* . . . *labiovelar* is dissimilated to *labial* . . . *labiovelar* (p. 255). Heubeck expressly rejects Gallavotti's connection of this phenomenon with the Aeolic change of *k^we* to πε whether another labiovelar was present or not (p. 261).

29. At the same Colloquium Risch proposed to explain Mycenaean *tereja* by a sound law that **eije* became *eija* in Mycenaean (p. 311; more fully *Mus. Helv.* 16.226 [1959]). *Tereja* would thus be for τελείει, the regular and well attested denominative to the noun stem τελεσ-, and not a derivationally monstrous and inflectionally somewhat dubious τελεία. Similarly its infinitive *terejae* (PY Eb 940, Ep 617.1, 4, fragmentary Eb 495) will be a regular thematic *τελείεεν, not a morphologically dubious athematic infinitive in -εν. The Arcado-Cyprian athematic inflection of contract verbs can then be altogether a post-Mycenaean innovation, not shared by Attic-Ionic. The difficulty, of course, is that Risch attributes to Mycenaean a sound change somewhat unlikely in itself and not shared by any later dialect, so that we would have to see here a development of the type envisioned by Georgiev (§19), with its attendant difficulties.

30. This was not the only specific Mycenaean innovation that Risch was finding. In *BSL* 53.96–102 (1957–1958) he pointed to apparent accusative plurals in -ες, an innovation not found in Arcado-Cyprian or Attic-Ionic, and so probably unrelated to similar forms appearing later in West Greek, Lesbian, and Koine.[27] In *Anthropos* 53.160 n. 40 (1958) he mentioned Mycenaean instances of *o* from *n̥ and *ə next to labilals, for example, *anowoto* 'ανοϝατον', *enewopeza* 'ἐννεάπεσα', *pemo* (beside *pema*) 'σπέρμα', *kowo* (PY Un 718.4) 'κῶας'. Since other Greek dialects seem to have *o* from *n̥ and *m̥ only as the result of anthology (cf. §36), Mycenaean would here have another unshared innovation. It would follow, too, that the coexistence of *pemo* and *pema* at Pylos would indicate not the presence of an Arcado-Cyprianlike dialect opposed to an Attic-

---

[25] "Myk. *pe-re-qo-no*," *IF* 65.252–262 (1960).

[26] I have taken this term from Stimson, *Lg.* 38.378 (1962).

[27] But Scherer, *Hdb. der gr. Dial.* 2.343 (Heidelberg, 1959) takes the Mycenaean forms as nominatives.

Ioniclike dialect, as Ruipérez and Lejeune thought in 1956 (§18), but rather a specifically "Mycenaean" *o*-dialect opposed to an *a*-dialect which could, as far as this one feature is concerned, be ancestral to *any* of the later-known dialects of Greek.

31. As remarked in note 16, I find some difficulty in supposing that the shared non-Mycenaean innovations of Arcadian and Cyprian all originated during a time of Arcadian-Cyprian contact after 1200. The situation is made even more complicated by Kathleen Forbes' article on "The relations of the particle ἄν with κε(ν), κα, καν," *Glotta* 37.179–182 (1958). Miss Forbes plausibly suggests that ἄν, peculiar to Attic-Ionic and Arcadian (Mycenaean unfortunately gives no evidence), was an innovation for καν (preserved in Arcadian εἴκαν), an ablaut variant of the κε(ν) of Cyprian and Aeolic. This "points to a period of unity" between the ancestors of Attic-Ionic and Arcadian "after the emigration of Achaeans to Cyprus" (p. 182). Since a feature shared by Attic-Ionic and Arcadian but foreign to Doric can hardly have originated after the intrusion of Dorians into the lands separating Arcadia and Attica, it is very likely that the innovation ἄν is already Mycenaean in date. Yet such a characteristic Arcado-Cyprian innovation as ιν for εν can hardly have got its start after the Dorian invasion either.[28]

It appears then that the beginnings of the differentiation of Attic-Ionic, Arcadian, and Cyprian can be traced back at least to the late days of the Mycenaean empire. So long as we lack Linear B evidence to the contrary, we can suppose that ἄν for κε was a widespread mainland feature, lacking in the colonial area of Cyprus. Arcado-Cyprian innovations not found in Linear B texts evidently were limited to styles or social levels that did not find their way into the palace records of the chief rulers.

32. Anton Scherer's revision of the second volume of Thumb's *Handbuch der griechischen Dialekte* (Heidelberg, 1959) presents a full sketch of Mycenaean and takes its evidence into account in discussing the interrelationships of the other non-West Greek dialects. Of Mycenaean, Scherer says that it "scheint . . . der gemeinsamen Vorstufe des Arkadischen und Kyprischen nahezustehen" (p. 326). Similarly, Ebbe Vilborg's *A tentative grammar of Mycenaean Greek* (Göteborg, 1960) provides a good summary of the Mycenaean features that had already been

[28] Indeed Lejeune, *Mémoires de philologie mycénienne* 169 (Paris, 1958), and Heubeck, *Glotta* 39.161, have suggested that examples of this change are found in the Linear B tablets; but none of their examples are sure. Hamp, *Glotta* 38.200 (1960), adopts the view of Schulze, *Quaestiones epicae* 323 n. 3 (Gütersloh, 1892), that Hom. πινυτός is a development of *πενυτός, and suggests very plausibly that the word is one inherited by the Epic language from Mycenaean times in a specifically "Achaean" shape.

noted as diagnostic for dialect grouping (pp. 19–23). Vilborg's conclusion is that if Risch is right in thinking that Attic-Ionic and Arcado-Cyprian were a "rather uniform dialect group in Mycenaean times," Mycenaean would belong to that group; otherwise, "there is no serious objection to . . . regarding [it] as . . . specifically Arcado-Cyprian" (p. 22).

33. More independent ideas are to be found in Alfred Heubeck's "Zur dialektologischen Einordnung des Mykenischen," *Glotta* 39.159–172 (1960–1961). Heubeck accepts Risch's position that before 1200 the ancestors of Attic-Ionic and Arcado-Cyprian were quite close to each other, and Mycenaean was close to both (p. 160). But he contends that Mycenaean has a number of specific innovations that show that it is not precisely the ancestor of any later dialect. One is the development of *-thiV-* to *-siV-*, as in *korisijo* 'Corinthian'; Attic examples of this development like Προβαλίσιος 'from Probalinthos' are, he thinks, borrowed from Mycenaean (p. 164). But surely Ventris and Chadwick are right (*Documents* 73) in seeing Προβαλίσιος as a regular Attic-Ionic form, and Κορίνθιος, and so on, in Attic, as analogic or borrowed,[29] so that this feature is not unique to Mycenaean.

34. More cogent is the dissimilation of labiovelars already mentioned in §28. The apparent syncope in *-CiV-* and *-CeV-* sequences (which Mühlestein [§20] and Gallavotti [§27] had used as evidence for grouping with Aeolic) in words like *kazoe* for *κακίοες, *kuruso* for χρύσιος (pp. 167–168), and the apparent alternation of *ke* and *ze* in words like *aketirija*, *azetirija*, are both somewhat unsure because of our uncertainty about the precise range of values of the signs *za ze zo* and because it is possible that Mycenaean scribes were more prone to write allegro forms than were the writers of later centuries. Heubeck's final point (p. 169) is the development of *n̥ to *o* in words like *pemo* and *amo*, already noted as uniquely Mycenaean by Risch in 1958 (§30).

From these four specific Mycenaean features Heubeck, if I understand him correctly, infers (p. 171) that it was not Dorians but the ancestors of the later Arcadians and Cyprians who destroyed the Mycenaean palaces. I strongly doubt that the number and importance of well-established differences between Mycenaean and Arcado-Cyprian are enough to lend any significant support to such a view, which as far as I know is also quite unsupported by either archaeology or Greek legend.

35. In 1960 Porzig returned to the problems of Greek dialectology,[30] and not surprisingly found occasion to modify some of the views in

---

[29] So also Risch, *Mus. Helv.* 14.71 n. 23 (1957); a priori, one would expect that if **thy* participates in the change of **ty* to σ, **thi* would at least some of the time participate in the notoriously spotty change of **ti* to σι.

[30] In his review of Thumb-Scherer, *Gnomon* 32.585–596 (1960).

his predecipherment article of 1954. In particular, he gave up the idea of an Aeolic invasion of the South (pp. 594–596).

36. In 1961 Risch's views continued to be attacked, this time by Ruijgh, in "Le traitement des sonantes voyelles dans les dialectes grecs et la position du mycénien," *Mnemosyne* 4:14.193–216. Ruijgh first establishes that in Arcado-Cyprian and Aeolic the regular treatment of *r̥ and *l̥ is ορ, ρο and ολ, (λο) (pp. 194–198), but that for *n̥ and *m̥ these dialects, like others, regularly have α. Exceptions occur only in numerals, for example, Arc. δέκο(τος), ἑκοτόν, Lesb. ἔνοτος; and the aberrant development is shared by Attic-Ionic in words like εἴκοσι and διακόσιοι. Ruijgh explains all these credibly as analogic, eventually to δύο and the decades in -κοντα (p. 200); likewise for Epic ὀ- from *sm̥- he has a credible analogic explanation (p. 201).[31]

37. Mycenaean clearly treats *r̥ like Arcado-Cyprian and Aeolic. But for *n̥ and *m̥ there seem to be two developments. *a* occurs, for instance, in the negative prefix *a*-, the accusative ending -*a*, and the participle *apeasa* from **apesn̥tya* (p. 202). But *o* is found in the numeral *enewo*- and in neuter *n*-stems like *amo* and *anowoto* 'ἀνούατον'. The occurrence of *ekamateqe* ἐχμάτεικ^{w}ε and *ekamapi* ἔχμαφι on tablets inscribed by the same hand that wrote *enewo* and *amotewija* refutes (p. 203) Risch's view (§30) that the development to *o* is phonologically conditioned by a neighboring labial. Ruijgh's solution is to take *enewo* as analogic, like Arc. δέκο,[32] and to explain the *o* of *n*-stems as starting in *r*/*n*-stems like ἄλειφορ, ἀλείφατος: leveling to ἄλειφορ, ἀλείφοτος and ἄλειφαρ, ἀλείφατος; hence also σπέρμο, σπέρμοτος beside σπέρμα, σπέρματος (p. 205). This solution is ingenious but not very convincing. There is no obvious reason why the few and unproductive nouns in *-r̥, -*n̥tos* should exert an influence on the common and productive type in *-*mn̥*, -*mn̥tos*, especially when that influence consists in the creation of new doublets, rather than the favoring of one or another inherited form or the leveling of some anomaly; and it is just as difficult for me to believe that one idiolect would have analogically introduced *o* in ἀρμοτ- but not in ἐχματ- as to believe that one idiolect would combine forms taken from two or more different phonologic strains. The Mycenaean treatment of syllabic nasals remains problematic; but for dialectological

[31] J. Taillardat, *REG* 73.3 n. 10 (1960), points to πάρο in an Alcaeus papyrus (Lobel-Page 130.12). Ruijgh, 202 n. 2, rather unconvincingly explains the final vowel of Myc. *paro* as analogic to πρό (similarly Scherer 359, who also cites the model of ὑπό). But it is by no means certain that the final vowel of παρά goes back to a syllabic nasal.

[32] Depending on the form of the unattested Arcado-Cyprian word for 'nine', this would be either another Mycenaean specialty or an important shared innovation of Mycenaean and Arcado-Cyprian.

purposes, we can say that Mycenaean clearly shows something different from any later known Greek dialect, regardless of whether with Risch we view the development to *o* as a conditioned sound change, or with Ruijgh see in it the result of various analogies.

38. Ruijgh further (p. 207) tries to show that the early differences between Aeolic and West Greek are greater than Risch supposes. In this he is probably right, but the lack of texts from the ancestors of these dialects in the second millennium makes it impossible to say for sure when the characteristic differences between them began developing. Thus it is conceivable (albeit very unlikely) that in the North PIE **r̥* and clusters of *s* with resonant existed unchanged much longer than in the South, and had assumed their characteristic West Greek and Aeolic shapes barely in time to predate the population movements at the end of the Mycenaean period. For the dating of the Aeolic dative plural in -εσσι, see §24.

39. In the South, Ruijgh emphasizes the old differences between Attic-Ionic and Arcado-Cyprian, and the agreements of Mycenaean with the latter, against Risch's view of relative homogeneity of all three. Of the points raised by Ruijgh, the most cogent is the agreement of Mycenaean *posi* with Arcado-Cyprian πός against Attic-Ionic πρός (§§15, 16). The differing treatment in Attic-Ionic and Arcadian of lengthened ε and ο I have discussed in §12; I still do not see how it can be proved to be a particularly old feature. Ruijgh tries to show that the Attic-Ionic and Arcado-Cyprian difference in the *s*-tenses of ζω-verbs[33] must be old, because the Arcado-Cyprian distribution of -ξ- and -σ- recurs in Argolic and so must go back to a pre-Dorian substratum. But why cannot the agreement between Arcadian and Argolic be the result of borrowing between neighboring dialects after the Dorian invasion? More to the point is the agreement (as far as the evidence goes) between Arcadian and Cyprian: it seems quite unlikely that the two dialects would have hit on exactly the same distribution of -ξ- and -σ- by chance. The most reasonable interpretation of the presently available evidence is that aorists (if not also futures) to ζω-presents had been created already in the second millennium, and that one group of southern speakers, those whose language was to develop into Arcadian and Cyprian, had already given them the shape -σ- after velars, -ξ- elsewhere (cf. §21).[34]

[33] Arc. ἐδικάσαμεν, παρετάξωνσι, Cypr. *kateskeuwase*, *oruxe* vs. Att. ἐδίκασα, ἐξήτασα.

[34] Hence also Ruijgh seems right in tracing Homeric forms with ξ to Achaean, since Homeric language observes the Arcado-Cyprian rule to the extent of never using ξ if either of the two preceding syllables contains a velar. Yet Pelasgiotic Thessalian, which is relatively little influenced by West Greek, has ψαφιξαμένας

In the matter of the contract verbs, Ruijgh (p. 211) is skeptical of Risch's derivation of Myc. *tereja* from τελείει; but, paradoxically, if Ruijgh is right in considering *tereja* an athematic form (which I very strongly doubt), its inflection is possibly (but cf. §13) an inherited archaism, of no diagnostic value for dialectology, while if Risch is right, *tereja* would contain an innovation shared by neither Attic-Ionic nor Arcado-Cyprian.

40. The apparent agreement of Myc. *pei*[35] with Arc. σφεις against Attic-Ionic σφίσι (p. 212) can also be an archaism, so long as the prehistory of this pronoun remains unclear. The view that Mycenaean shares with Arcado-Cyprian the use of dative rather than genitive with prepositions meaning 'from' (*ibid.*) has been dealt a heavy blow by Householder's article, "*pa-ro* and Mycenaean cases," *Glotta* 38.1–10 (1960).[36]

41. More recent discussions that I have seen do not seem to introduce any important new viewpoints. In his article of 1956, "The Greek dialects and Greek pre-history," *Greece and Rome* 25.38–50 (which I failed to treat at its proper place in this survey), Chadwick suggested (p. 44) that the innovations in which Attic-Ionic agrees with West Greek against Arcado-Cyprian and Mycenaean can be explained by supposing "that round about 1000 B.C. a dialect of the Arcadian type came for a period under Doric influence; but this soon ceased. . . ."[37] This explanation does not seem adequate to account for all the agreements involved (cf. the skepticism of Ruijgh, *Mnemosyne* 4:11.106 n. 4). The distribution of ἐνς for ἐν with accusative, which may be a post-Mycenaean innovation, could perhaps be explained by Chadwick's view (although I don't see why it couldn't equally well have started in a variety of South Greek and spread from there to the super- and ad-jacent varieties of West Greek). But other agreements of Attic-Ionic and West Greek are almost

---

and ἐργάξατο (Scherer 70, Bechtel 1.190). The latter, to be sure, violates the rule against ξ after velars; but who can say that in the Thessalian of 900 B.C. it was not still observed? It seems theoretically possible to attribute the Homeric ξ-forms to Aeolic still, but even so the pattern must be old, perhaps Proto-Greek: Attic-Ionic with Lesbian and the bulk of Boeotian would have leveled in one direction, West Greek (except Argolic) in the other. Some relevant Mycenaean forms would be very welcome here.

[35] Read σφει(ς) with plene writing of a monosyllable, as in *qoo* for $\gamma^w\omega(\nu)s$? Or σφε(ι)ï with the same **-si* as in *-oi* from **-oisi*? Cf. *Documents* 87, 189.

[36] Householder concludes that *paro* often, perhaps always, is used in a locative sense; if it ever means 'from', the case following it can be ablative, not yet syncretized with either dative or genitive (9).

[37] Similarly in "The prehistory of the Greek language" (*Cambridge Ancient History*[2] 2:39.16 [1963]).

certainly older: these are the choice of ἀπό rather than ἀπύ, and the development of α rather than ο next to syllabic liquids.

42. So far, one innovation of clearly Mycenaean date had been established for the whole South (Mycenaean, Arcado-Cyprian, Attic-Ionic): the assibilation of *t(h)i to σι and of *t(h)y to σ(σ). There appear to be also some choices common to the whole South: adverbs in -τε, and perhaps athematic infinitives in -εναι.[38] If Mycenaean material were not so limited, this list could probably be extended.

43. But it seems equally clear that the South was already somewhat differentiated in the second millennium, despite the near uniformity of Linear B texts from Pylos, Mycenae, and Knossos. It is indeed hardly thinkable, even supposing the language brought to Greece at the beginning of the second millennium was quite homogeneous, that it could have gone on being spoken there for nearly a thousand years without developing considerable local and social differences. The Mycenaean empire may have led to the creation and spread of a koine, but clearly this koine, if it existed, did not entirely obliterate internal differences. Mycenaean shares some choices with Arcado-Cyprian against Attic-Ionic: ορ from *r̥, ποσί, ἀπύ. It is not certain that Mycenaean shares any innovations with Arcado-Cyprian against Attic-Ionic archaisms. If my doubts about Ruipérez's view of the primary middle verb endings (note 14) are justified, the ending -τοι for -ται would be one such innovation. The interpretation of *tereja* and *terejae* as forms of an athematic verb stem τελεια- is far too insecure to be used as evidence that Mycenaean shares athematic inflection of contract verbs with Arcado-Cyprian. As far as I see, Mycenaean does not share a single innovation or choice with Attic-Ionic against Arcado-Cyprian.[39]

44. Mycenaean seems to have a few innovations unknown elsewhere, indicating that the language of the tablets cannot be a direct ancestor even of Arcado-Cyprian, so that we have evidence for a minimum of three varieties of speech in the Mycenaean empire (four, if we take into account the evidence mentioned in §31 that the dialect of Cyprus had already begun diverging from that of the homeland). Specific Mycenaean innovations include the vocalization of *pemo* and similar words (§37); the apparent dissimilation of labiovelars (§28); possibly *eija* from *eije* (§29) and accusative plurals in -ες (§30). The apparent syncope of -ι- and -ε-

[38] On this last point Mycenaean has no certain evidence. If *terejae* should prove after all to be an athematic infinitive, the South Greek form would have to be amended to -εν(αι), with the same final variation as North Greek -μεν(αι), and we would have to further specify that Lesbian forms like κέρναν are a late independent innovation on the analogy of thematic stems.

[39] On Myc. *toto*, cf. Lejeune, *Mémoires de philologie mycénienne* 231, and Humbert, *BSL* 55.92 n. 1 (1960).

before vowels (§34), while recurring in Aeolic, is not normal in Attic-Ionic and Arcado-Cyprian, and so probably belongs here.

45. For Homeric, both Achaean (Mycenaean) and Aeolic (Thessalian?) layers seem firmly established.

46. The one point I would like to elaborate a little further is the puzzling position of Ionic in the second millennium. As I have just said, it is apparent that "Ionic" and "Arcado-Cyprian" speech forms coexisted in the Mycenaean empire. But what was their distribution? It would be rather simple to suppose that "Ionic" was the speech of the upper classes, who remained in control in Attica and elsewhere went into exile, eventually ending up in the Cyclades and Asia Minor, while "Arcado-Cyprian" was the speech of the lower classes, which became standard in Arcadia and Cyprus, in the former owing to the disappearance of the old upper class, in the latter owing to events about which we have no information. But this feature is hard to square with the "Arcado-Cyprian" features of Linear B and the Achaean layer of Homer's language. Granted that accountants may have written a different dialect from that which their employers spoke, it seems incredible that poets would have used forms (e.g., aorists and futures in -ξ-) that would have seemed substandard in the ears of the audience on whom their livelihood depended, and equally unlikely that poems on the heroic deeds of Mycenaean princes would have been composed and preserved by their former serfs.

An alternative would be to imagine a geographic distribution, with "Ionic" spoken perhaps in Attica (and elsewhere?), and "Achaean" in at least Pylos, Mycenae, and Knossos. But, leaving aside the minor detail that there is no direct evidence at all for any such distribution, this would result in the anomalous situation that Achaean and Aeolic, which share presumably diagnostic features, would be cut off from each other by Ionic—unless indeed we imagine that Boeotia was "Achaean," too, in which event Attic-Ionic would be cut off from West Greek, and the old agreements between these two would have to be explained as owing to chance. The situation can be diagrammed as follows:

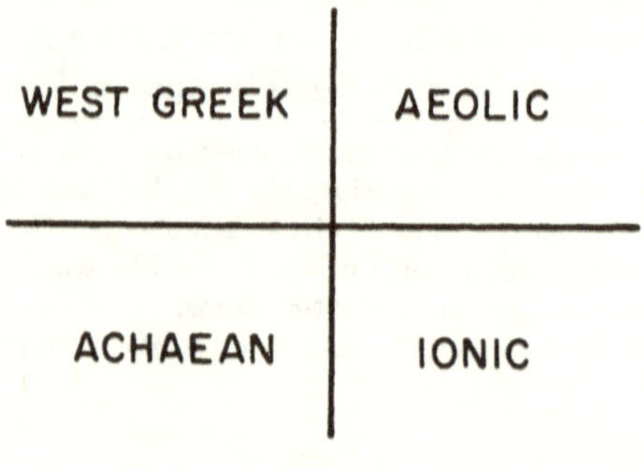

Each dialect shares significant features with its horizontal neighbor and the dialect diagonally opposite, but few or none with its vertical neighbor. Things would be much simpler if we could posit a prehistoric distribution like this (or with the same configuration, but reversed or rotated):

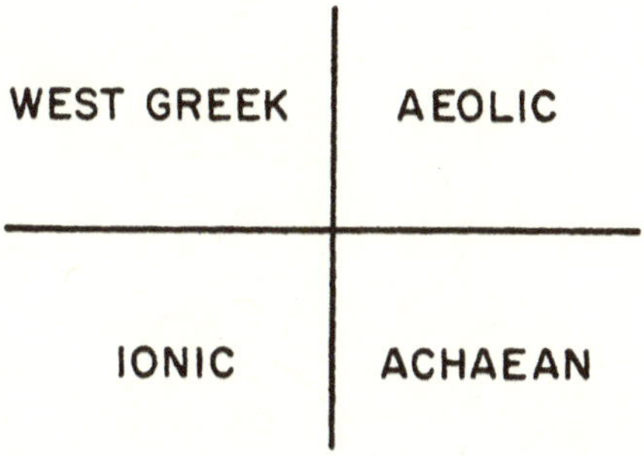

Now each dialect shares exclusive features with both its neighbors, but not with the dialect in the opposite corner. To be sure, I do not know of the faintest shred of nonlinguistic evidence for such a prehistoric arrangement of the Greek dialects. But it is perhaps not a complete waste of time to speculate that such an arrangement may have existed, perhaps in Greece in the (early?) second millennium, perhaps even earlier and outside of Greece.

(Participants in the discussion following the conference presentation of the first version of this paper: Watkins, Winter, Puhvel, Hamp, Emeneau, Collinder.)

The Position of Albanian

Eric P. Hamp

UNIVERSITY OF CHICAGO

1. It is fashionable at conferences to come out with no clear affirmative assertion, but rather with a statement of all the many difficulties. While I have no taste for fashion, this should prove a fashionable paper, on this ground if on no other. It is often hard enough to say conclusively where the IE features of Albanian lie, let alone to identify them unambiguously and assign them to a restricted relationship of shared innovation. This is not to say that things are as G. Meyer is all too well known to have put it; there is plenty of good Indo-European material in Albanian but it is often ambiguous and represented by small numbers of examples for each feature and combination.

Furthermore, I am not yet in a position to say what I hope will be possible when the dialect materials from most enclaves have been sifted and compared. This applies particularly to the verb.

There are also relative unknowns that are important in the total question on which I do not feel adequately informed to hold a worthwhile opinion: Thracian, with Dečev's bewildering material, is the notable example here.

2. There are ways in which our subject has been synthesized in the past that lighten our task somewhat: N. Jokl (Eberts *Reallexikon der Vorgeschichte*; articles "Albaner," "Illyrier," and "Thraker") gives a very just review; but he does nonetheless have his point of view. W. Porzig (*Die Gliederung des indogermanischen Sprachgebiets* [Heidelberg, 1954]) gives a fair and fairly complete summary, but he has no incisive point of view. Moreover, there has been a good bit of activity recently, for such a small field, and I have tried to sift through the output as fully as I could. Thus I hope to reach a fair degree of completeness in reporting, although, I suppose, at the same time some of my prejudices will show through.

3. When one looks over the ground to be covered, it seems that our subject falls naturally into three parts: the geographic position of Albanian in the Balkans; the corpus, location, and relations of Illyrian, Thracian, and their congeners; and the genetic ties of Albanian to its sister IE subgroups. These, in fair part, match three rather separate

fields of expertise: "Balkan linguistics"; Classical linguistics, philology, and epigraphy; and Indo-European studies in the traditional sense. No one can be equally competent in all.

4. On the question of the earlier location of the Albanians, there is a good summary and batch of references in A. Rosetti, *Istoria limbii romîne. II. Limbile balcanice*[3] 41–44 (București, 1962). Rosetti, however, mistakenly repeats the myth that some Tosk dialects show Geg characteristics, thus pointing, allegedly, to a more recent dialect split. The isogloss is clear in all dialects I have studied, which embrace nearly all types possible. It must be relatively old, that is, dating back into the post-Roman first millennium. As a guess, it seems possible that this isogloss reflects a spread of the speech area, after the settlement of the Albanians in roughly their present location, so that the speech area straddled the Jireček line.

In this context it is possible to find almost every opinion. Many agree that Albanian lacks an old maritime terminology, yet D. Dečev (*Charakteristik der thrakischen Sprache* 113 [Sofia, 1952]) thinks they have had it and lost it!

More positively, one may say that the mere absence of inherited maritime vocabulary can prove nothing. Recently, however, E. Çabej (*VII Congresso internazionale di scienze onomastiche, 4–8 Aprile 1961*, 248–249) has argued for the actual presence, insufficiently noticed heretofore, of certain preserved old terms. But it seems to me that these are for the most part inconclusive in themselves: *dēt* 'sea' (related to 'deep') could refer to any deep water; *vâ* 'ford, anchorage', *mat* 'beach' *valë* 'wave' could be applied to various bodies of water. A word like *grykë* 'narrows' is an easy metaphor ('throat'); *aní* (: *an*(*ë*) 'vessel') and some names of parts of boats (*ballë* 'forehead', *pëlhurë* 'sail', *shul* 'mast', *lugatë* 'rudder', belonging with *lugë* 'spoon') are also easily understood as metaphors; *likurishtë* 'polyp' (cf. *likurë* 'skin') and many other names, often fairly transparent compounds (p. 249), are descriptive and could presumably have arisen in their attested uses at almost any time. The word *ngjalë* 'eel' < **engella*, even if related correctly to Illyrian 'Εγγελᾶνες, does not necessarily presuppose the sea. Thus, we still lack a demonstrated body of native marine morphemes, with no other morphological or semantic connections in the language to make transfer possible. For such an argument, only isolated forms will be convincing.

Even recent history is checkered: *Shqiptar* first appears in the fourteenth century. *Albi* occurs in an Angevin document of 1330; according to Ptolemy, in the second century the *Albanoí* lived around *Albanópolis* (Kruja), where the ethnic has been recorded in modern times. The enclaves of Italy and Greece, to the extent that they use a traditional name, use this term: *arbrésh* (e.g., Vaccarizzo Albanese), *arbërishte* (Greece). The earlier data are rehearsed, with references, in H. Barić's *Lingvističke studije* (Sarajevo, 1954; abbr. *LS*), and *Hŷmje në historin e gjuhës shqipe* 7 (Prishtinë, 1955; abbr. *Hymje*; = trans. *Istorija arbanaškog jezika* 30 [Sarajevo, 1959]).

The question of the names *Elbasan, Arbëni, Albanopolis, Shqipëtar, Shqipëri* is discussed at length, but somewhat inaccessibly, in Dh. S. Shuteriqi, *Buletin për shkencat shoqërore* 1956:3.189–224 (abbr. *BShkSh*) and *Buletin i Universitetit Shtetëror të Tiranës* 1958:3.45–70 (abbr. *BUShT*) .

It is clear that in the Middle Ages the Albanians extended farther north (Jokl, *Albaner* §2); that there are persuasive arguments which have been advanced against their having extended as far as the Adriatic coast—the fact that *Scodra* 'Scutari' (*Shkodër*) shows un-Albanian development (see §6 below), that there is no demonstrated old maritime vocabulary (see above), and that there are few ancient Greek loans (Jokl, *Albaner* §5; but see §5 below); and that there are arguments in favor of old Dardania: *Niš* < *Naíssos*, with development as in *pyll* 'forest' < **pëýll* < **padūle(m)* : *palūdem* (Jokl, *Albaner* §5). Admittedly, many of the arguments are negative; they are dealt with further below.

In a series of studies, G. Reichenkron has recently elaborated on Albanian-Rumanian correspondences, and has even brought in Armenian. This latter argument is not new, having been first forcefully set forth by H. Pedersen (*KZ* 1900:36.340–341). Pertinent aspects of Reichenkron will be discussed below, but his work does not essentially alter the borrowing situation as it has been understood. S. Puşcariu (trans. *Die rumänische Sprache* [Leipzig, 1943], from which citation is here made) reviews these matters under "Das autochthone Element" (pp. 203—210) and in his discussion of common Latin inheritances (pp. 326–336). Although he deals with other views (pp. 336–338), he sees (p. 205) the Abanian-Rumanian elements as derived from Thracian, and thinks them inherited (as substratum) in Rumanian but loans into the Illyrian ancestor of Albanian. The richest account of this subject now is Rosetti *Istoria II*³, which commendably treats the Balkans as a historic unit. For Albanian-Rumanian the phonological correspondences are set out (pp. 103–106), as well as the lexical (pp. 106–121); many of these are too well known to need exemplification here—in the gross, they are obviously true, and largely well understood. They point solidly to (1) a local native language, and (2) a special dialect of Latin.

G. Reichenkron (*Romanistisches Jahrbuch* 1960:11.19–22) rehearses succinctly a number of hypotheses, which I summarize here:

a) Not all Albanian-Rumanian correspondences are loans from Albanian into Rumanian; they may be from Illyrian and Daco-Thracian as sources.

b) "Autochthonous" elements of Rumanian show only in part Illyrian-Thracian-Albanian regularities; in part proto-Romance developments appear.

c) Most Albanian-Rumanian correspondences come from borrowings by Vulgar Latin (as precursor of Rumanian) in Dardania from an Illyrian substrate. Then, we suppose, pre-Rumanian moved north of the Danube and merged with a Daco-Romance dialect, which contained Thracian elements showing correspondences with Armenian (allegedly a sound shift, and certain affixes dealt with in *Rom. Jb.* 9; for details, see below).

d) Daco-Thracian yields Rumanian *č* < IE **q* before *eu*; *ţ* < IE **s* + front *V*, and IE **k*; *-f-* < IE **p* (> *p*‘).

e) Of the residue of unexplained words, loans from Slavic and Magyar account for many.

f) Some ancient Greek loans are to be reckoned with, even though one would not expect Rumanian to borrow wholesale in areas where other Romance did not.

g) There are also some Germanic loans. Therefore, we must reckon with five IE components: Germanic, Latin, Greek, Dacian, Slavic.

h) We must be prepared for the situation where two unrelated etyma fall phonologically together but continue two meanings, such as OFr. *mont* 'world, mountain' < *mundum*, *montem*; this possibility has too often been overlooked.

Reichenkron's reasoning (*Rom. Jb.* 1958:9.59–105, esp. 59–62) on the Albanian-Rumanian sound correspondences runs as follows: Such correspondences might reflect either (1) Daco-Thracian to Rumanian, and to Illyrian, which later becomes Albanian; or (2) Illyrian, which later becomes Albanian, to Getian Thracian to Rumanian. On the basis of the assumption of a Thracian sound shift from IE, similar to that in Armenian, Reichenkron follows Gamillscheg's theory that the West Rumanian dialects (i.e., Dardanian and South Danubian) go with Albanian in their loan reflexes, while East Rumanian dialects go with Thracian and show sound-shifted reflexes. Thus

IE	*dh*	*d*	*th*	*t*	*ĝh*	*ĝ*	*k̂h*	*k̂*	etc.
Dacian	*d*	*t*		*t*‘	*z*	*ş*		*ş*‘	
Rumanian	*d*	*t*			*z*	*ţ*			

Hence, the main diagnostic reflexes are: IE *d*, *g*, *g*ᵘ, *ĝ* > East Rumanian *t*, *k*, *k*ᵘ, *ş*.

On the basis of this Daco-Thracian theory, Reichenkron tries to explain various difficult Rumanian words involving *z*, some of which may be related to some Albanian words. He tries to elucidate certain Rumanian words in *zg-* as being originally borrowed from Thracian forms with a prefixed **ǵhō-*, comparing certain Armenian developments. His attempt, which I consider unsuccessful or at best dubious, I criticize elsewhere, at least so far as the Albanian evidence goes. In any event, his main argument, whether right or wrong, would not need to affect our conclusions on Albanian, as it really has to do with the nature of Daco-Thracian and its putative reflexes in Rumanian.

Reichenkron argues repeatedly on the supposed direction of borrowing in a way that assumes that linguistic borrowing always moves from a higher sociological structure to a lower one. Without entering into the probably unprovable factuality of these aspects of the cultures in question (the Dacians, Getes, and pre-Albanians), nor into the anthropologically unclear concept of equality and superiority of cultures, it is worth noting that in the case of cultures we know much about we could scarcely hypothesize in advance which way many categories of loans would move.

In the course of discussing *shtrungë* 'enclosure for milking animals', Rumanian *strungă*, Reichenkron (*Rom. Jb.* 11.51–52) has an excursus on Baltic and Slavic *pa/po-* 'Art, After-, Nach-'. This argument loses force when we consider E. Westh Neuhard's article in *Scando-Slavica* 1959:5.52–63, showing that these Slavic compounds are calques on German, built on a very slender inherited Slavic base; moreover, they seem to reflect a rather literary (or literate) cosmopolitan intrusion of German culture rather than contact on the folk level. Therefore, it would be all the less likely to see such an origin in this item of Rumanian folk culture. As for the interesting Baltic forms adduced by Reichenkron, two types of explanation seem to suffice to dispose of them as calques, too. The *step* terms of kinship seem clear calques on the long established Slavic use of this prefix (*pásynokъ*). The other compounds of "approximation" seem again traceable to German diffusion, particularly when one considers how strong this influence has been, specifically in Lettish and Old Prussian. Thus the restricted size of the Old Prussian corpus, emphasized by Reichenkron in connection with the relatively large attestation of this feature, loses its probative value. Reichenkron goes on to urge a special relationship embracing Thracian, Slavic, and Baltic, based on a *po/pa-* prefix, in turn associated with dialect variants comprising the lone Rumanian *postrungă* (beside *strungă*) and the obscure and otherwise unelucidated *pociump* and *pozmóc*. With the above considerations, the assumption of such a special relationship dissolves into thin air. It should be noted, in fairness, that Reichenkron (p. 53) allows the possibility that the dialect form *po-strungă* may arise from early Serbian contacts.

Reichenkron's further argument (pp. 52–53), giving an alternative to the conventional (i.e., Jokl's) accounting for *pârîu* 'brook', is, independently of the above question, susceptible of a different solution. Jokl had *pârîu* < pre-Albanian **per-rēn-* (> Albanian *përrua, përroni*; cf. Latin *frēnum* > Rumanian *frîu*); Reichenkron suggests Thracian *pa-* (assimilated to *pâ-*) + Latin *rīvus* > *rîu* 'river'. Equally possible, if one insists on an alternative to **per-rēn-*, is **per-rīvus*.

5. Before continuing with the dimmer Balkan past, there are two sets of old loans in Albanian which lead us to a slender, but valuable, conclusion. It has long been recognized (since A. Thumb's basic article, *IF* 1910:26.1–20) that the ancient Greek loans are rare. Pre-Albanian was scarcely in close contact with Greek in antiquity. This places the Albanians north of the Jireček line.

However, Çabej has recently argued (*VII Congresso internazionale di scienze onomastiche* 250–251) that these Greek loans do not necessarily remove the pre-Albanians far from Greek territory; that is, that they fit well with a location in present-day Albania, in contact either with Doric Greek colonists or with the Northwest Dorians. His points on the Doric character of the loans certainly look persuasive: *drapën*, Tosk *drapër* 'sickle' < **δράπανον* rather than *δρέπανον*; *kumbull* 'plum' < *κοκκύμηλον*, *brukë* 'Tamariske' < *μυρίκη*, *trumzë* 'thyme' < *θύμβρα* ~ *θρύμβη*. The last three (and, for that matter, reflexes of the first) occur in parallel forms in the Greek enclaves of southern Italy (though the Doric nature of these dialects is another famous debate!). But this still does not tell us precisely where the Dorians in question were at the time of contact.

There are a few ancient Germanic loans: *fat* 'spouse', *shkum* 'foam', *tirq* 'trousers' (Goth. *þiubrōkis*) look best. Barić (*LS* 73–91) has up-to-date pertinent detail. These are supporting evidence, but do not place things any closer geographically. Presumably the farther north and east the Albanians were, the better were their chances of contacts at this time with Goths, but the whole question is uncertain in the extreme.

6. W. Cimochowski (*BUShT* 1958:3.37–48) displaces the Albanians much less than others: to the mountains near the Mati, north to Niš. Çabej (*BUShT* 1958:2.54–62) is even less willing to see them moved: on the basis of toponyms, he argues for a coastal region.

Particularly because of the relative inaccessibility of these articles, and because their theses have tended to be out of favor, it is worthwhile discussing them at some length. Cimochowski starts by reviewing, briefly and critically, Weigand's arguments (*Balkan-Archiv* 3.227–

251) for a Thracian background for Albanian, and for an earlier home east of its present location:

a) Toponyms of Latin origin in Albania show Dalmatian, not Albanian, phonological development.

b) Inherited nautical and fishing terms are absent in Albanian. These facts are easily understood, says Cimochowski, since Albanian must have continued in remoter areas where Romance would not absorb it completely—hence not in areas where such place names of Latin origin continued strongest. The Albanians would have lived inland from the seacoast, in the mountains, but not necessarily beyond the border of Albania.

c) Certain words, such as *man* 'mulberry, blackberry' are shared with Thracian (μαντεία). But this could merely show that there were contacts; besides, Thraco-Phrygian Βρίγες are known to have lived near Durrës. Moreover, Çabej thinks that even these words can be shown to be Illyrian. Cimochowski goes on to point out (p. 48) that *karpë* and *mën* are shared in the Italian pre-Romance area; hence this alleged Thracian correspondence is vitiated.

d) Certain Thracian names are supposedly explained with the help of Albanian. Of these, only *Dacia Maluensis* (: *mal*) is well explained in this way; *Decebalus* (: *ballë*) and *Burebista* (*burrë* + *bisht*) are surely wrong.

e) Albanian toponyms known from antiquity do not show Albanian phonological development. That should not be surprising; from the end of the tenth century the whole of southern Albania was overrun by Bulgarians. But that does not necessarily mean that there were no Albanians anywhere in Albania.

f) Old loans in Rumanian from Albanian and shared Albanian-Rumanian developments from Latin point to an eastern origin. But the nomadic habits of the Vlachs and the herding culture of the Albanians would have brought them into contact for perhaps long periods in the past. Moreover, granting that the Albanians may well have had eastern contacts, we still do not know exactly where the Illyrian-Thracian line was, and Ναῖσσος (Niš) is regarded by many as Illyrian territory.

From these observations Cimochowski concludes only that the south of Albania, the north around Shkodër, and the Adriatic seacoast are excluded as earlier Albanian territory; but this does not prove a Thracian relationship. There then follows a long discussion of the evidence for an Illyrian relationship, which will be taken up in part below, after which Cimochowski concludes, with Stadtmüller, that the home of the Albanians was somewhere in the vicinity of the Mat, stretching to Niš.

Çabej's claim is even stronger than Cimochowski's. He first runs through the history of views on the early Albanian habitat in a convenient way: The Albanians continue the habitat of Illyrian (claimed by Thunmann, Hahn, Kretschmer, Ribezzo, La Piana, Sufflay, and Erdeljanović). Half-Romanized Illyrians spilled south from the mountains between Dalmatia and the Danube (the view of Jireček). In the third through sixth centuries, as nomads, they moved from the Carpathians south (Pârvan, Puşcariu, Capidan). They came from Pannonia (Procopovici, Philippide). Albanians and Rumanians were in Thracian territory between Niš, Sofija, and Skopje (thus Weigand). Albanians were in Dardania, where Illyria and Thrace meet, and moved to Albania in the late Roman period, so that the Slavs found them in the Bojana basin (Jokl, Durham, Skok). From the Balkan and Rhodope mountains they moved to Albania before the Slavs (Barić). They were in the Mati basin in Northern Albania, and expanded south in the Middle Ages (Stadtmüller). This last location is too restrictive, according to Çabej. However, in *VII Congresso internazionale* 245, Çabej relates *Mathis fluvius* (Vibius Sequester) to *mat* 'river bank'.

Çabej points out that villages in the Balkans are generally of recent date and changeable settlement. Hence for the study of toponyms city names and rivers are best. If we inspect such names attested by ancient sources, we find that many follow Albanian phonological development: *Scardus* > *Shar*, with no metathesis, as in *Scardona* > *Skradin*. *Scodra* > *Shkodër*; Çabej remarks that *sk-* > *h-* belonged to the pre-Balkan period, and compares (*VII Congresso internazionale* 244), for phonology, *shkamb* < *scamnum* and *kulshedër* < *chersydrus*. (*Rogame* is a recent suffixation in *-ame* of *rogë*, and therefore no problem because of the medial *-g-*.) *Barbanna* > *Buenë* is regular, as shown by Jokl (*IF* 1932: 50.33 ff.), *Slavia* (1934–1935:13.286 ff.), *Glotta* (1936:25.121 ff.). *Lissus* > *Lesh* (cf. *missa* > *meshë*, etc.); Çabej points out (*VII Congresso internazionale* 245) that Latin *ĭ* + *CC* is regular, a statement I can neither affirm nor control at the moment. *Dyrrachium* > *Durrës*, *Isamnus* > *Ishm*, *Drivastum* > *Drisht* show, as Krahe claims, the Illyrian initial accent. *Shkum(b)î* < *Scampinus* is regular in the Central Albanian dialect, where pretonic *ë* > *u* and *mb* > *m* are expectable (*VII Congresso internazionale* 246). Αὐλών > *Vlorë* may perhaps involve a Slavic intermediary. *Thyamis* > *Çamëria*, as Leake saw in 1814, is accepted by Çabej; however, one might expect *s* < *ti̯* (cf. *pus* 'well' < Lat. *puteus*). *Arachthos* > *Arta* is supposedly better explained by Albanian than by Greek; but, apart from the surprising syncope, *kt* should yield *ft* or *jt*, and not *t*, from that time level. *Ragusium* (*Ragusa*) is *Rush* in Bogdan (1685).

Thus, says Çabej, the seacoast has remained Albanian since antiquity.

The foreign names represent several layers of later intrusions, which Weigand failed to weed out, and treated indiscriminately, according to Çabej (*VII Congresso internazionale* 243).

Barić (*LS* 25 ff.) gives an account that is as plausible on the other side of the debate, based on the careful work done by Skok on Balkan toponyms in relation to Romance. He sees Albanian as sharing with Thracian **kt* > *t* (p. 26), but it should be noted that, as we shall see, V. Georgiev's "Thracian" has this, but that excludes his Daco-Mysian. Using the known symbiosis with the pre-Rumanians and the place names *Niš*, *Škup*, and *Štip* (p. 26), Barić places the Albanians in the Dardanian-Peonian region (p. 27). He then goes on to discuss (pp. 30–34) the problem of the location of the pre-Rumanians; whether they were spread out and far north of the Danube at that time need not concern us here.

It has long been recognized that there are two treatments of Latin loans in Albanian. Barić sets forth (*LS* 27–28, and *Godišnjak, Balkanološki Institut, Sarajevo* 1.1–16 [1957], esp. 7–11) a very convincing looking solution for this duality. Latin *ct*, *cs* gives Albanian *ft*, *fš* (*luftë* 'war', *kofshë* 'thigh'), which matches Rumanian *luptă*, *coapsă*; these would easily represent sound substitutions after IE **kt* had become **t*. (One problem I see in this is *ftua* 'quince' < *cotóneum*, which would have to have become **ct-* almost immediately to avoid falling in with *këta* 'this [n.], these [m.]'.) This group also includes Albanian *traftār* < *tract-*. On the other hand, we have in *derjt* 'straight' < *d(i)rectus* and *trajtonj* a different outcome, which matches Old Dalmatian *traita* < *tract-*. Similarly, there are both Albanian *a* and *e* as reflexes of Latin *a*, which match Rumanian and Dalmatian developments. These, then, would look back to two chronological and geographical layers, one an "inner Balkan" and the other a "coastal Adriatic." Barić (*Godišnjak* 13) considers that since Rumanian has loans from Albanian, but Albanian has practically none in the opposite direction, these Rumanian shapes must all be "Restwörter," not "Lehnwörter"; but, as Reichenkron (above) takes into account, the loan situation may easily be more complex than this.

7. There is, then, the question of where the Albanians were when the Slavs arrived. Barić discusses this (*LS* 28–29). Seliščev thought that the Slavs met only Romans in Albania. He showed clearly that most Albanian territory was at least exposed to Slavs in the Middle Ages; only the central region is thin on Slavic toponyms, perhaps pointing to early concentration there by the Albanians. In my opinion, the chronology of the Slavs and Albanians in Albania is uncertain in the extreme. Barić (*Hymje* 77) considers the loss of intervocalic voiced *C* in Albanian as post-Slavic, after Jokl (*IF* 1926:44.37 ff.). This would explain *Shkinikë*

'Bulgaria' < *Sclavinica*; the etymon recurs clearly in the Greek enclavee as *škñerište* 'in the other [Greek] language'. But these could well havs had a Latin etymon in the first place. *Labërija* in the south has Tosk *-r-* from intervocalic *-n-* and the Slavic metathesized *la-*, but we could posit either order for the occurrence of these. Skok has *Durrës* 'Durazzo' < *Dъ́račь* < *Dyrrachium* (but note */dú-/ is required!). Yet pre-Serbian must have accented *Drač* on the second syllable. Moreover, to make matters more vexed, Cimochowski (*Ling. Posn.* 1960:8.133–145) posits Δυῤῥάχιον [dur:akhii̯on], taken into Illyrian as *dúrraki̯u-* (after **o* > *a*) > **dúrrać*(*An*) > **dúrrëć*(*ë*) > *Dúr̃ës*; this enlarges on and sharpens the account referred to above in Çabej's treatment of these names.

Perhaps it is naïve to look for neat, unbroken settlement areas, and doubly so for those familiar with the prenational state of the Balkans. On the present evidence, I cannot accept as a whole any one of the above vexed solutions; nor can I reject totally any one as clearly wrong.

An improvement of Barić's presentation of the name of the Bojana river (*LS* 29) might be to posit from Livy's *Barbanna* a form **barƀanna* (note that *Berat* lost its Slavic *-g-*) = /baru̯anna/ > **borjan*(*n*)*a* (by Slavic adoption) > **bojana* (in earlier Albanian; cf. *ujë* 'water' < **udrjā*). Here we would have all changes explained by known rules but no clear chronology.

Of course, in any event we could only prove the Albanians did, and never that they did *not*, precede the Slavs.

On the question of the erstwhile spread of the Albanian speech area, I. Popović (*Istorija srpskohrvatskog jezika* 23 [Novi Sad, 1955]) points out clear evidence of earlier remains in Crna Gora. But no argument can be raised on this, however well it may fit in with our general picture of the percolation south and west of the Albanians, for a similar argument could then be constructed for the older spread of the Tosk area to the south.

8. We must turn now to the troublesome and inconclusive question of Illyrian and Thracian, and their possible relation to Albanian.

Without entering into his arguments in detail—for I find their longer range aspects unconvincing, and his safer observations of concordances no advance over those of earlier workers—Barić (*LS* 24 and elsewhere) plumps for an Albanian-Armenian relationship, with Thracian as intermediate. More precisely, he would posit an Albano-Thracian and Phrygo-Armenian continuum. Note that this is quite a different relationship from that assumed by Reichenkron, above.

I. I. Russu (*Cercetări de lingvistică* 1958:3.89–107) finds Illyrian to be a *satəm* language, and Thracian likewise; but since they have a clearly different toponymic and onomastic lexicon, they are not one and the same language. Illyrian would have been Romanized at an early date, and Albanian, since it survived as an independent, would more likely be from Thracian. But, Russu declares, the problem of Albanian is still not solved.

Rosetti (*Istoria II*[3] 51–63) reviews the question generally. The two areas of Illyrian and Thracian were divided by the Morava-Vardar river line. While asserting what I take to be his considered conclusion that Albanian is a Thracian dialect, Rosetti mentions Georgiev (p. 53) and Barić (p. 54), citing V. V. Ivanov and Hamp to the effect that Albanian is neither *satəm* nor *centum* typologically (see more on this below in relation to Illyrian), and mentioning Russu and Cimochowski as defending a *satəm* character for Illyrian (see below also), while C. de Simone (*IF* 1960:65.33) doubts the latter. A good list, of the proposed lexical equations with Illyrian and Thracian, follows (pp. 56–62). A proper consideration of this list would easily generate a good-sized essay, for there are problems on all sides, and Rosetti is essentially reporting the state of scholarship as he sees it.

While opinion may differ on the above matters, none of the positions differs essentially from positions long held by one or another worker in the field. When we turn to the recent work of Georgiev, a new ingredient is added. In his *La toponymie ancienne de la péninsule balkanique et la thèse méditerranéenne* (Sofia, 1961; = *Linguistique balkanique* 3.1), he sets up seven regions, which number among them the three groups Daco-Mysian, Thracian, and Phrygian. (Roughly, the first two match the "Thracian" of many others.) The first of these groups is evidenced by toponyms in *-deva/-dava/-dova* (the variants are explained by chronology) < **dhēwā*, is the ancestor of Albanian, and illustrates its relation by the sound changes in the above form. Georgiev posits a whole set of phonological changes for this language, which match known developments in Albanian phonology: **é, o, ā, ē, ō, ū, au, ei* (> *e*), *eu* (> *e*), *ń̥* (> *a*), *r̥* (> *ri*), *k̂* (> *s, þ*), *ĝ*(*h*) (> *z, đ, d*), *tt* (> *s*), *s* (> *š*). This is discussed in his *Toponymie* 7–8, as well as in *Issledovanija po sravitel'no-istoričeskomu jazykoznaniju* 145 (Moscow, 1958). I am not sure that I understand what is posited for **ei* and **tt* in the light of what I understand for Albanian. This prelanguage would have arisen in Dacia and spread to Dardania and Eastern Macedonia, and thence down the Axios (Vardar). Georgiev mentions chronologies, but I do not know how he arrives at them.

Georgiev's Thracian is defined (p. 9) by *para* 'river', *bria* 'town', *diza* 'fortress'; as is customary in such matters, there are etymologies for all these. The Thracian area occupied the region bounded by the Black Sea, the Propontis, the Aegean, and the Timachus, Strymon, and Danube rivers. If Georgiev's phonological rules were to turn out to be correct, we are still faced with a formidable lexical job, in view of the sparsity of manageable items: *Darda-* appears as both Daco-Mysian and Thracian. The following, which we could try to fit into the Albanian schema, are declared Thracian (*Issledovanija* 119–121): *-bistas* (*Boure-bista*) 'πιστός', *b(o)ur-* (to *burrë?*), *zeiz-*, *zis-* (*i-zi?*), *mal-* (*mal?*), and the gloss *skiắrē* 'Kardendistel' (*sh-qer?*).

Again, Illyrian (pp. 32–34) occupies Illyria, Dalmatia, and southern Pannonia. Here we find *Delm-* (*delmë* 'mouton'; the ordinary form is *dele*, and we may wonder where other such forms are found), *Ulc-* (*ulk*, *ujk* 'loup'). Daco-Mysian supposedly penetrated Illyria and Dalmatia by the first millennium B.C. Also, Venetic and Keltic came in from the northwest, thus giving the analyst a wide range of possible alternatives. This would allegedly explicate the two traditional conceptions of "Illyrian": Hirt, Krahe, Barić, Pokorny, Popović (*centum*), versus Kretschmer, Jokl, Ribezzo, Pisani, Mayer (*satəm*, with an ingredient of *centum*).

In *Issledovanija* (pp. 133–137) Georgiev goes on to elaborate his Daco-Mysian/Albanian/Thracian relationship; there are two theories, which he elaborates but which we can pass over here. In the "Mysian" of Asia Minor, the solitary well-known inscription yields *patrizi* = Greek πατράσι; this would show Albanian *ri* < *r̥. An inscription in Bulgaria comes up with *diernēs*, which is derived from **k^w^ersnā* = *Černa*; here, supposedly, the labiovelar is palatalized and spirantized, as in Albanian. Thus Albanian and the relevant elements of Rumanian come from Daco-Mysian; *Athrus* > *Jantra* and *Utus* > *Vit* in northern Bulgaria show that that region was never Thracian, but rather Daco-Mysian.

The concrete evidence for the above claims is wholly beyond my control.

V. Pisani is well known to be against simple "Stammbaum" connections, yet he has from time to time pointed out apparent parallels in Albanian and Illyrian. In *Paideia* (1958:12.271) he draws an isogloss for "Macedonia-Tracia" with the words for 'name': Alb. *emen*, Slavic *imę*, Baltic *emnes/emmens*, Keltic *ainmN*, etc. Doric would also show Illyrian relics in Ευυμακρατίδας, Ευυμαντιάδας (both Laconian); and to these Pisani adds Laconian δίζα 'capra' = Albanian *dhi*. In *Paideia* (12.298) he adduces Laconian γριφᾶσθαι = γραφεῖν, with "Illyrian" *r̥ > *ri* and Hellenized phi; and δεῖσα 'sterco', first attested in δείσοζος in Leonidas of Tarentum, which he equates with Albanian *dhjes* 'defecate'. In his review of Volume I of A. Mayer's *Die Sprache der alten Illyrier* (*Paideia* 1958: 13.319–320) Pisani lists various Illyrian glosses, most of which show no hopeful connection with Albanian, but do show considerable philological difficulty: πέλιος, πελία 'vecchio, -a' might conceivably be put in relation with *plak* 'old man'; we could guess at *τριτώ* 'testa' alongside *trû* 'brain'; *μέδος* 'hydromel' does not occur in Albanian (see below); perhaps the most interesting is *δύβρις* '*θάλασσα*' ("senza etnico"), which has been suggested in connection with Albanian *dêet,* but which Pisani thinks probably Phrygian.

Dečev thinks that Albanian is from Thracian, not from Illyrian. R. Gusmani (*Paideia* 1957:12.164–165) remarks: "Ora qui il D. non ha tenuto calcolo del fatto che ogni lingua è la confluenza di diverse e molteplici tradizioni linguistiche, non di un filone unico, com'egli implicitamente pensa." Thus, Albanian would possibly be from an ancient Balkan *koiné linguistica,* but this evades the central quesiton of how the "mixture" came about.

Jokl's Illyrian-Albanian correspondences (*Albaner* §3a) are probably the best known. Certain of these require comment: Strabo (7.314) ἕλος Λούγεον : *lëgatë* 'swamp'. This could be **lug-*, but there is also **lag-* 'wet', which might of course also represent **loug-*.

Ludrum : Tosk *lum* 'muck', Geg *lym,* Tosk *ler,* but there are also Latin and Greek cognates.

Aquae Balizae : *baltë* 'mud'. But Krahe (*IF* 1962:67.151–158) thinks *Balissae* is from *Bal-is(i)a* : **Bal-sa* in *Balsenz* < **Bal-s-antia* (: **Ap-s-antia* > *Absentia*) : Lith. *balà* 'swamp' : OCS *blato,* Alb. *baltë.* Therefore, for Krahe *Balissae/Balizae* is "Alteuropäisch" (see below).

Metu-barbis ∼ *-barris* is ambiguous.

Malo/untum, etc., involve root etymologies and are dubious.

Place names in *-V-ste/a/o* : *kopshtë* 'orchard', *vresht* 'vineyard' : (*Illyrier* §4) Lith. *-ysta* 'membership'. But even this seemingly solid item has been challenged by J. Hubschmid ("Substratprobleme," *Vox Romanica* 1960:19): "Letzten Endes sind sie aber vorindogermanischen Ursprungs. Sie drücken die Zugehörigkeit aus, haben ferner kollektive oder frequentative Bedeutung" (p. 177). Hubschmid claims the suffix occurs from Basque and Western Romania to Asia Minor, against Georgiev's Pelasgic *-s(s)-* (pp. 298–299).

Schulze's *-is-* in names is now Krahe's "Alteuropäisch."

That Alb. *-inj* is a plural-collective is clear, but what about the meaning of *Delminium*?

Jokl's fragile Thracian correspondences need a thorough overhauling in the light of recent work, on more than one count.

While we must exercise due caution in the use of supposedly Illyrian forms (see below), Cimochowski (*BUShT* 1958:2.41–46) has some important discussion to contribute to the lasting debate on the reflexes of Indo-European "gutturals" in Illyrian. He points (pp. 41–42) to evidence for both *satəm* and *centum* character for Illyrian (-Messapic). Doubtless, he says, some proposed etymologies have been wrong: *Volturex, Regontius, Regius, Rega, Genthius*; yet many good examples of palatals > velars remain. Likewise, *Barzidihi* could be < **Barzes* < **Bard-jo-s* (cf. Alb. *mjekrrosh* 'bearded'); yet there remain many presumably original palatals written *s, z, σ, ζ, θ* in classical sources. Also, in his view *Aquilis, Aquincum* indubitably show labiovelars. Cimochowski further argues (pp. 42–44) that all *satəm* languages show some erratics with velar reflex for original palatal, which many scholars have tried to explain away as loans of ancient date. Jokl (Eberts *Reallexikon der Vorgeschichte* 1.89–94, 6.38–45, 13.29) tried to show that this occurred in the presence of *r* and *n*. Against this, Cimochowski adduces *Gentius, Genusus, Epicadus, Magaplinus* (the last supposedly belonging with Skt. *mahant-*, Alb. *i madh* 'big'), *Bersumno* beside *Berginium* and *Bargulum, Barzidihi* beside *Bargilius* and *Bargulis*. Cimochowski thus believes that Illyrian (-Messapic) shows velars where uncontested *satəm* languages do, and that therefore these reflexes fail to make Illyrian a *centum* dialect. I agree provisionally with Cimochowski's conclusion here, but on other grounds. True, the facts speak against a *centum* status for Illyrian; but Cimochowski has too simple a formula for the *centum-satəm* dichotomy. In all of his examples, the following environment *always* involves a resonant, while the other cognates adduced are sometimes weak or dubious or susceptible of other explanations: *Vescleves, Can-davia* (for which **k̂u̯n̥-* is gratuitously reconstructed, but which points only to **k̂n̥-* at most), *Acra-banis, Bargulis/Bargilius, Skerdis*, Ἄγγρος. This environment matches exactly that posited by me for the merger of palatals and velars in Albanian (*KZ* 1960:76.275–280), and on no account depends on erratic matches in the *satəm* languages as conventionally understood.

A special feature of Illyrian claimed by Cimochowski is its separate reflex of the labiovelars (pp. 44–46). Before front vowels, as Pedersen and Jokl showed, Albanian distinguishes the labiovelars. Jokl correctly saw that Illyrian distinguished them, too, but tried wrongly to prove that Thracian did also. Jokl's argument rested on Ακυενισιον (which is simply Latin *Aquensium*), Κουιμέδαβα/Κουμουδέβα (of uncertain first element) Γουολῆτα (of uncertain segmentation), Ζουούστη(ρ) (unclear even for the Thracian values of the letters), and Κοαδάμα (whose analysis rested circularly on the first two). Thus, according to Cimochowski, the evidence for Thracian labiovelars crumbles away. The distinct reflexes of labiovelars in Albanian and Illyrian form, then, a capital proof of the Illyrian ancestry of Albanian.

But, in the face of all this, I feel we must bear in mind that the positive Illyrian labiovelar evidence is sparse and conjectural in the extreme. Moreover, as a retention it would be, strictly speaking, only weakly diagnostic.

Cimochowski also claims that Albanian shares with Messapic *au* > *a* and with Illyrian IE **ē* > *ā* (then **ā* > Albanian *o*); the last would be seen in *Spalatum* : Σπολήτιον in Italy. But O. Haas (*Messapische Studien* 173–174 [Heidelberg, 1962]) states that *au* > *a* occurs in Vulgar Latin adaptations (*Ascoli* : *Ausculum*; *Basta* : *Bausta*), and not in Messapic itself, which had *au* > *ao* > *o*.

On the loss of *C*'s before **s* in Illyrian and Albanian, see Hamp (*IF* 1961:66.51–52).

Furthermore, Krahe's "Alteuropäisch" has added a new ingredient. For example, in his "Baltico-Illyrica" (*Festschrift für Max Vasmer* 245–252 [Berlin, 1956]), we see various equations that for Jokl might have been marks of kinship between Illyrian-Albanian and Baltic. With such sparse evidence, too, there is a self-defeating aspect to this scholarship; consider Krahe's equations in *BzN* (1956:7.1–8): *Nette*, *Netze* would match Skt. *nadī́*, *nadyā́ḥ*, while *naʒ* would match *nadá-*; so far so good. But then **ned-* would also appear in *Neta* (Norway), Greek Νέδα, Νέδων. Which language do we have now, and how do we know when we meet a new language on this level, much less who its kin are? More recently (*BzN* 14.1–19 and 113–124 [1963]) Krahe has screened "Die Gewässernamen im alten Illyrien" and sorted them into "Alteuropäisch," Baltic-Adriatic, Northwest (Germanic) connections, and a newly defined "Illyrian." In the last category we find only Αρ-δάξανος, *Artatus*, Δίζηρος, *Drīnus*, Δρίλων (are these related?), *Genusus*, Κατ-αρβάτης, *Clausala*, 'Ρίζων.

Clearly, one must be very circumspect before assigning any form definitely to Illyrian.

9. We will deal separately with the Messapic problem, partly because I have dealt with it before (*Studies Presented to Joshua Whatmough* 73–89 [The Hague, 1957]) and wish here to revise my statement of the problem, partly because we should not too lightly lump Illyrian and Messapic together. On this latter point, see now Haas' eagerly awaited *Messapische Studien*: On his page 11, Haas states that he intends to discuss elsewhere his views on the insufficiently grounded assumption of Messapic and Illyrian unity; here he simply illustrates the flimsiness of some grounds that depend on quite arbitrary segmentations of words. On his page 12 he says that the Illyrian thesis for Messapic belongs to the past, and hopefully soon to oblivion. This is not to exclude a fresh proof, when Illyrian may in the future become better specified; it is only that no such demonstration has been made up to now. On his page 13 he states that it is possible that Illyrian names may be clarified on the basis of our knowledge of Messapic; but the reverse is methodologically unsound.

After the recent painstaking philological work on the texts by O. Parlangèli (*Studi messapici* [Milano, 1960]), Haas (*op. cit.*), and de Simone (largely in *IF*), no forms should be used without being freshly checked.*

Apparently without having seen my above-mentioned article (abbr. *A&M*), Çabej has dealt with some Messapic words in his "Unele probleme ale istoriei limbii albaneze" (*Studii şi cercetări lingvistice* 1959: 10.527–560, esp. 555), and some of our treatments overlap.

Although the question of Phrygian takes us beyond the scope of this paper, those interested should now consult further (ad *A&M* 76) the recent papers of Haas in *Die Sprache* and *Linguistique balkanique*.

Taking up specific points in *A&M*: (§3.1) Çabej (p. 555) has likewise remarked this. (§3.3) Çabej adduces *balias*, *balakriaihi*, *bálakros*, Pliny's *balisca vitis*, and Apulian dialect *bálaku*, all beside Albanian *balosh* (term for horses and cattle with a white forehead). On the other hand, de Simone (*IF* 1962:67.36–52) lucidly reads *baleψias* as *balei̯as* (= Illyr. *Diteius*, *Poteius*, *Ateia*, etc., in form); connects *Bales* (< **bali̯as*) with *balásh*; and says that Messapic *balasiiri*[*hi*] is not to be equated with *Bálakros*. But the connection of these forms directly with *balásh* is inexact, for this *-l-* comes from **-lC-* and not from **VlV* or **-li̯-*.

(§3.4) Haas (*Mess. Stud.* 144) posits for *bijë* **bhūli̯ā*, but that cannot be, for it would give **byjë*. If *bolles* and *bili*(*v*)*a* really reflect **bhūl*(*i*)*i̯-*, as Haas assumes (pp. 28, 41, 131, 142–144), then we must abandon the Albanian equation. On *bir*, Pisani (*IF* 1959:64.170 n. 1), after E. Risch, has *fīlia* primary to the secondary *fīlius* and **putlo-* remodeled to *puer* after *gener*, *socer*; here might be a parallel to bolster **biñ-* > *bir*. (§3.5) If the suggestion of *delme* 'sheep' to the name of Dalmatia is sound, then my suggestion falls away. (§3.10) If Alb. *mëz* really joins Basque *mando* 'mule', as Barić (*Hymje* 57) has it, then these go with the *-st-* suffix above. Barić also includes here (*h*)*ardhí* 'grapevine' : Basque *ardao* 'wine' and *bisht* 'tail' : Basque *buztan*. (§3.13) I hope to refine the account of *mjegullë* on another occasion.

(§3.14) Çabej also adduces *ndë* 'in', but not the others. (§3.16) Pertinent to the comparative aspect of the discussion of *atavetes* and *sivjet* now is Mycenaean *za-we-te* (opposed to *pe-ru-si-nwa* PY Ma 225) = *kjawetes* 'this year' according to Palmer and Killen (*Nestor* 240 [March, 1963]), and 85-*u-te*, which would *not* be **sjawetes*, as Palmer wants, according to Killen (*Nestor* 258). In Mycenaean **kj* and **tj* would perhaps give the

* This article had already been sent to press when I received, thanks to the courtesy of the authors, the marvelously meticulous joint work of C. de Simone (*Die messapischen Inschriften*) and J. Untermann (*Die messapischen Personennamen* [Wiesbaden, 1964]), continuing Krahe's *Die Sprache der Illyrier*. Likewise, I had not seen de Simone's article on the Messapic diphthongs (*IF* 1964:69.20–37), nor Parlangèli's review of Haas (*Kratylos* 1963:8.179–186).

same result in this instance. (§3.19) Krahe (*IF* 1959:64.248) sees here the Messapic suffix *-idi̯o*, also seen in *alzanaidihi* (gen.). This could then be compared to the Albanian plural and diminutive *-z-*. (§3.24) Çabej, too, adduces this equation. (§4.3) Çabej wonders whether *veinan* is not to be equated with Lith. *víenas*. Note that Haas (*Mess. Stud.* 37 and 221) continues the unacceptable reconstruction of Albanian *vetë* as **su̯e-ti-* by suggesting a comparison with Messapic *vetai* 'ihr selbst'.

In passing, it is worth observing that Haas (p. 95) makes an identification and Messapic reconstruction that is suggestive of a new line of thought. He translates *aran* as 'illam' (contrast *A&M* §3.1) and compares Umbrian *oro-*; this may or may not be so. Here (and again on p. 177) he translates *ennan* also as 'illam', reconstructing **eni̯ām* and comparing Greek ἕνη 'jenen Tag', OCS *onъ*, Latin *enim*. If so, this same reconstructed shape would also accommodate Albanian *një* 'one', and the sense is not too far off.

Also (Haas, 46 ff.), *graiva*, γραιβια (-ϝ-) (a feast in Tarentum), derivative of an old *u*-stem, allegedly seen in B.1.43 *grahis damatria* **grāūs* = γρᾶῦς (Haas, *op. cit.* 142 on *ū* > *i*), suggests Albanian *grā* plural of *grua* 'woman'. On this last word, see Hamp (*KZ* 1960:76.276).

(§4.6) I am glad to see that Haas agrees (pp. 184–185) with me (save for a few details on which I am unclear) on the developments of the "gutturals." The separate reflexes shown for the labiovelars (pp. 185–187) and the dentals derived from palatals (p. 188) are highly suggestive of Albanian, but the supporting examples are as yet insufficiently certain. On this matter, see also the discussion of Cimochowski's ideas above. Haas' discussion of the labiovelars in *Ling. Posn.* (1953:4.78–80) seemed to me inconclusive by comparison with his later work. Further, Barić (*LS* 9–14) discusses the *satəm* question; all his examples for Illyrian *centum* features (p. 11) are dubious, as is his treatment of *kr*. On palatal-before-resonant in Albanian, see Hamp (*KZ* 1960:76.275–280); and cf. the above observations on the Illyrian question. Popović (pp. 21–22) essentially follows Barić for Illyrian and *satəm-centum*. The matter of supposed palatalization of labiovelars in Thracian goes beyond our discussion. S. Josifović "Nova mišljenja o indoevropskim jezičkim supstratima na Balkanu," *Godišnjak Filozofskog Fakulteta u Novom Sadu* 1959:4.97–115) comments on Budimir's works of 1950 and 1956 on "Pelasti," and on Pavlović's of 1957 and 1958 on the Mediterranean substratum in the Balkans. Most of this need not concern us here, but Budimir allegedly (p. 99) separates *kohë* from *časъ* < **kʷēso-*, which he relates to *česati*, *česno*, *kosa*, ξαίνω, ξέω, ξόανον. "Thus Albanian preserved the explosive character of the palatal gutturals for a long time, which is not the case with the other satəm dialects, and besides it distinguished velars and labiovelars in contradistinction to satəm languages." It may be so, but I do not see how this statement follows naturally from the context.

(§4.7) On *haivaψias* (p. 89), see de Simone, *IF* 1960:65.31–34. The ghost word *ana* now falls away; see L. Ognenova, *Studia in honorem D. Dečev* 333–341 (Sofia, 1958) Κ(ύρι)ε βοήθη Ἄννα, and E. Çabej (*BShkSh* 1957:2.122–126, conveniently reported by M. Lambertz, *Südostforschungen* 1959:18.402–403) ἀνα[β]οήθη Ἰ(η)σ(οῦ) Κ(ύ)ρ(ιε).

In addition to the forms I have discussed, Çabej (p. 555) has also proposed the following equations: *Meduma* (place name) = Albanian *i-mje(t)më* 'middle' (which, however, it should be pointed out, is simply a productive derivative in *-më* of the particle *mjet*); *tabaras, tabarra* 'priest, -ess (?)' = Albanian preverb (fossilized) *të-* plus the root *bar-* 'carry'; *ma* = Albanian *mos* 'modal negative'; *(ma)kos* 'ne quis (?)', *(ai min)kos* 'si quis (?)' = Albanian *kush* 'who?'. Most of these Messapic forms are as yet of highly uncertain interpretation; consult Haas for more detail. Çabej also suggests Calabrese dialect *menna minna* = Albanian *mënd* 'suck, nurse'.

For Salentine Greek, G. Rohlfs (*Die Sprache* 1959:5.173–175) has proposed a Messapic etymon **squèros* for the word *s̑kero*, and puts this in relation with Albanian *hirrë* "Käsewasser."

W. P. Schmid (*IF* 1960:65.26–30) reads Messapic genitive + *no* and equates this with Letto-Lithuanian *nuo*; since Lettish shows gen. sg. and dat. pl. here, Schmid posits original ablative syntax, which Messapic would have lost.

10. We come now to the proposed relations between Albanian and other Indo-European groups. The material will be quickly passed in review.

M. Durante ("Etrusco e lingue balcaniche," *Annali . . . Napoli* 1961: 3.59–77) has some hazardous implications tied to a few observations on Albanian which do not convince me.

It is convenient here to reproduce Georgiev's subgrouping of Indo-European (*Issledovanija* 282–283):

North: Baltic-Slavic-Germanic, perhaps Tocharian
West: Italic-Keltic, Venetic, Illyrian
Central: Greek, Daco-Mysian (including Albanian), Indo-Iranian, Phrygian-Armenian, Thracian, Pelasgic
South: Hittite-Luwian, Etruscan

Apart from the many debatable points that fall outside the scope of this paper, since Albanian belongs to the largest group, there is little to say about crucial problems. If one thing is clear to me, it is that no special relations have as yet been proposed for Italic, Keltic, or Anatolian. But in this field perhaps anything can happen.

11. By way of orienting ourselves, summarizing open issues, and correcting some unevennesses in past scholarship, we will now consider matters dealt with in Porzig's *Gliederung*.

First, some corrections. *dorë* 'hand' (p. 187), *χείρ*, etc. are taken back to **ĝher-* 'greifen', i.e., **ĝher-s-*; of course, in the light of Hittite the preform is something like **ĝhē̆sr* (fem. in Albanian < old neut pl. ?). The apparent reconstructions for Albanian are sg. *dorë* < **ĝhē(s)rā*, pl. *duar* < **ĝhē(s)res* (C-stem). An alternative, preserving the gender considerations along with formal shape, is *dorë* fem. < (by form-class analogy) *neuter < **ĝhē(s)r-An* (in Jokl's symbols) = **ĝhē(s)r-om*, thematized from **ĝhē̆sr*; *duar* < **dōr* < **geră* < **ghē(s)ra*.

zjarr (p. 163) 'fire' is derived from an *n*-suffix form, and is equated with Skt. *ghṛṇá* m. 'Glut, Hitze'; but as I have demonstrated in a recent oral presentation, this is not a separate lexeme, but rather an old *n*-plural with suffix in suppletive relation to the sg. *zjarm*.

mjal-të (p. 203) is an interesting case where careful dialect study pays off. In a few villages of Greece that show the contrast, and in reflexes in some enclaves of Italy, we find that we have *mjáltë* 'honey', in contrast to *báñtë* 'mud'. Thus the first is not an original **lt* cluster, but has lost a vowel by syncope; on the other hand, the *l* (not orthographic *ll*) must come from an old cluster, and **ll* is the only plausible one. The etymon is, then, the Latin word, and not Indo-European. Thus, Albanian here goes with Balto-Slavic, Tocharian, and Aryan, after all. Culturally, this gains in interest when we recall that Jokl (*Linguistisch-kulturhistorische Untersuchungen aus dem Bereiche des Albanischen* 289–296 [Berlin, 1923]) has traced *bletë* 'bee' to Latin **mellētum*.

For 'hit' < 'split' (pp. 204–205) alongside Lat. *feriō*, ON *berja(sk)*, Lith. *bar(i)ù*, Lett. *baŕu*, OCS *borjǫ*, it is likely that we should posit Alb. *bie* < **b(h)erjō*, homophonous with *bie* 'carry' < **b(h)erō*.

Now to some more general matters. The fate of the syllabic resonants (pp. 66–68) is a vexed problem. It is difficult merely to establish the facts. Unfortunately, S. E. Mann's article on the subject (*Lg.* 1941:17.23) is correct or cogent only where the same solution has been proposed many years before him. The question must be entirely rediscussed, but we would do well to start from Jokl (*Die Sprache* 1963:9.120–122).

For the voiced aspirates (pp. 68–72), Albanian fits in with Baltic, Slavic, Macedonian, Illyrian, and Keltic; but this is not diagnostic.

On the matter of gutturals (pp. 72–76), I have already stated my position in *A&M* (see above); see also Jokl, *Die Sprache* 1963:9.123–127. On the *kl* (p. 75) of so-called Grenzdialekte, see Hamp, *KZ* 1960: 76.275–280 and above.

On dental-plus-dental (pp. 76–78), Indic *tt* and Iranian *st* point to **tst* (which we see in Hittite); see also A. Meillet, *Dialectes indoeuropéens*

60. Greek *st* and Balto-Slavic *st* point to **tst,* according to Meillet, *op. cit.* 61. Italic, Keltic, and Germanic, however, share *ss* (which could conceivably come from a mediate **ts*). Porzig refers (p. 77) to "die Lücke unserer Kenntnis beim Armenischen und Albanischen." Meillet (p. 57), however, has *st* for Albanian, Illyrian, Thracian, and Phrygian. The truth is that Albanian shows a present-day *s* (*pasë* 'had [participle]', *besë* 'faith, loyalty'); see Hamp, *KZ* 1961:77.252–253. This must go back to a groove affricate, perhaps **ts*.

Albanian preserves many interesting old suppletions in the verb-stem system, among them 'sit', 'stand', 'lie' (these latter are poorly distinguished in the Balkans), and 'see'; here the situation is unlike Balto-Slavic, Germanic, and Latin (Porzig, 91–92).

Porzig makes a number of Greek equations (pp. 177–179) which require comment: Hom. ὀδμή Att. ὀσμή : *amë* 'odor' is too ambiguous to be certain. καπνός : *kem* < **ku̯epnos* would be of unclear relationship. κοῖλος : *thellë* (not *thelë*). What is special about the **-ni̯ō* of ὑφαίνω : *venj* 'weave'? μάρη : *marr* 'take' is dubious. Why should ἄλφι : *elb* 'barley' be < *'white'? δημός : *dhjamë* 'fat' is not a correct match in vocalism. ξένϝος : *huaj* 'stranger' (not *huai*). δόρπον : *darkë* 'supper' also involves *drekë* 'noon meal' (in ablaut), and I think this is to be equated with the otherwise unexplained Breton *dibri* ~ *dribi* 'eat', which I deal with elsewhere. The (Greek-Armenian-)Albanian *ândërrë* 'dream' is an archaism, and thus nondiagnostic, as are many other items above.

Porzig (p. 179) notes that when some other subgroup is involved in an equation, Greek or Balto-Slavic always is. *zâ* 'voice' (p. 180) matches Balto-Slavic and Armenian. *djathë* 'cheese' (*dithë* is a ghost, *IF* 1962: 67.144), with Indic and Balto-Slavic matches, is a good comparison, yet a survival; but the others on pages 180–181 are trivial. (*h*)*yll* 'star' cannot be used in evidence, since it is still unclarified. *mjekrë* 'beard' has a perfectly regular *k*, and thus means nothing (see *KZ* 1960:76.275–280).

For Porzig (p. 181) Albanian is Eastern Indo-European and goes with Greek, and especially with Balto-Slavic. In Western Indo-European it is supposed to be connected with Illyrian only.

12. Meillet (pp. 109–113) summarizes the distributions of *-ye-* presents: Greek and Indo-Iranian have *-y^e/o-*; Balto-Slavic and Armenian have *ī* for "state" and *-y^e/o-* for derived verbs; Germanic and his Italo-Keltic have *-yo/ī*, almost leveled out for both verb types. In the avant-propos to the reprinted edition (p. 14), Meillet adds Albanian to the last set.

He states erroneously (p. 17) that **prəwo-* is limited to Indo-Iranian and Slavic; Albanian has *i-parë* 'first'. Another set in agreement (Skt. *dáhati*, Lith. *degù*, OCS *žegǫ*, Alb. *djeg* 'burn') is probably too routine to be important.

To Meillet's "northwest" vocabulary (which includes Balto-Slavic) we could add *grurë* 'wheat' (p. 18) *shat* 'hoe'(p. 21), and *mos* (modal negative; p. 23). There is not much positive evidence here; these are, in the main, retentions.

Perhaps of considerable importance are the following two traits. Baltic and Slavic lack perfect reduplication, the archaic state of affairs (Meillet 104–107); Albanian agrees. Balto-Slavic also shows an old indicative aorist, but an active participle from the perfect; Germanic, Keltic, and Italic have pooled the old aorist and perfect. Here Albanian seems to agree on a slender base with Balto-Slavic. In obscure ways we may see agreement in *mora* 'took' : *marrë, lashë* 'left' : *lënë, erdha* 'came' : *ardhurë, hëngëra* 'ate' : *ngrënë.*

Albanian is particularly rich in *ē preterits, and this belongs to a lengthy discussion—too long for this paper—of the role of the long ablaut grade in Albanian, a discussion that Jokl (*IF* 1916:37.90–122) only opened and failed to see in its far-reaching main issues. Such a discussion would find a new base in the studies of Kuryłowicz.

13. F. B. J. Kuiper (*Annali . . . Napoli* 1960:2.159–164) has shown that OP *θātiy* 'says' is a root present *θā-* in suppletion with *θah-*. I think we must abandon the old equation with Latin *cēnseō* (on other grounds, too) and place Albanian *thom, thotë* (3 sg.), aor. *tha,* alongside these. What has never been adequately brought out is the fact that if *thom* 'I say' is **k̂ē(n)smi* (which it could be), *thotë* cannot be **k̂ē(n)st . . .*, which should give **thoshtë.* Since **k̂ēn(s)t . . .* would give **thând* (or perhaps **thân*), we must posit **k̂ēti* for the 3 sg.

14. A very important item has recently appeared, which relieves us to a large extent of the task of exposition that would otherwise be called for to bring together the very scattered earlier literature; that is the posthumous long article of Jokl, "Die Verwandtschaftsverhältnisse des Albanischen zu den übrigen indogermanischen Sprachen" (*Die Sprache* 1963:9.113–156), which was located only a few years ago among Jokl's *Nachlass*, now housed in the Vienna National Library, in the original draft in Gabelsberger shorthand. This article sets forth the distinctive phonological developments of Albanian from Indo-European from the point of view of what is shared with other groups (pp. 116–129); the similar morphological characteristics (pp. 129–148); and the lexical correspondences (pp. 148–156). There is not space here to criticize Jokl's points in detail, and I intend to consider the more interesting points on another occasion. Moreover, some have been implicitly dealt

with in the foregoing discussion; finally, since Jokl's article is about forty years old, there should be no wonder that even in so neglected a field as Albanian many items now simply fall away, overtaken by more recent scholarship, some of which is reflected in the preceding pages.

Fundamentally, Jokl's presentation suffers from two technical defects by current standards: an atomistic approach to the data, and a failure to distinguish conservative features from innovations. I shall deal with Jokl's results as concisely as is consistent with clarity.

15. Jokl summarizes his phonological results (p. 129) by stating that they fit well with a North European affiliation, specifically with Balto-Slavic. Jokl's considered opinion that Albanian goes most closely with Balto-Slavic, if often on the basis of far-from-obvious evidence, is well known from various of his publications; on this, see the relevant sections of Porzig's *Gliederung*. I have also expressed in print my agreement with Jokl on this to the extent that a clear-cut opinion can be held at this stage of our knowledge. However, the phonological evidence now in question scarcely manages to support this, no matter how correct the view may be. The Albanian merger of **o* and **a*, of **ē* with earlier **ā*, the phonetic drift of *[ā] to *ō*, the treatment of **ə*, and of **ou̯o*, and the change of **s* to [š], are all too isolated structurally (as presented) and too nonunique as events to associate Albanian clearly with any one group of dialects; they merely make certain trivial exclusions likely. The "helle Färbung" associated with **r̥* > *ri* does not really match Balto-Slavic and Keltic either in allophonic distribution or in phonetic detail without a great many more supporting considerations. Perhaps we may ultimately be able to sharpen these claims; at present I see no clinching phonological link, in the form of a structured shared innovation, with any other Indo-European group.

16. The conclusions presented (pp. 147–148) for the morphology make similar claims. We will inspect here only the correspondences that include Balto-Slavic; that is not to say that on a complete reëxamination of the problem we might not find further fundamental shared features involving other groups more intimately. One immediate disadvantage is noted in the nature of the features identified: they are almost all derivational morphs and processes of some sort; thus, they belong to a less structured, more open-ended, part of the grammar.

The development of the type *φόρος* (shared with Greek, too) was of old formation, and is not diagnostic. Long-grade nouns (also shared with Germanic) and preterits (more broadly shared) seem ultimately important to me, but cannot be assessed on this brief survey basis. Participles in *-mo-* (shared with Armenian) and in *-eno-* (also Aryan and Germanic) belong to an old layer of adjectival derivation. Nouns in

-imo-, if related to similar feminines (e.g., in Keltic), are also difficult to assign a precise innovational status to. Collectives in *-īno-* (also claimed for Latin and Germanic) are of ambiguous standing. Verbal nouns in *-lë* are claimed also for Armenian, but surely Tocharian and Hittite further complicate this picture.

The spread of *-m* to the neuter of interrogatives, if true, and the formation of the accusative of 1 sg. and 2 sg. personal pronouns, are features that are most difficult to evaluate at such reconstructive distance. The use of active plus reflexive for a passive is not quite parallel in Balto-Slavic and Albanian (where it is restricted by tense); but, if pertinent, that and the syntax of the 'teens of the numerals and perhaps the combination of interrogative and demonstrative pronouns seem good candidates for diffusional origin.

This leaves as possible uniquely shared items: diminutives in *l* + *-i̯o*, *-ti̯o* in ethnica, alternation of *-ti* and *-tā* (a weak possibility), verbal nouns in *-g-* and *-es* + *i̯ā*, and secondary adjectives in *-usto*. Considering that many of these call for searching discussion, and might not stand up very well in all cases, it is scarcely an impressive list. Moreover, our views of Indo-European have altered greatly since Jokl was writing, and only a full reëxamination *ab initio* could take proper account of this.

Clearly, the whole question remains completely open. But perhaps we have been able to clear a little ground.

17. For convenience, and by way of summary of the main fields covered, a selective bibliography is appended.

Bibliography

POSITION OF ALBANIAN IN INDO-EUROPEAN:

Barić, H. "Porkelo Arbanasa u svetlu jezika," *Lingvističke Studije* 7–48. Sarajevo, 1954.

Bàrtoli, M. "Accordi antichi fra l'albanese e le lingue sorelle," *Studi albanesi* 1932:2.5–72. P. 42: Alb. agrees with Balt. more in conservations than in innovations; with Gk. and southern languages more in innovations.

Çabej, E. "Unele probleme ale istoriei limbii albaneze," *Studii şi cercetări lingvistice* (abbr. *SCL*) 1959:10.527–560. Alb. version: *BUShT* 1963:3.69–116.

Cimochowski, W. "Prejardhja e gjuhës shqipe," *BUShT* 1958:2.37–53. Supports Illyrian kinship of Albanian.

Georgiev, V. "Albanisch, Dakisch-Mysisch und Rumänisch," *Linguistique balkanique* 1960:2.1–19.

Hamp, E. P. "Albanian and Messapic," *Studies Presented to Joshua Whatmough* 73–89. The Hague, 1957.

Jokl, N. "Kelten und Albaner," *Symbolae grammaticae in honorem Ioannis Rozwadowski* 1.235–250. Cracoviae, 1927.

———. "Die Verwandtschaftsverhältnisse des Albanischen zu den übrigen indogermanischen Sprachen," *Die Sprache* 1963:9.113–156.

Pedersen, H. "Albanesisch und Armenisch," *KZ* 1900:36.340–341.

Pisani, V. "L'albanais et les autres langues indo-européennes," *Annuaire de l'Institut de philologie et d'histoire orientales et slaves* 1950:10.519–538 (= *Saggi di linguistica storica. Scritti scelti di V. Pisani* 96–114. Torino, 1959).

Polák, V. "La position linguistique de la langue albanaise," *Philologica* 1957: 9.29–33.

Porzig, W. *Die Gliederung des indogermanischen Sprachgebiets.* Heidelberg, 1954. Esp. pp. 149–150, 174–181, 185–186, 209–211, for features shared by Alb. with other IE groups; good bibliography on previous work.

ADJACENT LANGUAGES AND DIFFUSION:

A. Balkan linguistics

Boissin, H. "Une formation balkanique aberrante de composés," *Godišnjak Naučnog Društva NR Bosne i Hercegovine* (abbr *GNDBiH*) 1957:1.17–28.

Gołąb, Z. *Conditionalis typu bałkańskiego w językach południowosłowiańskich.* Cracow, 1964. Esp. pp. 167 ff.

Hamp, E. P. "The Interconnection of Sound Production, Perception, and Phoneme Typology," *Proc. 4th International Congress of Phonetic Sciences, Helsinki, 1961* 639–642. The Hague, 1962.

Michov, D. M. "Die Anwendung des bestimmten Artikels im Rumänischen, verglichen mit der im Albanesischen und Bulgarischen," *Institut für rumänische Sprache, Jahresb.* 1908:14.1–111.

"Një konferencë mbi gjuhësinë balkanike e E. Çabejt," *BUShT* 1963:2.292–298.

Piotrovskij, R. G. "O sravnitel'noj xronologii postpozicii opredelennogo artiklja v tak nazyvaemyx balkanskix jazykax," *Voprosy slavjanskogo jazykoznanija* 1959:4.8–20.

Rohlfs, G. "La perdita dell'infinitivo nelle lingue balcaniche," *Omagiu lui Iorgu Iordan cu prilejul împlinirii a 70 de ani* 733–744. București, 1958.

Sandfeld, K. *Linguistique balkanique: problèmes et résultats*[2]. Paris, 1930. Rev. N. Jokl, *Litteris* 1927: 4.191–210. Summarizes and integrates previous work.

Schuchart, H. "Albanisches und Romanisches—Zu Miklosich's Albanischen Forschungen," *KZ* 1872: 20.241–302.

B. Rumanian

Barić, H. "Albanisch, Romanisch und Rumänisch," *GNDBiH* 1957:1.1–16.

Brîncuș, Gr. "Paralele frazeologice romîno-albaneze," *SCL* 1960:11.913–918.

Meyer-Lübke, W. "Rumänisch, Romanisch, Albanesisch," *Mitteilungen d. Rumän. Instituts an der Univ. Wien* 1914:1.1–43.

Polák, V. "Quelques idées concernant les rapports lexicaux albano-roumains," *Omagiu lui Iorgu Iordan* 693–699. București, 1958.

Puşcariu, S. *Die rumänische Sprache*. Leipzig, 1943. Esp. 188–210, 326–338.
Reichenkron, G. "Vorrömische Bestandteile des Rumänischen: III and IV. Albanisch-rumänisch-armenische Gleichungen," *Romanistisches Jahrbuch* 1958:9.59–105; 1960:11.19–53.
Rosetti, A. "Albano-romanica: I. De l'influence du grec et du slave méridional sur l'albanais et sur le roumain," *Bulletin linguistique de la Faculté des lettres de Bucarest* 1942:10.76–90.
———. *Istoria limbii romîne*. II³, III⁴. Bucureşti, 1962. On the Balkan and Slavic components in Rumanian; up to date.
Russu, I. I. "Raporturile romînei cu albaneza şi cu substratul balcanic," *Cercetări de lingvistică* 1962:7.107–130.
Treimer, K. "Albanisch und Rumänisch," *Zeitschrift für romanische Philologie* 1914:38.385–411.

C. Slavic

Djamo, L. "Contributii la studiul unor sufixe de origine slavă limba albaneză," *SCL* 1961:12.231–261.
Polák, V. "Albanci a Slovené (Vznik a počátky dnesnich nářečních variant albánských)," *Časopis pro moderní filologii* 1957:39.85–90.
Popović, I. "Albano-Slavica: Zur Geographie und Chronologie der albanischen Spracheinflüsse auf die Südslaven," *Südostforschungen* 1956:15.512–526.
———. "K voprosu o proisxoždenii slavjan severnoj Albanii," *Slavjanskaja filologija. Sbornik statej* I, Moscow, 1958.
———. "Slaven und Albaner in Albanien und Montenegro: Zum Problem der slavisch-albanischen Sprachchronologie," *Zeitschrift für slavische Philologie* 1958:26.301–324. Based on place names.
Seliščev, A. M. *Slavjanskoe naselenie Albanii*. Makedonskij naučnyj institut, Sofia, 1931. Penetrating use of place names.

TOPONYMS

Çabej, E. "Die älteren Wohnsitze der Albaner auf der Balkanhalbinsel im Lichte der Sprache und der Ortsnamen," *VII Congresso internaz. di scienze onomastiche, 1961* 241–251; Albanian version *BUShT* 1962:1.219–227.
———. "Problemi i autoktonisë së shqiptarëvet në dritën e emravet të vendeve," *BUShT* 1958:2.54–66. Also summarized in *Bibliotheca Classica Orientalis* (1960):5.20.
Cimochowski, W. "Des recherches sur la toponomastique de l'Albanie," *Ling. Posn.* 8.133–45 (1960). On Durrës.
Markelaj, G. "Rassegna di toponomastica albanese," *Università di Bologna, Istituto di glottologia, Quaderni* 1961:5.31–52.

(Participants in the discussion of the conference version of this paper: Hoenigswald, Birnbaum, Winter, Marku.)

The Dialects of Old Indo-Aryan

M. B. Emeneau

UNIVERSITY OF CALIFORNIA, BERKELEY

The most obvious fact about Sanskrit, or Old Indo-Aryan (OIA), when we are interested in its dialects, is that the records show large corpora in what are essentially two rather divergent dialects—Vedic and classical. But, as soon as this statement is made, it is seen to be too simple. Classical Sanskrit is a literary language written according to the book—that is, Pāṇini's grammar, and following it more or less correctly. We find in it no dialects, no chronological development, except loss and at times invasion from the vernaculars of the users, and no geographical divergences. Vedic Sanskrit, however, is different. It is anything but a unified language, a language of one dialect only. It shows even within the oldest member of the corpus, the Ṛgveda, linguistic features that can be explained only by positing their origin in slightly differing dialects, and within the total Vedic corpus there is a sliding scale of clusters of dialectal features that run all the way from those that are most different from classical Sanskrit to those that are, in fact, taken by most scholars in the field to be essentially the dialect that Pāṇini described as his norm. No dissent from this sketch need be caused by Pāṇini's label of "Vedic" for many forms that differ from those of his norm. It is the prose of the latest Brāhmaṇa texts and the Upaniṣads that is nearest to his language. His "Vedic" variants are those of the earlier, essentially "canonical" collections.[1]

Pāṇini described, presumably, a dialect of Northwestern India (his birthplace Śalātura was there), and he is dated in the middle of the fifth century B.C., with the usual plus-or-minus of Indian chronology, this time perhaps plus or minus a hundred and fifty years.[2] Besides his references to Vedic forms, he mentions geographical variants, but not so that we can do much in the way of identifying dialects. All that we are really told is that there were other dialects in North India besides the one he described. As has been said by L. Renou,[3] his information allows us to

[1] So I understand P. Thieme to hold in *Pāṇini and the Veda* (Allahabad, 1935).

[2] V. S. Agrawala, *India as Known to Pāṇini* 475 (Lucknow, 1953), for the attempt at precision; M. B. Emeneau, *JAOS* 75.146 n. 3 (1955) for a very short summary of views.

[3] *Histoire de la langue sanskrite* 67 (Lyon, 1956).

draw no isoglosses. And the same is true of what little dialectal information we are given by the two great commentators Kātyāyana and Patañjali (the latter in the second century B.C.).

A very crucial point in this matter of dialects is the relationship between classical Sanskrit and the extreme Vedic dialect of the Ṛgveda. A chronological difference, one of from five hundred years up, is the first matter to be mentioned. In saying five hundred years it is possible that there is exaggeration, but I incline to think that Burrow's, Renou's, and others' guess of circa 1200–1000 B.C. for the period of the composition of the hymns of the Ṛgveda is not far out. In a period of five hundred years we could expect much linguistic change to have taken place, if Ṛgvedic Sanskrit were the genetic origin of classical Sanskrit. It is worthwhile to assume for a moment that that is the relation between the two and to identify some of the changes.

Some of the differences that we might superficially hit upon turn out to be something else. For example, as we usually learn Sanskrit, whether it is Westerners or students in India, classical Sanskrit has a strangely indeterminate sort of stress accent and Vedic Sanskrit is characterized by a pitch-accent system. However, Pāṇini's Sanskrit had the same pitch accent as Vedic Sanskrit, and the learning of classical Sanskrit without the pitch accent, which is really what the uncertain stress accent amounts to, results from an invasion of classical Sanskrit by the Middle Indo-Aryan (MIA) and Modern Indo-Aryan (NIA) stress-accent systems which are a historical development diverging from the OIA state of affairs. Similarly, the general equation in meaning of the three past tenses, imperfect, perfect, and aorist, in classical and epic Sanskrit is certainly different from the Ṛgvedic state of affairs (even if we are not completely certain of the Vedic distinctions between these three tenses in all instances). But it is fairly certain that Pāṇini's Sanskrit had the same meanings for these tenses (or perhaps we should prefer to call them tense aspects) that the Veda had. The difference that we see in the epic and classical texts should be characterized as loss during the long period of the use of Sanskrit as a literary language. I would assume that it came about because of the invasion of the literary language by vernacular speech habits of the kind seen in our oldest voluminous MIA material, that in Pali. In this language there had evolved from the OIA system (the Vedic and that described by Pāṇini) a verbal system with one past tense only, formally an amalgam of imperfect and aorist, with very few forms descended from the perfect. In the Prakrits there is much less even than this, and passive constructions using the past participle are usual (when the present is not the narrative tense), prefiguring what is found in the modern vernaculars. It is from the oldest MIA stages, then, that the use of the narrative tenses in epic and classical Sanskrit literature derives.

Some changes may, however, be identified that might be quite straight-line developments from Vedic to classical. Most involve simplification or loss of one sort or another. A straightforward example is loss of the subjunctive except for the retention of first person forms as part of the imperative paradigm. Another is loss of augmentless aorist and imperfect forms in modal use except for the occurrence of such aorist forms with *mā* in prohibitions; they are completely lost in indicative use, with a very few epic exceptions, which are often treated as lapses from the normative grammar, but which in fact need a different treatment. Simplification in syntax is seen in the classical language's treatment of prepositions and verb forms as inseparable compounds, whereas in the Vedic language they had been freely separable.

Phonologically, some such simplifications are identifiable, in spite of the unhappy historical accident that the R̥gveda, and all other archaic Vedic texts as well, were written down only late within the Vedic period by speakers of what was apparently, for all that is relevant here, classical Sanskrit, and as if the old Vedic texts were in many details, especially of phonology, classical Sanskrit. Reconstruction of the Vedic text with the aid of the meter has allowed the recovery of the law that we know as Sievers-Edgerton's,[4] with all that this involves of an allomorphy much more complex than that of classical Sanskrit.

In fact, as has been amply demonstrated, classical Sanskrit contains so little of this allomorphy that on the basis of it alone the Vedic state of affairs could not be more than suspected. It is certain that the system of the classical language had already come into existence before the R̥gvedic corpus was composed in the condition in which we have it, and that this was prior to the writing-down. This condition involves two forms of the text, one by complete utterances (*saṃhitā-pāṭha*) and one with the utterances analyzed into separate words (*pada-pāṭha*). A considerable body of linguistic analysis is presupposed by this edition of the corpus. Such analysis, which states in all detail the relationship between the two forms of text, is provided by the R̥gveda-prātiśākhya treatise. Its date is, as usual, unknown, and even its relative chronology within the sequence of grammatical works as a whole is not certain. However, informed scholars, with such a notable exception as Thieme, place it prior to Pāṇini, but later, though how much later is very uncertain, than the two text forms of which it states the relationship. As so often in Indian literary scholarship, it is thought that the present treatise is the end result of a development from less developed to more developed and that the original treatise, which is presupposed by the R̥gveda text forms, was much enlarged to reach the present form and has itself been lost.

[4] F. Edgerton, "Sievers's Law and IE. Weak-grade Vocalism," *Lg.* 10.235–265 (1934); "The Indo-European Semivowels," *ibid.* 19.83–124 (1943).

The point of going into the matter of the prātiśākhya analysis is (1) that this analysis is of a R̥gvedic text which was, at the time of the first exegesis, that is, that of the word-by-word text form, already recited, whether in ritual use or otherwise, with classical Sanskrit phonology insofar as Sievers-Edgerton's law is concerned, but (2) that the prātiśākhya analysts had some sort of knowledge of the allophony of semivowels that is stated in the law, even if recitation, both then and in all later times in India, ignored the matter.[5] How was this knowledge derived? Was it something handed down by tradition, or was it theory based on the Vedic practitioners' study of metrics, as Edgerton suggests? That some fragments of tradition remained is at least suggested by the collection of written forms with *iy* and *uv* allophones from Vedic texts later than the R̥gveda.[6] Whichever it was, we must of course regret that more was not said or recorded by the prātiśākhya scholars, when we consider how much of the detail involved in the law is still uncertain. For example, the form written *pūrva-* is never pronounced **pūruva-* according to the law, for the reason that it is descended from **pr̥̄va-*, or whatever else is required or suggested by the use of laryngeals. Is it possible that it was actually pronounced **pr̥̄va-* (or what not) in the period of the composition of the R̥gvedic hymns? Certainly, while Sievers-Edgerton's law was in full working order, something other than *pūrva-* must have been the phonemic form; this means a time very close to the period of our hymns. To sum up, this phonological simplification is going from the R̥gveda to classical Sanskrit, a simplification that is generally the result of analogical spread for each morpheme of one allomorph at the expense of the other, would provide a chronological isogloss, relative rather than absolutely datable, if our assumption were tenable that classical Sanskrit is genetically derivable from R̥gvedic Sanskrit.

This assumption, however, is not tenable. The contrary evidence is familiar, and the hypothesis drawn therefrom. The evidence includes such phenomena as the R̥gvedic correspondence of retroflex *ḷ* where classical Sanskrit has *ḍ* intervocalically. R̥gvedic has innovations in the noun declension, such as the nom. pl. masc. in *-āsas*, which contrasts with *-ās*, which latter is found also in the R̥gveda and is the only form in the classical language. It has been demonstrated that, in the R̥gveda, *-āsas* is the form proper to its dialect, from metrical considerations, viz. that written *-ās* many times has to be read *-āsas* to mend defective meter,

---

[5] For the prātiśākhya passages (RPr. 8.22, 17.14 [ed. Regnier]), J. Wackernagel, *Altindische Grammatik* 1^2.202 (with much bibliography), and Edgerton, *loc. cit.*, esp. *Lg.* 19.92 n. 24.

[6] As given by Wackernagel 1.200 f.

while *-āsas* never has to be read *-ās*.[7] Since Iranian also shows entirely parallel phenomena in archaic and archaizing Avestan *- åŋhō* and Old Persian *-āha*, with also *-å* and *-ā* respectively in these languages, it follows that for both branches of Indo-Iranian it must be assumed that there were dialects that retained the monosyllabic ending, which is guaranteed as Indo-European by Oscan **-ús**, Umbrian **-us**, Gothic *-ōs* (but is presents difficulties as, e.g., Prokosch presents them), Old Irish *-u* (vocative: *firu* 'men!', etc.). Such an assumption of a dialect with at least several features that are more archaic than the corresponding features in the R̥gvedic dialect is necessary to explain for Indo-European *o*-stems the classical instr. pl. *-āis* beside R̥gvedic *-ebhis* and *-āis*. Again, Iranian has both forms, this time Old Persian only *-aibiš* and Avestan only *-āiš*. The R̥gvedic (and Old Persian) form is for these nouns an innovation found nowhere else in Indo-European; classical *-āis* has congeners in Italic, Greek, Lithuanian.

The R̥gvedic dialect, then, is clearly not the direct ancestor of classical Sanskrit. There must have been, even on this much evidence, several closely related dialects in the period of the R̥gveda composition, one of which is the basic dialect of this text, another of which is basically the ancestor of the classical language of some centuries later. But it is also clear that the R̥gvedic linguistic norm, even apart from hymns that represent something very close to the classical language, was a mixed dialect, and that one of the elements in the mixture was something near to classical Sanskrit. Only such a hypothesis will explain such mixtures as those of *-āsas* and *-ās*, of *-ebhis* and *-āis*, of the instr. sg. endings *-ā* and *-ena* of IE *o*-stems, of the neuter plurals of Indo-European *o*-stems in *-ā* and *-āni*, and so on. The composers of the older R̥gveda hymns, that is, not those that are for all practical purposes in classical Sanskrit, must have been speakers of many dialects, and the R̥gvedic language represents a mixture, probably of most of them; one very like, or even identical with, the ancestor of classical Sanskrit probably formed one very important element in the mixture. We have an inkling, therefore, so far as direct evidence goes, of the oldest Indo-Aryan of North India as a large dialect area whose speakers were unified by a common culture and by the religion that provides us with the evidential documents; there probably were other dialects as well, outside of this social and religious milieu, as we shall see. The dialects seem to have been subject to interborrowing, even the one which in theory was most free from such borrowing because it was the sacrosanct vehicle of the holy texts. It was a dialect area subject to typical Schmidtian "wave" effects. No other reconstruction will explain the R̥gvedic dialect as we know it, nor its relations with the

[7] So Wackernagel 3.100, following C. R. Lanman, "Noun Inflection in the R̥gveda," *JAOS* 10 (1878), esp. 345.

Sanskrit of Pāṇini. If it is impossible to be very certain about much of this, the chronological differences in the records account for some of the uncertainty, and the many gaps in the record, both synchronic and diachronic, account for more.

The earliest documents that we have in MIA are the Aśokan inscriptions of the middle of the third century B.C. This date, though post-Pāṇini, is prior to the whole corpus of the classical Sanskrit literature. It should not be surprising, then, to find words of MIA origin in the classical literature, even if their numbers are not excessive and if some of them are of fairly late attestation or only lexical. Exx. *masṛṇa-* 'soft, smooth, tender, mild' (kāvya) < Pkt. *masaṇa-*, *masiṇa-* < Skt. *mṛtsna-* or *mārtsna-* 'ground fine or small'; *mārṣa*, *māriṣa* 'friend!' (epic, etc.; *mārṣa* in Bhāsa's dramas, see Emeneau,*Lg.* 39.104 [1963]) < Pkt. *mārisa-* < Skt. *mādṛśa-* 'like me'; *prāgbhāra-* 'mountain slope' (kāvya) < Pkt. *pabbhāra-* 'sloping' (cf. also BHS *prāgbhāra-* id.[8]) < Skt. **prahvāra-*, cf. *hvṛ-* 'to bend, slope', probably *prahva-* 'sloping'; and *prāgbhāra-* 'mass, multitude, heap' (late kāvya) < Pkt. *pabbhāra-* id. < Skt. *pra* + *bhāra-*.[9]

But it is strictly relevant to our interest to determine how far back in the OIA record such borrowings from MIA can be attested, since, in default of other records, such borrowings are almost the only evidence available on the relative chronology of the emergence of MIA linguistic traits. To be sure, we have already pointed to several features of classical Sanskrit as being probably MIA in origin. One of these is the merging of the old past tenses into one meaning in epic and classical Sanskrit. Pāṇini still knew the differences. There has been discussion whether the epic in fact does not have an origin that is pre-Pāṇinean in time. If it had, it would follow that its use of the tenses might have derived from a MIA tendency already existing before Pāṇini. But there are too many gaps in the evidence for this to be anything but speculation.

Phonological Middle-Indicisms in the Vedic texts later than the Ṛgveda have already been pointed out by many scholars, in greatest mass by Bloomfield and Edgerton, *Vedic Variants* 2.20–25 and *passim*. Some of the material collected there is open to uncertainty,[10] but not all,

---

[8] B(uddhist) H(ybrid) S(anskrit) material must, of course, not be treated as Sanskrit, but as MIA.

[9] Emeneau, *Lg.* 36.541 (1960).

[10] The most striking and puzzling example is perhaps *avatá-* 'a well', three times in Ṛgveda passages and replaced by *avaṭa-* in the Sāmaveda and the Taittirīya Yajurveda. The *Vedic Variants* interpretation is followed by Mayrhofer. Wackernagel, 1.167, takes *avaṭa-* to be a Middle-Indicism from **avar* 'down,' with *rt* > *ṭ*. Even though Burrow (*The Sanskrit Language* 129 [London, 1955]) would refine this and posit an *r/n* formation (**avṇ-ta-* > *avata-*; **avṛ-ta-* > *avaṭa-*), this ignores the fact that *avaṭa-* is only post-Ṛgvedic and may well be secondary to *avata-* and not

and it seems to follow clearly enough that there were dialects that were contemporary with at least later Vedic texts and that had phonological features that we know from the later attested MIA dialects.

It will be more satisfactory, however, to pinpoint the matter as sharply as possible. In the first place, there is some clear evidence in Pāṇini. This we should expect because of his chronological proximity to Aśoka and, even more, to the Buddha. The latter's doctrine was that teaching of religion should take place in the colloquial dialects rather than in "Vedic."[11] This, together with the historical outcome, viz. Aśoka's Prakrits, Pali, Gāndhārī Prakrit, Buddhist Hybrid Sanskrit, all used as vehicles of Buddhist doctrine, means that in the Buddha's time there were MIA dialects. One of Pāṇini's words is *māireya-* 'an intoxicating drink' (6.2.70). It is from Pkt. *maïreya-*, which is an extension derived from Skt. *madira-* id. (R̥gveda +). As has been pointed out by earlier scholars, loss of OIA intervocalic *d* (and other voiced stops) is attested in general only in Māhārāṣṭrī Prakrit. Pāṇini's word is attestation of a dialect with this feature centuries earlier than we would otherwise expect it.

It is hardly profitable to go into details about Middle-Indicisms in the later Vedic texts. Identifications of such in the R̥gveda are of chief interest for the chronology we wish to establish. Some scholars have been rather unwilling to admit that they are to be found in this oldest corpus. Renou[12] seems very reluctant, and writes of "justes remarques de Mansion contre l'hypothèse d'un prâkrit contemporain du RV." In translating the introduction to the 1957 edition of Wackernagel's *Altindische Grammatik* Renou had to write (p. 7) of the existence of a MIA dialect "dès l'époque des Hymnes," "une langue . . . qui portait en elle les traits principaux de la phase la plus ancienne du moyen indien, ce qu'on appelle le niveau pāli." But he is here only translating Wackernagel, and in note 80, which gives a large bibliography pro and con, he again refers to Mansion, "qui proteste avec raison contre l'idée . . . d'un pkt contemporain du RV." The bibliography (on p. 7 and in note 80) is very useful in that it provides a large sample of the evidence on which one must rely in finding a MIA dialect contemporary with the R̥gveda.

Quite sound pieces of evidence would seem to be the following. *Múhu*, *múhur* 'suddenly', *muhūrtá-* 'a moment' are connected with Avestan *mərəzu-* 'short' (in compounds), Greek *βραχύς*, Latin *brevis*; here **ml̥r̥* > *u* would be MIA. The connection of the *m-* and the *b-* forms has been ac-

---

an inheritance from pre-Sanskrit. It should be noted, moreover, that even as a Middle-Indicism a sporadic *ṭ* < *t* is difficult.

[11] Edgerton, *Buddhist Hybrid Sanskrit Grammar* 1–2 (New Haven, 1953). For Gāndhārī Prakrit, see now J. Brough, *The Gāndhārī Dharmapada* (London, 1962).

[12] *Histoire de la langue sanskrite* 30 n. 1 (1956).

cepted in general with less than enthusiasm (*muhur*, etc., not given in WP, WH, Boisacq; given in Burrow; Mayrhofer seems to have no qualms), but even so, to connect Ṛgvedic *múhur* with the Avestan form requires the assumption of MIA phonology in the Ṛgveda. Words like *víkaṭa-* 'enormous' (< **vikṛta-*) and *śithirá-* 'loose' (< *śṛth . . .*) have MIA phonology. So also does *púruṣa-* 'man', which in the Ṛgveda occurs written both *púruṣa-* and *pū́ruṣa-*, and in MIA shows such forms as Pali *posa-*, *porisa-*, BHS *poṣa-*, Pkt. *purisa-*; the old theory[13] that all these are derived by MIA developments from **pūrṣa-* still seems most useful, even if Edgerton has qualms.[14]

The very frequent noun *jyótis-* 'light' has long been recognized as having in its initial *jy-* the MIA reflex of *dy-*, viz. *j-*, with *y* written perhaps because of some thought of the various forms of the origin morpheme *dyut-* 'to be bright'; the noun in Prakrit is *joï-*. That the Ṛgvedic pronunciation of the noun, whether as a simplex or as first member of a compound, was *jotis-*, is clear from a metrical examination of all the many Ṛgveda passages that could be found for it by use of Grassmann's dictionary. The stem is always disyllabic, never showing *jiy-* according to Sievers-Edgerton's law, in spite of the very great majority of its occurrences in a heavy situation (heavy 102 : light 40).[15]

Finally, we should note the nom.-acc. sg. neuter of the interrogative pronoun, viz. *kím*, which P. Tedesco[16] has demonstrated very beautifully to be a Middle-Indicism in the Ṛgveda. The Ṛgveda had the series *tát*, *yát*, *kát*. Later, MIA had the series *taṃ*, *yaṃ*, *kiṃ*, the latter replacing **kit*, which was an analogical replacement for still earlier *cit*, which in the Ṛgveda had already become 'adverbial' and been replaced by *kát* on the analogy of

---

[13] Wackernagel 1, §51; R. Pischel, *Grammatik der Prakrit-Sprachen*, §124 (Strasbourg, 1900); Wilhelm Geiger, *Pāli Literatur und Sprache*, §30 (Strasbourg, 1916); etc.

[14] *Buddhist Hybrid Sanskrit Dictionary*, s.v. *poṣa*. Ṛgvedic meter in two passages may be mended by assuming **pū́rṣa-*. RV 10.90.4d *tripā́d ūrdhvá úd ait púruṣaḥ*, would be a good anuṣṭubh line with *pū́rṣaḥ*. Oldenberg rather favored mending the bad meter of 10.87.16c by reading *páuruṣeyeṇa* as *páurṣeyeṇa* (*yáḥ páuruṣeyeṇa kravíṣā samaṅkté*), with the secondary derivative **páurṣeya-* from **pū́rṣa-*. He inconsistently thought it probably better to mend 10.90.4d by secondary crasis of *ūrdhvá úd*.

[15] The word is not treated in Edgerton's two papers. In addition, it is possible that the many exceptions, or some of them, to Sievers-Edgerton's law for the 'sky, day' word, when it is written with *dy-* in a heavy situation, should be explained by a MIA pronunciation *j-*. This morpheme certainly needs further study, if only to sort out the occurrences of exceptions, as Edgerton said in *Lg*. 10.253. The further note in *Lg*. 11.120 does not exhaust the matter.

[16] *Lg*. 21.128–141 (1945).

kás, *kā́*, and so on, *tát*, *yát*. Tedesco makes it clear that there must at an early period have been, beside the R̥gvedic hieratic dialect, a colloquial with the series *tam*, *yam*, *kim*. He attempts several complicated, inconsistent, and not entirely convincing arguments as to why the whole Rgvedic series was not replaced by the whole MIA series. The preferable one of his arguments is perhaps that in which *tam* and *yam* were avoided as being "low" and (I suppose) "mistaken" forms for *tát* and *yát*, while *kím* was too unlike *kát* to need to be so avoided. Another possible argument is that *tam* and *yam* were avoided because of their inconvenient homonymy with the acc. sg. masculine and feminine forms (it is an inconvenient homonymy in MIA—*taṃ* and *yaṃ* for all three genders), while *kím* did not suffer from this disability and could be admitted. I prefer this type of argument, feeling that the avoidance of "low" forms might well have excluded *kím* as well as *tam* and *yam*. Neither Tedesco nor I can explain why *kím* displaced only some of the occurrences of *kát* and not all—in fact, why there was dialect mixture, even to occurrence of both forms in the same verse in three instances. Tedesco tackles the problem of nomenclature boldly and prefers to call this dialect parallel to R̥gvedic "archaic Middle Indic"; probably "Proto-Middle-Indo-Aryan (or Indic)" is as good. No absolute chronology is possible for it, since the R̥gvedic corpus is so impossibly vague in its chronology, beginning from the time when composition was going on in something close to the colloquial and reaching down to the time when epigonoi were composing in an archaic dialect far different from their colloquial or colloquials, some Sanskrit-like, some Proto-Middle Indo-Aryan. But we can guess that the latter type of dialect was in existence almost from the beginning of the time span.

Once this Proto-Middle-Indo-Aryan is admitted, it is not necessary to discuss further the appropriateness (or lack of it) of referring as MIA to the change of **ĝh*, **gh*[front vowels and **g^wh*[front vowels, *dh*, and *bh* to *h*. For as much of the change as is contained within the time span of the Indic documents, MIA would seem to be the proper designation. The adverb *ihá* 'here', which is both R̥gvedic and classical, is MIA and presumably was borrowed first from a PrMIA dialect, while Pali, Gāndhārī Prakrit, BHS, Śaurasenī, and Māgadhī have *idha* (cf. Avestan *ida*), and *iha* is the form of most other Prakrit dialects, including Māhārāṣṭrī.

The net of dialects we have posited for OIA includes, then, at some rather indefinitely placed period, dialects that have already gone some way on the MIA road. At a later period all vernacular dialects are of the MIA type and, also, we must posit, form a net. This net is represented in the written record by a considerable number of literary languages.

And later, of course, comes the dialect net that we know as the NIA vernaculars, with literatures representing a dozen or so nodes in the net.

The general question arises whether we can recover from the MIA and NIA records material of Indo-Iranian or Indo-European origin which is not represented in the OIA documentary record. An *a priori* answer will not do, since it is conceivable that we could argue either way—either that our OIA records are representative of all and the only Indo-European speakers who penetrated Indic territory, or that they represent the speech of only some, perhaps even only a few, of such immigrants. Frankly, we are totally uninformed of the history of the migration. If the former linguistic hypothesis were the case, the picture would be like that of the Romance languages coming from Indo-European through the Latin channel only and adding nothing to our knowledge of Indo-European that we do not already get from the Latin record—this at least seems to be implicitly, or even more or less explicitly, the standard doctrine about the Romance languages, though it is at least possible that the picture is overdrawn and that there are a few scraps of evidence for Indo-European to be extracted from the Romance languages (so Malkiel, in conversation). The other case would be more like that of Germanic, where the literatures of the medieval period do not remotely exhaust all the languages and dialects of that period and where even scraps of other medieval evidence and much of the modern material is employable for Indo-European research.

There has been both implicit adoption of one point of view or the other, and some explicit discussion of the problem. In fact, neither point of view can be adopted in an extreme way. A conservative approach will not rule out the possibility, or even the probability, of the OIA records representing only a part of the OIA net—there is some evidence from the Dardic and Xafir languages looking in this direction. Nor will such a view fail to exercise the utmost caution in examining MIA and, *a fortiori*, NIA evidence which it is claimed represents IE material that bypassed OIA. It is *a priori* unlikely that MIA, and *a fortiori* NIA, will preserve, for example, ablaut grades that are divergent from those found in OIA, considering that the OIA ablaut structure no longer exists as a structure anywhere in MIA, and also considering how much the analogical process has remade those parts of the total OIA structure that showed most of the old ablaut system. Renou's somewhat differently slanted statement is worth quoting:[17] "The time is past when one could hope to use Indo-European to explain many developments

[17] *Lg.* 29.186 (1953).

peculiar to the historical period; today innovations are considered more important than survivals."

In practice, there have been divergent approaches to the problem. Research in this area has usually been of a piecemeal sort, overeager to find an Indo-Europeanism for any small problem that was being investigated. Only so can we evaluate the long lists of items collected, such as those by T. Burrow, Jules Bloch, or Wackernagel,[18] these lists overlapping very considerably; the same evaluation is needed also for L. H. Gray's determined onslaught against MIA in "Fifteen Prākrit-Indo-European Etymologies."[19] Negative reactions to many of the items have been shown by many scholars, of whom I may perhaps mention Edgerton and myself. Mayrhofer alone, I think, has perforce, in the work on his etymological dictionary, had to be seriously explicit about the possibilities. His article, "Das Problem der indogermanischen Altertümlichkeiten im Mittelindischen,"[20] has upheld an even more strongly negative attitude than I am willing to voice.[21]

As examples where we can be sure of most of the relevant facts we can adduce *gūtha-* 'excrement' and *pard-* 'to break wind' (*pardate*). Both are found in the Sanskrit lexica, but not in the literature, except that a late commentator, who is notorious for his use of lexical words, uses the first, and a writer of poetics the second (presumably to label it a word to be avoided in literature). Both words must have been items of the vernacular vocabulary, adjudged too "vulgar" to be used in literature. Both have very good Indo-European etymologies. The first, *gūtha-*, is known from MIA and NIA, the latter, *pard-*, only from NIA. If it had not been that the Hindu grammarians and scholars constructed lexica, dredging up words from many sources besides the literature, these words would not have been known as existing in OIA dialects. What other items does MIA show that are either not attested in OIA or that are more archaic than the corresponding items in OIA? The adverb *idha*, that was adduced above, is clearly one and cannot be explained otherwise.

But hardly any other item in the lists mentioned above can be, or has been, wholeheartedly accepted. To find other than the OIA ablaut grades as explanations for MIA *supina-* 'sleep' (: Greek ὕπνος; contrast Skt. *svapna-*), Pali *garu-*, Pkt. *garua-* 'heavy' (: Greek βαρύς; contrast

[18] Burrow, *The Sanskrit Language* 45 ff.; Jules Bloch, *L'indo-aryen du Veda aux temps modernes* 14 f. (Paris, 1934); Wackernagel 1, reproduced by Renou in Introduction 8 f.

[19] *JAOS* 60.361–369 (1940).

[20] *Studia Indologica, Festschrift für Willibald Kirfel* 219–241 (Bonn, 1955).

[21] *Lg.* 34.409–15 (1958), 39.103–104 (1963).

Skt. *guru-*), Pkt. °*metta-* 'measure; only' (: Greek μέτρον < IE **mǝtróm*; contrast Skt. *mātrā-*), hardly seems justified when very easy analogies are at hand in Skt. *supta-* 'asleep', Skt. *garīyāṃs-* 'heavier', *gariṣṭha-* 'heaviest', Pkt. *gariṭṭha-* id., MIA *mia-* (< *mita-*), *mii-* (< *miti-*), *mijjanta-*, *mijjamāṇa-* (< passive *mīya-*).[22] MIA *tārisa-* 'like that' is certainly derived from OIA *tādṛśa-* (whatever the explanation of *r*), and not to be compared with Greek τηλίκος. Tempting as it might be, with R. L. Turner,[23] to derive MIA *ghara-* 'house' (and the derived NIA forms) from IE **gʷhoro-* 'fire, hearth (> home)', cognate with Greek θέρος, Skt. *gharma-* 'heat', it is hardly likely that *ghara-* is anything more than a metathesized form from OIA *gṛha-* 'house', especially since there is no trace elsewhere in this 'heat' group of etyma of the required meaning development (whatever there may be in the **aydh-* group). Even more tempting is the connection of BHS, Pkt. *se*, the third person enclitic pronoun, with the Iranian forms, Old Persian *šaiy*, Avestan *hōi*, *hē*, *šē*, and even possibly the Old Latin anaphoric pronouns *sum*, *sam*, *sos*, *sās*; and yet the extension of *s*-forms in the MIA demonstrative pronoun (from *sas*, *sā*),[24] and the absence of *se* in Pali make it highly probable that MIA *se* is merely an analogical formation on the model of first person *me* and second person *te*.

Pischel and Geiger[25] had proposed that the reason Skt. *kṣ* was variously represented in MIA by *cch*, *kkh*, *jjh*, *ggh* was that the latter were reflexes, at least in part, of the different Indo-European combinations that fell together in Skt. *kṣ* but that were kept apart in Iranian. Geiger found that there were too many exceptions for him to accept Pischel's doctrine completely. Mayrhofer and Katre[26] pointed out even more exceptions, and were unwilling to accept even the points that Geiger kept, to such an extent that Mayrhofer wished to find only secondary dialectal variations and developments in the whole body of MIA instances.[27] H. W. Bailey accepts the older doctrine,[28] though he must acknowledge the exceptional character of some instances. Most recently Burrow[29] has combatted Mayrhofer's skepticism, especially by ingenious

---

22 Cf. Edgerton, *JAOS* 73.117 (on *supina-*); Emeneau, *Lg.* 39.103 (on °*metta-*); also in Mayrhofer. For *supina-* it should be noted that MIA has no forms in the verb with any vowel but *u/o*.

23 *BSOS* 3.401–404 (1924). But Turner now (*A Comparative Dictionary of the Indo-Aryan Languages* 239, entry 4428) says that his earlier view is "very unlikely," apparently persuaded by Mayrhofer's skepticism (1.357).

24 Pischel, §423; Edgerton, *BHS Grammar*, chap. 21, esp. gen. pl. *sānaṃ* in 21.45.

25 Pischel, §§317–326; Geiger, §56.

26 Mayrhofer, *Studia Indologica . . . Kirfel* 227–233; Katre, *JBORS* 23.15 (1937).

27 Edgerton, *BHS Dictionary*, s.v. *pragharati*, shows skepticism of the older doctrine.

28 *BSOAS* 13.137 (1949).

29 *JAOS* 79.255–262 (1959), esp. 261 f.

new etymological combinations and philological interpretations. He probably has made advances, but even so he is forced to posit *ad hoc* interdialectal borrowings and influences on MIA from Sanskrit, and the end result is probably too complicated to be really cogent. In my opinion, the matter is still *sub judice*; my guess is that Mayrhofer's skepticism is better justified than the old doctrine.

If MIA adds only a very little that is certain to the OIA picture of Indo-European inheritances in Indic, it can hardly be expected that NIA will contribute much, and in fact there are few suggestions. Hindi *āṭā* 'meal', and so forth, and the fourteenth-century A.D. Sanskrit lexical *aṭṭa* 'food', which is surely only a Sanskritization of an NIA form, are hardly to be derived from Indo-Iranian **ar-* (IE **al-*) 'to grind', which otherwise has no representative in Indo-Aryan.[30]

The most notable of such suggestions is that the past passive stem of the verb meaning 'to give', as seen in Hindi *diyā* and other NIA forms, is derived from IE **dətó-*, through **dita-* of an unattested OIA dialect and such an unattested MIA form (with an added OIA *-ka-*) as **diaa-*; so Tedesco[31] argues most ingeniously and brilliantly and with much reconstruction to which one can take no exception. His central thesis, however, has been much discussed, and independently (so I think) in recent years has been rejected by three scholars—Mayrhofer, myself, and Turner.[32] The two latter find in the NIA forms analogical formations based on a present stem of the type *dē-*, which is found early in MIA

---

[30] *Kurzgefasstes Etymologisches Wörterbuch des Altindischen* 1.546 (Heidelberg, 1956).

[31] "Geben und Nehmen im Indischen," *JAOS* 43.358–390 (1923). In saying that **dita-* is unattested in OIA, I am not ignoring Epic Skt. *vyādita-* 'opened' (*vi-ā-√dā*), which has been discussed often. It is generally agreed (e.g., by M. Leumann *IF* 57.231, and Wackernagel-Debrunner, *Altindische Grammatik* 2.2.561 f. [Göttingen, 1954]) that this form can be only a late formation of MIA type, on the basis of a present **vy-ā-deti*. What seems not to have been put in evidence so far is that the form is found only in the compound *vyāditāsya-* 'with opened mouth' and usually only in the simile *vyāditāsya ivā 'natakaḥ* (Mbh. 6.58.33d), *vyāditāsyam ivā 'ntakam* (6.59.20d, 102.18b, 110.38d, 112.74f; according to E. W. Hopkins, *The Great Epic of India* 436 [New York, 1901], also in Rāmāyaṇa, Bombay ed., 3.2.6); otherwise *vyāditāsyair mahānādaiḥ* (Mbh. 2.22.23a) and *vyāditāsyā mahāraudrā* (3.146.46c). The synonymous equivalent of the simile, *vyāttānanam ivā 'natakam*, is found in Mbh. 3.125.1d, 6.55.45b, 59.23b, 78.23d, 103.93b, 104.37f (and also in Rāmayāṇa according to Hopkins). Nothing at the moment seems to follow from this coexistence of synonymous compounds, one with the Pāṇinean form and one with the other problematic one; nor, of course, are the collectanea complete for the epic at the present stage of epic studies (probably only for Mbh. books 1, 2, 3, 6).

[32] Mayrhofer, *Studia Indologica . . . Kirfel* 237–239, and *Kurzgef. etym. Wb.* 2.13 f. (my interpretation is that he has rejected it); Emeneau, *Lg.* 34.409 f. (1958); Turner, *Journal of the Gypsy Lore Society*, 3rd ser., 39.28–30 (1960), in spite of earlier acceptance, e.g., in *BSOS* 5.131 (1928).

and which (as I stated it) led to the analogy *eti* 'goes' : *ita-*, *jeti* 'conquers' : *jita-*, *(s)theti* 'stands' : *sthita-*, *dheti* 'places' : *hita-*, *deti* 'gives' : x, x being **dita-*.

Not quite all the data have yet been included by any of those who have treated the matter. Evidence for the NIA languages of the northern section of the Indo-Iranian border, the Dardic and Kafir languages, is still somewhat scanty, and not all the material relevant to this problem is yet in hand. However, Khowar (otherwise Chitrali), one of the Dardic languages,[33] provides some interesting forms. For the verb 'to give', the perfect participle is *dirū*, which Morgenstierne derives from **ditaka-*, which is the OIA origin of MIA **diaa-*, whence Hindi *diyā* (**t* > Khowar *r* intervocalically). It is hardly necessary to separate this participle in origin from those of other NIA languages already presented. It is interesting, however, that the *r* of Khowar is independent evidence for **t*, which those NIA languages that have descended through the normal MIA languages do not actually show (Hindi *diyā*, etc.). Since we have posited that this participle is analogically based on a present stem *dē-*, we should examine the Khowar verb to try to determine whether our explanation will hold for it, too. The Khowar present (really present and future, labeled 'aorist-future') is *dōm*, *dōs*, *dōi*, *dōsi*, *dōmi*, *dōni*. The Dardic languages in general, however, have a stem *dē-*.[34] The stem *dō-* of Khowar must be analogically formed on the basis of the small class of verbs that have this type of stem, cf. *korōm* 'I do' (< Skt. *karōmi*), *bōm* 'I become' (Skt. *bhavāmi* > MIA [e.g., Pali] **bhōmi* > Khowar *bōm*); it is not of an origin parallel to that of the Balto-Slavic **dōmi*, *dōsi*, and so on (cf. Senn's paper, p. 149 of this volume). Etymologies are uncertain or unknown for the other verbs of the class. We may posit, then, for Khowar the same formations that enter into the analogy given above, and should probably assume that, at the early MIA period when the analogical formation took place, the ancestor of Khowar formed part of the MIA dialect net.

The general run of NIA languages thus seems unpromising in yielding material of the sort we are looking for. It has been claimed that the Dardic and Kafir languages already mentioned occupy a different position in NIA, and it is possible that when we have more descriptive data on them there may be found, rather abundantly, Indo-European evidences that appear in neither the OIA nor the MIA records. It was claimed by Grierson (as well as by some before him) that these two

---

[33] G. Morgenstierne, "Some Features of Khowar Morphology," *Norsk Tidsskrift for Sprogvidenskap* (*NTS*) 14.5–28 (1947). Some lexical material is presented also by him in an article, "Sanskritic Words in Khowar," *Felicitation Volume presented to Prof. Sripad Krishna Belvalkar* 84–98 (Banaras, 1957).

[34] Turner, *Dictionary of the Nepali Language* (London, 1931), s.v. *dinu*.

groups of languages form a third branch of Indo-Iranian, in that "they seem to have left the parent stem after the Indo-Aryan languages, but before all the typical Iranian characteristics, which we meet in the Avesta, had become developed."[35] The material that was gathered by Morgenstierne after Grierson's volume appeared led Morgenstierne to the conclusion (which has been accepted by, for example, J. Bloch and Burrow[36]) that the Dardic languages (Kashmiri, Shina, Indus Kohistani, Khowar, Kalasha, Pashai, Tirahi) are Indo-Aryan but did not pass through the MIA developments represented by the records, while, on the other hand, the Kafir languages (Kati, Waigali, Ashkun, Prasun, and to some extent Dameli) may occupy some sort of special position.[37] The task of sorting out the evidence is considerably complicated by loanwords in the Kafir languages from neighboring Iranian languages and from other neighboring Indo-Aryan languages, and also by loans in the other directions, that is, from the Kafir languages into neighboring Iranian and Indo-Aryan languages. But, neglecting such items (insofar as they can be identified), one finds that in the Kafir languages there is retention with Indo-Aryan of *s*, which Iranian changes to *h*, and retention with Iranian of two separate palatal series, which Indo-Aryan let fall together. I.e., **ǵ*, *ǵh* > Kaf. *j* (= *dz*)/*z*; palatalized **g* and g^w, *gh* and g^wh > Kaf. *ǯ*/*ž*; e.g., Kati *j*/*zå̄*, Waigali, Ashkun *zā̃* 'knee'; Kati *j*/*zīm*, Waigali *zīm*, Prasun *zəma*, Ashkun *žīm* (secondary palatalization before *ī*) 'snow'; Kati, Waigali *ǯī*, Prasun, Ashkun *žī* 'bowstring'; Kati *ǯā̃ŕ-*, Waigali *ǯā̃-* 'to kill'. In addition, there is the following feature in which the Kafir languages are more archaic than either Iranian or Indo-Aryan, viz., in having to a large extent affricates (dental) for the Indo-European palatal series, even though the matter is at times obscured by borrowings from Indo-Aryan, especiallyin Waigali and Ashkun. Examples: Kati *duċ* 'ten', Prasun *leze* id., *čpu-lċ* 'fourteen', Waigali *dōš*, Ashkun *dus* 'ten'; Kati *ċå̄w*, Waigali, Prasun *ċāw*, Ashkun *ċ*/*sau* 'branch'; Kati *ċuī̃*, Waigali *ċūne-*, Ashkun *ċuni-* 'empty'; and 'knee' and 'snow'

[35] G. A. Grierson, *The Piśāca Languages of North-western India . . .*, p. iii (London, 1906). Sköld held that the Kafir languages are not Indo-Iranian at all, but an independent branch of Indo-European (so reported by Morgenstierne, *NTS* 2.196, with reference in note 1 to an unavailable paper by Sköld). This is surely fantasy.

[36] Bloch, *L'indo-aryen* 18 f.; Burrow, *The Sanskrit Language* 32.

[37] Morgenstierne, *Report on a Linguistic Mission to Afghanistan* (Oslo, 1926), *Report on a Linguistic Mission to North-western India* (Oslo, 1932), "The Language of the Askhun Kafirs," *NTS* 2.192–289 (1929), "Additional Notes on Ashkun," *NTS* 7.56–115 (1934), "Indo-European *ḱ* in Kafiri," *NTS* 13.225–238 (1945), "The Language of the Prasun Kafirs," *NTS* 15.188–334 (1949), "The Waigali Language," *NTS* 17.146–324 (1954). Recent fieldwork by Georg Buddruss in this area may have included the Kafir languages, as it did Dardic, but it has not yet been published.

above.[38] Morgenstierne argues for another archaism in the occurrence of *s* after original *u* (e.g., Kati *dūs*, Waigali, Ashkun *dōs*, Prasun *ulus* 'yesterday': Dardic *dōṣ* id.: Skt. *doṣā* 'in the evening'; Kati *mū̃sə*, Ashkun *musā*, Prasun *mūsu* 'mouse'), and *š* after *i* (with secondary palatalization; e.g., Kati *wiš* 'poison', *niš-* 'to sit down'), as against *ṣ* initial (Kati, Waigali, Ashkun *ṣū*, Prasun *wuṣu* 'six') and after *r* (Kati, Waigali *waṣ* 'rain'). But this distribution might equally well result from conditioned development at a late period (unless there are reasons, unknown to me, for thinking otherwise); there are exceptions to the conditions just stated, but either interpretation will divide the material in the same way.

In general, the Kafir vocabulary agrees with Indo-Aryan rather than with Iranian. There are a very few instances of agreement with Iranian; e.g., Kati, Waigali *kan-*, Ashkun *kōn-* 'to laugh' (Persian *xand-*).

Morgenstierne's final view on the position of Kafiri[39] is that "the remarkable archaisms of Kaf. and its geographical position render it probable that it contains a residuum going back to the language of tribes which split off from the main body of Aryans and penetrated into the Indian borderland before the invasion of the Indo-Aryans." Kafiri is in the main Indo-Aryan in vocabulary and phonology, but it retains the pre-Indo-Aryan treatment of the two palatal series, and, if Morgenstierne is correct in his view of the relationship of the Kafiri dental affricates to the Indo-European palatal series, it represents a very archaic state of things in this matter, perhaps a stage of development that may be called Proto-Indo-Iranian.

Close examination of the Dardic and Kafir languages has already yielded to Morgenstierne more details than I have reported here, of a very archaic layer of vocabulary. For example, he gives Khowar *bispī* or *bispiki*, Waigali *vašpīk* 'wasp', which is represented in Iranian by Baloch *gvabz*, but is not otherwise found in Indo-Iranian. Some of the other suggestions are not equally convincing. Further collection of field material to supplement the fairly meager collections already made, and further detailed study by Iranianists and Indo-Aryanists, will undoubtedly yield more material of the type we have been interested in here. The Indo-Iranian border area is both neglected and of extreme interest. Without its evidence the dialect jigsaw-puzzle picture, whether of Indo-Aryan or of Iranian, shows many missing pieces.

(Participants in the discussion following the conference presentation of the first version of this paper: Puhvel, Hoenigswald, Lane, Lehmann, Polomé, Hamp.)

---

[38] Morgenstierne argues that this is an archaism against M. Leumann (*IF* 58.3 [1941]), who would find in this material a change from sibilant to affricate in some dialects. Morgenstierne makes the good point (*NTS* 13.230) that no instances of IE **s* show *č* in Kafiri, except in a few cases of assimilation.

[39] *NTS* 13.234 (1945).

The Relationships of Baltic and Slavic

Alfred Senn

UNIVERSITY OF PENNSYLVANIA

A discussion of the relationships between Baltic and Slavic must start from Oswald Szemerényi's article, "The Problem of Balto-Slav Unity—A Critical Survey," published in *Kratylos* 2.97–123 (1957), in which my views are criticized. A more significant article, however, is Manu Leumann's "Baltisch und Slavisch" in *Corolla Linguistica. Festschrift Ferdinand Sommer* 154–162 (1955).[1] I have kept silent so long because my work on the Lithuanian dictionary, started forty years ago, has allowed me very little free time. Even now I am unable, for lack of time, to enter into all details. I shall limit myself to a discussion of most of the points raised by Szemerényi, hoping to find the necessary leisure for a fuller treatment very soon.

Szemerényi is not completely right in his reproach (pp. 111 f.) that I used Baltic and Germanic in their "Ur-forms," but "Urslavic" in its latest phase. He failed to recognize that at the time when Proto-Slavic was in its latest phase, let's say about A.D. 700–800, the appearance of Proto-Baltic was still very much the same as it had been a thousand years earlier, that is, about the time of the first phase of Proto-Slavic. Consequently, the Baltic and Slavic forms used by me were both taken from the latest phase of "Urslavic" and "Urbaltic" respectively. It is true that Proto-Slavic in its first phase still had IE *oi* (or *ai*), *ei*, *ou* (or *au*), *ū*, as had Proto-Baltic. But the same is true also of Proto-Germanic. However, about A.D. 700–800, when the Proto-Germanic unity had long been dissolved and Proto-Slavic was in its latest phase, the picture had completely changed in Slavic while remaining unchanged in Baltic.

Szemerényi defends the idea of a Balto-Slavic unity. According to him (p. 120), the separation of the Balts and the Slavs, that is, the breakup of the Balto-Slavic community and unity, was "largely due to the Germanic invasions along the Vistula and Dnepr about the beginning

[1] In the discussion, Henrik Birnbaum pointed out that several Scandinavian, Polish, and Soviet scholars who expressed themselves on the problem after Szemerényi are not mentioned in my presentation. I defended their omission with the statement that they have not brought any new argument into the discussion, in contrast to Manu Leumann.

of our era." Here one might point out first that the reference to the time of the Germanic invasions is rather vague. The Roman historian Livy (59 B.C.–A.D. 17) reports that the Germanic nation of the *Bastarnae* or *Basternae* helped the Macedonian King Perseus in the war against the Romans which resulted in his defeat in the year 168 B.C. The *Bastarnae* lived at that time on the northern shore of the lower Danube. They must have settled there after the fourth century B.C., as Alexander the Great of Macedonia met only non-Germanic *Getae* on the other side of the lower Danube.[2] The *Bastarnae* must have had contacts with the Slavs, but could not have had any with the Balts. The Gothic migration from the shores of the Baltic Sea to the east and to the Black Sea started in the second century of our era.

Szemerényi's statement quoted above is taken over from André Vaillant, *Grammaire comparée des langues slaves* I.14 f. Consequently, I have to address myself in this matter to Vaillant. He attributes to the migrations of the Goths a special role in breaking up the Balto-Slavic unity. However, a separate branch of Baltic people had been known to the world some time before the start of the Gothic migration. Consequently, there was no Balto-Slavic unity left for the Goths to break up.

Vaillant sees a period of Balto-Slavic unity, which continued for some time after the Indo-European unity had vanished, and lasted until quite recently. The time of this unity was not as remote as that of the Italo-Celtic unity, but more or less contemporary with the Germanic unity. Vaillant thinks that the *Venedi* mentioned by Pliny and Tacitus were really the Balto-Slavic "Urvolk." He says nothing about the *Aestii* of Tacitus who were the Baltic Prussians. Tacitus describes the *Aestii* in chapter 45 of his *Germania* and then mentions the *Venethi* (other spelling for *Venedi*) in chapter 46 in the statement: "I am in doubt whether the nations of the *Peucini* and *Venethi* and *Fenni* should be assigned to the *Germani* or the *Sarmati*." Clearly, the picture presented by Tacitus is not one of unity and uniformity, since he deals with the *Aestii* in one chapter and with the *Venethi* in another. It is surprising that no mention at all is made of the *Aestii* in the detailed enumeration of peoples and tribes living in European Sarmatia which was given by the Greek Claudius Ptolemy (living in Alexandria around A.D. 140).[3] Judging by the description of the habitat, there is only one solution to the problem, namely, the amber-fishing *Aestii* of Tacitus are called Οὐενέδαι by Ptolemy: they are said to be a "major nation" sitting all along the part of the Baltic Sea called Οὐενεδικὸς κόλπος (the Bay of

[2] See Kaspar Zeuss, *Die Deutschen und die Nachbarstämme* 127–137 (1837; reprinted 1904).

[3] *Geographia* III, 5.

Danzig with the Frisches Haff). Furthermore, the Γύθωνες (Goths) are placed "below the *Venedae* along the Vistula River." The sixth-century historiographer Jordanes reports[4] that Hermanarich, the king of the Goths, conquered both the *Venethi* (who were known by three names: *Venethi*, *Antes*, *Sclaveni*) and the *Aesti*. These were events of the fourth century of the Christian era.

The picture presented by historical records certainly refutes the idea of a single Balto-Slavic community for the time claimed by Vaillant, though it need not necessarily deny the existence of a linguistic unity, just as we have today a large number of English-speaking, French-speaking, and Spanish-speaking countries. However, I must categorically reject Vaillant's claim that the difference between the modern Baltic and Slavic languages is hardly more than that between Swedish and German. An educated German not knowing Swedish can still see some rays of light in a Swedish text, but this is not true of any Slav (under the same conditions) concerning a Lithuanian or Lettish text. It is shocking that a scholar of Vaillant's high reputation should make such a lighthearted claim.

Previously I could not make up my mind whether to consider the *Aestii* of Tacitus as Indo-European (that is, "Baltic") or non-Indo-European (i.e., Finnic).[5] Jordanes' and Wulfstan's testimony, however, seems to leave no doubt, since it must refer to the same people. On the other hand, both the *Aestii* of Tacitus and the *Aesti* of Jordanes being coastal dwellers, they cannot include the totality of the Baltic tribes, some of whom lived several hundred miles inland, north of the Pripet Marshes. They can only be Prussians, as had already been pointed out by the Lithuanian scholar K. Būga four decades ago.[6]

Szemerényi further (p. 110) calls my method "aprioristic (geological)" and "uneven in the evaluation of the linguistic evidence." Then (p. 113) he states:

> I cannot pronounce on Senn's geological argumentation; but then I am convinced that our problem is a linguistic one. . . . Senn . . . has some illuminating discussions of historical interrelations between Baltic and Slavic. But when it comes to

---

[4] "Post Herulorum cede item Hermanaricus in Venethos arma commovit . . . hi, ut in initio expositionis vel catalogo gentium dicere coepimus, ab una stirpe exorti, tria nunc nomina ediderunt, id est Venethi, Antes, Sclaveni. . . . Aestorum quoque similiter nationem, qui longissimam ripam Oceani Germanici insident, idem ipse prudentia et virtute subegit. . . ." Jordanes, *De origina actibusque Getarum*, Chap. XXIII in *Jordanis Romana et Getica* recensuit Theodorus Mommsen (Berlin, 1882), *Monumenta Germaniae Historica. Auctorum Antiquissimorum* Tomi V Pars Prior 88 f.

[5] Cf. my article "A Contribution to Lithuanian Historiography," *Studi Baltici* 9.107–120 (1952).

[6] K. Būga, *Lietuvių kalbos žodynas* 2.LXXII (1925).

the earlier stages, his approach loses sight of quality, and the quantitative method (acquired in his new home?) threatens to crush all linguistic reality!

This is strong language. He himself (following Vaillant) refuses to recognize realities of history and geography. As to "linguistic reality" being threatened by me, let us hope that the present paper will throw some light on it.

Is it not linguistic reality when the study of river and place names in the area between Vilna and Moscow has uncovered Baltic traces indicating that the old homes at least of the Eastern Balts were in that region? Szemerényi calls this "geological," apparently because he did not check my references of Lithuanian publications. Actually, this new direction of research was opened by the Russian A. I. Sobolevskij in 1911, in his article "Gde žila Litva?" ("Where was the home of the Lithuanians?"), published in *Izvestija Akademii Nauk*, VI serija, Nos. 12–18, 1051 ff. Scholars like K. Būga and Max Vasmer contributed most significantly to the elucidation of the problem, as can be seen from the most recent pertinent publication *Lingvističeskij analiz gidronimov verchnego Podneprov'ja* ("Linguistic Analysis of Hydronyms of the Upper Dnepr Basin") by the two Soviet scholars V. N. Toporov and O. N. Trubačev, published by the Academy of Sciences of the USSR in Moscow in 1962, and containing 270 pages and 13 extra charts. Chart 1 presents the river network with the names of the most important rivers and their tributaries. On chart 2 the relative density of Iranian, Finnic, and Baltic hydronyms is shown: Baltic names are very dense northeast of the Pripet River, much less dense (and covering a much smaller territory) south of it, and occasionally interspersed with Iranian and Finnic names (in the eastern half). Chart 3 shows 22 dots indicating Baltic hydronyms south of the Pripet River, and at least 500 to the north, northeast, and east of it.

During the first millenium of the Christian era, the Lithuanians and the Letts lived much farther to the east than they do today. In that northeastern habitat there was no possibility of direct contact with the Proto-Slavs because of the impenetrable Pripet Marshes. It is interesting to note that in figure 1 (map showing localities mentioned in the text) of Marija Gimbutas' book, *The Prehistory of Eastern Europe*,[7] the wide area of the Pripet Marshes contains no excavation sites, that is to say that it was not inhabited.

Ptolemy's Γαλίνδαι (var.: Γαλίδαναι) and Σουδινοί (var.: Σουδηνοί) must refer to these eastern Balts.

On the basis of Tacitus' information, the homeland of the Slavs, during

[7] *The Prehistory of Eastern Europe. Part I: Mesolithic, Neolithic and Copper Ages Cultures in Russia and the Baltic Area* (Cambridge, Mass., 1956).

the first Christian century, was the area east of the middle part of the Vistula River, south of the Pripet River, west of the Dnieper (Dnepr) River, north of the Carpathian Mountains.

According to Wenzel Vondrák, *Vergl. slav. Grammatik* I².3, the Polish scholar Jan Rozwadowski, who believed in a Balto-Slavic unity, was the first to postulate a long rupture between Proto-Slavs and Proto-Balts, a rupture that followed the original unity and preceded the historical contacts. He placed the period of the original unity in the third millennium B.C., and the period of separation in the second and first pre-Christian millennia.

Anthony Salys, in his article "Baltic Languages," *Encyclopaedia Britannica*, vol. 3 (1955), makes the following well-founded statement:

> The evident and commonly accepted affinity of these two linguistic groups is well explained by assuming their development from two neighbouring IE dialects which still remained in contact during the final stages of the disintegration of the proto-Indo-European unity. The migration of the pre-Balts to the northeast, probably about 2000 B.C., severed the contact with the pre-Slavs and thus led to a separate linguistic development on both sides. A new contact, as late as the 6th century A.D. in the east, but much earlier in the southwest, was established again by the Slavic expansion.

I could admit the term "Balto-Slavic" in the sense of "Baltic and Slavic" and in the meaning of "Proto-Indo-European of Northeastern Europe in its last phase." It is the residue of Proto-Indo-European, the remainder left after all adjacent parts had entered into history and developed into independently regulated languages.

In Szemerényi's article (p. 120), the reader finds fourteen items that, in the author's view, decide the question in favor of the theory of Balto-Slavic unity, and "against Meillet and his present-day followers." These fourteen items are said to be "the most important innovations, which cannot be ascribed to chance or 'parallel' development and thus prove a period of common language and life." To this I wish to state first of all and most emphatically that I do not believe in "parallel" development in two adjacent languages whose speakers have lived in close symbiosis for over a thousand years. In this sense, I am not a follower of Meillet. In a large number of Baltic and Slavic similarities and uniformities I see the imprint of past political and cultural domination of the Letts and the Lithuanians by Russians and Poles. This statement may remind you of Professor Beeler's statement heard yesterday when, speaking of the undeniable similarities existing between Latin and Oscan-Umbrian, he asked whether they cannot "just as well be accounted for by borrowing and convergence within a symbiosis in central Italy which must have endured for hundreds of years." The one-sided Slavic-Lithuanian symbiosis lasted at least 1,200 years.

It is a well-known fact of documented history that the Lithuanian language has always been under strong Slavic (Russian and Polish) influence. In the Grand Duchy of Lithuania, the administrative language was first a sort of Russian[8] and then Polish. Lithuanian and Lettish did not become administrative languages until 1918.

In the twelfth century, that is, before the arrival of the German conquerors, at least the eastern part of the present-day Latvian territory was under Russian domination. Heinrich's *Chronicle of Livonia*[9], written in 1225–1226, reports (I.3) that about the year 1180 the Livonians paid tribute to Prince Vladimir of Polock. In 1207, the German priest Alabrand preached the Word of God to the Letts living by the river Imera. According to the Chronicler, these Letts received the Word of God with joy. First, however, they cast lots and asked the opinion of their gods as to whether they should submit to the baptism of the Orthodox Russians of Pskov, as the Letts of Tholowa had done, or to that of the Latins and Germans. For the Russians had earlier come to baptize their own Letts of Tholowa, who had always been their tributaries.[10]

The fourteen allegedly common Balto-Slavic innovations enumerated by Szemerényi are:

1) Balto-Slavic palatalization.
2) The development of *i*, and, after velars, *u* before IE $\underset{\circ}{r}$ $\underset{\circ}{l}$ $\underset{\circ}{m}$ $\underset{\circ}{n}$.
3) *s* > *š* after *i/u/r/k*.
4) Accent innovations.
5) Definite adjective.
6) -*i̯o*- declension of active participles.
7) Genitive singular of -*o*- stems in -*ā* (< -*āt*).
8) New comparative formation.
9) **men*-(*mun*-) in oblique cases of the pronoun of the first person

[8] Described by Chr. S. Stang in his book *Die westrussische Kanzleisprache des Grossfürstentums Litauen* (Oslo, 1935).

[9] *Heinrici Chronicon Lyvoniae*, in *Monumenta Germaniae Historica*, *SS*, XXIII, 231–332 (Hanover, 1874). Cf. the English translation by J. A. Brundage, *The Chronicle of Henry of Livonia* (Madison, 1961).

[10] My translation of this passage differs somewhat from the one given by Brundage (p. 75). Here is the original Latin text from XI, 7: "Alobrandus . . . Letthgallis, circa Ymeram habitantibus, verbum Dei de suscipiendo baptismo alloquitur . . . At illi . . . cum gaudio verbum Dei recipiunt: missis tamen prius sortibus et requisito consensu deorum suorum: An Ruthenorum de Plescekowe habentium Graecorum fidem cum aliis Letthigallis de Tholowa, an Latinorum et Teutonicorum debeant subire baptismum? Nam Rutheni eorum tempore venerant baptizantes Lethigallos suos de Tholowa, sibi semper tributarios."

singular; genitive **nōsōm* of the pronoun of the first person plural.

10) *tos/tā* for IE *so/sā*.
11) Balto-Slavic **dōmi/dōsi/dōst-/dōdn̥t-*.
12) *Balto-Slavic preterit in -ē-/-ā-*.
13) Verbs in Lithuanian *-áuju* = Slavic *-ują*.
14) Morpholexical elements.

I agree or agree tentatively with Szemerényi on numbers 4, 6, 8, 9, 12, and 14, in the sense that they go back to "Balto-Slavic" as defined by me above. Some of them had been stated in my own earlier writings. Time does not permit me to discuss these items at this time. I disagree (or disagree partly) with Szemerényi on the remaining items.

Ad 6): *-i̯o-* and *-i̯ā-* stem declension of present active participles is the rule in Old High German, Old Saxon, and Old English. This must be an innovation (limited to West Germanic), since a number of masculine nouns of agency with a stem in *-nt-* or *-nd-* respectively, which are substantivized former participles, show that the present active participle had been inflected as a consonantal stem in Proto-Germanic. The question arises whether this West Germanic innovation was completely independent of the Slavic and Baltic innovation.

In numbers 1 and 2, Szemerényi depends completely on Kuryłowicz's theory presented in his book *L'apophonie en indo-européen* (Wrocław, 1956), §26: "Le double traitement des sonantes vocaliques en balto-slave" (227–243). In §21 of his survey, Szemerényi says with reference to Kuryłowicz:

> We have already mentioned his ingenious solution of the *u*-colour in the syllabic sonants, see §1 (1). But even more important is his cogent demonstration that the process presupposes a stage, a BS innovation, in which palatalization was introduced into the consonantal system as a phonological feature.

On p. 99, Szemerényi says:

> He [i.e., Kuryłowicz] proves that the normal development, *iR*, was impossible after a velar because, owing to the BS palatalization, the sequence *KiR* would have resulted in *K'ir*, with a phonological palatalization, contrasting with the normal *K*; to avoid this, the developing short vowel was formed further back, as *u*. The new explanation is important, not only because it shows that the BS development has nothing to do with, e.g., Germanic, but also because the identity of the process reveals it as a BS innovation.

Here is what Kuryłowicz actually states (p. 241):

> Donc: balto-slave *R̥* devient *uR* après les vélaires, *iR* après toutes les autres consonnes. Cette répartition ne coincide pas avec les faits, bien que la prépondérance relative de *kuR*, *guR* ait laissé une trace distincte. Non seulement *iR*

est-il introduit après les vélaires, mais aussi, quoique plus rarement, *uR* apparaît après les autres consonnes.

And (pp. 239–240):

La répartition des vélaires est garantie par le slave, où *k*, *g* devant voyelle palatale aboutissent aux mêmes résultats que *ki̯*, *gi̯*: *plačǫ* (< **plākiō*) et *rečetъ* (< **reketi*), *mǫžь* (< **mongi̯o-*) et *možetъ* (< **mogheti*). . . . Elle est aussi démontrée par le lette, p. ex. *lìecu* 'je courbe' = lit. *lenkiù*, *stèidzu* 'je me hâte', cf. lit. *steigiúos*—comme lette *lùocit* = lit. *lankýti*, lette *aũdzinât* 'élever', cf. lit. *augìnti*.

Most important is Kuryłowicz's statement (p. 243): "L'explication de *iR*, *uR* esquissée ici se fonde sur une seule supposition, d'ordre *chronologique*: l'antériorité de la palatalisation balto-slave au passage *R̥* > *iR*."

Kuryłowicz's claim that sonantic *r̥* became *ur* after velars was first posited by Vaillant. In my opinion, it might really be true for Slavic, but only as a Slavic innovation, not common Balto-Slavic. It must have spread among the contiguous Baltic languages later, just as the Byelorussian and Polish *cekan'e* and *dzekan'e* in the Dzukish dialect of Lithuanian. It is significant, though by no means a cogent argument, that of the Baltic loanwords in Finnish none containing an original sonantic liquid or nasal shows the vowel *u*.

This means that Szemerényi's number 2 can be true only if number 1 can be proven correct, that is, if the type of "Balto-Slavic palatalization" envisaged by Kuryłowicz did not take place in the Balto-Slavic period and prior to number 2, both postulates collapse.

Kuryłowicz identifies the second Slavic palatalization (cf. Lith. *káina* 'price' with Slav. *cěna*, Lith. dat. sing. *rañkai* 'hand' with OCS *rǫcě*, Lith. nom. pl. *vaikaĩ* 'children' with OCS nom. pl. *člověci* 'people') with the Lettish palatalization.

According to Vaillant, *Grammaire comparée des langues slaves* I.52 f., Gothic loanwords that entered Slavic in the third and fourth centuries A.D. took part in both the first and the second palatalization. Būga's hydronymic studies, in *Tauta ir žodis* I.7, 30, have shown that at the time when the Russians broke into the territory inhabited by the Eastern Balts (sixth century A.D.), the Baltic phoneme *k'*, when taken over into Russian, could still change into Russian *č*, while remaining *k'* in Lithuanian: as in the Lithuanian river names *Laukesà* (Lettish *Laucesa*) and *Merkỹs*, which became *Lučesa* and *Mereč'* respectively in Russian. At the outset we could say that a change that took place only in Lettish, but not in Lithuanian and Old Prussian, cannot be assigned to the period of Balto-Slavic unity.

However, according to Būga,[11] the split of East Baltic into a Lithua-

[11] *Lietuvių kalbos žodynas* I.LIX (1924).

nian and a Lettish dialect was prompted by a difference in the treatment of the velar stops *k* and *g* before the front vowels *i*, *ī*, *e*, *ē*, and before *j*. The Letts started to palatalize these consonants in such position: they pronounced *k'i*, *k'ī*, *k'e*, *k'ē*, *k'j* and *g'i*, *g'ī*, *g'e*, *g'ē*, *g'j*, while the Lithuanians continued their hard or unpalatalized pronunciation **kelja·s*, **kepō*, **gerv·ē*, **gerjō*. Had the Lithuanians, at the same time as the Letts, introduced the pronunciation *k'*, *g'*, they would today say **čẽlias*, **čepù*, **džérvė*, **džeriù*, instead of the actual forms *kẽlias*, *kepù*, *gérvė*, *geriù*.

In the Lettish the development resulted in the affricates *c* and *dz*, while in Lithuanian the stops were preserved as such and then, at a later stage, palatalized. Examples:

LETTISH		LITHUANIAN	
cept	:	*kèpti*	'to bake'
cìest	:	*kę̃sti*	'to suffer'
ciêts	:	*kíetas*	'hard'
cits	:	*kìtas*	'another'
cìrvis	:	*kir̃vis*	'hatchet'
caũrs	:	*kiáuras*	'with holes'
dzèlzs	:	*geležìs*	'iron'
dzert	:	*gérti*	'to drink'
dziêdât	:	*giedóti*	'to sing'
dzija	:	*gijà*	'thread'
dzîvs	:	*gývas*	'alive'
dzìt	:	*giñti*	'to chase'

The terminus post quem for this change in Lettish was about the seventh or eighth century A.D., the time when the Letts first invaded Latgala, the eastern part of present-day Latvia. Toponymic studies have shown that at that time there was hardly any difference between their language and that of the Lithuanians.

The terminus ante quem for the change of Lettish *k'* > *c* and *g'* > *dz* is the beginning of the German occupation of the Lettish lands, that is, about the year 1200. The thirteenth-century documents of the German invaders show that the Lettish language at that time already possessed the affricates *c* and *dz* in place of the older soft velar stops *k'* and *g'*. In agreement with this situation, all of the numerous German loanwords (which could only enter Lettish after 1200) having a guttural before a front vowel have a soft velar, and none of them has an affricate; for example, Low German *käke* 'kitchen' > Lettish *k'èk'is*, Low German *gelden* (G. *gelten*) 'to be worth' > Lettish *g'eldêt*.

The German evidence of the thirteenth century is supported by the Russian language which gave the Letts the food name *k'īselis* (< Russian *kisél'*) 'Danish pudding', which did not change to **cīselis*.

Number 3 is not an exclusive Balto-Slavic innovation, since the same change occurred also in Indo-Iranian. Only exclusive innovations can count as support for the theory of units.

Ad 5): According to A. Salys,[12] the formation of the definite adjective by adding the pronoun **jo-* (Lithuanian *basàsis* < *bãsas* + *jis* : Proto-Slavic **bosŭjĭ* < *bosŭ* + *jĭ* 'the barefooted one') is a "comparatively late development." If this feature were old, one would expect in Slavic **bosošĭ*, or at least **bosŭšĭ* (< **bosos* + *jis*). Salys also pointed out discrepancies in the Baltic forms: Lithuanian standard *baltàsis* 'the white one', dialectal *baltàjis* and *baltùjis*, Lettish *baltaĩs*, Old Prussian *pirmoys* 'the first one'; Old Lithuanian genitive singular *pajoprasto* for modern *pãprastojo* 'the simple one'.

Salys' explanation assumes that Proto-Slavic in its earliest phase still maintained final *-s*.

Final *-s* did not survive in any Slavic language. Vondrák (*loc. cit.*, 425–449) does not mention it at all.

Vaillant (*op. cit.*, p. 200) says: "Le *-s* final est régulièrement maintenu en baltique, et régulièrement tombé en slave." And (p. 201): "De toute façon, la disparition de *-s* a été générale en slave. Mais elle ne doit pas être très ancienne, puisque *-s* a exercé une action sur le traitement de groupes comme **-ans* (§88)."

And further (p. 214): "Et devant *-s* ancien on a *-i* de **-ins*, *-y* de **-uns* : acc. pl. *nošti*, lit. *naktìs* de v.pr. *-ins*, got. *-ins*, gr. dial. *-ινς*, et *dŭšteri*, lit. *dùkteris*, de i.-eu. **-n̥s*, gr. *θυγατέρας*; *syny*, lit. *sū́nus* de **-uns*, got. *-uns*, gr. dial. *-υνς*."

Ad 7): This feature is not even common Baltic and can hence not be common Balto-Slavic. The innovation in the genitive singular Lithuanian *vil̃ko* 'wolf', Lettish *vìlka*, Old Church Slavic *vlĭka* (originally an ablative form) is not shared by Old Prussian where the ending is *-as*, e.g., over 50 occurrences of *deiwas* 'God's' (nom. *deiws* 30 times, *deywis* once, *deiwas* once), 11 occurrences of *tāwas*, *tawas*, *thawas* 'father's' (nom. *tāws*, *taws*, 9 times, *tawas* once). On p. 102, Szemerényi disputes the derivation of the OPruss. ending from IE *-oso*, which he calls "hardly tenable." He overlooked the fact that R. Trautmann[13] considered primarily IE *-osjo* (beside *-oso*), when he said: "So steht einer Erklärung von *deiwas* aus idg. *deiwósjo* oder *deiwóso* nichts im Wege: dass *deiwósjo* im Preussischen *deiwas*, *deiwos* aber *deiws* ergab, hat seine Parallele im ags. *dómaes* neben *dóm* und beruht auf dem verschiedenen Silbenakzente." I do not understand Trautmann's reference to Old English *dómaes*. However, the genitive *-osjo* does appear in Sanskrit (*vṛ́kasya*) and Homeric Greek

[12] *Encyclopaedia Britannica, loc. cit.*

[13] *Die altpreussischen Sprachdenkmäler* 216, 319, 447 (Göttingen, 1910).

(οἴκοιο).[14] Szemerényi postulates a choice between two alternatives: (1) Gothic influence on Old Prussian, (2) Vaillant's assumption that *deiwas* represents the Balto-Slavic type in *-ā*, which took *-s* over from the regular genitives in *-s*. He himself considers Gothic influence somewhat doubtful, and rightly so, for more reasons than the one mentioned by him. Actually, it is astonishing that Gothic influence could be invoked at all.[15] If Trautmann's explanation were not to be accepted, I do not see why Vaillant's theory should deserve preference over that of Leskien and Berneker (see Trautmann, *loc. cit.*) who saw in this genitive *-as* a transfer of the genitive ending *-ās* of the feminine *ā*-stems.

Ad 10): In Slavic and in Baltic, the Indo-European *s*-forms of the nom. sing. masc. and fem. of the demonstrative pronoun were replaced by *t*-forms. This may have been a gradual development, starting in Slavic and later spreading into Baltic, after Slavic and Baltic were already established as separate languages. Germanic has *s*-forms in Gothic, Old Norse, and Old English, but *t*-forms in Old Saxon, Old High German, and in Modern English. Thus we see that in West Germanic the *s*-forms were gradually replaced by *t*-forms. The same could happen in the Slavic and Baltic area, except that the development is hidden by the absence of pertinent Baltic records for almost eight hundred years after the earliest Slavic texts. However, this innovation is common only to Slavic and East Baltic, since Old Prussian has only forms beginning with *sta-* (nom. sing. masc. *stas*, nom. sing. neuter *sta*, nom. sing. fem. *sta*, *stā*), a combination of two Indo-European demonstrative elements: *k-* and *te/to*; cf. the Lith. interjection *štaĩ* 'there! lo!'.

Ad 11): There is a striking Balto-Slavic agreement in the present-future tense forms of the Indo-European verb for 'to give': Greek δίδωμι, Sanskrit *dádāmi*, OCS *damĭ* (third sing. *dastŭ*), OLith. *dúomi* (third pers. *dúosti*), OPruss. *dāst* (third pers.). The traditional explanation[16] sees in these forms reduplication, the reduplicating syllable containing the long-vowel root **dō-*. The root syllable could have been *-də-* or *-d-* (cf. Sanskrit *dadmáḥ*). The peculiar form (*dōd-mi*) of the reduplicating syllable in Slavic and Baltic was brought into relationship with two facts: (*a*) Indo-European *dh* and *d* coalesced in these languages to *d*; (b) both the root **dhē-* and the root **dō-* were preserved simultaneously, both roots forming a reduplicating present tense. In the zero-grade forms, both **de-d*(ə)- and **dhe-dh*(ə)- had to become **ded-*. Under these circumstances, the

[14] H. Hirt, *Handbuch der griechischen Laut- und Formenlehre*² 346 (1902).

[15] Cf. my article "Deutsche und germanische Lehnwörter im Litauischen," *Germanisch-romanische Monatsschrift* 34 (N.F. 3). 332–344, esp. 342 f.

[16] K. Brugmann, *Grundriss*² II.3. 110 f; W. Vondrák, *Vergl. slav. Grammatik* I² 705; Stang, *Das slavische und baltische Verbum* 21, 268 (Oslo, 1942).

root form *$d\bar{o}$- appearing in the aorist penetrated into the present-tense system ("Homonymenfurcht"). Szemerényi proposes the simpler explanation, given earlier by Kořínek, that it was simply an unreduplicated *$d\bar{o}$-*mi*. He states: "Now the fact that Baltic and Slavic should start from an unreduplicated form, is no more remarkable than that English has *do*." By this he admits that Germanic does not use reduplication in the formation of the present tense. Thus, since the lack of reduplication is shared by Baltic, Slavic, and Germanic, there would be no exclusive Balto-Slavic innovation. Since the root *dhē- survives in Germanic in two ablaut varieties, **dhē*- and **dhō*-, the root **dō*- 'give' was given up in pre-Germanic times. However, in Baltic and Slavic the verb **dō*- cannot be separated from **dhē*-. Both have reduplication, that is, if we hold to the traditional explanation. Certainly both have reduplication in modern Lithuanian: *dúodu* and *dedù*. Clearly the two verbs have influenced each other in recent times just as they had done earlier. Conclusion: A theory based merely on the stem **dō*-, without consideration of **dhē*-, is unsatisfactory. I concede the existence of a Balto-Slavic similarity, on the basis of Manu Leumann's reasoning (p. 160).

Ad 13): Brugmann, *Grundriss*², II.3.220 f., has shown that the Slavic denominative verbs in *-ovati* and the Lithuanian denominatives in *-auti* are related to the Greek denominatives in -εύω < -ηϝι̯ω, e.g., ἱερεύω 'I offer sacrifice' from ἱερεύς 'one who offers sacrifice' < *-ηυς. It may be indicative of the situation that of the three Lithuanian (and Old Prussian) examples given by Brugmann two are foreign words, namely, *rykáuju* 'I rule' (Germanism) and *griekáuju* 'I reproach somebody his sins' (Slavism). In my view, Brugmann was right in connecting the Lithuanian *-auti* verbs with those in *-uoti*, e.g., Lith. *sapnúoti* 'to dream' (from *sãpnas* 'dream'), *juõduoti* and *juodúoti* 'to appear black' (from *júodas* 'black'). The verbs in *-uoti* have the same preterit endings as those in *-auti*, e.g., *tarnáuti* 'to serve' : present *tarnáuju*, preterit *tarnavaũ*; *sapnúoti* : present *sapnúoju*, preterit *sapnavaũ*. According to Brugmann, *uo* (= IE ō < ōu̯) was originally limited to the infinitive stem, while the tense system would have been *-auju -avau -uoti*. The Lithuanian infinitive ending *-uoti* would correspond to the Slavic *-ati*. The Lithuanian infinitive *-auti* would be a new formation on the basis of the present tense form *-auju*, and in some instances the Slavic infinitive ending *-ovati* could be a replacement for earlier *-ati*. Cf. also Vondrák, *Vergl. slav. Grammatik* I².718 f.

Postscript

The ensuing discussion (participants: Birnbaum, Hoenigswald, Hamp, Winter, Collinder) centered mainly around the question of whether my admission of the term

"Balto-Slavic" in the sense of "Baltic and Slavic" and in the meaning of "Proto-Indo-European of Northeastern Europe in its last phase" did not in fact mean a separate Balto-Slavic unity. This question cannot be answered without consideration of the relationship of both Slavic and Baltic to Germanic, all the more since, in Vaillant's opinion, the alleged Balto-Slavic unity must have been more or less contemporary with the Germanic unity.

The Dialects of Common Slavic

Henrik Birnbaum

UNIVERSITY OF CALIFORNIA, LOS ANGELES

0. *Preliminary remarks*

0.1. *Terminology: Proto-Slavic and Common Slavic, their delimitation and periodization*

Proto-Slavic (PSl) and Common Slavic (CSl) are used in this paper as overlapping, not synonymous terms. By PSl we mean the language partly recovered by methods of linguistic reconstruction, comparative as well as internal,[1] ranging from its emergence from Balto-Slavic—or, as some scholars prefer to put it, from the group of Indo-European (IE) dialects which subsequently developed into Proto-Baltic and PSl respectively—and down to the centuries immediately preceding the oldest attested Slavic linguistic data of Old Church Slavic (OCS), a language first written down in the second half of the ninth century (the oldest preserved records, manuscripts, and inscriptions dating from the last decades of the tenth century, e.g., King Samuil's inscription of 993). PSl is, therefore, in all its stages a purely hypothetical, reconstructed

[1] Discussions on methods of comparative IE linguistics have lately again been emphasized by Soviet scholars; cf., e.g., the volume *Voprosy metodiki sravnitel'no-istoričeskogo izučenija indoevropejskix jazykov* (Moscow, 1956), and the book by A. V. Desnickaja, *Voprosy izučenija rodstva indoevropejskix jazykov* (Moscow and Leningrad, 1955). Among recent contributions to the methodology of internal reconstruction, cf., e.g., H. M. Hoenigswald, *Language Change and Linguistic Reconstruction* 68–69, 99–104, 132–134, 151 (Chicago, 1959); and J. Kuryłowicz, "On the Methods of Internal Reconstruction," *Proceedings of the Ninth International Congress of Linguists, Cambridge, Mass., August 27–31, 1962*, H. G. Lunt, ed. (The Hague, 1964), pp. 9–36. Some confusion seems still to prevail as to the scope of internal reconstruction of lost parental languages as opposed to comparative reconstruction of such languages. Thus, in the case of CSl, some scholars would label "internal" all reconstruction derived from the attested individual Slavic languages, reserving "comparative" to reconstruction based on comparison with non-Slavic IE languages (Baltic, Indo-Iranian, etc.), while other linguists would rather limit the use of the term "internal" to such reconstruction deducible from the evidence of one single (in this case, Slavic) language only; e.g., inferring the existence of (strong and weak) reduced vowels ("jers") in CSl from the morphophonemic /e/ : /o/ vs. ø (zero) alternations in Russian.

language. CSl, on the other hand, is used here to denote the later periods of PSl—definable only in terms of relative chronology: roughly after the change of closed syllables into open ones, or rather into syllables with increasing (rising) sonority[2]—as well as the subsequent periods in Slavic linguistic development, during which general, common innovations occurred simultaneously with locally restricted changes, that is, until approximately the end of the ninth century—the time of the Magyar invasion—including the first decades of OCS literary activities. Moreover, this period is followed by one of disintegration of CSl, its gradual divergence into the separate Slavic languages, ending with the fall of the so-called reduced vowels or jers in weak position, a process the result of which conflicted with the late PSl principle of syllable structure. Since we can speak about truly individual Slavic languages only for the period after the fall of the weak jers, we should also include in our considerations of the dialects of CSl this early phase of attested Slavic linguistic evolution, that is, the tenth through early twelfth centuries, provided we are to recognize as correct the traditional view according to which the fall of the jers began to take place in East Slavic or Old Russian (OR) only in the eleventh century and the full vocalization of the strong jers even later (late twelfth and thirteenth centuries). OCS *sensu stricto* (i.e., Old Macedo-Bulgarian), early OR, as well as certain other Old Slavic ecclesiastical texts with marked local characteristics, such as the "mixed" OCS-Old Czech *Kievan Missal*, the Old Czech *Prague Fragments*, or the Old Slovene *Freising Texts*, would, consequently, have to be considered specimens of late CSl dialects rather than of individual Slavic languages.[3]

---

[2] Cf., e.g., A. Martinet, *Economie des changements phonétiques* 349–369 (Berne, 1955), ("Les syllabes ouvertes du slave commun"). The broader concept of syllables with increasing (rising) sonority was suggested by N. van Wijk; see his *Geschichte der altkirchenslavischen Sprache* 1.39–40, 46–47 (Berlin and Leipzig, 1931), ("Die Neigung zur steigenden Sonoritätswelle"); *Les langues slaves. De l'unité à la pluralité*[2] 20–22 (The Hague, 1956). Most recently this problem is discussed by G. Y. Shevelov in his paper "Prothetic Consonants in Common Slavic. An historical approach," *American Contributions to the Fifth International Congress of Slavists*. Vol. I: *Linguistic Contributions* 41–60 (The Hague, 1964). On the periodization of PSl and CSl cf. also F. P. Filin, *Obrazovanie jazyka vostočnyx slavjan* 99–110 (Moscow and Leningrad, 1962); on the beginning of the dialectal differentiation of CSl see ibid., 161–166. For cautiously used quantitative methods of dating the separation of Slavic dialects and languages (based on lexical data) see also I. Fodor, "The Validity of Glottochronology on the Basis of the Slavonic Languages," *Studia Slavica* 7.295–346 (1961), esp. 325–330.

[3] See, e.g., P. Ja. Černyx, *Istoričeskaja grammatika russkogo jazyka*[3] 110–111 (Moscow, 1962), where, among other things, also the early evidence of the *Gnezdovo inscription* (dating, as it seems, from the first decades of the tenth century) for the preliterary fall of the jers (read by him as *gorušna* < **gorušьna*) is cited; see

We can, in other words, discuss problems of dialectal differentiation for CSl as a whole, that is, for the entire period of its duration from the early (= late PSl) reconstructed stages down to its more recent, recorded epoch. As for PSl, on the other hand, we could speak about its local varieties only with regard to its later stages, no evidence being available for any early PSl spatial diversity.[4] The controversial problems of Balto-Slavic linguistic relationship (cf. A. Senn's communication at this conference), of the *terminus a quo* of PSl, and of the original homeland ("Urheimat") of the Slavs, are of little if any direct relevance for the matter to be discussed here. CSl dialects presuppose an expansion of the primitive Slavic tribes from their original habitat—wherever this is to be

---

also Constantine VII Porphyrogennetos' spellings Νεασήτ = *nejasytь*, πραχ = *pragъ*, i.e., /praγ/, (OR *porogъ*), or *praxъ* (OR *poroxъ*), not rendering the final jers, in the middle of the tenth century. Further arguments, to be discussed elsewhere, can perhaps be adduced against the traditional view, as expressed and indeed partly supported by some new material in E. Koschmieder's article "Schwund und Vokalisation der Halbvokale im Ostslavischen," *Die Welt der Slaven* 3.124–137 (1958). If therefore the date of the fall of the weak jers possibly could be pushed back to somewhere around or even before A.D. 1000 all over the Slavic linguistic territory, the *terminus ad quem* for CSl (in the sense defined above) could also be set at approximately that date. This would render the OCS language spoken and written by Constantine-Cyril, Methodius, and their collaborators in the ninth century a late CSl dialect, but the language of virtually none of the extant OCS or other earliest Old Slavic texts (with the possible exception of the *Kievan Missal*, with its consistent use of the jers) would qualify for such labeling. It may be added, however, that the problem of dating the fall of the weak jers in East Slavic is not really essential for CSl dialectology. At any rate, it can be assumed that even if the reduced vowels physically disappeared as vowels ("fell") in weak position in OR only relatively late (eleventh–twelfth centuries) the front vs. back (acute vs. grave) distinction had already earlier ceased to be phonemic in them. The phonemic distinction was instead carried on by the preceding consonant, which could be palatalized or nonpalatalized (sharp vs. plain). This transphonologization and retraction of the phonemic feature could, for example, for word-final position be denoted as follows: /-T'ь/ vs. /-Tъ/ > /-T'ə/ vs. /-Tə/ (> /-T'/ vs. /-T/). The correlation /-T'ə/ vs. /-Tə/ was parallellized under stress and in the *okan'e* dialects generally by /-T'o/ vs. /-To/, i.e., graphically [-*Te*] vs. [-*To*]; the implication of [-*Te*] being phonemically equal to /-T'o/ already anticipates the later shift of /'e/ > /'o/ in Russian. Similarly, on this problem see also C. L. Ebeling, "Questions of Relative Chronology in Common Slavic and Russian Phonology," *Dutch Contributions to the Fifth International Congress of Slavicists, Sofia, 1963* 27–42, esp. 39–41 (The Hague, 1963). See also note 37.

[4] On the simultaneous emergence in PSl of dialectal features and a tendency toward open syllables cf. also S. B. Bernštejn, *Očerk sravnitel'noj grammatiki slavjanskix jazykov* 182–184 (Moscow, 1961).

located[5]—to a territory reaching, at any rate, from the Oder (Odra) river to the mid-Dnieper basin, and limited in the south by the Carpathian (and possibly also the Sudeten) Mountains. For the late CSl period we must of course take into account also the new territories settled by Slavs—those on the Balkan Peninsula, in Russia, and west of the Oder.[6]

0.2. *Scope of linguistic evidence: Features to be eliminated from establishing CSl dialects*

It is worth mentioning that, since this paper is concerned with the dialects of CSl as just defined (including the period of its disintegration), only phenomena falling into this period, or rather these periods, will be included in our deliberations. Phenomena arising in subsequent periods, though they may be shared by several individual Slavic languages (or some of their dialects) not even necessarily belonging to one and the same group or subgroup, will therefore not be discussed in this report. This applies for example to such isoglosses as: /g/ > /γ/ (> /h/) in South (Great) Russian dialects, Byelorussian, and Ukrainian, as well as in Czech, Slovak, High Sorbian, and partly also in certain Slovene dialects (this is an old feature in southern and parts of western and central Russia, but dates in West Slavic only from the late twelfth or early thirteenth century); various consequences of so-called compensatory lengthening resulting from the fall of the weak jers in most West Slavic languages and in Ukrainian; /jь̑-/ > /j-/ (> /Ø/), with a few exceptions, in roughly the same geographic area; /t'/, /d'/ > /ć/, /ʒ́/ in Polish and Byelorussian ("cekan'e/dzekan'e" or "ciakanie/dziakanie"), though these are probably independent developments in the two languages; /r'/ > /ř/ (> /ž/š/) in Polish and Czech; /ě/ > /i/ in Old Novgorod records, but also in South Russian dialects, Ukrainian, and certain Serbocroation dialect areas ("ikavism"); merging of hushing and hissing fricatives and affricates into one (mostly hissing) series in dialects of Polish ("mazurzenie"), Russian ("cokan'e"—here primarily affecting only the voiceless affricates), and Serbocroatian ("cakavism"); certain "Balkan" features in the morphology and syntax of South Slavic: a compound future tense formed by means of the auxiliary *xotěti* (or its reflexes) in Bulgarian, Macedonian, and Serbocroation; the loss of the

[5] The two main hypotheses about the original homeland of the Slavs still deserving consideration—the "eastern" and the "western" (or "autochthonic") respectively—may be represented here by M. Vasmer, "Die Urheimat der Slaven," *Der ostdeutsche Volksboden* 118–143 (Breslau, 1926), and T. Lehr-Spławiński, *O pochodzeniu i praojczyźnie Słowian* (Poznań, 1946). Cf. most recently also F. P. Filin, *op. cit.* 35–49, and 147–151 (where the author adheres, partly on the basis of new evidence, to the "eastern" hypothesis advocated by L. Niederle, M. Vasmer, and others).

[6] For further details see, for instance, S. B. Bernštejn, *op. cit.* 75–86.

infinitive in Bulgarian, Macedonian, and a considerable part of Serbocroatian; the analytic structure—with prepositional phrases replacing case forms, and so on—in Bulgarian and Macedonian; postpositive articles in the same area, but also in some North Russian dialects; and so forth.[7] These and similar features, great as their importance may be for a typological classification of the Slavic languages, will be omitted in the subsequent considerations regarding the dialects of CSl.

0.3. *Participation of linguistic and other disciplines in establishing CSl dialects*

Of the traditional linguistic disciplines—phonology, morphology, syntax, and lexicology—not all can be equally utilized for the purpose of establishing criteria differentiating the dialects of CSl. It goes almost without saying that by far the greatest number of connecting and separating isoglosses that can be traced back to CSl are of a phonological nature (isophones).[8] Only to a lesser extent will morphological criteria prove useful for such classification; see below, §§1.1 and 1.2.

---

[7] These and similar features are, of course, listed in most of the pertinent standard textbooks. Of recent treatments of these isoglosses one may refer, e.g., to the brief sketches by Z. Stieber, "Wzajemne stosunki języków zachodnio-słowiańskich," W. Kuraszkiewicz, "Ugrupowanie języków wschodnio-słowiańskich," and F. Sławski, "Ugrupowanie języków południowo-słowiańskich," in the *Biuletyn Polskiego Towarzystwa Językoznawczego* 14.73–93, 94–102, 103–111 (Wrocław-Kraków, 1955). As to "mazurzenie" in Polish, which earlier was thought to be of CSl dialectal origin, its relatively recent date (beginning, probably, in the late twelfth century) seems now to have been convincingly demonstrated; see Z. Stieber, *Rozwój fonologiczny języka polskiego*³ 64–66 (Warsaw, 1962). For the isoglosses of South Slavic cf. also the excellent treatment by P. Ivić, *Die serbokroatischen Dialekte. Ihre Struktur und Entwicklung* 1.25–49 (The Hague, 1958) ("Die skr. Dialektologie als Teil der Dialektologie des südslavischen Sprachraumes"); see further F. Sławski, *Zarys dialektologii południowosłowiańskiej*, *passim* (Warsaw, 1962). In "Balkan linguistics," otherwise, K. Sandfeld's *Linguistique balkanique* (Paris, 1930) remains the unequaled classic, even though, of course, many general as well as special studies in this field have been published since. For some new approaches, with particular emphasis on the Balkan Slavic languages, see, most recently, H. L. Klagstad's congress paper "Toward a morphosyntactic treatment of the Balkan linguistic group," *American Contributions* 1.179–189 (The Hague, 1964); and H. Birnbaum, "Balkanslavisch und Südslavisch. Zur Reichweite der Balkanismen im südslavischen Sprachraum," *Zeitschrift für Balkanologie* 3 (in press). On the status of the OCS periphrastic future expressions formed by means of the auxiliary *xošto̧*, etc., + infinitive as a predecessor of the general Balkan future tense see H. Birnbaum, *Untersuchungen zu den Zukunftsumschreibungen mit dem Infinitiv im Altkirchenslavischen* 260, 277 (Stockholm, 1958).

[8] The Organizing Committee of the Third International Congress of Slavists, which was to have been held in Belgrade in 1939, even formulated a special question on the possibility of defining the dialects of CSl by means of criteria other

As for lexical criteria, including CSl borrowings from other ancient languages or language groups, such as Iranian, Greek, and Germanic, our knowledge is still far too fragmentary to enable us to draw any definitive conclusions. However, we can expect important additional classificatory criteria with regard to the dialects of CSl, once more complete pertinent data are available.[9]

Virtually nothing of real value for our purpose seems, finally, to be likely to result from future inquiry into the syntactic structure of the earlier, unrecorded stages of CSl. While syntax is in my opinion one of the domains of language most susceptible to foreign influences, no refined and reliable methods of syntactic reconstruction have yet been developed. This holds true at any rate as far as the recovery of lost stages of Slavic syntactic evolution is involved. All that has been actually done in this respect serves primarily to winnow out of the oldest recorded form of Slavic (i.e., OCS, largely influenced by foreign, in particular Greek, syntactic patterns) such features as can be attributed with fair probability to an underlying non-Slavic model, thus establishing—still in only a rather vague and fragmentary way—certain patterns of word combination (types of syntagms), word order, and sentence structure that may be considered genuine Slavic, that is, inherited from preliterary CSl.[10] But still, by comparing, for example, OR (East Slavic), OCS

---

than phonological; see the reply by B. Havránek in *III Međunarodni kongres slavista. Odgovori na pitanja—Saopštenja i referati, Dopune*, 20 (Belgrade, 1939).

[9] Only a first groundwork was laid by such pioneering works as those on early Slavic-Iranian and Slavic-Greek linguistic relations by M. Vasmer, on CSl loanwords from Germanic by V. Kiparsky, and others, not to mention the many studies on Baltic-Slavic lexical ties, R. Trautmann's Balto-Slavic dictionary being the best known of them. The forthcoming General Slavic Dialectological Atlas will, no doubt, greatly contribute to the elucidation of these matters; see Z. Stieber, "O projekcie ogólnosłowiańskiego atlasu dialektologicznego," *Slavjanskaja filologija* 1.129–135 (Moscow, 1958). See also the recent semischolarly booklet by K. I. Xodova, *Jazykovoe rodstvo slavjanskix narodov (na materiale slovarja)* (Moscow, 1960). Only quite recently was a first attempt made to present in a systematic way lexical data (including CSl words inherited from IE as well as borrowings) for the purpose of classifying CSl dialects: F. P. Filin, *op. cit.*; see §0.4. for further references.

[10] For methods of syntactic reconstruction see, *inter alia*, the introductory remarks by C. Watkins in his recent contribution to the Ninth Congress of Linguists, "Preliminaries to the Reconstruction of Indo-European Sentence Structure," *Proceedings* 1035–1045. For the methodology of winnowing out foreign syntactic features, see, on a general level, V. N. Jarceva, "Problema vydelenija zaimstvovannyx èlementov pri rekonstrukcii sravnitel'no-istoričeskogo sintaksisa rodstvennyx jazykov," *Voprosy jazykoznanija* 1956:6.3–14; as applied to OCS see the present author's contribution to the Moscow Congress of Slavists, "Zur Aussonderung der syntaktischen Gräzismen im Altkirchenslavischen. Einige metho-

(South Slavic), and Old Czech or Old Polish (West Slavic) sentence structure we can hardly determine any potential syntactic dialectal variations in the earlier, unrecorded development of CSl. Any attempt to establish CSl local differences in syntactic patterns and models on the basis of features such as a presumed predilection of East Slavic for nominal sentences must seem methodologically highly dubious if not inadmissible.

0.4. *Current state of research in CSl dialectology*

The literature dealing with problems of CSl dialects is very extensive. Most authors of text- and handbooks of CSl, Comparative Slavic linguistics, and the history of individual Slavic languages have treated or at least touched upon these problems. The same applies to works on Slavic linguistic relationship, CSl and its disintegration, and so forth. Of older special monographs treating this subject one deserves particular mention, viz., D. Džurovyč's *Govory obščeslavjanskogo jazyka* (Warsaw, 1913). However, only after a strictly phonemic approach had been introduced could considerable progress be made also in the field of CSl dialects. Pioneering works in this respect were N. S. Trubeckoj's articles "Essai sur la chronologie de certains faits phonétiques du slave commun," *Revue des études slaves* 2.217–234 (1922), and "Über die Entstehung der gemeinwestslavischen Eigentümlichkeiten auf dem Gebiete des Konsonantismus," *Zeitschrift für slavische Philologie* 7.383—406 (1930), as well as several contributions by N. van Wijk, in particular his lectures on CSl and its divergence into the separate Slavic languages, delivered at the Sorbonne and later published also in book form, *Les langues slaves. De l'unité à la pluralité*[2] (The Hague, 1956), and his posthumous article "K istorii fonologičeskoj sistemy v obščeslavjanskom jazyke pozdnego perioda," *Slavia* 19.293–313 (1950). Furthermore, of several contributions by N. N. Durnovo, at least his sketch "K voprosu o vremeni raspadenija obščeslavjanskogo jazyka," *Sborník prací I. Sjezdu slovanských filologů v Praze 1929*, 514–526 (Prague, 1932), should be mentioned here. Of great interest in this context is the profound article by F. V. Mareš, "Vznik slovanského fonologického systému a jeho vývoj do konce období slovanské jazykové jednoty," *Slavia* 25.443–495 (1956). Among more traditionally oriented contemporary scholars, T. Lehr-Spławiński has dealt on several occasions with different aspects of our topic; cf. his articles "O dialektach prasłowiańskich," *Sborník prací* . . .

---

dische Bemerkungen," *Scando-Slavica* 4.239–257 (1958); see also my reply to the question "Kakvi sa dosegašnite slabosti na sravnitelnoistoričeskoto izsledvane na sintaktičnata sistema na slavjanskite ezici?" *Slavjanska filologija*. I. *Otgovori na văprosite za naučnata anketa po ezikoznanie* 88–91 (Sofia, 1963).

577–585 (reprinted in his *Studia i szkice wybrane z językoznawstwa słowiańskiego* 207–214 [Warsaw, 1957]); "Problem ugrupowania języków słowiańskich," *Biuletyn Polskiego Towarzystwa Językoznawczego* 14.112–121 (1955) (reprinted in *Studia i szkice* ... 42–51); "Das Problem der Zusammenfassung der slavischen Sprachen zu Gruppen," *Vorträge auf der Berliner Slawistentagung (11.–13. November 1954)* 46–56 (Berlin, 1956); his reply to the question "K kakim periodam otnosjatsja fakty razdelenija slavjan na osnovnye vetvi?" in the *Sbornik otvetov na voprosy po jazykoznaniju (k IV Meždunarodnomu s"ezdu slavistov)* 192–196 (Moscow, 1958); and "Szkic dziejów języka prasłowiańskiego," *Studia z filologii polskiej i słowiańskiej* 3.243–265 (Warsaw, 1959). An original, "quantitative" approach pertaining to data of CSl dialects was suggested by J. Czekanowski in his paper "Różnicowanie się dialektów prasłowiańskich w świetle kryterium ilościowego," *Sborník prací* ... 485–504, and also in the corresponding section of his book *Wstęp do historii Słowian*[2] 177–201 (Poznań, 1957) ("Różnicowanie się Słowiańszczyzny pierwotnej"). The role of the Carpathian Mountains as a main borderline dividing late CSl dialects was particularly stressed by M. Braun in his brief introduction *Grundzüge der slawischen Sprachen* 29–40, 53–55 (Göttingen, 1947).

Recently, problems of CSl, its delimitation in time and space, its periodization, and dialectal differentiation, have been discussed from a partly new and occasionally rather original angle by S. B. Bernštejn in his book *Očerk sravnitel'noj grammatiki slavjanskix jazykov* 42–86 (Moscow, 1961). Some of the opinions expressed in his book will be discussed on the following pages. A thorough account of the disintegration of CSl and the present state of its investigation has been given by A. Furdal in *Rozpad języka prasłowiańskiego w świetle rozwoju głosowego* (Wrocław, 1961). This impressive book contains, among other things, the most comprehensive bibliography (up to 1959) on the subject. Much of the following will, in fact, be a report on and discussion of the conclusions arrived at by Furdal. The latest contribution to our topic, F. P. Filin's book *Obrazovanie jazyka vostočnyx slavjan* (Moscow and Leningrad, 1962), containing also a chapter on "The Beginning of the Disintegration of Common Slavic" (152–223), where particularly lexical data are taken into account (cf. §4, 167–174, "The Disintegration of Common Slavic in the Light of Lexical Borrowings"; §6, 205–218, "Old Slavic Dialectal Zones in the Light of Lexical Data"), became available to me only while I was writing this report. In fact, it seems to constitute a first attempt to systematize lexical data for the purpose of classifying CSl dialects. Although, in Filin's words, "a detailed study of the ancient lexical dialectal features is a task for the future" (p. 222), some of his conclusions point in the same direction as those based on phonological as well as on certain morphological features to be reported in this paper.

It goes without saying that the titles listed above represent a mere cross section of the many contributions to CSl dialectology made, in particular, in recent years.

1. *Linguistic evidence*

1.1. *Phonological criteria*

As already mentioned (see section 0.3.), linguistic conclusions with regard to CSl dialectal differentiation will have to be based primarily on phonological data of the separate Slavic languages, particularly in their earliest available form, that is, in their oldest recorded stages of development. Before attempting any interpretation in terms of spatial grouping or chronology, let us therefore envisage those major phonological isoglosses within the Slavic linguistic territory which can be attributed, with a fair degree of probability, to the period of CSl and its disintegration (see §§0.1. and 0.2.).

In order to facilitate the schematic presentation of these CSl isophones we can, a posteriori, assume here the existence of certain CSl dialect groups: A, B, C, D, E, and F. These dialect groups will be shown to correspond to East Slavic (or "Russian" in the broad sense, = A), Lekhitic (including Polish and the Pomeranian and Polabian dialects, = B), Sorbian (or Lusatian, = C), Czechoslovak (= D), Sloveno-Serbocroatian (= E), and Macedo-Bulgarian, (= F). Although this division will subsequently turn out to coincide with the basic late CSl dialect groups to be established, at this stage of our discussion it serves merely practical purposes, and its underlying implications remain so far to be proven correct.

1.11. *Dialect A (East Slavic)*

Starting out from dialect A (and the point of departure is, of course, chosen arbitrarily) we will find that this dialect as a whole is characterized by two exclusive phonological features, both involving a shift from high to low tonality (to use the term of distinctive feature theory). One is the rounding of the back jer, presumably only in strong position, resulting in the full vocalization /ъ̥/ > /o/ in OR. A similar development, parallel with /ь̥/ > /e/, is, to be sure, also found in Macedonian, including its oldest OCS evidence; cf. OCS *sъnъ*/ *sonъ*, Mac., R. *son*; OCS *dьnь*, Mac. *den*, R. *den'* (= /d'en'/). However, there is a fundamental difference in these otherwise similar processes between Macedonian and East Slavic: while in Macedonian the /e/ : /o/ distinction, reflecting the earlier /ь̥/ : /ъ̥/ opposition, was phonemic, in OR the original front vs. back distinction of the strong jers was phonemically sufficiently carried on by the soft vs. hard distinction of the preceding consonant (or, in other words, by the consonantal correlation of palatalization vs. lack of palatalization cf. *infra*), in the same way as, for example, in Polish; cf. *dzień* (= /ʒ́eń/), *len* < *dьnь*, *lьnъ* vs. *sen*, *łeb* < *sъnъ*, *lъbъ*. The fact that in OR /ъ̥/ developed specifically > /o/ (i.e., to a vowel different from that resulting from /ь̥/) proved to be phonemically irrelevant and it must therefore be explained in terms of a general, nonphonemic tendency toward labialization.[11] The other isogloss of shifting to low tonality is the change /e-/ > /o-/, rather than /je-/ > /o-/ as usually presented, found in OR from the very beginning of its recorded evolution.[12] In this context one may also mention the consistent use of /u-/ in OR, corresponding to /ju-/ of other Slavic languages, where the /j-/ is either original (reflecting /jow-/, /ew-/) or owing to prothesis. Words with /ju-/ in OR are of Church Slavic origin; in modern Russian /ju-/ is of course also found in more or less recent loanwords, such as *jubka*, *jubilej*, *jumor*.

In addition to these two features there are some phonological isoglosses characteristic of dialect A only, but as such forming part of a larger system of isophones which cover all of CSl. One such feature is "pleophonic" /ToroT/ as a reflex of PSl /TorT/. We are here using the symbol /TorT/ to represent any of the combinations /-or-/, /-ol-/, /-er-/, /-el-/ in medial (interconsonantal) position, disregarding at this point the special varied development of /TelT/ in dialect A (cf. *infra*). The reflex of PSl /TorT/ in dialects D, E, and F is /TraT/ (/TrěT/, etc.); in dialect C and the bulk of dialect B the corresponding reflex is /TroT/; only a northwestern fraction of dialect B seems to have the

[11] See for further details A. Furdal, *op. cit.* 83. B. Calleman, *Zu den Haupttendenzen der urslavischen und altrussischen Lautentwicklung* 27–31, 144–161, and *passim* (Uppsala, 1950), stresses the phonetic ("articulatory") tendency of velarization in late CSl and OR, separating, however, labialization from velarization and rejecting on phonetic grounds the concept of labiovelarization. I agree with Furdal, considering labialization (rather than velarization) a general phonetic tendency of East Slavic (dialect A); cf., however, /Tl̥'T/ > /Tl̥T/ below. The notion of low (vs. high) tonality, accounting for both labial and velar, as opposed to nonlabial (unrounded) and nonvelar (front), can conveniently be used if one wants to avoid determining whether a sound change primarily involves labialization or velarization. Notice, however, that by "primarily" we do not even necessarily mean "phonemic" (as opposed to "redundant").

[12] Cf. A. Furdal, *op. cit.* 82–83; R. Jakobson, *Remarques sur l'évolution phonologique du russe comparée à celle des autres langues slaves* (*TCLP* 2) 38–45 (Prague, 1929), (= *Selected Writings* 1.44–52, [The Hague, 1962]); R. Ekblom, *Der Wechsel (j)e- ~ o- im Slavischen* (Uppsala and Leipzig, 1925); S. B. Bernštejn, *op. cit.*, 226–227.

reflex /TarT/, used, incidentally, rather inconsistently and largely alternating with /TroT/.[13] Another such isogloss of dialect A is /TъrT/ as reflecting late PSl (= early CSl) /Tr̥T/. Similarly, we are here using the symbol /TъrT/ for any of the groups "reduced vowel + liquid" in medial position, disregarding for the time being the merging of /TъlT/, /TьlT/ > /TъlT/ in dialect A (cf. *infra*). The further OR development of /Tъ̥rT/ > /TorT/ and, partly, by so-called second pleophony ("vtoroe polnoglasie"), > /ToroT/ falls beyond the scope of the present paper on CSl dialects. The assumption of the reflex /Tъ̥rT/ < /Tr̥T/ presupposes, however, the controversial development /TъrT/ > /Tr̥T/ in PSl. Some linguists still prefer to consider OR /Tъ̥rT/ a direct continuation of early PSl /TъrT/, corresponding closely to Baltic (and Balto-Slavic) /-ur-/ (/-ir-/, /-ul-/, /-il-/).[14] In dialects B and C late PSl [Tr̥T/—but not /Tr̥'T/!—is represented by /TArT/, where /A/ stands for any back vowel. In dialects D, E, and F /Tr̥T/ corresponds to late PSl /Tr̥T/ (as well as /Tr̥'T/. In many Slavic languages the ultimate outcome of PSl /Tl̥T/, and in dialect A and a northwestern branch of dialect B also of PSl /Tl̥'T/, was /TolT/. However, this convergent evolution cannot be considered an isophone connecting East Slavic and the Pomeranian and Polabian idioms with High Sorbian, Slovene and Macedonian. It must be explained rather as due to the inherent limitations of the different phonemic systems.[15] Finally, to the same type of phonological isoglosses of dialect A belong also /č/, /ž/ as reflexes of PSl /tj/, /dj/. In dialects B, C, and D PSl /tj/ was reflected by /c/. The same applies also to PSl /kt'/ (partly < /gt/, before front vowel). In the languages that subsequently developed from what is here called dialects E and F we encounter a variety of reflexes, which may however be traced to the two basic types /ć/ in dialect E (and perhaps in late PSl in general), and /št'/ in dialect F. In this context I refrain from discussing whether in dialect F ("Proto-OCS," Cyrillo-Methodian Slavic) /št'/ and its voiced equivalent /žd'/ should be interpreted as being biphonemic, as is usually assumed, or rather monophonemic, as was asserted by N. S. Trubeckoj, following a suggestion made by N. N. Durnovo.[16] Similarly, the reflex of PSl /dj/

---

[13] See A. Furdal, *op. cit.* 56–59 (with ample bibliographical references).

[14] See S. B. Bernštejn, *op. cit.* 207; A. Furdal, *op. cit.* 40–41.

[15] See A. Furdal, *op. cit.* 59 (with notes 19 and 20).

[16] See N. Trubetzkoy, "Die altkirchenslavische Vertretung der urslavischen **tj, *dj,*" *Zeitschrift für slavische Philologie* 13.88–97 (1936), as well as his treatment in *Altkirchenslavische Grammatik* 27–28, 81, and *passim* (Vienna, 1954); see also W. K. Matthews's criticism in "Trubetzkoy's ψ/ϯ and the Old Bulgarian groups *št/žd*," *Beogradski međunarodni slavistički sastanak* 485–490 (Belgrade, 1957).

can be reduced to /ʒ́/ in dialect E (and possibly in late PSl in general). In dialect B PSl /dj/ was represented by /ʒ/, though subsequently partly simplified > /z/ in Pomeranian, whereas in dialect C the same PSl cluster ultimately resulted in /z/. Dialect D falls in this regard into two parts, one western (developing later into Czech) adhering to dialect C with its reflex /z/, and one eastern (developing into Slovak) adhering in this respect to dialect B, that is, retaining the reflex /ʒ/. Contemporary standard Macedonian /k'/, /g'/ do not represent a special treatment of PSl /tj/, /dj/, but are to be considered as owing to the influence of Serbian /ć/, /ʒ́/ or some of their phonetic variants. Many Macedonian dialects have the reflexes /št/, /žd/, the same as Bulgarian.[17]

Furthermore, dialect A is intersected by two other isoglottic lines, one of which is the ramification of a major CSl phonological line of demarcation, while the other forms the northeastern end of such a line. Within dialect A both these lines separate only minor areas from the bulk of the territory of this dialect. The first of these two isophonic lines is the one dividing the reflexes /l/ : /kl/, /gl/ < PSl /tl/, /dl/. Most of dialect A, coinciding in this respect with dialect F and the major part of dialect E, reflects the PSl clusters /tl/, /dl/ by /l/, whereas in a smaller section of dialect A PSl /tl/, /dl/ are represented by /kl/, /gl/. The main isoglottic line separating western /tl/, /dl/ from eastern /l/ as reflexes of PSl /tl/, /dl/ does not intersect the territory of dialect A, leaving it entirely east of this line. Incidentally, the simplification /tl/, /dl/ > /l/ occurs also in a small part of dialect E (NW Slovenian dialects; cf. the forms *modliti* vs. *crilatcem* attested already in the *Freising Texts*) and occasionally even in dialects D (as reflected in South Slovak) and C (as reflected in West Low Sorbian). The /kl/, /gl/ reflexes of PSl /tl/, /dl/ are characteristic of certain Northwest Russian dialects in the Pskov, Novgorod, and Leningrad areas. In texts from these areas (primarily Pskov, occasionally also Novgorod) they have been recorded since the fourteenth century. The same phenomenon, /tl/, /dl/ > /kl/, /gl/, is known also from the contiguous Baltic linguistic territory, and its presence in Russian dialects has therefore often been explained as being owing to the underlying Baltic substratum of these areas. In favor of an explanation based on the assump-

[17] See A. Furdal, *op. cit.* 17–19. On the different treatment of PSl /dj/ in Czech and Slovak see also R. Auty, *Transactions of the Philological Society* 145 (1953) (in his article "The Evolution of Literary Slovak"), and, in particular, N. van Wijk, "Die älteste Gruppierung der čechoslovakischen Mundarten," *Slavia* 11.425–436 (1932), esp. 426–427. The regular reflex of /dj/ in Kashubian-Slovincian is /z/; however, in idioms of this area also forms with /ʒ/, and even /ʒ́/, can be found; as to their explanation see A. M. Seliščev, *Slavjanskoe jazykoznanie*. 1. *Zapadno-slavjanskie jazyki* 304 (Moscow, 1941).

tion of a Baltic substratum, one could also adduce the fact that in certain West Slavic areas adjacent to the original Baltic linguistic territory, viz., in Kashubian and Masovian (North Polish) dialects, /kl/ and in particular /gl/ (< /tl/, /dl/) are occasionally encountered. However, a mere phonetic, internal Slavic explanation has also been suggested.[18]

The second isophonic line intersecting the territory of dialect A concerns the reflexes of PSl /sk/ when preceding a secondary front vowel, that is, /ě$_2$/ or /-i$_2$/ derived from an original diphthong. East and south of this line the reflex of /sk/ in such position, henceforth denoted /sk'$_2$/, was /sc/ (or, to be exact, originally /sc'/ or even /s'c'/), from which subsequently developed /st/, as frequently encountered already in OCS. West and north of it, the reflex was /šč/, from which ultimately, though only in a late phase, could develop /št'/, as found in modern Czech (loc. sg. *vojště*), opposed in this respect to Old Czech (*vojšče*). It seems less satisfactory, in my opinion, to prefer an explanation deriving OCS /st/ directly from PSl /sk'$_2$/, thus an alleged series */sk'$_2$/ > /st'/ > /sc'/ > /sc/, to the traditional view assuming dissimilation in the last step of the development: /sk'$_2$/ > /sc'/ > /sc/ (i.e., /sts/) > /st/. Also this isophonic line separates only a minor, northwestern fraction of dialect A (reflected, e.g., in the OR idioms of Novgorod and Smolensk; cf. OR *vъ Smolenscě* vs. *Smolenščě*) from the rest of it. And, again, this line interesects the territory of dialect E in roughly the same way as the /tl/, /dl/ vs. /l/ line, dividing the linguistic territory of Slovenia. What has been said here about the development of PSl /sk'$_2$/ applies, *mutatis mutandis*, also to /zg'$_2$/. However, the reflex of PSl /zg/ in this position is partly obscured in OR by other factors (orthography, OCS influence). For the expected reflex */žǯ/ we find in the northwestern area of OR /žg'/, at least graphically ([žgь]).[19]

---

[18] See A. Meillet, *Le slave commun*^{2} 138–139 (Paris, 1934), and, in particular, A. Furdal, *op. cit.* 27–31. For further details see also N. Trubetzkoy, "Die Behandlung der Lautverbindungen *tl, dl* in den slavischen Sprachen," *Zeitschrift für slavische Philologie* 2.177–121 (1925); M. Rudnicki, "Grupy *tl, dl* w językach słowiańskich," *Prace filologiczne* 12.30–34 (1927); and, above all, the thorough treatment by L. Tesnière, "Les diphones *tl, dl* en slave," *Revue des études slaves* 13.51–100 (1933), analyzing in great detail, among other things, the pertinent Slovenian data. For South Slovak and West Low Sorbian idioms see also Z. Stieber, "Wzajemne stosunki" 75–78 and 88. See also F. P. Filin, *op. cit.* 181–188 (with further bibliographical references).

[19] See A. Furdal, *op. cit.* 19–20, 31–33 (with note 73); S. B. Bernštejn, *op. cit.* 204; N. Durnovo, "Le traitement de *sk* dans les langues slaves," *Revue des études slaves* 6.216–223 (1926); on the reflexes in West Slavic (= dialects B, C, and D) see also T. Lehr-Spławiński, "Jedna z izofon północno-zachodnio-słowiańskich (Formy typu *w Polszcze* itp.)," *Slavia Occidentalis* 10.153–159 (1931) (= *Studia i szkice* 251–256); on OR orthography (/žg'/ also < /zgj/, /zg'$_1$/) cf. further R.

Two more isoglosses may be considered part of the general tendency of dialect A (East Slavic) toward low tonality (labialization or possibly velarization; see *supra*, with note 11). Both seem to imply a modification unrounded > rounded and/or front > back of the timbre of vowels (or vocaloids) in front of tautosyllabic /l/. Both these isophones cover basically the same area, viz., in addition to all of dialect A also a smaller, northwestern section of dialect B (Pomeranian-Polabian). The first of them may be denoted /TьlT/ > /TъlT/ or /Tl̥'T/ > /Tl̥T/, or even /TilT/ > /TulT/. The problem of how to interpret phonologically and hence how to symbolize this isogloss of dialect A and a fraction of dialect B is connected with the somewhat controversial question of its chronology. No doubt this isogloss is of very old date. Using the symbols applicable to the earliest phase of PSl or even the Balto-Slavic period, that is, /TilT/ > /TulT/, we could explain this development phonetically in terms of labialization of the vocalic element preceding the liquid, thus /i/ > /ü/ > /u/, generally characteristic of dialect A. If, on the other hand, we interpret it as /Tl̥'T/ > /Tl̥T/, this process can phonologically only be termed velarization (or depalatalization). The same would, incidentally, also apply to /TьlT/ > /TъlT/, if, as we probably should, we assume an early lax (unrounded) pronunciation of both reduced vowels, the front as well as the back jer. Chronological, if not phonological, considerations may, however, speak in favor of the /Tl̥'T/ > /Tl̥T/ interpretation. For it was asserted above (§0.1., with note 4) that dialectal features could be ascertained only for the CSl period (including late PSl), but not for early PSl. The rise of a tendency toward syllables with increasing sonority, or simply toward open (unchecked) syllables, was said to mark the transition from early to late PSl (and CSl). Now the development /TъrT/ (or /TurT/) > /Tr̥T/, and so forth, assumed for PSl, must be considered to constitute one of the manifestations of this tendency (cf. above, with note 14). Hence, even if for phonological reasons (assuming labialization rather than velarization) we would have preferred to posit /TilT/ > /TulT/ instead of /Tl̥'T/ > /Tl̥T/ or /TьlT/ > /TъlT/, chronological deliberations might nevertheless force us to postulate the latter, namely, velarization (depalatalization). The parallel development /TelT/ > /TolT/, less problematic though it may be, is also ambiguous in this very respect; in other words, it can be interpreted as owing to either labialization or velarization and is therefore of little value in determining the underlying

Jakobson, "Spornyj vopros drevnerusskogo pravopisanija (dъžgь, dъždь)," *Belićev Zbornik* 39–45 (Belgrade, 1937) (= *Selected Writings* 1.247–253); and G. I. Gerovskij, "Drevnerusskie napisanija *žč*, *žg* i *g* pered perednimi glasnymi," *Voprosy jazykoznanija* 1959:4.52–59.

cause of the comparable /TilT/ > /TulT/ or /Tl̥'T/ > /Tl̥T/ change; on /T'elT/ > /T'ölT/ > /T'eloT/, see below. It is for such reasons that we prefer to speak about low tonality rather than about labialization and/or velarization. Henceforth we will as a mere matter of convenience refer to the controversial change just discussed only as /Tl̥'T/ > /Tl̥T/. Incidentally, in dialect B it is largely obscured by the subsequent velarization or depalatalization (often referred to as umlaut, Polish "przegłos") /l̥'/ > /l̥/ > /oł/, /uł/, /łu/, /eł/, with /l̥'/ developing to /il/ only when occurring after a labial and before a consonant other than hard dental (Polish *milczeć*, *wilk*, *wilgoć*). (For more on chronology, see §2.2. below.)

The second isophone covering roughly the same geographical area is, as mentioned, the change /TelT/ > /TolT/. Anticipating here again some chronological conclusions, it is readily evident that this change must have preceded in time the /TorT/ > /ToroT/ modification ("pleophony") mentioned above. It is, in other words, proper to assume only a series /TelT/ > /TolT/ > /ToloT/, not */TelT/ > /TeleT/ > /ToloT/. As is well known, the /TelT/ > /ToloT/ process does not operate if /T-/ stands for an originally soft (palatal) consonant, /T'-/. Here the result was instead /-elo-/, thus /T'elT/ > /T'eloT/. As an intermediate stage in this development some linguists posit /TölT/. It is at least highly doubtful whether beside /T'eloT/ also /T'eleT/ can be considered a normal East Slavic reflex of PSl /T'elT/; cf. Russian dial. *oželedica*, Ukr. *oželed'*, *oželeda*. It seems even less probable that /TelT/, a sound sequence beginning with a nonpalatal consonant in PSl, could ever result in /TeleT/. Most of the not-too-numerous pertinent examples require a special explanation; cf., for example, Russian (partly dialectal) *pelëva*, *peled*, *pelega*, *pelena*, *pelësyj*, *peleskat'sja* (: *poloskat'sja*), *selezënka*, *selezen'*, *velet* (: *volot*).[20]

Moreover, there are some important phonological isoglosses of dialect A which are shared by other CSl dialects in their entirety as well. These isophones are the following: the so-called epenthetic /l'/ after labials, namely, the reflexes /pl'/, /bl'/, /ml'/, /vl'/ for PSl /pj/, /bj/, /mj/, /vj/ in other than word-initial positions; /cv/, (/ʒv/ >) /zv/, /sv/ reflecting /kv/, /gv/, /xv/ when followed by /$\check{e}_2$/ or /-i_2/; /s'/ resulting

[20] On /Tl̥'T/ > /Tl̥T/ and /TelT/ > /TolT/ in general see A. Furdal, *op. cit.* 53, 58–59, 72 and 96. See also T. Lehr-Spławiński, "O mieszaniu prasłowiańskich połączeń *telt z tolt* w językach północno-słowiańskich," *Prace filologiczne* 15:2.345–361 (1932) (= *Studia i szkice* 219–230). On /T'elT/ > /T'ölT/ > /T'eloT/ cf., e.g., P. Ja. Černyx, *op. cit.* 82–83; on this, and /TilT/ > /TülT/ (> /TъlT/ > /TolT/) in East Slavic see also R. Jakobson, *Remarques* 20–22 (= *Selected Writings* 1.25–27). For the words containing /-ele-/, /-elë-/ see further under the relevant entries in M. Vasmer, *Russisches etymologisches Wörterbuch* 1–3 (Heidelberg, 1953–1958).

from the so-called second and third palatalization of PSl /x/, here denoted /x'₂/; /roT-/, /loT-/ < PSl /ŏrT-/, /ŏlT-/; and the general palatalization of consonants when followed by front vowels.

Dialect A had in common with dialect E the feature of inserting /l'/ after the soft labials /p'/, /b'/, /m'/, /v'/ derived from /p/, and so on, +/j/, not only in word-initial (intramorphemic) but also in medial position (i.e., on the morpheme boundary). Dialect F seems originally also to have participated in this development but subsequently again abandoned the epenthetic /l'/. The oldest evidence from this area, OCS, already indicates the gradual loss of this /l'/; while the oldest West OCS (Old Macedonian, glagolitic) manuscripts still by and large preserve the epenthetic /l'/ fairly well (e.g., the *Codices Zographensis* and *Marianus*, the *Glagolita Clozianus*, and the *Euchologium Sinaiticum*, to say nothing of the highly consistent *Kievan Missal*), the younger East OCS (Old Bulgarian, cyrillic) texts (such as the *Savvina Kniga* and, in particular, the *Codex Suprasliensis*) show an increasing tendency to drop the /l'/. To forms like Russian *kuplju* (OCS *kupljǫ/kupjǫ*), *ljublju* (OCS *ljubljǫ/ljubjǫ*), *zemlja* (OCS *zemlja/zemja*), *lovlju* (OCS *lovljǫ/lovjǫ*) correspond Polish *kupię*, *lubię*, *ziemia*, *łowię*. Thus West Slavic (dialects B, C, D) does not have the epenthetic /l'/ in this position. Words like Polish *kropla*, *grobla*, *skomleć*, or *niemowlę* seem, however, to indicate that the medial /l'/ after labials once existed also in this part of the CSl linguistic territory. If, therefore, /pj/ > /p'/ > /pl'/, and so on, may be considered a general CSl feature, then the loss of the /l'/ in dialects B, C, D, and F, rather than its retention in dialects A and E, can be termed an isogloss. In word-initial (intramorphemic) position the postlabial /l'/ has been preserved all over the Slavic linguistic territory; cf. OCS *pljujǫ*, Bg. *pluvam*, R. *pljuju*, P. *pluję*. The change /vj/ > /v'/ > /vl'/ in CSl must be considered secondary (and partly analogical), since the original diphthongs in /w/ were monophthongized in front of /j/; cf. R. *torgovlja* < **tъrg-ov-ja* : *torguju* < **tъrg-u-jǫ* < **turg-ow-j-ō-m*. Both the fact that original diphthongs in /w/ + /j/ developed into /uj/, and also that the /j/ in /ju/ derived from /ew/ affected preceding labials, causing the insertion of /l'/, speak against dating its rise too far back in early PSl; cf. OCS *bljudǫ*, R. *bljudu* < IE **bhewdh-* (Gr. *πεύθομαι*).[21]

[21] See, e.g., A Furdal, *op. cit.* 71–72, 88, 91–92 (with note 26); for the evidence of "epenthetic" /l'/ in OCS see P. Diels, *Altkirchenslavische Grammatik* 1.131 (note 4) and 139 (Heidelberg, 1932). On the development of /wj/ see further the article by P. S. Kuznecov, "O povedenii sonantov na granice osnov glagolov III i IV klassov v slavjanskix jazykax," *Slavjanskaja filologija* 3.5–57 (Moscow, 1958). On the development of /pj/, etc., in dialects B, C, D, and F, cf. also N. Trubetzkoj, *Zeitschrift für slavische Philologie* 7.394–403 (1930).

The isogloss /kv/ > /cv/, and so on, is shared by dialects A, E, and F. Whether, in addition to the position in front of /ě₂/, /-i₂/, it occurred regularly also before some original front vowels, /i/ < /ej/, /ь/ < /i/, is a matter of controversy. Possibly /cv/, etc., in such position can be explained as due to analogy; cf. OCS *cvětъ* as well as *cvъtǫ, cvisti*, R. *cvet* vs. P. *kwiat*, Cz. *květ*; OCS *ʒvězda, zvězda*, R. *zvezda* vs. P. *gwiazda*, Cz. *hvězda*; nom. pl. OCS *vlъsvi*, OR *vъlsvi, volsvi*, etc. Apart from certain fluctuations that can be explained by analogy (cf., e.g., also R. dial. *kvet, kvët* /kv'ot/, Ukr. *kvit*, along with the regular reflexes *cvet, cvit*), there are some instances of irregularity due to onomatopoeia and West Slavic influence.[22]

The /kv/ > /cv/ isogloss coincides in its geographic distribution with the reflex /s'/ < /x'₂/. In dialects B, C, and D the corresponding reflex was /š/. Cf., e.g., dat. and loc. sg. OCS, OR *musě* vs. P. *musze*, Cz. *mouše*; R. *seryj* vs. P. *szary* (< **xojr*-); OCS *vъsego*, R. *vsego* vs. Cz. *všeho*. The fact that this /s'/ was originally palatalized is somewhat obscured by the general palatalization of consonants before front vowels in dialect A, as well as by the corresponding lack of palatalization in dialects E and F (see below). However, when resulting from the so-called third (progressive) palatalization and followed by the unshifted back vowel /a/, the softness of the /s'/ is still apparent in dialect A (East Slavic); cf., e.g., R. *vsjakij* /fs'ak-/ with the same suffix *-ak-* as in *takoj, kakoj*.

Dialect D shared, as we have seen, with dialects E and F the same treatment of the /TorT/ isogloss, showing the reflex /TraT/, as opposed to /TroT/ and exceptionally /TarT/ of dialects B and C, and /ToroT/ of dialect A. It is therefore remarkable that in its reflection of PSl word-initial /orT/, /olT/ with circumflex pitch, here denoted /õrT-/, /õlT-/, dialect D coincides by and large with dialects A, B, and C, showing /roT-/, /loT-/. Only the central Slovak dialects agree in this respect (as well as in many others) with South Slavic (CSl dialect E). Presumably the difference between dialects A, B, C, and D, on the one hand, and dialects E and F (> /raT-/, /laT-/) on the other, amounts phonetically to vowel shortening in the northern group: /rå̄T-/ /lå̄T-/ > /raT-/, /laT-/ vs. /råT-/, /låT-/ > /roT-/, /loT-/. In dialect A, the original reflexes /roT-/, /loT-/ were subsequently largely obscured by South Slavic influence, with Church Slavic forms replacing genuine East Slavic words, and by the effect of "akan'e"—the /a/-pronunciation of un-

[22] For more details see H. Birnbaum, "Zu urslav. *kv-*," *Scando-Slavica* 2.29–40 (1956); H. Bräuer, *Slavische Sprachwissenschaft* 1.192 (Berlin, 1961); F. V. Mareš, *Slavia* 25.469–470 (1956) (in his article "Vznik"). See also N. Trubetzkoj, *Zeitschrift für slavische Philologie* 7.393–394, 402–403 (1930), and *Voprosy jazykoznanija* 1959:2.63–64.

stressed, pretonic /o/. It is worth mentioning, incidentally, that in Bulgarian, starting from the language of the OCS *Codex Suprasliensis*, throughout the Middle Bulgarian period, and down to modern Bulgarian dialects, we also find a reflex /roT-/; cf. OCS *rabъ/robъ, raz-/roz-*; Bulg. dial. *rob, robuvam, robski*; similar reflexes of this word and its cognates (*ròb*, etc.) are also to be found in Serbocroatian. No reflex /loT-/ can be ascertained for the CSl dialects E and F. On the other hand, the oldest evidence here shows a fluctuation /alT-/ ~ /laT-/; cf. OCS *al(ъ)dii / ladii, al(ъ)kati / lakati*. Also the nonmetathetic forms already have vowel lengthening: /å/ > /o/ vs. /å̄/ > /a/; to be sure, this seems to apply primarily to instances of acute intonation, but in the case of *al(ъ)dii / ladii* the original pitch was apparently circumflex (cf. Lith. *aldijà*, acc. sg. *al̃diją*).[23]

Finally, there remains to be mentioned the isophonic feature of palatalizing all consonants before front vowels. This isophone is often referred to as the consonantal correlation of palatalization or softness. While palatalization (or even what has sometimes been called "semi-palatalization" or "slight palatalization") in PSl certainly was not a phonemic but only a phonetic feature characteristic of all consonants preceding front vowels, this very feature became phonemic in the northern dialectal area of CSl, that is, in dialects A, B, C, and D. The subsequent depalatalization in varying degrees of soft consonants before front vowels or their reflexes in a part of dialect A (Ukrainian), as well as part of dialect B (Polabian), and in dialect D (to a greater extent in Czech, to a lesser in Slovak), is of more recent, post-CSl date. The same is true of such a further development as /t'/, /d'/ > /ć/, /ʒ́/ in adjacent parts of dialect A (Byelorussian) and B (Polish); see above (§0.2.).[24]

1.12. *Dialects B, C, and D (West Slavic: Lekhitic, Sorbian, Czechoslovak)*

In the preceding treatment many isoglosses of CSl dialects other than A have already been discussed. In the following only brief reference will therefore be made to them. Other isophones not mentioned so far must, on the other hand, be treated at somewhat greater length.

---

[23] Cf. A. Furdal, *op. cit.* 56–57 and 64–65 (with further bibliographical references); see also, e.g., R. Nahtigal, *Die slavischen Sprachen* 13–14 (Wiesbaden, 1961).

[24] On the consonantal correlation of palatalization as an isogloss within CSl see A. Furdal, *op. cit.* 46–55 (with extensive bibliographical references); S. B. Bernštejn, *op. cit.* 259–260. See further, in particular, F. V. Mareš, *Slavia* 25.482–483 (1956) (in "Vznik"); E. Koschmieder, "Die Palatalitätskorrelation im Slavischen," *Zeitschrift für slavische Philologie* 27.245–255 (1959); and G. Y. Shevelov, "Konsonanten vor *e*, *i* in den protoukrainischen Dialekten," *Festschrift für Max Vasmer* 482–494 (Wiesbaden, 1956).

Fixed stress is not a dialectal CSl feature. Although dialects B, C, and D, with the exception of a very small area of dialect B only (North Kashubian), have a fixed stress pattern—Polish stressing the penult, South Kashubian, Sorbian, and Czechoslovak (as well as Old Polish) having initial stress—this feature must be regarded as of considerably later date than CSl. The fixation of stress must therefore be relegated to those features that cannot serve to establish CSl dialects (see §0.2.).[25] Nor do other prosodic features (pitch and quantity) yield any applicable data for the classification of CSl dialects.

Turning to dialect B (Lekhitic), we have already mentioned the isophones intersecting this dialect's territory and cutting off a northern part of it: the /Tl̥'T/ > /Tl̥T/ and the TelT/ > /TolT/ isoglosses connecting this area with dialect A (East Slavic), and the North Lekhitic /TarT/ ~ /TroT/ fluctuation as opposed to the regular reflex /TroT/ in the bulk of dialect B as well as in dialect C (Sorbian), and contrasted with the normal /ToroT/ of dialect A and /TraT/ of dialects D (Czechoslovak), E (Sloveno-Serbocroation), and F (Macedo-Bulgarian). The isophonic /TarT/ ~ /TroT/ vs. /TroT/ line of North Lekhitic forms in other words a ramification of the basic division of the CSl dialects according to their reflection of PSl /TorT/ : dialect A—/ToroT/, dialects B and C—/TroT/, dialects D, E, and F—/TraT/.

A feature characteristic of dialect B is the retention of an open pronunciation of CSl /ě/, both of the original front vowel /$\check{e}_1$/ and of the product of monophthongization /$\check{e}_2$/. Tentatively this open (and lax) pronunciation may be denoted by /ä/. The Lekhitic alternation /'e/ ~ /'a/, as in P. *bielizna* ~ *biały* (cf. *infra*), is generally thought to reflect this original open (and wide) pronunciation; of course, Polabian /'o/ represents here only a further development of /'a/; cf. Polab. *l'otü*, P. *lato* < *lěto*. Apart from Lekhitic we find the same open pronunciation of CSl /ě/ also in dialect F. As is well known, the oldest Slavic writing system, the glagolitic alphabet, did not even differentiate graphically /ě/ and /ja/, /'a/. In the OCS language of Cyril and Methodius both sounds probably merged into one, realized as /'ä/, /ä/. There is, however, no compelling reason to consider this pronunciation in Lekhitic and Bulgarian (as well as East Macedonian dialects) a geographically conditioned common innovation, as has been suggested by B. Conev and S. B. Bernštejn. It may be explained rather as a characteristic of the periphery of the CSl linguistic territory, and the closed (and tense) pronunciation /ê/ of CSl /ě/, as found in dialects A, C, D, and E and tending toward a development > /je/, /ije/ > /i/, encountered in Novgorodian OR, Ukrainian, partly in Czech, and in

[25] See Z. Stieber, *Rozwój* 44–45.

"ikavski" Serbocroatian (while, e.g., certain East Slavic dialects as well as "jekavski" Serbocroatian represent the intermediate stage /je/, /ije/), can be considered a novelty. However, not even here must we necessarily, with T. Lehr-Spławiński, assume a closer connection between dialects A, C, and D on the one hand, and dialect E on the other.[26] (For more on grouping and chronology of dialectal features of CSl, see below, §2.)

The preservation of nasal vowels is usually considered another characteristic of Lekhitic or our dialect B. As a rule, the loss of nasal vowels is assumed to fall into the late CSl period of disintegration, since the presence of nasal vowels is recorded also from dialect F, viz., in OCS. It can also be shown that nasal vowels still existed in dialect A during the ninth century, when combinations of the type "oral vowel + nasal consonant" in foreign names and loanwords, primarily of Scandinavian origin, were rendered by sounds, the OR reflexes of which are traceable to nasal vowels, that is, by /u/ and /ja/, /'a/; cf., for example, OR *sudъ*, *varjagъ* < OScand. *sund*, *varing*(*r*). On the other hand, these sound combinations seem to have been pronounced by the East Slavs as purely oral vowels already around 950, since in two of the names of the Dnieper rapids mentioned by the Byzantine emperor Constantine VII Porphyrogennetos in his famous work "Περὶ ἐθνῶν" ("De administrando imperio") such combinations are rendered by the Greek graphemes for /u/ and /a/ : Βερούτζη—OR *vъruči* < **vъrǫtji*; Νεασήτ = OR *nejasytъ* < **nejęsytъ*. It should be noticed that what here in a traditional manner is termed "nasal vowels" were not, it seems to me, in the CSl period (including OCS up to the period of the loss of the weak jers) phonemically autonomous nasal vowels. Adhering to, and slightly modifying, an opinion expressed by N. S. Trubeckoj, I assume that the CSl (and early OCS) "nasal vowels" must be interpreted as allophones of combinations consisting of an oral vowel (one of the "archiphonemes" /E/ or /O/) + a nasal consonant (the neutralized "archiphoneme" /N/). Although these allophones might very well have been realized (pronounced) as nasal vowels already in CSl, that is to say, as /ę/, /ǫ/, these sounds seem to have become phonemic only after the fall of the jers in weak position. Even though remnants of nasal vowels are known also from Slovenian and Macedonian dialects, it is primarily Lehitic that has

---

[26] See A. Furdal, *op. cit.* 80–81; B. Conev, *Istorija na bălgarski ezik* 1^2 38 (Sofia, 1940); S. B. Bernštejn, *op. cit.* 72; T. Lehr-Spławiński, "O dialektach prasłowiańskich," *Sbornik prací* 583 (= *Studia i szkice* 213). On the merging of /ě/ and /ja/ in the Cyrillo-Methodian dialect see, e.g., H. G. Lunt, *Old Church Slavonic Grammar*^{2} 19 (§1.24.) and 25 (§2.04.) (The Hague, 1959).

preserved nasal vowels reflecting /ę/, /ǫ/ > /ą̈/, /ą̊/ (> OP /ą/). However, in the light of the above it may appear doubtful whether the retention of nasal vowels in the Lekhitic languages can properly be considered an isophone of the CSl dialect B, from which these languages subsequently emerged. For, as mentioned, we can reckon the nasal vowels independent phonemes only in the post-CSl period (i.e., after the fall of the jers, here considered the *terminus ad quem* for CSl; see §0.1 *supra*). For the preceding time I assume the existence of what phonetically might have been nasal vowels but phonemically must be considered allophones of /EN/, /ON/ also in other areas of the CSl linguistic territory, for instance, in dialect F (OCS) and, up to the middle of the tenth century, in dialect A.[27]

Whatever the phonemic analysis of the CSl "nasal vowels" may be, nasality was not preserved in their reflexes except in the Lekhitic group; in this context we thus ignore certain archaic features of South Slavic dialects already mentioned: /ą/ < CSl /ę/ in long syllables in North Slovene (the Jauntal dialect), vestiges of so-called rhineism in North Slovene, South and East Macedonian, and so forth. The reflex of CSl /ǫ/ was /u/ in dialects A, C, and D; in dialect E we find the double reflex /o/, in Slovene and Kajkavian Serbocroatian, and /u/, in the rest of Serbocroatian (Čakavian and Štokavian). In dialect F, where nasal vowels seem to have persisted longer than elsewhere (apart from Lekhitic), CSl /ǫ/ was first delabialized > /ą̊/, ultimately resulting in /ă/, /a/; cf., e.g., Bulg. *răka, nesa* < OCS *rǫka, nesǫ*. This feature thus constitutes an isoglottic particularity of dialect F (Macedo-Bulgarian). The reflex of CSl /ę/ was /e/ in both dialect E and F, i.e., all over the South Slavic territory. In dialects A and D, as well as a part of dialect C (viz., High Sorbian), CSl /ę/ developed into /ä/, with subsequent minor modifications (> /a/, /ě/, /i/) which may be ignored here. Only in a part of dialect C (viz., Low Sorbian) was the result instead /ě/, pronounced as a tense (narrow) vowel, i.e., /ê/; cf., e.g., HSorb.

[27] For a basically traditional presentation of the problem of nasal vowels in the Lekhitic languages, as well as their reflexes in other Slavic languages, see A. Furdal, *op. cit.* 76–80; some new ideas can be found in S. B. Bernštejn, *op. cit.* 241–246 and 286–287. A phonemically more adequate, though not entirely satisfactory, interpretation was given by N. S. Trubeckoj (N. Troubetzkoy) in his article "Les voyelles nasales des langues léchites," *Revue des études slaves* 5.24–37 (1925), provoking, however, immediate criticism by T. Lehr-Spławiński; see his "Les voyelles nasales dans les langues léchites," *ibid.* 6.54–65 (1926). For a full account with detailed bibliographical references as well as certain modifications of Trubeckoj's analysis, see my contribution to the Fifth International Congress of Slavists, "Reinterpretacje fonologiczne nosówek słowiańskich," *American Contributions* 1.21–42 (The Hague, 1964).

mjaso vs. LSorb. *měso*. This difference in the treatment of CSl /ę/ seems to be the only old isophone splitting up dialect C into two sections.[28]

Before leaving dialect B we must mention certain phenomena involving depalatalization (or velarization), triggered, as it seems, by similar phonetic conditions, though not completely coinciding in time and space: /eT/ > /oT/, /ěT/ > /aT/, /ęT/ > /ǫT/ (or possibly already /ą̈T/ > /ą̊T), and also /ṛ'T/ > /ṛT/, where /-T/ stands for a hard dental in a broad sense, i.e., for /t/, /d/, /n/, /r/, /ł/, /s/, or /z/. Furdal has convincingly shown that the umlaut ("przegłos") /eT/ > /oT/ was, in fact, not a Common Lekhitic but a merely Polish, or rather Polish-Kashubian (i.e., East Lekhitic) development. He has also pointed out the fundamental differences between this change and the comparable, though by no means identical, development /e/ > /o/ in dialect A (East Slavic), the latter being considerably later and, perhaps, due to labialization rather than velarization (see above, §1.11., with note 11). Thus the /eT/ > /oT/ change is not Common Lekhitic, embracing only a part of dialect B, and falls beyond the scope of this paper; we can therefore ignore it here. As to the change of /ęT/ > /ǫT/ (or /ą̈T/ > /ą̊T/), our assumptions can be based only on the evidence of the *Gniezno Bull* of 1136 and some other early ecclesiastical documents of the twelfth and thirteenth centuries (written in Latin, but containing Polish onomastic material), since its consequences have subsequently been entirely obscured by the merging of /ę/ ~ /ą̈/ and /ǫ/ ~ /ą̊/ in Old Polish (> /ą/). For this reason, Bernštejn does not even recognize this process (reflected, e.g., in such writings as *Landa* < **lęda*) as firmly established. However, his counterargument (P. *rząd*, and not **rąd*, < CSl *rędъ*) does not withstand criticism. I therefore see no reason why we should not assume a Lekhitic development /ęT/ > /ǫT/ (or /ą̈T/ > /ą̊T), granting that evidence for it is scanty. Concerning /ěT/ > /aT/, neatly singling out dialect B, no doubts have ever been expressed, as far as I know. The depalatalization of /ṛ'T/, finally, embraced not only dialect B, but also dialect C (Sorbian). As shown by examples like P. *śmierć* < OP *śm̓irć* as compared to P. *martwy*, it must chronologically have preceded the change /TṛT/ > /TArT/ mentioned above (see § 1.11.). Otherwise **m̓ṛ'tvъ* would not have developed > *martwy*, as it actually did, with **mṛtvъ* as an intermediate stage.[29]

[28] For further details see, in addition to the relevant paragraphs in A. Furdal's and S. B. Bernštejn's books referred to in note 29, also R. Nahtigal, *op. cit.* 109–110.

[29] See, in particular, A. Furdal, *op. cit.* 72–76; cf. also S. B. Bernštejn, *op. cit.* 286, and Z. Stieber, *Rozwój* 11–13 and 19. For the details of the Polish reflex *rząd* < CSl *rędъ* and its phonemic implications, see H. Birnbaum, "Lautwandel und

The other two phonological isoglosses separating dialects B and C from dialect D (Czechoslovak), viz. /Tr̥T/ > /TArT/ vs. /Tr̥T/, and /TorT/ > /TroT/, and exceptionally also > /TarT/, vs. /TraT/ have already been mentioned. The reflexes of dialect D, /Tr̥T/ and /TraT/, connect this dialectal group with the southern branch of CSl dialects, E and F. Also the isophones separating dialect D (or at least the bulk of it) from dialects E and F have already been discussed: /roT-/, as opposed to /raT-/ < PSl /ŏrT-/, and the consonantal correlation of palatalization (i.e., general and only subsequently again partly limited palatalization of consonants preceding front vowels), these features being shared also by dialects A, B, and C; and /kv/ vs. /cv/, /š/ vs. /s'/ < /x'₂/, /šč/ vs. /sc/ < /sk'₂/, and /tl/ vs. /l/, having these latter features in common with dialects B and C, and some of them also with small fractions of dialects A and E; see §1.11. *supra*.

1.13. *Dialects E and F (South Slavic: Sloveno-Serbocroatian and Macedo-Bulgarian)*

As a matter of fact, very little remains to be added about the phonological isoglosses characteristic of dialects E and F. All the isophones separating these dialects from the rest of CSl dialects have already been listed.

Possibly the most important of them all, the consonantal correlation of palatalization, characteristic of dialects A, B, C, and D, but absent from dialects E and F, implies also such features as /i/ < PSl /i/ ~ /y/ in dialects E and F. In the other CSl dialects /i/ and /y/ correspond to South Slavic /i/; however, these vowels are not independent phonemes in these dialects either, but only positionally conditioned allophones; cf., e.g., SCr. *bȉti* = R. *bit'* /b'it'/, *byt'* /bit'/, P. *bić* /b'ić/, *być* /bić/. On soft consonants in dialects E and, particularly, dialect F, see below. Of course, in the northern branch of CSl the original phonemic distinction between /i/ and /y/ ceased to exist only after the establishment of the consonantal correlation of palatalization, when the phonemic opposition /i/ vs. /y/ was replaced by the palatalized vs. nonpalatalized distinctions of the preceding consonant. In those languages emerging from the northern CSl dialects, in which this correlation subsequently was reduced to only a few members, the /i/ vs. /y/ distinction could again become phonemic. This was true in Ukrainian, with its further complications of the vocalic system, but not in Czech, where the distribution of the letters [i], [í] vs. [y], [ý] is purely orthographic and etymological, but not phonemic. In fact, /i/y/, /í/ý/ are not even allophones in Czech

Phonologisierung, erläutert an zwei dialektischen Erscheinungen des Spätgemeinslavischen," *Zeitschrift für slavische Philologie* 32:2 (in press).

(as, e.g., in Russian or Polish). In the languages that have retained the consonantal correlation of palatalization to its full extent (as Russian and Polish), /i/ and /y/ remain merely allophones of one and the same phoneme, /i/.[30]

Some of the isophonic lines dividing dialects E and F have already been discussed. This applies to the delabialization of /ǫ/ > /ă/, /a/, the loss of the "epenthetic" /l'/ after (soft) labials, and the retention of an open pronunciation /ä/ of CSl /ě/ in dialect F (Bulgarian, but only a small eastern fraction of modern Macedonian dialects). For all of these features we have found corresponding phenomena also in dialect B, without assuming, however, any closer geographically conditioned links between dialects B and F; see §§1.12. *supra* and 2.2. *infra*. In this connection only one more feature deserves mention, although it can hardly be considered an independent isogloss of dialect F, but is rather a concomitant effect of the dropping of postlabial /l'/ and the change /ě/ > /a/ reflecting the pronunciation /ä/ of /ě/ in dialect F. I am referring to the genesis in dialect F of new palatal consonants apart from those derived from PSl clusters consisting of a consonant + /j/ and preserved also in dialect E; cf., e.g., Bg. *zeḿa* < *zeml'a* (*zemlja*), *bŕag* < *brěgъ* (but *bregove*), and so on. In addition, we encounter in certain East Bulgarian dialects further soft consonants, the palatality of which is, however, not necessarily a distinctive feature. Some of these phenomena of palatalization seem to require special explanations.[31]

What remains to be mentioned are two phonological phenomena involving a process of merging (fusion) of originally distinct sounds or sound combinations: of the front and back jers in strong position in dialect E, and of the reflexes of /tj/ and /stj/, /skj/, /sk'ı/, and of /dj/ and /zdj/, /zgj/, /zg'ı/ in dialect F. (By /k'ı/, /g'ı/ I here indicate the position of the velars in front of primary front vowels.) The former (merging of strong jers) is perhaps the most important single isophone within South Slavic, separating dialects E and F. It is of course not correct to assert that the merging of strong jers in dialect E (> /a/ in Serbocroatian; > /ə/ [graphically e] in short syllables, /â/, dialectally also /ȇ/, in long syllables in Slovene) has a direct continuation in the north in the merging of the strong jers into one vowel in dialects B, C, and D

---

[30] See, e.g., for Russian, M. Halle, *The Sound Pattern of Russian* 45–46, 161, and *passim* (The Hague, 1959); R. I. Avanesov, *Fonetika sovremennogo russkogo literaturnogo jazyka* 94–105 and *passim* (Moscow, 1956); for Polish, Z. Stieber, *Rozwój* 49–51; for Ukranian, Ju. Šerex [= G. Y. Shevelov], *Narys sučasnoji ukrajins'koji literaturnoji movy* 365–367 (Munich, 1951); for Czech, H. Kučera, *The Phonology of Czech* 25–26 (The Hague, 1961) (with further references mentioned in note 7). See also A. Furdal, *op. cit.* 85.

[31] Cf. A. Furdal, *op. cit.* 90–93.

(> /e/ in Czech, Polish, and Pomeranian, with more diversified reflexes in Slovak, Sorbian, and Polabian). For, even though the vocalic timbre of the reflexes of /ь̥/ and /ъ̥/ happens to be identical in Czech and Polish, the original phonemic distinction between front and back jers was here perpetuated, incidentally in strong as well as weak position, by the soft vs. hard opposition of the preceding consonant, or, in other words, by the consonantal correlation of palatalization; see also what has been said in note 3 about the phonemic implications of the "fall" of the jers in OR. This "transphonologization" was only subsequently obscured by the depalatization ("hardening") of certain consonants in Czech and, to a lesser extent, in Slovak; see §1.11. *supra* (last paragraph). Hence SCr *sȁn, dân*, Sln *sen, dân* (dial. *dên*), Cz. *sen, den*, Slk. *sen, deň* : P. *sen, dzień*. In South Slavic, which lacked the consonantal correlation of palatalization, the merging of the strong reduced vowels into one vowel in dialect E was an instance of complete neutralization of two originally distinct phonemes. Moreover, the isophonic line marking the merging of the two jers is the one that, of all isophonic lines cutting through the South Slavic linguistic territory, most closely corresponds to the present demarcation between Serbocroatian on the one hand, and Macedonian and Bulgarian on the other.[32] On /ъ̥/ > /o/ in Macedonian, see above (first paragraph of §1.11.).

As to the second isogloss, characteristic of dialect F, i.e., the merging of the reflex of PSl /tj/ (representing here also PSl /ktj/ as well as /kt'/) with those of PSl /stj/, /skj/, /sk'$_1$/ > /št/, and of the reflex of PSl /dj/ with those of PSl /zdj/, /zgj/, /zg'$_1$/ > /žd/, it must be considered an early feature of this dialect. Toponomastic evidence seems to indicate that the Slavs, when establishing contact with the Greek and Albanian population of the southern Balkans in the sixth to eighth centuries, had already developed the phonemes or biphonemic clusters /št/, /žd/; on the phonemic interpretation of these sounds, see *supra*, §1.11. with note 16. Cf. such place names as Gk. Κορύστιανη, Μεσδάνι = Slavic **Koryštane* (SCr. *Koričani*), **Meždane* (SCr. *Međani*), or Alb. *Pešter*, *Graždеn*.[33] All OCS texts (except the *Kievan Missal* with its special treatment of /tj/, /dj/ corresponding to Czech) have the uniform reflexes /št/, /žd/ for the different PSl clusters listed above. Cf., e.g., OCS *meštǫ* < **metj-* (inf. *metati*), *puštǫ* < **pustj-* (inf. *pustiti*), *blъštǫ* < **blъskj-* (inf. *blъštati* < **blъskěti*); *viždǫ* < **vidj-* (inf. *viděti*), *prigvoždǫ* < **prigvozdj-* and *prigvoždenъ* < **prigvozdjenъ* (inf. *prigvozditi*), *roždъje* / *raždije* < **rozgъje* / *razgъje* (cf.

[32] Cf. for this and the following feature the schematic map in P. Ivić, *op. cit.* 31; see also A. Furdal, *op. cit.* 89.

[33] On Slavic place names in their Greek form see M. Vasmer, *Die Slaven in Griechenland* (Berlin, 1941); for the names quoted, see pp. 38 and 94.

rozga / razga). In the rest of the Slavic linguistic territory the reflexes of PSl /tj/ and /stj/, /skj/, /sk'₁/, and of PSl /dj/ and /zdj/, /zgj/, /zg'₁/ were kept apart. Already in the *Kievan Missal*, where PSl /tj/ is represented by /c/, we thus find /šč/ for PSl /stj/ and /sk'₁/ : *očiščenię* = OCS *očištenija* (cf. *čistъ*), *zaščiti* = OCS *zaštiti* (cf. OCS *štitъ* < **skejtos*, Lith. *skiẽtas*, OPr. acc. sg. *scaytan*). This isogloss of merging, once apparently including all of dialect F, today covers Bulgarian and an eastern and southern strip of Macedonian only.[34] On /enn/ > /ęn/ (> /jan/, /'an/) in dialect A vs. /ěn/ elsewhere, see below (§2.3.).

1.2. *Other linguistic criteria*

Compared with the overwhelming evidence of phonological isoglosses, which, incidentally, could be outlined here only in a sketchy manner, other linguistic criteria for the classification of CSl dialects seem rather meager. For reasons suggested above (see §0.3.) we will here limit ourselves to discussing, in addition to the phonological evidence just presented, a few morphological (and phonomorphological, but not morphophonemic) phenomena, leaving aside syntactic and lexical data for the time being.

What is originally clearly a phonological feature, though prominent in certain grammatical endings owing to its restriction to word-final position, is seen in the double reflection of PSl /-jens/ (</-jans/, /-jons/), in the gen. sg. and nom. acc. pl. of the nominal and pronominal *ja*-stems as well as the acc. pl. of the corresponding *jo*-stems. Dialects A, B, C, and D present here the reflex /-jě₃/, /-'ě₃/, whereas dialects E and F have /-ję/, /-'ę/. For the development /-jens/ > /-jě₃/, /-'ě₃/ some linguists posit (ever since F. F. Fortunatov) the highly questionable intermediate stage /-ję̌/, /-'ę̌/ ("nasal jat' "). Cf., e.g., OR *zemlě*, OP *ziemie* vs. OCS *zemlję*, SCr *zèmlje* (< *zemlję*); OR *duše*, Ukr. *duši* (< *duše*), OP *dusze* vs. OCS *dušę*, SCr *dúše*; OR acc. pl. *koně*, Ukr. *koni*, P. *konie* vs. OCS *konję*; OR gen. sg. f. *jejě*, *vьsejě* vs. OCS *jeję*, *vьseję*, etc. While the reflex in South Slavic (dialects E and F) does not occasion any doubts, the different development in the rest of CSl has so far not been satisfactorily explained. However, it can be assumed that the North Slavic reflex is an innovation as compared to the nasal vowel of dialects E and F.[35]

The same geographical distribution as in the case of the /-ę/ vs. /-ě₃/ isogloss is seen in the different nom. sg. masc. endings of the present active participles: /-a/ in dialects A, B, C, and D (N CSl) vs. /-y/ in

[34] Cf. A. Furdal, *op. cit.* 18 and 87–88; for the OCS evidence see also P. Diels, *op. cit.* 12 and 136–137; for the present isogloss line of the South Slavic linguistic territory, see the schematic map in P. Ivić, *op. cit.* 31.

[35] Cf., e.g., A. Furdal, *op. cit.* 60–62.

dialects E and F (S CSl). Cf., e.g., OR *nesa, veda, moga, rъka*, OP *rzeka*, Cz. *nesa, veda, moha, řka* vs. OCS *nesy, mogy, reky*, OSerb. *mogi*. The South Slavic ending /-y/ is usually traced back to /-on(t)s/. For the North Slavic ending different explanations have been suggested. The most original, at least phonetically plausible conjecture was advanced by J. Zubatý, operating with an IE sandhi variant in /-ō/ along with /-ōn/, the latter being attested in forms like Gk. φέρων. For the South Slavic reflex /-y/ one could in such an instance assume the IE doublet in /-ōn/ with the same auslaut development as in *kamy* < **kāmōn* (cf. Gk. ἄκμων).[36]

A third isogloss coinciding geographically with the two just mentioned is clearly morphological; the early replacement of the ending /-omь/ in the instr. sg. of the *o*-stems by that of the *u*-stems, /-ъmь/. Thus OCS *vlъkomь, gněvomь* correspond to OR *vъlkъmь, gněvъmь* (forms like *vъlkomь, volkomь, gněvomь* are here owing only to the subsequent full vocalization of the strong back jer or to OCS influence), P. *wilkiem, gniewem*, etc. Similarly, in the *jo*-stems: OCS *ložemь* vs. OR *ložъmь*, P. *łożem* (where, however, the original difference is obscured also in West Slavic, by the subsequent /ь̥/ > /e/ change). Wherever we encounter OCS forms of original *o/jo*-stems ending in /-ъmь/ ∼ /-ьmь/, these are either hypercorrect or explicable in terms of the general fusion of the *o*- and *u*- declensions. The *Kievan Missal*, representing in this respect as in others West Slavic, consistently has /-ъmь/, not /-omь/. Since the ending of the instr. sg. of the *o*-stems in Slavic is an innovation that cannot be traced back directly to an IE form, it is perhaps possible that the CSl dialectal distribution, /-ъmь/ in the north vs. /-omь/ in the south, generalized for both *o*- and *u*-stems, should be considered a common, simultaneous PSl innovation, rather than labeling only the introduction of /-ъmь/ in the *o*-stems a north CSl neologism.[37]

Less consistent, though in general agreement with the geographical distribution into North vs. South Slavic, is the use of two other morpho-

---

[36] See J. Zubatý, "Zur Deklination der sog. -i̯ā- und -i̯o-Stämme im Slavischen," *Archiv für slavische Philologie* 15.493–518 (1893) (with an additional note by V. Jagić, *ibid.* 518–524), esp. 503 ff.; criticism of Zubatý's hypothesis can be found, e.g., in N. van Wijk's article "Zur Entwicklung der partizipialen Nominativendung *-onts* in den slavischen Sprachen," *Zeitschrift für slavische Philologie* 1.279–286 (1925) (with ample bibliographical references), suggesting /-onts/ as the common origin of both /-y/ and /-a/. Cf. also A. Furdal, *op. cit.* 62.

[37] Cf. A. Furdal, *op. cit.* 62; see further A. Vaillant, *Grammaire comparée des langues slaves*. 2.*Morphologie*. 1.*Flexion nominale* 31–33 and 121–122 (Lyon and Paris, 1958). Incidentally, the OR ending *-ъmь*, typical of genuine East Slavic (and West Slavic) as opposed to South Slavic (including OCS), can be adduced against the assumption of a very early, possibly even preliterary, change /ъ̥/ > /o/ (and /ь̥/ > /e/) in OR, since forms with this ending cannot, of course, be considered as displaying an artificial spelling influenced by OCS orthographic

logical features: the pronominal dative-locative *tobě/sobě* vs. *tebě/ sebě* opposition, and the prefixes *vy-* vs. *iz-* contrast, the latter to be termed morphological or lexical as it concerns word formation. Thus, while in dialects A, B, C, and D the pronominal forms with /-o-/ seem to have prevailed, we find only the forms with /-e-/ in the South CSl dialects E and F; cf. OR *tobě*, Ukr. *tobi*, P. *tobie*, Cz. *tobě* vs. OCS *tebě*, SCr *tèbi*. However, the *o*-forms do perhaps represent a PSl innovation, having their vocalism transferred from the instr. (*tobojǫ, sobojǫ*). On the other hand, the modern Russian forms *tebe, sebe* have to be explained as being of Church Slavic origin and/or influenced by the forms of the gen.-acc. (originally only gen.) *tebja, sebja* < *tebe, sebe*. It is also possible that in OR parallel *tobě/tebě, sobě/sebě* coexisted from the beginning. In that case the lack of *o*-forms (in the dat.-loc.) in South Slavic, rather than their presence in North Slavic, should be considered an isogloss. In Slovak, *tebe, sebe* presumably originate from Slovene (cf. also instr. *tebou, sebou*).[38]

The distribution of the verbal prefixes *vy-* vs. *iz-* (*izo-*, WSl *z-*, *ze-*, etc., < **jьz-*) in North and South Slavic should perhaps rather be termed a tendency than a neat and consistent dialectal isogloss. Thus we encounter *vy-* also in OCS, although only exceptionally and limited to a few texts: *vygoniti, vygъnati, vyrinǫti, vyvrěšti* (in the *Psalterium Sinaiticum*), *vynesti* (in the *Glagolita Clozianus*). On the other hand, the prefix *iz-* is largely attested also in North Slavic, particularly in OR, where not all instances of its occurrence are necessarily to be explained as Slavonisms. In view of the higher degree of consistency in South Slavic one should consider the absence of the prefix *vy-* (*vi-*), or the near-to-exclusiveness of *iz-*, in dialects E and F, rather than the predominance of *vy-* in dialects A, B, C, and D, if not an isogloss proper then at least a dialectal tendency of CSl[39].

norms. On the other hand, granted that we must assume the existence of reduced vowels (and not of /e/, /o/) in strong position in the earlier stages of OR (eleventh–twelfth centuries), we could still maintain that in weak position the reduced vowels had already disappeared or, at any rate, had become nonphonemic, and that the retention of the jers in this position only served to indicate whether or not the preceding consonantal segment (simple consonant or cluster) was palatalized; see also note 3.

[38] See, e.g., R. Nahtigal, *op. cit.* 51, 54, and 211–212; on the possibility of considering /-ob-/ original or of Balto-Slavic origin, at any rate in the locative, see A. Vaillant, *Grammaire comparée 2.2. Flexion pronominale* 446 and 450–451 (Lyon and Paris, 1958). On Slovak-Slovenian isoglosses (including *tebě, sebě*) see S. B. Bernštejn, *op. cit.* 79–80.

[39] For *iz-* in East Slavic see, e.g., A. Šachmatov-G.Y. Shevelov, *Die kirchenslavischen Elemente in der modernen russischen Literatursprache* 35 (Wiesbaden, 1960), as well as the relevant entries in I. I. Sreznevskij, *Materialy dlja slovarja drevnerusskogo jazyka* 1 (Moscow, 1958) (reprint).

Turning to further derivational and inflectional criteria characteristic of certain areas of the CSl linguistic territory, we have to mention two features encountered in the West Slavic pronoun. One is the substitution of the nom.-acc. sg. *čto* (or other reflexes of *čьto*) by the original gen. sg. *co* < *čьso* (a parallel form of OCS *česo*). Only High Sorbian retains the nom. *što* (but acc. *co*), whereas all the other West Slavic languages have replaced it by *co*. Obviously this is an old dialectal CSl feature, despite the High Sorbian archaism. The second feature is the use of the suffix *-nъ* in the nom. sg. masc. of certain pronouns; cf. P., Cz., Slk., LSorb. *ten*, HSorb. *tón* < **tъ-nъ*; Cz. *jenž*, OCz. *jen*, OP *jen(że)* < **jь-nъ(-že)*. Other Slavic languages use here different means of word formation, such as reduplication (cf. R. *tot* < OR *tъ-tъ*, and with a deictic particle, *ètot* < **ė-tъ-tъ*) or other suffixes, primarily *-jь* (cf. OR *tъi* = *tъjь*, Ukr. *toj*, SCr. *tâj*, etc.).

The difference in the endings of the long adjectival forms as apparent in OCS gen. sg. *-ajego*, dat. sg. *-ujemu* (> *-aago* > *-ago*, *-uumu* > *-umu*) vs. R. *-ogo*, *-omu*, P. *-ego*, *-emu* , SCr *-oga*, *-omu*, etc., cannot be considered isoglottic features of CSl, since the OCS forms here simply seem to represent an older stage of evolution, subsequently adapted to the "hard" pronominal declension (of the type R. *togo*, P. *tego*, etc.) in the entire Slavic linguistic territory; the literary forms of Russian up to 1917, *-ago*, *-jago*, represent of course just an artificial Slavonism, though supported by "akan'e"-pronunciation.

Finally a few words on verbal endings. It seems very doubtful indeed whether any importance at all in terms of classificatory criteria for the dialects of CSl can be attributed to the distribution of the endings *-šę* vs. *-xǫ* in the 3rd p. pl. of the sigmatic aorist. As is well known, it is a characteristic of Bulgarian and the West Slavic languages (in their older stages of evolution when aorist forms still were used) that the original athematic ending *-šę* (< **-x-n̥t*), partly also *-sę* (< *-s-n̥t*), was replaced by the thematic ending *-xǫ* (< **-x-ont*) belonging originally to the corresponding form of the imperfect. Cf., e.g., Bg. *vladjaxa* < *vladěxǫ*, OCz. *řechu* (< **rěxǫ*), *pichu* (< **pixǫ*), OP *wzdachø poczøchø* (OP /ø/ = /ą/, /ą̈-å/). At least for dialect F (Bulgarian) this feature can be proved to be post-CSl, since OCS in the corresponding forms still regularly has *-šę* (*-sę*): *rěšę*, *pišę*, *vъzdašę*, *vladěšę*, *počęsę* (1st p. sg. *počęsъ*). Therefore, while the date of this change can be approximately set for Bulgarian, it is impossible, for lack of evidence, to establish the time of its occurrence in West Slavic. However, here, too, there is hardly any necessity to attribute this feature to the late CSl period. Probably this is just another characteristic of the peripheral areas of the Slavic linguistic territory.[40]

Highly controversial is the origin of the OCS ending *-tъ* in the present

---

[40] See, e.g., R. Nahtigal, *op. cit.* 85.

tense of the third person (singular and plural). As is well known, this is in OCS the regular ending, while *-tъ* occurs here only exceptionally and primarily in the athematic verbs.[41] Other Old Slavic languages have in these forms, apart from zero ending (resulting from the dropping of *-t*), the ending *-tь*; so consistently in OR (cf. also the archaic forms of modern Russian: *jest'*, *sut'*, *vest'*). In OP we encounter *jeść* along with *jest* (= modern P.) and *je*; for Old Slovene compare already in the *Freising Texts* *jest* / *je*; SCr. *jȅ(st)* / *je*, etc. Only Russian (and the same applies partly also to Bulgarian) eventually generalized the ending *-t*. South Russian dialects and Ukrainian, however, have also retained the ending *-t'*. Whether the zero ending (as opposed to *-tь*, *-tъ*) can be considered a CSl dialectal isogloss seems doubtful, since we encounter endingless forms occasionally also in OCS; cf., e.g., forms like *bǫde*, *može*, *leži* in the *Codex Suprasliensis*.[42] Presumably this therefore is basically a post-CSl, though old general feature of Slavic (except by and large for Russian, and, to an extent, Bulgarian; notice, however, that endingless forms are also known from certain North Russian dialects, particularly the Pskov and Novgorod areas). It thus belongs to the features to be excluded from establishing the dialects of CSl (see §0.2. *supra*). The ending *-tъ* of OCS, on the other hand, could possibly represent a CSl isogloss. While *-tь* can be easily identified with IE *-ti*, various explanations have been suggested for the origin of OCS *-tъ*. They can be classified as phonological (A. Meillet's theory, modified and improved by Chr. S. Stang; differently J. Rozwadowski and A. Vaillant), morphological (F. F. Fortunatov, cautiously supported by P. S. Kuznecov, similarly also S. P. Obnorskij; differently N. van Wijk, R. Nahtigal), and combined phonomorphological explanations (I. Lekov, F. Liewehr).[43] For our present purpose it may be sufficient to point out that if OCS *-tъ* can be explained phonologically (and I am personally inclined to adhere to Stang's improved version of Meillet's interpretation), then we do not have to set up this feature as a separate (morphological) isogloss of CSl, since it may be explained in terms of the South Slavic lack of the consonantal correlation of palatalization already discussed (see last paragraph of §1.11. above) as combined

---

[41] See P. Diels, *op. cit.* 227; N. van Wijk, *Geschichte* 213–214.

[42] See further P. Diels, *op. cit.* 227–228; for the pertinent details of the *Codex Suprasliensis* see also A. Margulиés, *Der altkirchenslavische Codex Suprasliensis* 159–201 (*passim*) (Heidelberg, 1927).

[43] For more information on this controversial problem see, in addition to the references given in note 41, especially Chr. S. Stang, *Das slavische und baltische Verbum* 215–219 (Oslo, 1942); P. S. Kuznecov, *Očerki po morfologii praslavjanskogo jazyka* 93–96 (Moscow, 1961); L. A. Bulaxovskij, *Istoričeskij kommentarij k russkomu literaturnomu jazyku*[5] 209–212 (Kiev, 1958), all with further references; R. Nahtigal, *op. cit.* 81–82.

with the fall of the jers in weak auslaut position. Only forms like OCS *postavity-i* (< *postavitъ jь*, Matth. XXIV, 47 in the *Codex Marianus*), *možeto-s* (< *možetъ sь*, J. VI, 52, *ibid.*), *ležito-sь* (< *ležitъ sь*, Lc. II, 34 in the *Codex Assemanianus*), *sъměrito-i* (< *sъměritъ jь*, *Psalterium Sinaiticum*, 10b, 1–2), etc., instead of **postaviti-i*, **možete-sь*, etc., seem to present here certain, though not necessarily insurmountable, difficulties. If on the other hand a strictly morphological explanation should actually account for the *-tъ* vs. *-tь* distinction (though hardly Fortunatov's or Obnorskij's, considering *-tъ*, or even *-tь*, to be of pronominal origin), we would most probably have to reckon with a pre-Slavic, and presumably IE, differentiation of the verbal ending of the third person, which only subsequently was to be inherited by PSl and CSl. In the light of the aforesaid, I shall in the further discussion of CSl dialects refrain from taking the OCS ending *-tъ* into consideration.

Equally questionable as a criterion for the classification of CSl dialects are, finally, the different endings of the first person plural in Slavic: *-mъ*, *-mo*, *-me*, *-my*. The predominant form of OCS is *-mъ*. Also in OR, forms in *-mъ* (subsequently > *-m*) prevail, although all the other endings can be found here, too. Occasional OCS forms in *-my* can be explained either in terms of the so-called tense jer in front of a following /j-/ : *-my i* = *-mъ jь*, or, in certain parts of the *Codex Suprasliensis*, as owing to extension by means of the pronoun *my*.[44] The ending *-my* is also found in OR, in Polish, High Sorbian, and partly Low Sorbian (here along with *-me*). At least the West Slavic forms must most probably be explained as influenced by the personal pronoun (of the first person plural). It is certainly of post-CSl origin and therefore need not be considered here any further. In late OR texts—starting from the fourteenth century, and particularly in Muscovite records—we encounter, in addition to the endings just mentioned, also *-mja*, viz., in *jesmja*. If considered an archaism (< **jesmę*), this form could easily be identified with Gk. ἐσμέν. However, it may be safer to interpret OR *jesmja* as due to Bulgarian influence (Bg. *esme*), reinforced during the period of the so-called Second South Slavic Influence in Russia.[45] Of the remaining endings *-mo* and *-me*, we find *-mo* in Ukrainian, Slovak dialects, Slovenian, Serbocroatian, and North Macedonian, as well as in West Bulgarian dialects. Its presence in parts of Macedonian and Bulgarian is obviously due to Serbocroatian, in a part of Slovak to Slovene influence.[46] Still, it seems difficult to assume here a special, strictly genetically conditioned central CSl isogloss

[44] See P. Diels, *op. cit.* 228; for details of the *Codex Suprasliensis* see A. Margulies, *op. cit.* 187, 191–192.

[45] Cf. L. A. Bulaxovskij, *op. cit.* 101–102.

[46] Cf. P. Ivić, *op. cit.* 32; S. B. Bernštejn, *op. cit.* 79.

embracing a southern section of dialect A (as reflected in certain OR texts, and in Ukrainian) and dialect E (as reflected in Slovene and Serbocroatian). Besides, the earliest record of Slovene, i.e., the *Freising Texts*, do not have *-mo*, but *-m* (< *-mъ*): *nesem, pijem, klańam se, modlim se, jesm*. Cf., however, also, the possibility of a different interpretation of a feature like *-mo* below, in §2.3. The ending *-me* is found in Macedonian (generalized), Bulgarian (along with *-m* in the present tense, but used exclusively in the aorist and imperfect), Czech (along with *-m*; cf. OCz. aorist *vedechme* vs. present *vedem*), Slovak, and Low Sorbian (along with *-my*; see above). Possibly Slavic *-me* reflects an IE secondary ending (**-mē/mō, *-me/-mo*, cf. Skt. *ábharāma*, Lith. *nẽšame* < **-mḗ*), and was originally restricted to the simple past tenses, aorist and imperfect. At any rate, both *-mъ* (> *-m*), *-mo*, and *-me* can be traced back to various IE origins, although it also seems conceivable to derive all three of them from a common IE origin (**-mos/-mes*, but hardly **-mon/-men*), explaining the different endings in Slavic by PSl rules governing the auslaut evolution. Nevertheless, it seems virtually impossible—and I agree in this respect with L. A. Bulaxovskij rather than with S. B. Bernštejn—to use the present (or even historically attested Old Slavic) distribution of the endings *-m(ъ)*, *-mo*, *-me* (*-my*, *-mja*) throughout the Slavic linguistic territory as a diagnostic classificatory criterion for CSl dialects.[47]

To sum up, of all the morphological or phonomorphological features discussed in this section only three, viz., -(*j*)*ě*$_3$ vs. -(*j*)*ę*, *-a* vs. *-y*, and *-ъmъ* vs. *-omъ*, seem actually to yield sufficient, unambiguous evidence with regard to the grouping of CSl dialects. Some other criteria (*tobě* vs. *tebě*, *vy-* vs. *iz-*) display basically the same geographical distribution, though with less consistency. As they do not add essentially to our understanding, they will be ignored in the following. A few additional criteria such as *co* (< *čьso*) vs. *čto, ščo, što, šta*, etc. (< *čьto*), or the pronominal derivation by means of a *-n* suffix (*ten, jen*, etc.), do not, to be sure, provoke any serious doubts; but they are of less overall importance, particularly since they also coincide geographically with other more essential West Slavic isoglosses. They, too, will therefore be omitted in the subsequent discussion. Still other morphological features, important as they may be, are, as has been shown, either of no relevance to the particular problem here discussed (e.g., *-ajego* > *-ago* vs. *-ogo*, etc.; *-šę* vs. *-xǫ*), or are too contro-

---

[47] In addition to literature just quoted, see also Chr. S. Stang, *op. cit.* 222–223; R. Nahtigal, *op. cit.* 82–83; S. B. Bernštejn, *op. cit.* 73; P. S. Kuznecov, *Očerki* 98–99; L. A. Bulaxovx'kyj, *Pytannja poxoždennja ukrajins'koji movy* 75 and 200–201 (Kiev, 1956). For details on PSl auslaut evolution, see further T. Milewski's article mentioned in note 51.

versial to serve as a basis for further deliberations (*-tь* vs. *-tъ*, *-mъ* vs. *-mo* vs. *-me*). Thus we end up with only the three most important morphological (and phonomorphological) features utilized as classificatory criteria also by Furdal.[48]

2. *Interpretation: Grouping and chronology*

2.1. *Ultimate grouping of CSl dialects*

Such is then in brief, apart from lexical data that have been omitted here for reasons suggested above (see §0.3.), the evidence available for discussing problems of grouping and chronology of the dialects of CSl. I have so far abstained from any more general comments on questions of internal grouping and relative chronology of the dialectal characteristics of CSl, making only a few occasional remarks pertaining to problems such as the order of succession of changes like /Tr̥'T/ > /Tr̥T/ and /Tr̥T/ > /TArT/ in dialects B and C, or the striking resemblance of certain developments in dialect B (or even all of the West CSl dialects, B, C, and D) and dialect F: /pl'/ > /p'/, etc., /ě/ > /ä/ (> /a/), retention of nasal vowels, *-xǫ* replacing *-šę*. Basically, however, I have just listed the more important isoglosses of CSl, adding only, wherever it seemed apt, a few elucidative comments.

Already from the linguistic, primarily phonological, evidence presented in the preceding sections we can draw certain definitive conclusions as to the ultimate arrangement of CSl dialects. By simply drawing the isophonic and isomorphic lines indicated above on a schematic diagram (and leaving out the less pertinent as well as the more controversial isomorphs) we can satisfy ourselves that the dialectal CSl groups A, B, C, D, E, and F, which at the outset were assumed a posteriori, actually correspond fairly well to a grouping that can be established on the basis of the ascertained isoglosses. From the incomplete evidence of lexical data currently available it seems hardly probable that their inclusion would substantially change the general picture at which we have arrived. (See diagram on next page.)

Key to symbols used in diagram.

The areas of the various CSl dialects are schematically indicated by dotted circles. Solid lines and Arabic numerals represent boundaries of phonological isoglosses (isophones); additional letters denote subtypes. The sign)(is used to symbolize merging of originally distinct sounds and clusters or their reflexes. Broken lines and Roman numerals represent boundaries of the most important phonomorphological and morphological isoglosses (isomorphs).

---

[48] See A. Furdal, *op. cit.* 59–62, and on diagram (between 96 and 97).

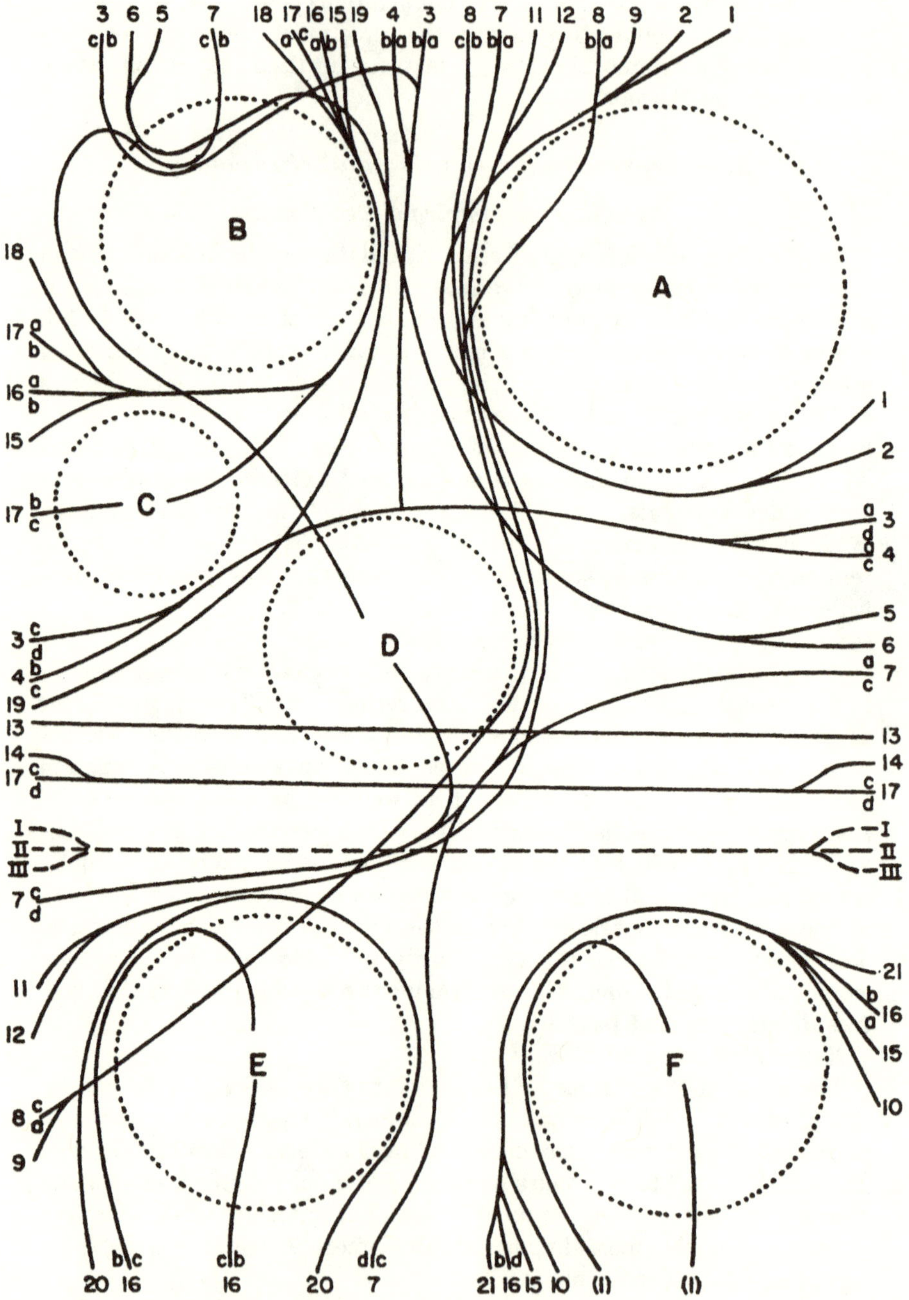
A
B
C
D
E
F

1) labilialization of /ъ̥/ (> /o/)
2) /(j)e-/, /ju-/ > /o-/, /u-/
3) /TorT/ > a) /ToroT/
b) /TarT/ ~ /TroT/
c) /TroT/
d) /TraT/
4) /Tr̥T/ > a) /Tъ̥rT/ (> /TorT/ ~ /ToroT/)
b) /TÅrT/
c) /Tr̥T/
5) /Tl̥'T/ > /Tl̥T/ (> /Tъ̥lT/ > /TolT/ ~ /ToloT/)
6) /TelT/ > /TolT/ (> /ToloT/; /T'elT/ > /T'ölT/? > /T'eloT/
7) /tj/ (/kt'/), /dj/ > a) /č/, /ž/
b) /c/, /ʒ/
c) /c/, /z/
d) /ć/, /ʒ́/
e) /št/, /žd/
8) /tl/, /dl/ > a) /l/
b) /kl/, /gl/
c) /tl/, /dl/
9) /sk'$_2$/ > /šč/ (> /št/) vs. /sc/ (> /st/)
10) (/pj/, etc. >) /pl'/ > /p'/ vs. /pl'/
11) /kv'/ (or /kv'$_2$/ only?), etc. > /cv/ vs. /kv/
12) /x'$_2$/ > /s'/ vs. /š/
13) /ŏrT-/, etc. > /roT-/ vs. /raT-/
14) /TE/ > /T'E/ vs. /TE/, i.e., presence vs. lack of consonantal correlation of palatalization
15) /ě/ > /ä/ (> /'a/) vs. /ê/ (> /je/, /ije/ > /i/)
16) /ǫ/ (= /ON/) > a) /ǫ/ > /ą̊/ (> /ą/)
b) /u/
c) /o/
d) /ą̊/ > /ă/, /a/
17) /ę/ (= /EN/) > a) /ę/ > /ą̈/ (> /'ą/)
b) /ě/
c) /ä/ (> /'a/)
d) /e/
18) /ěT/, /ęT/ (or /ą̈T/) > /aT/, /ǫT/ (or /ą̊T/)
19) /r̥'/ > /r̥T/ (> /ArT/, see 4b *supra*)
20) /ь̥/)(/ъ̥/
21) /tj/ (/kt'/), etc.,)(/stj/, /skj/, /sk'$_1$/, etc.

I) **-jens* (**-jēns*) > *-ě*$_3$ vs. *-ę*
II) **-on*(*t*)*s* (**-ō* : **-ōn* ?) > *-a* vs. *-y*
III) *-ъmъ* vs. *-omъ*

This diagram is with slight modifications adapted from the one elaborated by Furdal. Of course, we can now also substitute East Slavic (or "Russian" in a broad sense), Lekhitic, Sorbian (Lusatian), Czechoslovak, Sloveno-Serbocroatian, and Macedo-Bulgarian, as we have already done occasionally, for the respective letter symbols. It is worth pointing out on examination of this diagram that no major CSl isogloss cuts through either the territory of Sloveno-Serbocroatian (which would divide this dialect into two distinct subdialects, Proto-Slovene and Proto-Serbocroatian respectively), or that of Macedo-Bulgarian (which would similarly separate Proto-Macedonian from Proto-Bulgarian; these terms are used here, of course, as referring to ancient Slavic idioms). Hence there are certain difficulties in classifying a dialect like Kajkavian as Slovenian or Serbocroatian (although it seems clear that the basis of Kajkavian is Slovene rather than Serbocroatian), and in assigning certain East Macedonian or West Bulgarian idioms to one of the two languages involved. The fact that some of the isoglosses assumed as characteristic of dialect F do not cover all of modern Macedonian must be explained in terms of the strong influence exerted upon the only recently created standard literary language of Macedonia as well as on many Macedonian dialects by the adjacent Serbocroatian. In fact, a bundle of isoglosses fans out over the Macedonian linguistic territory.[49] One important phonological feature separating Macedonian from Bulgarian, viz., CSl /ъ̣/ > Mac. /o/, Bg. /ǎ/ (= /ə/, graphically ъ) seems to be essentially post-CSl, although its beginnings can be traced in OCS texts; see line number 1 on diagram. Moreover, this double reflex must be seen as part of the common Macedo-Bulgarian maintenance of the CSl front vs. back distinction: /ь̣/ vs. /ъ̣/ > Mac. /e/ vs. /o/, Bg. /e/ vs. /ǎ/; see also above (first paragraph of §1.11.). The occasional Bulgarian reflex /ǎ/ also for CSl /ь̣/ (as in *pǎn* < *pьnь*) must be seen in the light of the South Slavic lack of general (correlational) palatalization of consonants, but requires an additional explanation. Turning to dialect E, one could, to be sure, perhaps claim the double reflex of CSl /ǫ/, Slovenian (and Kajkavian) /o/ as opposed to Serbocroatian /u/, to constitute a late CSl isophonic boundary within this dialect; see line number 16b and c on diagram. However, the Slovenian-Kajkavian reflex /o/ does not form part of a larger, overall CSl continuum, since it is surrounded in the north (Slovak) as well as in the South (Serbocroatian) by /u/. We have to do here, in other words, with an "insular" feature within one CSl isogloss area. Both dialect C (Sorbian) and dialect D (Czechoslovak) are, on the other hand, each intersected by at least one important isophonic line of CSl: Sorbian by line number

[49] See P. Ivić, *op. cit.* 41–44; F. Sławski, *Zarys* 117–119.

17b and c of our diagram, i.e., /ę/ > /ě/ vs. /ä/ (> /'a/), forming part of an overall CSl continuum, and Czechoslovak by line number 7b and c, i.e., /dj/ > /ʒ/ vs. /z/, which at the same time separates most of dialect B from dialect C and therefore cannot be considered an "insular" feature in the same way as the reflex /o/ < /ǫ/ in Slovenian-Kajkavian. These isophonic lines already point to the subsequent partition into the subdialects (and eventually separate languages) of Low vs. High Sorbian (Lusatian), and Slovak vs. Czech. For reasons why Sorbian should perhaps not be set up as a separate, full-fledged CSl dialect group, see the following section.

2.2. *Earlier grouping of CSl dialects. Relative chronology*

What remains to be done, then, is to shed more light on the genesis of this ultimate grouping of CSl dialects, and to contrast this evidence with the traditional division of the Slavic languages into three main branches, an eastern, a western, and a southern.

According to T. Lehr-Spławiński (cf. writings mentioned in §0.4.), it is possible to distinguish at least four successive phases in the process of dialectal differentiation of CSl. The first is said to have implied an initial division into a western and an eastern branch of CSl. It is during this phase (or rather at its beginning) that the so-called second palatalization of velars took place, and this first dialectal split supposedly manifested itself in such instances of a double sound reflection as /kv'$_2$/, etc., > /cv/ vs. /kv/, etc., /x'$_2$/ > /s'/ vs. /š/, /sk'$_2$/ > /sc/ vs. /šč/—all being related to the second palatalization, and—without such relation—/tl/, /dl/ > /l/ vs. /tl/, /dl/. The second dialectal phase in the development of CSl embraced, in Lehr-Spławiński's opinion, certain phenomena to be seen in the light of the migrations of a part of the Slavs southward across the Carpathian Mountains, viz., /ŏrT-/, /ŏlT-/ > /roT-/, /loT-/ vs. /raT-/, /laT-/, as well as the double phonomorphological reflections **-jens* (**-jēns*) > -(*j*)ě$_3$ vs. -(*j*)ę, and **-on*(*t*)*s* > *-a* vs. *-y* (if one is not to reckon with an old IE opposition **-ō* vs. **-ōn*, as suggested by J. Zubatý; cf. above §1.2. with note 36). A third phase or stage of dialectal evolution of CSl included, according to the Polish scholar, the sound changes that unite the dialects of the ancestors of the Czechs and the Slovaks with those of the South Slavs and at the same time separate the rest of the West CSl dialects (i.e., our dialects B and C) from the East Slavs (dialect A). These sound changes concern primarily the transformation of sound combinations containing a liquid in word-medial position, i.e., the groups /TorT/, etc., and /Tr̥T/, etc. The fourth and last of these successive phases should then have implied a renewed approximation or closing of the gap between the ancestors of the Czechs and Slovaks and their northern neighbors, the speakers of Sorbian and Lekhitic dialects. In addition, during this very period a first loosening of the South CSl dialects is supposed to have occurred, resulting in a splitting into a western and an eastern group (our dialects E and F). The main phonological characteristic of this last period of dialectal differentiation within CSl is said to have been the varying treatment of the PSl clusters /tj/ (/kt'/), /dj/ or rather of their late CSl reflexes (presumably /t'/, /d'/).[50]

On at least one point, another Polish linguist, T. Milewski, has suggested a different chronology of the linguistic data of CSl dialectology. According to Milewski, the divergences of the CSl development in word-final position mentioned above (*-ě̆*$_3$ vs. *-ę*, *-a* vs. *-y*) must be referred to an earlier period of CSl dialectal differentiation, preceding even the first of Lehr-Spławiński's phases, that of the first West-East division.[51] It seems doubtful, however, whether such an assumption can be actually supported by indisputable arguments.

In his recent book on the disintegration of CSl, A. Furdal has subjected Lehr-Spławiński's chronological concept to a far-reaching critical scrutiny. While agreeing with the assumption of the two first stages of dialectal evolution suggested by Lehr-Spławiński, Furdal takes up at the outset of his monograph, and from a standpoint of principle, the question of whether it can seem justified to assume also a third and fourth phase in the development of CSl dialects. In this context he points out that the hypothesis of a phase (number 3) of rapprochement between the CSl dialect labeled D in this paper (from which subsequently Czech and Slovak developed) and the southern CSl dialects (E and F) is in fact based on only one single phonological innovation that these dialect groups as a whole share, viz., the /TorT/ > /TraT/, etc., change. The other phonological feature separating Czechoslovak from the rest of the West Slavic languages as well as from East Slavic (or more exactly, dialect D from dialects B, C, and A), and connecting it with South Slavic (dialects E and F), viz., the treatment of CSl /Tr̥T/, etc., did as a matter of fact not imply a common innovation of these dialects (D, E, F), as was true with /TorT/ > /TraT/, and so on, but only a retention of the CSl (= late PSl) situation: /Tr̥T/ = /Tr̥T/, and so forth. The rest of the CSl dialects showed here a novel development; dialect A: > /TъrT/ > /TorT/ ~ /ToroT/, dialects B and C: > /TArT/. But if, consequently, there is no real necessity to assume such an intervening

[50] See in particular T. Lehr-Spławiński, "Problem," *BPTJ* 14.114–115 (1955), and the account given by A. Furdal, *op. cit.* 9–10.

[51] See T. Milewski's article "Rozwój fonetyczny wygłosu prasłowiańskiego," *Slavia* 11.1–32 and 225–264 (1932).

third phase, there is no need either for setting up a separate fourth phase in the dialectal development of CSl. Thus the many features linking the West Slavic languages (and the underlying West CSl dialects) can, in Furdal's opinion, be referred to only two basic stages of CSl linguistic evolution. To untangle and elucidate the intertwining phonological details, in time as well as in space, of these two main dialectal phases of CSl, is the primary endeavor of Furdal's book. He has in this respect, as far as I can judge, been quite successful. We will return to his general conclusions.[52]

A basically different theory of the earlier grouping of CSl dialects has lately been advanced by the Soviet linguist S. B. Bernštejn.[53] He, too, starts out from an initial west-east dichotomy, extending geographically from the Oder-Neisse (Odra-Nysa) rivers in the West to and beyond a line formed by the rivers Dnieper and Desna in the East. The border line between the original west and east CSl dialects was supposedly formed by the (western) Bug and its northward prolongation (where the river turns westward). The main characteristics of these earliest dialectal groups were, according to Bernštejn, the following: (1) /t̄'/, /d̄'/ (< /tj/, /kt'/; /dj/); the alleged long quality of these consonants (!) was given up by means of developing off-glides, hissing in the western, hushing in the eastern dialect.[54] (2) /$p^{l'}$/, /$b^{l'}$/, /$m^{l'}$/; the lateral off-glide developed into an independent sound ("epenthetic" /l'/) only in intramorphemic position in the western dialect, while this development occurred in all positions (thus including morpheme boundary) in the eastern dialect.[55] (3) /tl/, /dl/; retention of the dental stop in the western dialect vs. simplification of the cluster (> /l/) in the eastern dialect. (4) twofold treatment of /x'_2/, > /š/ in the west, > /s'/ in the east. (5) /kv'_2/, /gv'_2/; these clusters were retained in the west, but shifted > /c'v/, /ʒ'v/ (> /z'v/) in the east. As can be seen already from this brief enumeration, only processes (3), (4), and (5) are such as were considered to fall into the earliest phase of CSl dialectal differentiation by Lehr-Spławiński (cf. *supra*). Even more important, though, is the fact that Bernštejn considers the western dialect the basis of the West Slavic languages, and the eastern dialect the basis of both the East and South Slavic languages. In this respect he follows an established tradition in Slavic linguistics, advocated by,

---

[52] See especially A. Furdal, *op. cit.* 10 and 94–99.

[53] See for the following S. B. Bernštejn, *op. cit.* 66–82.

[54] See *ibid.*, 228–229; see also F. P. Filin, *op. cit.* 195.

[55] For details, particularly for the allegedly inconsistent treatment within a branch of the eastern dialect (accounting for the lack of "epenthetic" /l'/ in Macedo-Bulgarian), see S. B. Bernštejn, *op. cit.* 213.

among others, A. A. Šaxmatov; however, this concept of an evolutionary stage of Common East-South Slavic does oversimplify complex matters and must, as a whole, be considered erroneous.

These main CSl dialects were, in Bernštejn's opinion, further subdivided. Thus, the western dialect consisted of two subdialects, a northern or Proto-Lekhitic, and a southern or Proto-Czechoslovak. It is therefore unfounded, according to him, to assume a homogeneous Common West Slavic language. The emergence of a West Slavic group was accompanied by its simultaneous breaking up into a northern and a southern subgroup. Characteristic of the northern subdialect was presumably the development /ě$_1$/, /ě$_2$/ > /ä/, the retention of /ʒ'/, and the pronunciation of /ǫ/ as /å̜/. The southern subdialect, on the other hand, was supposedly characterized by the change /ě$_1$/, /ě$_2$/ > /ê/, the simplification /ʒ'/ > /z'/ (cf. Slovak, however!), and the pronunciation of the back nasal vowel as /ų/. Although I cannot agree on all the points made by Bernštejn, it must be conceded that his interpretation of the West Slavic data just adduced is not without certain merits. First of all, I find myself in agreement with his assumption that there probably never existed one homogeneous Common West Slavic language. In addition, his refraining from singling out Proto-Sorbian as a separate CSl dialect may possibly be justified. After all, the Sorbian languages form in many respects an intermediate link between Lekhitic and Czechoslovak. In other words, they seem to be basically transitional idioms between the two main groups within West Slavic, with Low Sorbian adhering in some (but not all) respects more closely to Polish (Lekhitic), and High Sorbian to Czech;[56] see also above (§0.2. and, on *-my* : *-me*, §1.2.).

The East CSl dialect was, according to Bernštejn, characterized by even more important and more profound differences than the western one. Here he distinguishes between what he calls a central and an eastern subdialect. This latter, fairly homogeneous in itself, is said to have formed the basis of the subsequent East Slavic languages. Only in its southwestern part did certain features appear (like, e.g., the stressed ending *-mo* in the 1st p. pl. of the present) that were otherwise foreign to this subdialect. The central dialect, on the other hand, was supposedly very heterogeneous. It can be subdivided into at least two further subidioms, a northern one, remaining for a long time in close connection with the Lekhitic dialects and being the foundation of the subsequent Macedo-Bulgarian group, and a southern one, ultimately giving rise to Slovenian and Serbocroatian. Only subsequently, as a result of convergent developments, did new isogloss areas emerge, such as the Slovene-Slovak

[56] See, for further details, Z. Stieber, "Wzajemne stosunki," *BPTJ* 14.85–89 (1955).

(characterized by many agreements) or the more loosely connected Ukrainian-Serbocroatian area (characterized by only a few conformities).

Such is, then, in brief and omitting details and illustrative examples, Bernštejn's general conception of the dialects of CSl. While not lacking, to be sure, certain merits and original ideas, it seems to be as a whole less realistic than that elaborated by Furdal. Let us now, therefore, turn to Furdal's basic assumptions.

Summing up the results of his observations and considerations, Furdal points out that only two main chronological phases of CSl dialectal differentiation can be ascertained.[57] The first, identical with that suggested by Lehr-Spławiński and implying an early separation between east and west, is characterized by phonological isoglosses connected with the second palatalization of velars and the simplification of the clusters /tl/, /dl/. Dialectal innovations occurred during this period which lasted to somewhere around the middle of the first millennium of our era. The second phase is much more complex. Relative chronology does not suggest any establishment of clear-cut further subphases of dialectal development, since phenomena of linguistic change are here intermingled with dialectal features of different spatial distribution. On the basis of data of external history alone we can distinguish in this period two successive subphases, viz., one of cohesion and continuity of the CSl linguistic territory, and a second one, beginning circa A.D. 900, when this continuity was interrupted by the Magyar invasion of Pannonia, separating the South Slavs from the rest of the Slavs. The second evolutionary phase of CSl dialectal differentiation is characterized both by general or nearly general CSl innovations, such as the emergence of syllabic liquids, the positional distribution of strong and weak jers, and a widespread tendency to give up nasality in the nasal vowels, and by locally more or less restricted changes. Only in the ninth century did such geographically very limited developments take place as /ěT/ > /aT/ in Lekhitic, the merging of the reflexes of /tj/ (/kt'/) and /stj/, /skj/, /sk'$_1$/ in Macedo–Bulgarian, and so forth. During the later part of the second CSl dialectal period, when the northern Slavs were already separated from the South Slavs, innovations contrasting all of North Slavic with South Slavic increased. These innovations could be either independent (in a dialectological sense), as, e.g., the shortening /raT-/ (< /ŏrT-/) > /roT/ (or rather /rå̄T-/ > /råT-/) and the replacement of *-omъ* by *-ъmъ*, or they might in their turn depend on locally more restricted developments, such as /ę/ > /'a/, this change supposedly being one of the preconditions for the genesis of the consonantal correlation of palatalization as well as for the ending in -ě$_3$. Geographically the second period of CSl dialectological differentiation is marked not only

[57] See for the following A. Furdal, *op. cit.* 94–95.

by the separation of the South Slavs from the rest of the Slavs, as well as a deepening of the detachment between West and East Slavs, but also by the dissociation of the South Slavs into an eastern and a western branch, and of the West Slavs into a Lekhito-Sorbian group (subsequently subdivided into Lekhitic and Sorbian, with Lekhitic ending up divided into a northwestern and a southeastern branch) and a Czechoslovak group.

Although certain objections can also be raised against Furdal's interpretation of some of his data, such as his abortive attempt to establish a connection between a change like the non-Lekhitic /ę/ > /ä/ > /'a/ and general North Slavic (and hence also Lekhitic!) phenomena such as the correlational palatalization of consonants and the ending -$ě_3$, it is in my opinion by and large sounder and more realistic than the partly very speculative picture sketched by Bernštejn.

2.3. *Grouping of CSl dialects and tripartition of Slavic languages*

It should be clear from the preceding that the divergence from CSl into the individual Slavic languages, traditionally divided into the three branches of East, West, and South Slavic, cannot be conceived of as a uniform, rectilinear development from the common parental language through certain clear-cut intermediate stages of Common East Slavic, Common West Slavic, and Common South Slavic down to the separate languages. In reality the evolutionary process was far more complex. Of intermediate stages, only the existence of a Common East Slavic language—in a preliterary ("Proto-Russian") and a literary (OR) phase—can of course be assumed, since it can be considered as firmly established (with minor disagreements only as to certain details) that the beginning divergence into the separate East Slavic languages (Great Russian, Ukrainian, Byelorussian) is a matter of the high Middle Ages.[58]

[58] This does not mean, however, that OR could not have had certain dialectal variations, including such features as subsequently became characteristics of, for instance, Ukrainian and/or Byelorussian as opposed to Great Russian. One such peculiarity was the development /g/ > /γ/ (> /h/), typical of Ukrainian and Byelorussian (as well as of many South Great Russian dialects), but reaching back into the remote past on East Slavic soil, as possibly shown by such writings as the already quoted *πραχ* = OCS *pragъ* (= /praγ/) for ESl *porogъ* in Constantine VII Porphyrogennetos (mid-tenth century), while, as mentioned, the corresponding development in West Slavic was of a more recent date; see §0.2. and note 3. Another phenomenon displaying certain fluctuations in OR, which were gradually stabilized differently, in Great Russian on the one hand and Ukrainian and Byelorussian on the other, is the treatment of /ь̂/, /ъ̂/, i.e., of "tense" jers in strong position; cf. R. *-oj* in the modern standard language only when stressed, otherwise substituted by Church Slavic *-yi* <-*ъ̂jь̯* (though supported also by the *akan'e*-pronunciation of unstressed *-oj* as /-əj/) vs. Ukr. *-yj*; or R. *bréju*, *króju*, *móju* vs. Ukr. *bryju*, *kryju*, *myju* < *brъ̂jǫ*, *krъ̂jǫ*, *mъ̂jǫ*, OCS also *brijǫ*, *kryjǫ*, *myjǫ* (with strong jer because of its position in first stressed syllable); R. *bej*, *pej* vs. Ukr.

On the other hand, it remains unproven, and in fact highly doubtful in view of the complexity of the dialectal differentiation of CSl suggested above, that there ever existed anything like a Common West Slavic language. As for South Slavic, it is perhaps possible to assume that there did actually exist for a limited period of time a common parental language from which the current South Slavic languages subsequently emerged. A feature such as the nondevelopment of a phonemic consonantal correlation of palatalization, as well as isoglosses such as *-ę* (vs. *-ě*$_3$), *-y* (vs. *-a*), and *-omъ* (vs. *-ъmъ*) seem indeed to suggest the existence of a Common South Slavic language. On the other hand, I see no real reason to assume that there ever existed a Common East-South Slavic language, as once advocated by A. A. Šaxmatov, more recently by T. Lehr-Spławiński, and only lately by S. B. Bernštejn. The conformity of certain isophones connecting East and South Slavic (e.g., /l/ < /tl/, /dl/; /cv/ < /kv'$_2$/, etc.; /s'/ < /x'$_2$/) must be explained as part of a general complex system of intersecting isogloss areas. This negative assumption has recently also been corroborated by the evidence of lexical data studied by F. P. Filin.[59] Similarly, it seems impossible to reckon with a particular phase in the course of CSl dialectal differentiation during which the forefathers of the South Slavs should have formed a close linguistic unity with the ancestors of the Czechs and the Slovaks. Again, the isophones of Czechoslovak and South Slavic, above all /TraT/ (< /TorT/), etc., and /Tr̥T/ (< /Tь/ъrT/), etc., can only be interpreted as a subsystem of concordances integrated into a superior system which also included divergent dialectal features. As part of such an overall system we can also consider the agreements that can be ascertained between such distant languages as Polish (or all of Lekhitic) and Bulgarian (or Macedo-Bulgarian), e.g., /ě/ > /ä/ (> /'a/); original retention and delabialization of /ǫ/ > /ą̊/ (> /ą/; /ă/, /a/); or, embracing all of West Slavic and Macedo-Bulgarian, the loss of postlabial ("epenthetic") /l'/ at the morpheme boundary. To try to explain such isoglosses in terms of an earlier period of close, geographically conditioned affinities between the predecessors of these languages, as still suggested by S. B. Bernštejn, seems less realistic than to see in them developments (innovations) or the preservation of archaic features (retentions) characteristic of the peripheral zones of the CSl linguistic territory.

In this context it should, perhaps, be made clear that, in a way, all

byj, *pyj* < *bъ̥̂jь̂*, *pъ̥̂jь̂* (imperatives of *biti*, *piti*), etc. For some difficulties and controversial details with regard to the explanation of some of the forms just quoted see L. A. Bulaxovskij, *Istoričeskij kommentarij* 92–93 (especially also the alternative explanation mentioned in note 2).

[59] See F. P. Filin, *op. cit.* 215–216, and also his general conclusions on 219–220, justly criticizing the East-South Slavic hypothesis.

spatial classification of dialects based exclusively on the geographical-genetic notion of adjacency remains incomplete and is therefore misleading. As a matter of fact, the very concept of isoglosses and isogloss zones was introduced primarily just to overcome this often oversimplified, mechanistic approach. In addition to traditional geographical classifications of dialects, other spatial criteria, such as peripheralness vs. centralness of a dialectally varied linguistic territory, with its centrifugal or centripetal tendencies of (joint or parallel) development, must be taken into account. From this standpoint, which should, again, not be the only one to be considered, pre-Polish (or Lekhitic) and pre-Bulgarian (or Macedo-Bulgarian) would have to be singled out as displaying certain common features characteristic of peripheral CSl dialects. Similarly, a feature like the ending *-mo* of the 1st p. pl. could be considered a central CSl dialectism, even though its existence in, say, Ukrainian and Serbocroatian presumably should not be explained in genetic terms.[60]

In this context it is worth mentioning, incidentally, that although there obviously does exist a limited number of West-South Slavic (or even special West Slavic–Macedo-Bulgarian) isolexes, extending partly also into Baltic, we know of hardly any general West-South Slavic isophones.[61] The only exception would possibly be the reflex /ěn/ < /enn/. In West Slavic this reflex seems to be the rule, while South Slavic here shows a coexistence of /ěn/ and /ęn/. In East Slavic /ęn/ (> /'an/) seems to have been the only corresponding reflex; cf., e.g., OCS *ruměnъ*, P. *rumiany* (< *ruměn-*) vs. R. *rumjanyj* (< **rumęn-*); OCS *kaměnъ*, SCr *kȁmenī* (< **kamęn-*) vs. OR *kamjanъ* (< **kamęn-*, along with *kamenьnъ*); OCS *poměnǫti* and *pomęnǫti*, SCr *poménuti* (< **pomęn-*) vs. R. *pomjanut'* (< **pomęn-*); OCS *pěnęʒь*, *pěnęzь*, P. *pieniądz* < Gmc. *penning(az)*.[62]

[60] On the structure of dialectal differentiation see, e.g., E. Stankiewicz, "On Discreteness and Continuity in Structural Dialectology," *Word* 13.44–59, esp. 57–59 (1957) (applied to Slavic linguistic material); and in particular P. Ivić, "Osnovni aspekti strukture dijalekatske diferencijacije," *Makedonski jazik* 11–12.81–103 (1960/61); P. Ivić, "On the Structure of Dialectal Differentiation," *Word* 18.33–53 (1962), with ample further references; P. Ivić, "Structure and typology of dialectal differentiation," *Proceedings* 115–129; and P. Ivić, "Importance des caractéristiques structurales pour la description et la classification des dialectes," *Orbis* 12.117–131 (1963). For additional references see now also T. M. Sudnik, S. M. Šur, "O primenenii nekotoryx novyx metodov v rabotax po obščej i slavjanskoj dialektologii," *Voprosy jazykoznanija* 1963:4.115–119.

[61] For the lexical data see S. B. Bernštejn, *op. cit.* 73–75, and F. P. Filin, *op. cit.* 216–218 (with criticism of Bernštejn's view).

[62] For further details see, e.g., A. Vaillant, *Grammaire comparée*. 1. *Phonétique* 146–148; A. Meillet, *Etudes sur l'étymologie et le vocabulaire du vieux slave*² 2.434–438 (Paris, 1961); L. A. Bulaxovsk'kyj, *Pytannja* 129–130, quoting also the etymologically controversial R. *prjamo*, OCS *prěmo*, Cz. *přímo* (< *prěmo*) and cognates; cf. also M. Vasmer, *Russ. etym. Wb.* 2.455, s.v. (1955).

The complexity and stratification of the internal connections within the dialects of CSl in relation to the current generally accepted tripartition of the Slavic languages should, however, not be interpreted in such a sense as to suggest the substitution of some other, more adequate division to this firmly established one. There is, I believe, no need for such a substitution. For, on the contrary, it can be maintained that the present tripartition actually best corresponds to the statistical facts of CSl isogloss bundles. That is to say, more isoglosses connect each of the East, West, and South Slavic languages within their respective groups than do isoglosses embracing individual members of more than one of these main branches of the Slavic languages. It would be possible, in other words, to list more agreements between, for example, Russian and Ukrainian than between Ukrainian on the one hand and Polish or Czech on the other, or to list a greater number of concordances connecting Czech and Polish, for instance, than, let us say, Czech and Slovene, and so forth.

To sum up, it can be said that the traditional tripartition into East, West, and South Slavic languages respectively remains valid in the light of CSl dialectology. However, such a classification should be considered primarily as based on statistically derived synchronic data, since the underlying, many-layered diachronic phenomena do not represent any consistent, rectilinear evolution, as the adherents of the *Stammbaum* theory would have been inclined to believe.[63]

(Participants in the discussion following the conference presentation of the first version of this paper: Senn, Watkins, Beliakoff, Lehmann, Hamp, Cowgill, Winter.)

[63] Only when I had finished this paper did I have an opportunity to read B. V. Gornung's *Iz predystorii obrazovanija obščeslavjanskogo jazykovogo edinstva* (Moscow, 1963), one of the Soviet contributions to the Fifth International Congress of Slavists. In the preface to his report the author cites (on p. 4), with approval, the hypothesis first advanced by N. S. Trubeckoj about two original PSl dialect groups, one northwestern (or "Protolekhitic") and one southeastern. The Lekhitic branch of the West Slavic languages as well as a northern section of the subsequent East Slavic languages (the dialects of the *Kriviči* and the *Ilmen*-Slavs, the *Slověne* of the Novgorod area) allegedly originated from the dialects of the northwestern group, while the rest of the Slavic languages, i.e., Czechoslovak, South Slavic, and the major, central and southern, part of East Slavic, supposedly emerged from the southeastern group of the earliest PSl dialects. The ultimate tripartition of the "historically attested" Slavs into western, eastern, and southern is said to be due to a regrouping which took place between the seventh and tenth centuries. In the preceding, I have discussed some aspects of the regrouping process which ultimately led to the generally assumed tripartition of the Slavic languages. From this discussion it should be clear that I cannot accept the view now subscribed to by Gornung according to which an early division into "Protolekhitic" (including some northern part of what subsequently became East Slavic) and non-"Protolekhitic" is to be considered as the point of departure for CSl dialectology.

Distant Linguistic Affinity

Björn Collinder

UNIVERSITY OF UPPSALA

Summary

Holger Pedersen used to speak about a "nostratic" family of languages, comprising Indo-European, Semitic-Egyptian-Hamitic, Uralic, Altaic, Yukagir, and Eskimo. I do not think his thesis is proved. Can it be proved?

We start from the fact that a divergent development has taken place within the IE family. The Romance languages have developed from Latin. The differences between these languages have come about in four ways: (1) a meaning-bearer has undergone such phonologic changes that it cannot be recognized from one language to another; (2) a meaning-bearer has changed its meaning so that it cannot be recognized; (3) a meaning-bearer has changed both shape and meaning; (4) a meaning-bearer has disappeared in one of the languages, being preserved in another.

In the case of the Romance languages we know the mother language. It would be useless pedantry to deny that the partial identities of the Romance languages are fragments of a total identity that we call Latin, even if we do not think that all Latin-speaking individuals at any time spoke in absolutely the same way.

We postulate a total identity from which the different IE languages have developed—call it PIE (Proto- or Primitive or Primordial IE), or CIE (Common IE), or what you like. We say "total" with the same reservation as when we are talking of any language actually spoken.

This postulate does not mean that we adhere to Schleicher's *Stammbaumtheorie*. We prefer the *Wellentheorie* of Joh. Schmidt and Hugo Schuchardt, but it should not be forgotten that this theory implies both a divergent development, taking place continually, by imperceptible degrees, and a competition which leads to the extinction of dialects. Turkic is, except for Chuvash and Yakute, much more uniform than Swedish, although it is spoken in a much greater area. This may be owing to the fact that it has conquered many different speeches, both related and unrelated, just as Latin conquered almost all the other idioms of Italy in less than three hundred years.

Marrism, which was officially encouraged in Russia for political reasons, has raged as a kind of Asiatic flu in some European universities west of the Iron Curtain. Since the Russian authorities dropped Marrism—obviously because they had found out that Common Slavic could be used as a vehicle of Russian-driven Panslavism—there has been much less talk of "parallel glottogonic development."

When Rask and Bopp laid the foundations of comparative Indo-European linguistics, they started from morphologic identities, chiefly affixes forming systematic groups. It has been justly urged that merely identical word-stems cannot prove that two languages are related. Words are duty-free to a great extent. Affixes can be borrowed, but only as constituents of words. Once an affix is used in many borrowed words, it may be combined, by analogy, with genuine word-stems. This may even be true with inflectional endings, as the plural ending *-s* in the German sixth declension. But as far as we know, inflectional endings have never been borrowed en bloc.

Among the most frequent words of a language, the pronouns have a status of their own because they form an organized group. But their value as evidence in assessing linguistic affinity is restricted because they are especially liable to two sources of error: chance and symbolism. The pronominal stems are mostly short; often they consist of a consonant + a vowel, sometimes merely a vowel. The functions of the pronouns are few. Even the product of the functions (meanings) and the possible combinations of a vowel and a consonant constitutes so low a number that there is much room for chance. And there may be in pronouns an inherent psychophysic connection between sound and meaning, making for what Schuchardt called *elementare Verwandtschaft.*

It has been said that identical pronouns do not even give an indication of affinity, because you will find such identities anywhere, even if you compare two manifestly unrelated languages. The random checks I have made seem to indicate that this does not hold good. Outside the nostratic group, there are identities, but only a few, from one to four. Within the nostratic group the number of identities varies from, let us say, seven to ten. As the probability of mere chance decreases in geometric, not in arithmetic, proportion to the increasing number of identities, seven to ten identities means quite another level of probability than one to four. A global survey of the pronouns of the linguistic families is a desideratum.

I have worked out a simple—perhaps too simple—mathematical model in order to assess the probability of mere chance in problems of distant linguistic affinity. I have presented it in an article called "L'Affinité linguistique et le calcul des probabilités," in *Språkvetenskapliga Sällskapets Förhandlingar, Uppsala Universitets Årsskrift* (1948).

(Participants in the discussion following the presentation summarized above: Lehmann, Hamp, Hoenigswald.)

Traces of Early Dialectal Diversity in Old Armenian

Werner Winter

UNIVERSITY OF TEXAS

0. To the extent that they represent inherited features, the contrasting forms on either side of an isogloss line are, from a historical point of view, divergent developments from one single source form. Dialects are delimited by bundles of isoglosses; viewed historically, dialects are variants of one language that are characterized by a clustering of divergent developments from several unitary features of the protolanguage.

Given this reasoning, and given a solid knowledge of the protolanguage, it becomes possible to identify material from different dialectal sources even in a seemingly uniform linguistic corpus: if conflicting developments from identical or analogous forms can be found to cluster in a systematic fashion, the presence in the corpus of more than one dialectal component can be assumed with a high degree of confidence.

In the present paper I propose to investigate what appears to be evidence for dialectal diversity reflected in data from Old Armenian. I will be concerned only with genuine Armenian material; borrowings from other languages, Indo-European and non-Indo-European, will be disregarded.

To begin with, I shall document various conflicting developments by some selected forms; wherever possible, I will attempt to avoid unnecessary argument by a reference to standard works, viz., H. Hübschmann, *Armenische Grammatik I*: *Armenische Etymologie* (Leipzig, 1897), A. Meillet, *Esquisse d'une grammaire comparée de l'arménien classique*[2] (Vienna, 1936), and above all, G. R. Solta, *Die Stellung des Armenischen im Kreise der indogermanischen Sprachen* (Vienna, 1960), a useful, though unimaginative, compilation of etymologies as proposed by Hübschmann, Pedersen, Meillet, Adjarian, and others. To be practical, the arrangement within a group of conflicting developments will at least in part anticipate our eventual results.

1. The following conflicting developments were noted in the vocalism:

1.1. PArm. *-e-a-*, *-e-u-* > [A] *-e-a-*, *-e-u-* : [B] *-a-a-/-a-ə-*, *-a-u-/-a-ə-*.

Examples: [A] *veštasan* 'sixteen' < **sweḱs-deḱm̥ti-* (a slightly different reconstruction: Meillet, 100)

henum 'weave' : Lith. *pìnti* 'pleat' (Solta, 258–259)
skesur 'mother-in-law' : Skt. *śvaśrú-* (Solta, 57–58)
tesanem 'see' : Gk. *dérkomai* (Solta, 267)
heru 'last year' : Gk. *pérusi* (Solta, 108)
p'etur 'feather' : Skt. *pátatra-* (Hübschmann, 500; *Lg*. 31.5 [1955])

[B] *vat'sun* 'sixty' < **sweks-kontḀ* (cf. Meillet, 55)
hanum 'weave' : Lith. *pìnti* 'pleat' (Solta, 258–259)
całr 'laughter' (*u*-stem) : Gk. *gélōs* (Solta, 422–423)
anun 'name' : Gk. *enuma-* (cf. Solta, 23–25)
tasn 'ten' : Gk. *déka* (Hübschmann, 496)
vasn 'because of' : OPers. *vašnā* 'according to the will of' (Hübschmann, 494–495)
asr 'fleece' (*u*-stem) < **peku-* (cf. Solta, 125–126)

Comments: The assimilation phenomenon registered under 1.1.A must be older than the reduction of **an* from **n̥* in final syllable.

1.2. PArm. *-eha-*, *-ehu-* > [A] *-e-*, *-oy-* : [B] *-a-*, (*-aw-?*).

Examples: [A] *k'erb* 'sister' (instr.) < **swesr̥bhi* (cf. Meillet, 83)
jerb- 'hand' (instr.) < **ĝhesr̥bhi* (cf. Meillet, 99)
en 'they are' < **E̥sn̥ti*
k'oyr 'sister' (nom.) < **swesōr* (Meillet, 39)

[B] *ariwn* 'blood' < **E̥sḀr-* (cf. Solta, 129)
garun 'spring' < **wesr̥-* (Solta, 140)

Comments: A derivation of *en* from **E̥senti* (cf. Goth. *sind*) is not possible; an analogical replacement of the expected **in* (Meillet, 117) or **ein* does not seem likely.

1.3. PArm. *-efC-* > [A] *-ewC-* : [B] *-iwC-* : [C] *-awC-*.

Examples: [A] *ewt'n* 'seven' : Gk. *heptá* (Meillet, 38)

[B] *hiwsem* 'weave' : Lat. *texō*, Osset. *taxun*.
hiwsn 'carpenter' : Gk. *téktōn* (cf. *Lg*. 38.262 [1962]).
muruk' 'beard' : Lith. *smãkras* (Hübschmann, 476–477)

[C] *eōt'n* 'seven' cf. 1.3.A.
yawsem 'weave' : Lat. *texō*
mawruk' 'beard' cf. 1.3.B.

Comments: The 'younger' form *eōt'n* (Hübschmann, 445; Meillet, 46) seems to be a contamination of *ewt'n* and **awt'n*. It seems advisable to keep two Indo-European bases, **tek-s-* 'weave' and **tek-* 'work with a sharp tool', separate (cf. the discussion registered by Walde-Hofmann, *Lateinisches etymologisches Wörterbuch*[3] 2.678–679). *muruk'* is taken to be syncopated from **miwruk'* (cf. *patiw* 'honor', gen. *patuoy*); if that is correct, *hiwsem* must be a relatively late denominative form like *k'unem* 'have intercourse' beside *k'nem* 'sleep' from *k'un* 'sleep'.

1.4. PIE *-ewV-* > [A] *-egV-/-ew-(V)-* : [B] ?/*-iw-(V)-* : [C] *-ogV-/-ow-(V)-*.

Examples: [A] *ałbewr* 'source, spring' : Gk. *phréar* (Solta, 280 n. 1)
aregakn, arew 'sun' : Skt. *ravi-* (Solta, 407–408)
[B] *ałbiwr* 'spring' cf. 1.4.A. (Solta, 280)
iwr '(of) oneself' : Gk. *heós* (Hübschmann, 451)
[C] *loganam* 'wash' : Gk. *loúō* (Solta, 251–252)
nor 'new' : Gk. *nearós* (Solta, 229–230)
inn 'nine' < **Enewn* (cf. Solta, 112)

Comments: Meillet (45) assesses the contrast between 1.4.A and 1.4.B as "une hésitation graphique." For a discussion of *loganam* cf. *Evidence for laryngeals* (The Hague, 1965) 108. The form *nor* is derived from **newros* by Hübschmann (479). *inn* is very important for the insights it offers into the relative chronology of sound changes: **-wV-* > *-gV-* must be more recent than the change of **-an* in final position to *-n* (cf. also *ałbewr, ałbiwr* with *-wr* from **-war*); **-ow-* before *-n* apparently became *-u-* as in *k'un* 'sleep' (< **swopno-*); the resulting form **inun* was preserved in the plural *inunk'*, from which *inn* seems to have been derived in analogy to *tasn* 'ten' (cf. *Evidence* 101).

2. In the consonantism, the following conflicting developments were noted:

2.1. PIE *p- t- kʷ-* > [A] *p'- t'- k'-* : [B] *h-* : [C] *y-*.

Examples: [A] *p'esay* 'suitor' : Lat. *procus*
p'etur 'feather' cf. 1.1.A.
p'ul 'fall' : Lith. *pùlti* 'to fall' (Solta, 391)
t'ek'em 'twist' : Osset. *taxun* (Solta, 378)
t'anjr 'thick' : Lith. *tánkus* (Solta, 223)
k'an 'than' : Lat. *quam* (Solta, 455)
k'erem 'scrape' : Alb. *harr* 'weed' (Solta, 106–107)
[B] *harsn* 'bride' : Lat. *procus* 'suitor' (Solta, 172–173)
henum, hanum 'weave' cf. 1.1.A. and 1.1.B.
heru 'last year' cf. 1.1.A.
hiwsem 'weave' cf. 1.3.B.
hiwsn 'carpenter' cf. 1.3.B.
him 'why' cf. Lat. *quid* 'what' (Meillet, 89)
[C] *yawray* 'stepfather' : Gk. *pátrōs* 'father's brother' (Solta, 46)

yisun 'fifty' : Gk. *pentḗkonta* (Meillet, 30)
yawsem 'weave' cf. 1.3.C.
yesan 'whetstone' : Lat. *tēlum* 'projectile'

Comments: *p'esay* is viewed as containing the same suffixal configuration as *ark'ay* 'ruler'. If correctly interpreted, *p'esay* must be derived from a base **perk̂*- rather than **prek̂*-; is it more than coincidence that Lithuanian has *peršù* for 'ask for a girl's hand in marriage'? *t'ek'em* is a fairly recent formation derived from a noun **t'ek'*. - *k'an* has customarily been taken (since Hübschmann, 502–503, offered this etymology with a question mark) as a match of Lat. *quam*; in view of *k'ani* 'how much?' the alternative possibility that *k'an* derives from **k^wānt*- (cf. Lat. *quantus*) deserves continued attention (cf. H. Pedersen, *KZ* 39.374–377 [1906]; note the rejection by Walde-Hofmann, *LEW*³ 2.398). For *yisun* see the comments below in 2.7. The derivation of *yesan* 'whetstone' along with *hiwsn* 'carpenter' from PIE *tek̂*- (cf. 1.3.) rests on the parallel to the relationship between *yesan* and Lat. *tēlum* that can be found within Greek between *akónē* 'whetstone' and *ákōn* 'spear'.

2.2. PIE *ĝ ĝh* > [A] *c j* : [B] *t d*.

Examples: [A] *acem* 'lead' : Lat. *agō* (Solta, 75–76)
boyc 'nourishment' : Skt. *bhóga*- 'eating, etc.' (Meillet, 44)
barjr 'high' : Hitt. *parkus* 'high' (Solta, 68–69)
jeṙn 'hand' : Gk. *kheír* (Solta, 316–317)
[B] *art* 'field' : Lat. *ager* (Solta, 132)
but 'nourishment' : Skt. *bhóga*-, cf. 2.2.A.
tal 'husband's sister' : Gk. *gálōs* (Solta, 58–59)
berd 'fortress' : OHG *burg*
deln, *delb* 'yellow' : Skt. *hári*-

Comments: *art* is derived from **atsr*- > **atr*- by H. Pedersen, *KZ* 39.352 (1906); *tal* is taken to show the interference of the semantically related term *taygr* 'husband's brother' (: Skt. *devár*-) by Meillet, 144. However, if the other items listed here can be accepted, it becomes possible to ascribe at least the -*t*- in *art* to a regular development.

2.3. PIE *k̂w* > [A] *sk* : [B] *š*.

Examples: [A] *skesur* 'mother-in-law' cf. 1.1.A.
skund 'little dog' : Goth. *hunds* 'dog' (cf. Solta, 57 n.)
[B] *ēš* 'donkey' : Lat. *equus* (Pedersen, *KZ* 38.197, 205 [1905])
šun 'dog' : Gk. *kúōn* (Solta, 56)

Comments: As long as divergent developments of *$\hat{k}w$ are recognized for *skesur* and *šun*, there is no reason why the equations for *skund* and *ēš* should not be retained; it is hard to see why the semantic difference between 'horse' and 'donkey' should be too great to permit the transfer of the term for 'horse', the more so as no inherited word for 'donkey' seems to have existed; as evident from the use of ideograms, the Hittites at least appear to have considered the equines as related, as did the Sumerians: cf. ANŠU.KUR.RA 'mountain donkey' = 'horse'.

2.4. PIE *r$\hat{k}$* > [A] *s* : [B] *rs*.

Examples: [A] *p'esay* 'suitor' cf. 2.1.A
tesanem 'see' cf. 1.1.A.
[B] *harsn* 'bride' cf. 2.1.B.

2.5. PIE *rs* > [A] *ṙ* : [B] *rš*.

Examples: [A] *t'aṙamim* 'wither' : Gk. *társomai* 'become dry' (Solta, 154–155)
oṙk' 'buttocks' : Gk. *órros* (Solta, 323–324)
moṙanam 'forget' : Toch. A *märsneñc* 'they forget' (Solta, 384)
[B] *t'aršamim* 'wither' cf. 2.5.A.
garšim 'abhor' : Lat. *horreō* 'be horrified' (Solta, 371–372)
k'aršem 'drag' : Skt. *kárṣati* (Meillet, 40)

2.6. PIE *rt* > [A] *rd* : [B] *rt'*.

Examples: [A] *ard* 'shape' : Gk. *artús* (Solta, 127)
ard 'right now' : Gk. *árti* (Solta, 127)
mard 'man' : Av. *mərəta-* (Solta, 180)
leard 'liver' : Skt. *yákṛt* (Solta, 157–159)
[B] *ort'* 'calf' : Skt. *pṛthuka-* (Solta, 200–201)

Comments: The *-t'* in *ort'* is usually taken to represent PIE *th*. However, in view of the extremely dubious status of aspirated voiceless stops as Proto-Indo-European phonemes, and in view of the development PIE *-nt-* > Arm. *-t'-* (cf. 2.7.B.), it seems preferable to consider *-t'* in *ort'* the reflex of PIE *t*.

2.7. PIE *nt*, *nk^w* > [A] *nd*, *ng* : [B] *t'*, *k'* : [C] *n*, (*n*?).

Examples: [A] *skund* 'little dog' cf. 2.3.A.
ənderk' 'entrails' : Gk. *éntera* (Solta, 152)
hing 'five' : Gk. *pénte* (Meillet, 30)
[B] *arcat'* 'silver' : Lat. *argentum* (Solta, 129–131)

kut'k' 'harvest' : Gk. *génto* 'grasped' (cf. *Lg.* 30.198 [1954])
lk'anem 'leave' : Gk. *limpánō* (Solta, 96)
[C] *en* 'they are' cf. 1.2.A.
k'san 'twenty' : Dor. *wíkati* (Hübschmann, 504)
eresun 'thirty' : Gk. *triákonta* (Hübschmann, 444)
hun 'ford' : Lat. *pons* 'bridge' (Solta, 175)
gan 'whipping' < *$g^wh\d{n}ti$- (cf. Solta, 80–81)
yisun 'fifty' cf. 2.1.C.

Comments: *lk'anem* is not likely to reflect a form without nasal infix, since in that case one would expect to find the intervocalic development from *k^w (for which cf. *leard* 'liver'). For *k'*- in *k'san* cf. *Evidence for laryngeals* (1965) 107. *yisun* is taken to be from earlier **yinsun*, with common loss of nasal before *-s-*; however, it should be noted that such an assumption implies that this particular sound change remained active until a fairly late time, as the syncope of *i* and *u* is a rather recent phenomenon, and only after **i* from **ē* was syncopated did **yin-* and *-sun* come in direct contact. For a somewhat different argument see Meillet, 30, 40.

2.8. PIE *ndh, mbh* > [A] *?, mb* : [B] *n, m.*

Examples: [A] *amb* 'cloud' : Lat. *imber* 'cloudburst' (Solta, 119–120)
[B] *aner* 'wife's father' : Gk. *pentherós*
camem 'chew' : Gk. *gómphos* 'tooth' (Solta, 254–255)

Comments: It seems that Toch. B *keme*, A *kam* 'tooth' cannot be taken as an indication of a Proto-Indo-European form of the base without a **-bh-*. The agreement in meaning between Arm. *aner* and Gk. *pentherós* is striking. If the latter form is related to Skt. *bándhu-* 'bond; kinsman' (cf. M. Mayrhofer, *Kurzgefasstes etymologisches Wörterbuch des Altindischen* 2.408; E. Fraenkel, *Litauisches etymologisches Wörterbuch* 39), one would have expected to find **bner* (from **biner*) or perhaps rather **baner* in Armenian; it seems legitimate to assume that the onset of *aner* 'wife's father' reflects the influence of the word for 'father', now *hayr*.

2.9. PIE *-wt-, -yt-* > [A] *-wd-, -yd-* : [B] *-wt'-, ?*

Examples: [A] *awd* 'footwear' : Av. *aoθra-* 'shoe' (cf. Hübschmann, 411)
ayd 'that one' : Gk. *tón* (Hübschmann, 437, 487)
[B] *awt'* 'sleeping place' : cf. Gk. *aûlis* (cf. Hübschmann, 412–413)

2.10. PArm. *-Vst-* > [A] *-Vst-* : [B] *-Vy-*.

Examples: [A] *zgest* 'garment' : Lat. *vestis* (Solta, 247–248)
ost 'branch' : Goth. *asts* (Solta, 324)
[B] *ē* 'is' : Lat. *est*
ēk' 'you (pl.) are' : Lat. *estis*
goy 'being' : OIr. *foss* 'rest' (cf. Hübschmann, 435–436)
gari 'barley' : OHG *gersta*

Comments: Rather than derive *ē* from the present-tense ending *-ē* (< **-eti*), as does Meillet (p. 118), it seems advisable to ascribe the strangely leveled "thematic" *-em* present to the influence of the verb 'to be'. If *gari* is an Indo-European item, which seems likely in spite of Georg. *keri* 'barley' (cf. G. Deeters, *IF* 56.140–141 [1938]), it cannot be separated from OHG. *gersta*, Lat. *hordeum* (Gk. *krithḗ* poses problems of its own; cf. H. Frisk, *Griechisches etymologisches Wörterbuch* 2.18–19). *gari* can hardly be derived from PIE *ghr̥yo-* (Frisk, 19), since one would expect to find Arm. **gayr* or perhaps **garǰ*; it seems preferable to posit PIE *ghr̥sd(i)yo-* as the source form of Arm. *gari*, which closely resembles the source form of Lat. *hordeum* (cf. Walde-Hofmann, *LEW*[3] 1.657).

2.11. PIE *sk̂* > [A] *š* : [B] *ç*.

Examples: [A] *šuk'* 'shadow' : OE *scúa* (cf. Hübschmann, 480)
[B] *çuçanem* 'show' : OHG *scouwon* 'look' (Solta, 268–269)
haçi 'ash' : OHG *asc* (Solta, 312–313)

2.12. PIE *k̂s* > [A] *š* : [B] *ç*.

Examples: [A] *veštasan* 'sixteen' cf. 1.1.A.
gišer 'night' : Welsh *ucher* 'evening' (cf. Solta, 296–298, and fn. 30)
[B] *veç* 'six' : Lat. *sex* (Meillet, 40)
vat'sun 'sixty' cf. 1.1.B.

Comments: Welsh *ucher* is derived from **woyk̂sero-* by J. Pokorny, *ZCPh.* 15.377; precisely the same source form can be reconstructed for Arm *gišer*. *-t's-* in *vat'sun* is taken to be a simplification of **-çs-* (i.e., [-t'ss-]); **-ss-* has become *-s* in *es* 'you (sg.) are'.

3. The number of conflicting developments observed is rather high. We note, of course, that the number of contrasts can be reduced readily enough by the simple device of counting not individual developments, but classes of developments. Thus, 1.1.B. and 1.2.B. can be lumped together as phenomena of regressive vowel assimilation, while 2.6.A., 2.7.A., and 2.9.A. may be grouped together since they all show Armenian voiced-stop reflex of Proto-Indo-European voiceless stop after a resonant.

Still, rather numerous contrasts remain. To evaluate them we have to study the way in which these various conflicting developments cluster.

3.1. To accommodate the contrasts listed in 2.1. in terms of our general theory, we have to posit three different dialects. However, three dialects will not be enough to account for the combined evidence of 2.1. and 1.1.: to be sure, 2.1.C. combines only with 1.1.A. (*yesan*) and 2.1.A. only with 1.1.A. (*p'esay*, *p'etur*), but 2.1.B. combines with 1.1.A. (*henum*, *heru*) and 1.1.B. (*hanum*). We will therefore have to recognize two varieties of the 2.1.B. dialect. It will be helpful to map our findings from the very beginning; the features discussed up to this point can arranged as follows:

I: 2.1.A. (*p' t' k'*) 1.1.A. (*e* – *a*)	II: 2.1.B. (*h*) 1.1.A. (*e* – *a*)
IV: 2.1.C. (*y*) 1.1.A. (*e* – *a*)	III: 2.1.B. (*h*) 1.1.B. (*a* – *a*)

Our next task is to attempt to determine the alignment of further categories with these four dialects and to revise, if necessary, the pattern tentatively suggested here.

Under I, we can add 1.3.A. (*-t'-* in *ewt'n*), 1.4.A. (absence of umlaut [1.1.A.] and preservation of *-ew-* as in 1.3.A.), 2.4.A. (2.1.A. and 1.1.A. combined), 2.6.B. (agreement with 2.1.A.), 2.7.B. (do.), 2.9.B. (do.)

Under II, 2.3.A. and 2.7.A. are to be added: *hing* precludes an alignment with I or IV, *skesur* beside *skund* in 2.7.A. an alignment with III.

Under III, 2.12.B. is to be listed, as is 1.2.B.

Finally, under IV, 2.7.C. is to be listed (*yisun* combines 2.7.C. and 2.1.C.); since *en* occurs in both 2.7.C. and 1.2.A., the latter is to be added. *yawsem* lets us include 1.3.C. here, too.

Again, as in the case of 2.1.B. (*h*), we note that the feature 2.7.C. (*n*) extends over two areas: *yisun* made us assign it to IV, but *hun*, with the same loss of a reflex of voiceless dental, cannot be placed in IV, but only in II or III; since *vat'sun* (2.12.B.) likewise shows the development 2.7.C., and since it can only belong with III, *hun* is also to be registered here. Indirectly, this decision, which establishes a partial continuum between III and IV, makes us feel that the tentative mapping given above may reflect some historical reality: We note that a continuum exists between IV, I, and II in regard to feature 1.1.A. (*e-a*), between II and III as far as 2.1.B. (*h*) is concerned, and now also between III and IV with respect to 2.7.C.

Such an overlap between dialect areas in some features is a perfectly normal phenomenon; for our purposes, however, it may mean a serious handicap. While, for instance, 2.4.A. (*p'esay*) can safely be assigned to I, it remains impossible to determine whether 2.4.B. (*harsn*) belongs with II or with III, as both share the development 2.1.B. (*h*).

Clearly, no assignment to an established group can be made when forms showing a particular contrasting development do not show at least one more feature that has already been identified as a characteristic marker of a dialect affiliation. Thus, while it seems legitimate to view the contrast between 2.2.A. and 2.2.B. as one of dialects, none of the forms listed contains a further distinctive development.

3.2. Another complication should be mentioned at least in passing. When borrowing occurs, it need not lead to the elimination of a native form; both the old and the new may continue to coexist, or a blend may come into existence. This "mixed" form may contrast in one feature with dialect A, in another with B, and thus give the impression to the investigator that it really belonged to a third dialect C which shared certain features with A, others with B.

An example may be *t'anjr* 'thick'. Its initial places the form clearly in I. However, the voicing reflected in the interior is parallel to that noted in 2.6.A., 2.7.A., and 2.9.A., and 2.7.A. has been listed as a characteristic of II. One is tempted to assume that *t'anjr* resulted from a blend of **t'asr* (I) and **hanjr* (II), though of course no proof can be offered for an assumption of this kind.

4. Admittedly, the analysis of the composition of classical Armenian as presented here constitutes a tour de force. However, the alternative we are faced with is widespread anarchy. The proposed derivation of conflicting forms from different dialects permits us to maintain the essential principle of regularity in sound change; if we insist on viewing Old Armenian as one uniform corpus, we are faced with rather numerous unexplainable, haphazard changes. We can of course try to reduce the number of conflicting developments by challenging some of the proposed etymologies; an inspection of the list of forms given shows that this will eliminate individual items, but almost none of the contrasts adduced. Neither does it seem possible to eliminate one or more of the contrasting groupings: while it might be possible to consider *y*- in *yawsem* as the prefix *y*- (cf. *y-aṙnem* 'rise'), such an analysis seems precluded for *yisun* 'fifty' (in spite of H. Pedersen's insistence, *KZ* 39.371 [1906]); moreover, even if we could extract **hawsem* from *yawsem*, the *-aw-* vocalism would still force us to retain a separate category.

5. We will want to raise the question of which of the dialects posited should be considered the basis, that is, the principal source of classical

Armenian. Our decision has to be based on the membership observed for each of the dialects postulated. Our list will not give us the answer, since it is selective rather than comprehensive. Extendable are the following subclasses: 2.1.A., 2.1.B., 1.1.A., 2.2.A., 2.6.A. The subclass 2.1.A. includes more examples for PIE *t*- > Arm. *t'*-; 2.1.B., however, contains a considerable number of further cases of PIE *p*- > Arm. *h*- (*Ø*-), and the developments from clusters with Proto-Indo-European voiceless stop plus *r* or *l* belong at least in part here (for examples, cf. *Lg*. 38.259 [1962]). If one is to venture a suggestion, it would seem most likely that our dialect II was the principal source of classical Armenian, the dialect characterized by the features 2.1.B., 1.1.A., 2.3.A., 2.6.A., 2.7.A., 2.9.A.

6. In certain respects, our argument has been carried on in abstracto: forms used have been taken from dictionaries and linguistic treatises, not from actual texts. Our work then clearly needs to be supplemented by further studies. Taking such near synonyms or synonyms as *t'ek'em*, *hiwsem*, and *yawsem*, *henum* and *hanum*, *muruk'* and *mawruk'*, is it possible to determine whether one or the other of the alternants is limited to only some of the classical Armenian sources? To do this type of work, it will be necessary to prepare indices and concordances; by doing that, it may be possible to supplement phonological isoglosses as studied here by lexical ones.

Furthermore, it will be necessary to investigate the possibility that dialectal features of preclassical Armenian survived in modern Armenian dialects. The Armenian scholar, A. S. Garibjan, has initiated a lively discussion of this problem by his various articles on different reflexes of Proto-Indo-European consonants in Armenian dialects (*Izvestija Akademii Nauk Armjanskoj SSR* 1956:2.15–28; *Voprosy Jazykoznanija* 1959: 5.81–90; *Voprosy Jazykoznanija* 1962:2.18–23; for a summary of the entire discussion cf. V. M. Žirmunskij, *Voprosy Jazykoznanija* 1962: 5.32–46); his view is, of course, that preclassical features survived directly, while in our study the possibility is envisaged that preclassical dialectal features were incorporated in a classical koine which in turn should have been the source of at least the majority of the modern dialects. It must obviously be said that at present we know by far too little to arrive at clear decisions; we look forward with great anticipation to the completion of an Armenian dialect dictionary now being prepared by the Armenian Academy of Sciences at Erevan, a tool easily of as great an importance as the indices referred to above.

7. If the view presented here is even only partially justified, classical Armenian loses its monolithic character; it becomes a language marked by a high degree of incorporations from dialectal Armenian sources as well as from languages other than Armenian, both Indo-European and non-Indo-European. Incorporation of foreign materials has been a phenomenon long recognized; it is interesting to note that it seems to find its parallel in an internal, cross-dialectal borrowing of similarly impressive proportions.

(Participants in the discussion following the conference presentation of the first version of this paper: Hamp, Polomé, Hoenigswald, Lehmann, Watkins, Birnbaum, Cowgill.)

On the Interrelationship of the Tocharian Dialects

George S. Lane

UNIVERSITY OF NORTH CAROLINA

A good many years ago now I remarked, in a paper on comparative Tocharian phonology,[1] that the more one observes the similarities between the two dialects, the more forcibly one is struck by their sharp divergences. At that time I did not have at my disposal the texts nor the studies we now have, and comparisons had to be made bit by bit. The only complete ones were E. Sieg, W. Siegling, and W. Schulze, *Tocharische Grammatik*,[2] for Tocharian A, and *Tocharische Sprachreste I*.[3] If that was my impression then, how much deeper it has become now! The cleavage between the two dialects is nowhere brought forth more clearly than in the recent *Tocharisches Elementarbuch*, vol. I, of W. Krause and W. Thomas.[4] That is not an inconsiderable merit of this work, though it is, I presume, an unintentional one.

Inasmuch as it is perforce the agreements between the two dialects, rather than their disparities, that are dwelt on in comparative studies, I should imagine that the nonspecialists in the field are used to equating the use of the word dialect in "Tocharian dialects" with that in "Slavic, Germanic or Romance dialects," or possibly "Italic dialects." To be sure, the divergence of separate languages from one another in any of these "dialect groups" varies considerably, yet the differences between Tocharian A and Tocharian B are greater than between any two languages of the above groups, especially with regard to morphology, to a lesser extent perhaps in their phonology and vocabulary. But the vocabulary in particular will be the subject of special scrutiny here, for I am sure that many words common to both A and B which have been heretofore taken as cognate are actually the result of extensive borrowings from dialect B into dialect A. In this I am persuaded that Professor Werner Winter's conclusions are largely valid,[5] and in fact I am in-

[1] *Lg*. 14.20–38 (1938).

[2] Göttingen, 1931. Hereinafter abbreviated SSS.

[3] *Tocharische Sprachreste I. Die Texte. A.Transcription. B.Tafeln* (Berlin and Leipzig, 1921). Abbreviated as *Sprachreste I*.

[4] Heidelberg, 1960. Hereinafter abbreviated *TE*.

[5] "Lexical Interchange between 'Tocharian' A and B," *JAOS* 81.271–280 (1961).

clined to go a bit farther than he has. Moreover, the presence of such borrowings is of great importance to our conclusions about the interrelationship between the two languages.

Let us first, however, summarize briefly the more striking contrasts:

Phonological:

1) A *e* = B *ai* and A *o* = B *au* as the regular reflexes of inherited *i*- and *u*- diphthongs, e.g., A *tre*, B *trai* m. 'three'; A *pekat*, B *paiykāte* 'wrote'; A *klots*, B *klautso* 'ear', A *śol*, B *śaul* 'life', etc.[6]
2) A *a* = B *e* from PIE *o*, e.g., A *ak*, B *ek* 'eye' (Lat. *oculus*); A *kam*, B *keme* 'comb' (Grk. γόμφος), etc.
3) Apocope of final vowels in A which are retained in B, e.g.: A *kam*, B *keme* (PIE *-os*); A *pekat*, B *paiykāte* (PIE *-o*); A *śäṃ*, B *śana* 'woman, wife' (PIE *-ā*? cf. Grk. γυνή).
4) Also significant here are the results of the accent position as it affects weakening or syncope of medial vowels, especially the interplay of *ä* — *a* and *a* — *ā*. As Professor Winter has pointed out,[7] we have an alternation B *a*/*ä* corresponding to A *ä* or zero, e.g., B *palsko*, gen. *pälskontse* : A *pältsäk*, gen. *pälskes* 'thought'; and B *a* — *ā* corresponds to A *ā* — *a* in many words of three syllables in B but of two in A (where the final has been lost), e.g., B *aknātsa* : A *āknats* 'ignorant', and especially in many verb forms; B *waskāte* : A *wāskat* 'he moved'. While the details of Tocharian accentuation are far from clear in either dialect, and especially so in dialect A as regards "weak" and "strong" verb stems, yet these phenomena here referred to make it abundantly clear that the two dialects differed widely in this respect and had differed widely for a considerable period of time—during which the vowel weakenings and the syncope, which were dependent on accent position, had arisen.

Other distinctions in historical phonological development are, it seems to me, less significant of the long period of time during which the two dialects have gone their separate ways. Some others, however, might be mentioned as adding at least to the difficulty of mutual comprehensibility to speakers of the two, though for the most part they would affect merely individual pieces of vocabulary. Examples are: "palatalization" of w in B; B *yente* = A *want* 'wind', B *yasa* = A *wäs* 'gold', etc.; B *st* = A *ṣt*: B *stām*, A *ṣtām* 'tree', B *kest*, A *kaṣt* 'hunger'; B *ts* = A *ś* by a second palatalization in some categories of forms, e.g., B *tsmentär*, A *śamantär* 'they grow', B *tsälpentär* A *śalpantär* 'they go over, are released', etc. The alternation between *sk* and (palatalized)

---

[6] Further examples of all these equations are available in *TE* 50 ff.

[7] *Loc. cit.* 271.

ṣṣ in B corresponds to a simple *s* alternating with *ṣ* in A in *sk* presents, e.g., B sg. 1 *aiskau*, 3 *aiṣṣäṃ*, pl. 1 *aiskem*, 3 *aiskeṃ* but A sg. 1 *esam*, *eṣt*, 3 *eṣ* (*eṣṣ-äṃ*), pl. 3 *eseñc*. Toch. B shows a secondary palatalization of *k*, *p*, *m*, and *ts* to *ky*, *py*, *my*, and *tsy* in certain categories of the causative, e.g., subj. mid. *kyānamar*, pret. *kyānawa* to pres. *knastär*, caus. of *kän-* 'happen', beside A subj. act. *knāsam*, (pres. *knāṣtär*). Material of this same type could be cited abundantly, but much of it is significant only insofar as it affects the morphology of the two dialects, as is true, for example, in the last instance.[8]

It is indeed in morphology that the two dialects go most widely asunder. In the plural, where, to be sure, some originally identical formations are found, only rarely do we find cognate words with cognate plural endings, e.g., B *-wa* = A *-u* only in B *ostwa*, A *waṣtu* 'houses', and B *kwarsärwa*, A *kurtsru* (beside extended *kursärwā*), pl. of a measure of distance; B *-nta* = A *-nt* only in B *yärkenta*, A *yärkant* 'honors', and B *pälskonta*, A *pälskant* 'thoughts'. The later ending is for the most part extended by *-u* in Tocharian A : B *wranta*, A *wräntu* 'waters', etc.

Furthermore, in those plurals that distinguish the oblique from the nominative, the former is always in *-ṃ* (i.e., final *n*) in B but in *-s* in A, e.g., B nom. *meñi*, obl. *meñäṃ*, A *mañi*, *mañäs* 'months' (sg. nom. B *meñe*, A *mañ* 'moon, month'). This, it seems to me, is a more fundamental cleavage than the mere disagreement in vocabulary assigned to this or that plural formation, or even more significant than the later independent developments of the same original formation, as, for example, the widespread extension of original endings in A by *-ā* or *-u* (cf. the example above). For here we have in all probability an instance of the extreme divergence in the laws of finals in the two dialects, that is, vowel plus *-ns* becomes *-n* (spelled *ṃ*) in B, but *-s* in A. In other words, the full Proto-Indo-European ending must be postulated for Proto-Tocharian. The distinction is parallel (insofar as the final consonant group is concerned) to the contrast in the development, say, between Skt. *vṛkān* and Lat. *lupōs*.[9] There are of course two other possible solutions: one, B *-ṃ* and A *-s* result from different sandhi developments, which is improbable, since sandhi seems of little significance in the development of Tocharian; or, two, the endings have entirely different origins, which is of course possible.[10]

With regard to the oblique singular, the two dialects show one agreement, namely the ending *-ṃ* (= final *n*) which in all probability is to

[8] For further similar data, see *TE* 61–71.

[9] See *TE* 128.

[10] The derivation of the A ending *-s* from the *s*-stem, after loss of ending, might be possible.

be derived from the stem suffix of old *n*-stems after the case endings themselves have been eroded away. The ending is limited to masculine, rational beings in B and for the most part in A where, however, it has been extended to a few feminines. This is of course an important point of agreement between the two dialects and one which has its germ in pre-Tocharian, since it is to be compared with the development of epithets like Lat. *Catō* (*catus*), Grk. Στράβων (στραβός), and, especially, with the weak adjective inflection in Germanic.[11]

Otherwise the oblique singular in A is, with few exceptions, like the nominative, but in B we find a wide assortment of formations. The most striking of these, perhaps, is the ending *-ai* or *-yai*, especially for feminines *aśiyai*, nom. *aśiya* 'nun', *mñcuṣkai*, nom. *mñcuṣka* 'princess', *preśyai*, nom. *preśya*, *preściya*, *preśyo* 'time', but there are rarely masculines also, e.g., *yerkwantai* 'wheel' (nom. not attested). The only probable example of this type is the (highly irregular) A k_u*le*, to nom. k_u*li* = B *klai*, nom. *klyiye*.

Another important type of singular in B is that which ends in *-e* in the nom. but drops it in the obl., e.g., nom. *riye*, obl. *ri* 'city' (A nom. obl. *ri*), nom. *ytārye*, obl. *ytāri* 'way' (A *ytār*), nom. *arañce*, obl. *arañc* 'heart' (A *āriñc*). The identity of nom. and obl. in A results, of course, from the syncope of the final *-e* which is kept in B.

In dialect B, an archaic relic is found in the distinction of palatalized vs. unpalatalized *t* in nouns of relationship : nom. *pācer*, *procer*, *mācer*, *tkācer*, obl. *pātär*, *protär*, *mātär*, *tkātär*, but A nom.-obl. *pācar*, *pracar*, etc.

However, these and other differences in the nom. and obl. sg. and pl. formations are not so significant for the mutual comprehensibility of the two languages (and that is really what we are talking about here) as is the radical divergence in both the genitive and, especially, in the "secondary" cases, i.e., those based on the oblique.

In B the regular ending of the gen. sg. of nouns is *-ntse* (*-ṃtse*), but in A it is *-s*. The history of both is disputed and still, to me, uncertain. Moreover, in spite of the many attempts to derive both from a common origin, I am myself not persuaded, although there are many direct correspondences, e.g., B *ñäktentse* : A *ñäktes* 'of a god'; *yäkwentse* : A *yukes* 'of a horse', etc. Such agreements can hardly be considered significant, since the two endings are far and away the most frequent.[12]

Only three gen. sg. formations seem to me to have a claim to being cognate: (1) A B *-i*, e.g., in nouns of relationship A *pācri*, B *pātri*, and in A also extended (as *-y*) to some nouns in *-ā*, *-u* and *-i*, especially

---

[11] *TE* 108 f.

[12] Reference to discussions in *TE* 103 n, and 104 Anm.

Sanskrit loanwords, *ñäkteññāy* 'of a goddess', *upādhyāy* 'of a teacher', *Viṣṇuy*, etc.; (2) A -(*y*)*āp*, B *-epi*, originally an adjective ending; (3) B *-e*, A zero, in B *lānte*, A *lānt* 'of a king' (nom. B *walo*, A *wäl*), from PIE *-os*. But the first and the last of these are mere relics, and of the second only the final parts A *-p*, B *-pi* are equivalent. Besides, the extension to nouns occurs only in A.

The gen. pl. in B is normally *-ṃts*, less usually *-nts*, or merely *-ts*. In A we have two endings, the regular *-śśi* and the rarer *-is* (only for nouns which have a single nom.-obl. pl. ending), but these show also the alternant *-śśi*. Again any connection between the endings of the two dialects is most dubious (as is also that which has been suggested between *-is* and *-śśi* by deriving the latter from *-s-ts-i*).

With regard to the secondary cases, i.e., those clearly formed by postpositions added to the oblique, there is only one exact agreement, that of the locative A *-aṃ*, B *-ane*, and one other that seems probable, the dative (*TE* "allative") A *-ac*, B *-aś*, *-aśc*. Furthermore, there is not even agreement in the case functions, e.g., A distinguishes formally between an instrumental in *-yo* and a so-called perlative in *-ā* which shares with it the functions of agent and of manner, on the one hand, and usurps the function of the locative on the other. Most of these functions are expressed in B by the suffix *-sa* (usually called instrumental, but perlative in *TE*). On the other hand, B has a special causal suffix in *-ñ* (rare) 'through, on account of', e.g., *läkle-ñ* 'on account of suffering'.

Even more important perhaps than these formal (and functional) differences between the two dialects, is the fact that insofar as we can tell in dialect A the secondary case endings were firmly attached to the preceding oblique case, forming with it a unit in the same way that the various cases are units in any inflectional (or agglutinating) language, but in dialect B the evidence of vowel weakening of *a* to *ä* in the syllable before the accent would indicate that the secondary endings are really still postpositions and do not affect accent position at all, e.g., B nom. *yarke*, gen. sg. *yärkéntse*, inst. sg. *yárke-sa*, nom.-obl. pl. *yärkénta*, in contrast to A *yärk*, gen. *yärkes*, inst. *yärk-yo*, pl. *yärkant*, etc. To this extent are the endings to be considered free forms in both languages: in so-called "group inflection" both secondary and genitive endings may be attached to the final member only of syntactic groups consisting either of nouns or of a noun preceded by attributes: A *śäṃ sewās ckācräśśäl* 'with wife, sons, (and) daughters', B *kektseñ reki palskosa* 'by body, word, (and) thought'. However, this fact hardly makes them free forms any more than the possessive *s* is free in "the king of England's hat."[13]

[13] Further examples of group inflection in *TE* 91 f.

In adjective inflection the two dialects show a great deal more agreement than in the instance of the nouns, though in detail there is great divergence in the frequency of this or that particular formation. In B, for example, the pl. nom. *-ñ*, obl. *-(nä)ṃ* has seen a wide extension; e.g., B *ratre*, *rätreṃ*, pl. *rätreñ*, *rätre(nä)ṃ*; fem. *rtarya*, *rtaryai*, pl. *rätrona*, but A *rtär*, *rträṃ*, pl. *rtre*, *rtres*; fem. *rtri*, *rtäryāṃ*, pl. *rtraṃ* (i.e., like *āṣtär* : B *astare*, pl. *astari*, etc.).

Possibly more significant than other differences would be the divergence in the inflection of the preterit participle. The Indo-European origins of this form seem clear. It is based on the Proto-Indo-European perfect active participle in *-wos/us-*. In dialect B the *s*-stem has been kept throughout the inflection, except for the fem. pl., e.g., masc. sg. nom. *yāmu*, obl. *yāmoṣ*, pl. nom. *yāmoṣ*, obl. *yāmoṣäṃ*; fem. sg. nom. *yāmusa*, obl. *yāmusai*, pl. nom.-obl. *yām(u)wa*. But in dialect A the *-nt-* stem has largely taken over, e.g., masc. sg. nom. *yāmu*, obl. *yāmunt*, pl. nom. *yāmuṣ*, obl. *yāmuñcäs*; fem. sg. nom. *yāmus*, obl. *yāmusāṃ*, pl. nom.-obl. *yāmunt*. The reverse has happened in the masc. pl. nom. of the *nt*-stems, e.g., A *ymassuṣ* to *ymassu* (beside B *ymassoñc* to *ymassu*).

That the pronouns, especially the demonstratives, show considerable divergence is not surprising. Even more closely related languages, such as Germanic, show remarkably different forms. Pronouns are always subjected to continual reinforcing by added particles, which shortly become necessary and inseparable parts of the basic stems. One divergence does seem remarkable and possibly old, namely distinction of gender in A masc. *näṣ*, fem. *ñuk*, beside B masc. and fem. *ñäś*, *ñiś* 'I'. Historically all three forms are most unclear, but if we could ever find out what non-Indo-European influence brought about the distinction in gender in A, we might know considerably more about the wanderings and contacts of the "Tocharians."

But I must hasten on to the verb. At first glance the verb systems of the two dialects seem deceptively alike, but the longer one studies them, the more one is impressed by the remarkable differences. Possibly the mistaken notion of great similarity is caused by a first quick glance at the present system where many cognate present stem formations do occur, and where especially the *r*-endings of the middle catch the eye. The same illusion trapped early scholars, especially those few who had in their mind's eye the Old Irish deponent conjugation, into suggesting that Tocharian was a Celtic language.

The present middle endings are remarkably identical and do reflect a very significant common Tocharian development retained quite intact in both dialects. However, even a quick glance at the present active endings tells quite another story. Only one single ending here can be identified without equivocation as the same in the two dialects, namely the 2nd pers. sg. *-t*. Elsewhere we see such contrasts as sg. 1 A *-m*, B *-u*, 3 A *-ṣ*, B *-ṃ*, pl. 1 A *-mäs*, B *-m*, 2 A *-c*, B *-cer*, 3 A *-ñc*, B *-ṃ*. Some of these are clear as regards their origin, e.g., sg. 1 A *-m* < -**mi*, but B *-u* probably from *-ō*, i.e., athematic vs. thematic primary ending; pl. 1 A *-mäs* < -**mos* plus vowel, B *-m* < -**me* (or -**mo*), 3 A *-ñc* < -**nti*, B *-ṃ* < -**nt*,[14] i.e., primary endings in A but secondary in B. Such differences must be very old.

Of all the tenses it is the preterit that shows the greatest agreement both in possible stem formations and in endings, not only in the middle but also in the active. In the latter respect only a few are irreconcilable, e.g., active pl. 1 A *-mäs*, B *-m* (as in the present), and in the middle sg. 1 A *-e*, B *-mai*, pl. 2 A *-c*, B *-t*. And, while it is true that the same original stem formations are readily identifiable in both dialects, the details of development, possibly due to differences in accent, are very different, cf., e.g., (from *tärk-* 'release') act. sg. 3 A *cärk*, B *carka*, pl. 3 A *tarkar*, B *cärkāre*; mid. sg. 3 A **tärkāt*, B *tärkāte*, pl. 3 A **tärkānt*, B *tärkante*. To be noted especially is the regular interchange of *ä/a* in the sg. and pl. active in A, whereas in B the alternation is conditioned by the accent that apparently in such forms falls on the antepenult. In the subjunctive, too, in A we note a regular (but different) alternation (*kälk-* 'go', *kälp-* 'obtain') act. sg. 3 *kalkaṣ*, pl. 3 *kälkeñc*; mid. sg. 3 *kälpātär*, pl. 3 **kälpāntär*. In B, of course, the subjunctive is, to a great extent, independent of the preterit in stem formation, cf. to *tärk-*: act. sg. 3 *tārkaṃ*, pl. 1 *tarkam* (*ā*-subj.); to *kälp-* act. sg. and pl. 3 *kallaṃ* and *källaṃ* (*nā*-subj.; *lpn* > *ll*).

The usual derivation of the subjunctive and the preterit from the same stem in dialect A, as opposed to B, is one of the most marked contrasts between the two. There are, to be sure, many irregularities left in the former, but, as is remarked in SSS, the difference between preterit indicative and the subjunctive is most frequently only a matter of personal endings, "secondary" in the former, "primary" in the latter. In dialect B, however, the subjunctive formations show greater variation. In fact, except for two (those in *-i-* and *-ñ-*), all the "signs" of the subjunctive are found also in the present indicative, and conversely all the present "signs" except three (*-o-*, *-n*-infix, and *-s-*) are found also in the subjunctive.

It is, of course, the *ā*-subjunctive that is the dominant type in both

[14] The word for 'twenty' B *ikäṃ*, beside A *wiki*, poses a problem here. In my opinion neither form is derived directly from **wigenti*, though to be sure the A form may be compared with the "short" pl. 3 act. pres. A *-i* beside *-iñc*, e.g., *träṅki* : *träṅkiñc* (cf. SSS 326 f.).

dialects, and apparently increasingly so in A, which is in part due, it would seem, to the formalizing of the relationship between *ā*-subjunctive and *ā*-preterit (see above).

Even more indicative, however, of a long period of independent development of the two dialects is the almost complete divergence in the formation of the imperfect. In dialect B it is based completely on the Proto-Indo-European optative formation in *ī*. The sign *i* (*y*) is normally added to the present stem minus any final vowel, but present stems in *ā* keep the *ā* and form an imperfect in *oy*, e.g., *palkäṃ* 'shines', impf. *palyśi*; *mäsketär* 'is', impf. *mäskitär*; *śuwaṃ* 'eats', impf. and opt. *śuwoy*, etc. In dialect A only two instances of this type of imperfect are found, namely for the verbs 'be' and 'go', respectively sg. 3 *ṣeṣ* and *yeṣ* = B *ṣey*, *ṣai* and *yey*, *yai*. Otherwise in dialect A the regular imperfect is formed from the present stem. This basic and, it would appear, extremely old cleavage between the dialects is possibly of greater significance than would appear to be the case at first glance.

The development optative > imperfect (or preterit) is found sporadically throughout Indo-European, from Indic to Celtic.[15] Its roots are possibly even in the parent speech, i.e., in the use of the optative to signify repetitive or habitual action in the past. Yet, outside of Tocharian, it seems to be particularly characteristic of Iranian, and occurs especially in various Middle Persian dialects, such as Sogdian and Khotanese.

I am inclined to see in the development optative > imperfect in Tocharian the result of long and intimate contact between the speakers of dialect B and those of the northeastern Iranian dialects. On the other hand, if, as I shall undertake to demonstrate later, dialect A was a language of greatly restricted use in both area and function, then it is not surprising that it did not suffer the same influence. Besides, it was at a greater distance from intimate Iranian contacts than was dialect B. The use of the optative of the verbs "be" and "go" as imperfects in dialect A can be old. It is not surprising if two highly irregular verbs of this sort should be aberrant in their development from the general run. Or, and this is what I suspect, we may have here evidence of the tremendous influence of dialect B on dialect A throughout the period of its documentation and indeed perhaps long before that.

Of course it is possible that the development optative > imperfect

---

[15] For a general statement with bibliography, see W. Couvreur, *BSL* 39.247 f. (1938); E. Benveniste, *BSL* 47.17 f. (1951). Special discussions of the development in different languages are to be found in: F. Edgerton, *Buddhist Hybrid Sanskrit Grammar* 1.161 f.; J. A. Kerns, "The Imperfect in Armenian and Irish," *Lg.* 15.20–33 (1939); Krause, "The Imperfect in British and Kuchean," *Journal of Celtic Studies* 1.24 ff. (1949–50).

is independent of outside influences, but if so the divergence between A and B is stranger still. For if it is independent, it would seem to me to be necessarily of pre-Tocharian origin and would thus be a development shared in particular with Indo-Iranian, Celtic, and possibly Armenian. On the other hand, Armenian may show the same Iranian influence as Tocharian. The Celtic would then have to be completely independent.

Possibly some of the more significant data for our purposes here are to be gleaned from a comparison of the vocabularies.

Already in the introduction to his *Fragments de textes koutchéens*, 32 ff.,[16] Sylvain Lévi has commented on the independence of the technical vocabulary of Buddhism in the two Tocharian dialects. His list includes such terms as the following:

A	B	Sanskrit
lyalypu	yāmor	= karman
kārme	empreṃ	= satya
klop	lakle	= duḥkha
pñi	yärpo	= puṇya
märkampal	pelaikne	= dharma
śkatampeyum	śkamaiyya	= daśabala
plyaskeṃ	ompalskoññe	= dhyāna, samādhi

Such divergences as this are, of course, extremely important, in that they show the independence of the two languages at the time of the earliest translation of Buddhistic works, and therefore, it would seem, the independence of the activities of the Buddhist missions to the two peoples.

Some of the words above, though used in technical Buddhistic formulae, reveal a cleavage of more general and therefore more fundamental nature, e.g., *klop* vs. *lakle*. These appear to be old words in the two languages, though to be sure even their internal etymological connections are to me obscure. For the latter a connection with either *läk-* 'see' or *lyäk-* 'lie' could be defended from the formal but hardly from the semantic point of view. A *klop* seems to have no possible relatives in either dialect. Likewise A *śka-tampeyum*, B *śka-maiyya* show, in their second element, a similar cleavage. A *tampe* 'strength' belongs of course with AB *cämp-* 'be able, can', but so far as I know no cognate form with unpalatalized *t-* exists in B. The form must be very old in A. As for B *maiyya*, it is not only without cognate in A, but is of doubtful connections within Tocharian. Possible would be eventual relation to B *mai-*, A *me-* 'measure', but semantically the etymology is not satisfying.[17]

[16] Paris, 1933.

[17] Another etymology in A. J. van Windekens, *Lexique étymologique des dialectes tokhariens* 60 f. (Louvain, 1941).

A *plyaskeṃ* and B *ompalskoññe* are probably independent formations from the same root, cf. A *päl(t)sk-* 'think', *pältsäk* 'thought', B *pälsk-*, *palsko*. A *märkam-pal* and B *pelaikne* contain cognate nouns A *pal* = B *pele* 'right, order'. The first part A *märkam-* is still obscure (cf. *sne märklune* = Skt. *ahārya*? SSS 455), and the final part of the B form can be either *yakne* 'way, manner' or possibly *aikne* 'id'.[18]

Other remarkable contrasts that affect the vocabulary are A *wrasom* but B *onolme* for Skt. *jana, bhūta, sattva*, etc.,[19] and the words for 'good' and 'evil'. For the former as an adjective we have nom. sg. m. A *kāsu* but B *kartse* (also fem. sg. nom. *kartsa*, obl. *kartsai*; the rest of the forms are from A *krant* = B *krent-*). As substantives *kāsu* and *kartse* are termini technici 'the good'. While it may be possible to connect B *karts-* with *krent-*, A *kāsu* must stand quite apart.[20]

For 'evil' we have A *omäskeṃ* (adj. and sb.) and *umpar* (adj.) but B *yolo* (adj. and sb.). For the latter Sieg and Siegling suggest (*Sprachreste B* 1.158) "vielleicht iran. Lehnwort" without further identification, but they no doubt follow Hansen's derivation from Sacian (Khotanese) *yolo*, which might itself be of Turkish origin.[21] The important point here is, for us, the fact that we have a probable late borrowing from an Iranian dialect in B only, not in A.

These technical terms or words in technical use are not the only lexical divergences between the Tocharian dialects. I present here only a partial list. It embraces the greatest variety of terms, names of parts of the body, concrete and abstract nouns of all sorts, descriptive adjectives of all sorts, adverbs, etc.

A	B	
mrāc, lap	āśce	'head'
śāku	matsi	'hair (of the head)'
puskāñ (pl.)	ṣñor	'sinew'
āy, pl. āyäntu	āy, pl. āsta	'bone'
pāccās	saiwai	'right (hand)'
mokone	ktsaitsäññe	'old age'
śwal	mīsa	'meat'
naṣu	waṣamo	'friend'
yäslu	sāṃ	'enemy'

[18] Cf. SSS 248; *Toch. Sprachreste. Sprache B. Heft* 1 : *Die Udānālaṅkāra-Fragmente*, 100 (Göttingen, 1949). Hereinafter abbreviated *Sprachreste B*.

[19] Lévi, *loc. cit.*, lists A *śoṣi* = B *onolme*. But the B equivalent is rather *śaiṣṣe* = Skt. *loka*.

[20] Winter, privately, mentions the possibility of a connection between A *kāsu* 'good' and B *kāswo* 'leprosy'. The phonetic equivalence is impeccable.

[21] O. Hansen, "Toch.-iran. Beziehungen," *ZDMG* 94.162 (1940).

mäśkit	mñcuśke	'prince'
napeṃ	śaumo	'man'
śom	śamaśke	'boy'
yṣaṃ	tsrerme	'fortification ditch'
ṣukṣ-	k_uṣai (obl.)	'village'
tsmār	witsako	'root'
niṣpal	waipecce	'property'
sañce	sklok	'doubt'
smale	waike	'falsehood'
ṣont	nauntai	'street'
kunti	lwāke	'jar'
tsopats (sg.) śāwe (pl.)	orotstse	'large'
kupār	kätkre	'deep'
kāpñe	lāre	'dear'
aryu	walke	'long (of time)'
tsru	totka	'little, few'
tāpärk	ñake	'now'
lek	päst, pest	'away, off'[22]
letkār	waiptār	'apart'
oseñi	kästwer	'at night'
ksär	tsoṅkaik	'in the morning'

To this list, which could be greatly lengthened by the inclusion especially of more adverbs, conjunctions, prepositions and postpositions, I might add only a short list of verbs, again without any attempt to be complete. I would draw attention particularly to suppletive stems.

1) A *kälk-*, B *mas-* (sg.), *mit-* (pl.), pret.-subj. stem to AB *i-* 'go'.

2) B *ās-*, inf. and imptv. stem to AB *pär-* (pres.), *kām-* (pret.) 'bring'.

3) A *ken-*, B *kwā-*, *śauk-*, pres. to AB *kāk-*, pret.-subj. 'call'.

4) A *träṅk-* beside B *wesk-*, pres. to AB *weñ-*, pret.-subj. 'speak'.

5) B sg. 3 *ste*, *star*, pl. 3 *stare*, *skente*, pres. copula beside AB *nes-*, pres. 'be'.

Besides these suppletive forms may be mentioned here also:

1) A *knān-*, B *aik-* 'know, recognize'. The former is found as a verb stem in A only but has the derivative B *aknātsa* = A *āknats* 'ignorant'. Both dialects have another verb for 'know', *kärs-*.

2) A *kātk*, B *tsäṅk-* 'arise, come into being'.

3) A *pāt* (pret. pl. 3 *pātar*), verb beside noun B *āre* 'plow'.

Interesting and of some importance for our purpose here is the article by O. Hansen to which reference has been made above. Of the fifty-one words submitted as possible borrowings from Iranian, twenty-one

[22] Beside the cognate preverbs in much the same use A *lo*, B *lau* (rare) : A *lok*, B *lauke* adv. = Skt. *dūra*.

are attested in Saca (Khotanese), or on various grounds appear to be for the most part of Saca origin. For thirteen others Hansen assumes a Sogdian source. For the rest he indicates merely a "middle Iranian" origin.

This "middle Iranian" origin for all these probable or possible borrowings would perhaps speak against the theory often defended in the past, that Tocharian, and dialect A in particular, was reintroduced in northern and eastern Chinese Turkestan by a return migration of the Tocharians of classical reference, who were established in Tocharistan (Bactria, upper Oxus) before and around the beginning of the Christian era. If this were true, then certainly some of the borrowings should be expected to be of that date and would reflect an earlier Iranian phonology. A fuller investigation of the contacts between the Iranian languages and Tocharian is urgently needed.

In the article entitled "Lexical Interchange between 'Tocharian' A and B," already referred to above,[23] Werner Winter listed some forty words which he considered to be "certain or possible" borrowings from dialect B into A, including some words of Iranian origin (or transmission). On the other hand, only five words appear to have traveled in the opposite direction, from A to B, and these are by no means as probable as the greater share of the former list. If borrowed, one difficulty with them is that they came into dialect B at a fairly early date—earlier than those from B to A—and consequently suffered phonological changes in B which disguise their origins. On the other hand, many of the first group, those from B into A, appear to be of fairly recent importation.

There seems little to be gained by any attempt to classify the loanwords from a semantic point of view. They include both nouns and adjectives, not to mention adverbs and conjunctions, and range through the most concrete ('fruit' *oko*, 'knife' *yepe*) to the most abstract ('best' *śpālmeṃ*, 'annoyance' *krāso*). In this regard they are to be contrasted with the borrowings from Iranian which are to a great extent technical if not always Buddhistic: A *āmāś*, B *amāc* 'minister', A *aśi*, B *aśiya* 'nun', A *käṣṣi*, B *käṣṣi* 'teacher', A *ṣāmaṃ*, B *ṣamāne* 'monk', etc.

Professor Winter has also suggested that certain suffixes were borrowed by dialect A from B, namely the adjective suffix *-assu*, e.g., in *tuṅkassu* 'loving' (*tuṅk* 'love'), *śolassu* 'āyuṣmant' (*śol* 'life'), cf. B *täṅwassu*, *śaulassu* with the same meaning. The original form in A was probably *-su*, as in *kipsu* from *kip* 'shame'. A second suffix which might be borrowed, according to Winter, is the abstract formation *-rñe* (e.g., *ekrorñe* from *ekro* 'sick', *tālorñe* from *tālo* 'miserable', etc.). One par-

[23] Note 5.

ticular form AB *ykorñe* (: AB *yäk-* 'be negligent') may actually be borrowed in toto.[24] The proper suffix in A is simply *-ne*, cf. *pāpṣune* : B *papāṣṣorñe* (A *pās-*, B *pāsk-* 'observe').

In my opinion, Professor Winter has by no means exhausted the possible list of borrowings from dialect B by dialect A, but for the most part other words are merely suspect and there is no way to prove by their phonology or otherwise that they are not cognate. Indeed it appears to me that, in view of the wide divergence between the two dialects in most other respects, too exact a similarity between forms in the two dialects make such forms the object of immediate suspicion. The influence of dialect B upon dialect A in vocabulary is far greater than we have heretofore suspected or, indeed, than we shall ever be able to prove. The reason for my suspicions will be made clear in a moment.

Of particular interest are some words of Iranian origin of which dialect B has been the transmitter. Professor Winter lists AB *käṣṣi* 'teacher' and A *āmāṃ*, B *amāṃ* 'pride' from Hansen's list. I believe we may include a few others: A *āmāś*, B *amāc* 'minister' (Saka *āmāca*), A *āśari*, B *aśari* 'teacher' (Saka *āśiri* < Skt. *ācārya*), and perhaps A *kāṣār*, *kāṣāri*, B *kaṣār* '*kāṣāya*, 'yellow-red monk's dress', cf. *kaṣara* in Krorainian Prakrit.[25] In fact it is possible, even likely, that the greater share of the later Buddhist technical vocabulary common to the two dialects, and of Iranian origin, has been transmitted to A by B.

The transmittal of this common technical Buddhist vocabulary of Iranian origin is, like the other terms borrowed by A from B, of fairly recent date. It is to be contrasted with those Buddhist terms mentioned above which show such a remarkable divergence. Sylvain Lévi has, in the discussion referred to above, suggested a most plausible explanation.[26]

The original Buddhist missions among the Tocharians were of Iranian origin. Later came a more direct influence from India. This latter effort affected the region of Kucha more deeply than it did the more distant Karashar-Turfan territory, and overlaid the more original Iranian influence with later, more direct borrowings from Buddhistic Sanskrit. A particularly important form for Lévi is A *Metrak* 'Maitreya', which is preserved in its Iranian form. In dialect B the corresponding *Maitrāk* occurs once (74bl = T III. Š 65.2). Otherwise the

[24] For the forms, see SSS 20 f.

[25] T. Burrow, *The Language of the Kharoṣṭhi Documents from Chinese Turkestan* (Cambridge, 1937); and "Tocharian Elements in the Kharoṣṭhi Documents from Chinese Turkestan," *JRAS* 667–675 (1935). In view of the meager and doubtful nature of "Tocharian" remains in these materials, I have not considered it of any use to attempt to place them dialectally alongside Toch. A and B.

[26] Cf. note 16, above.

more direct *Maitreye* (Skt. *Maitreya*) is regular. In fact the name of the Buddha itself shows the later (or at least the continual) influence of Sanskrit in dialect B as opposed to A: B *pŭdñäkte* (*pañäkte* in prose) as opposed to the earlier form in A *ptāñkät*.

However, Lévi does not exploit his evidence further in any attempt to explain the anomalous distribution of the manuscript remains of the two dialects: A only in the east, Karashar-Turfan, but B both in the west and the east, Kucha-Turfan. In an early discussion he did prove beyond doubt that dialect B was the spoken language of the region of Kucha in the earlier part of the second half of the first millennium A.D.[27] No one has ever since, to my knowledge, attempted to dispute that fact. But there is no evidence that I know of which forces us to think that either dialect was a vernacular language of the time, spoken by the native population of the eastern area where the manuscripts of both A and B are found.

The solution is a simple one. At the time when the extant materials in dialect A were written it was purely a liturgical language in the monasteries of the east, and had been so preserved for several centuries at least. To what extent it was also a spoken religious language in the same circles, I shall not venture to say, but it had long since ceased to be a vernacular. Any one of several languages, or indeed several at the same time, could have been used as vernaculars in the region, though some form of Turkish was no doubt in the ascendancy. But the spoken language of the earlier Indo-European-speaking inhabitants had been lost. And no wonder. From the first two centuries preceding the Christian era down through the first six hundred years A.D. the Turfan oasis had been the object of continuous struggles between the Chinese and the various barbarian hordes from the north—the Hiung-nu, the Avars, the Turks, and probably a dozen other tribes related or unrelated ethnically and linguistically to these, whose names alone are recorded in the Chinese annals. It is possible that dialect A was at one time the spoken vernacular of the Turfan region alone, and not even of Karashar to the west. It could have been brought there by monks merely in its capacity as a written language for use in the monasteries. But there is no proof either way.[28]

On the other hand, the region of Kucha, better protected from the barbarians by the mountains to the north and farther from China, was

---

[27] *Journal asiatique* 1913:2.311 ff.

[28] For a detailed account with reference to the Chinese sources, see especially the study by W. Fuchs, "Das Turfangebiet. Seine äusseren Geschicke bis in die T'angzeit," *Ostasiatische Zeitschrift* 13.124–166 (1926). A briefer account will be found in Lévi's discussion in his *Fragments de textes koutchéens* (above, note 16), 8 ff.

better able to maintain its independence than Turfan or even Karashar. Besides, it had the latter as a buffer state to its east, to bear the brunt of the Chinese-barbarian tug-of-war for dominance over the cities along the caravan routes between east and west. Kucha itself was the center of an early and flourishing Buddhist monastery culture which came more and more under direct Indian influence from the time of the famous scholar Kumārajīva (A.D. 344–413), son of an Indian father with a Kuchean princess as mother. The article by Lévi referred to above[29] has collected for us from the Chinese documents the references to Kucha. The picture one gets here contrasts sharply with the history of Turfan, especially from the time of Kumārajīva until the end of the eighth century. Not the least significant of these accounts is that of the famous Chinese pilgrim, Hiuen-Tsang, who passed through Kucha in 630. Just previous to his arrival in Kucha, Hiuen-Tsang had passed through Turfan and Karashar, and his account leaves no doubt about the difference in political affairs which obtained in the east. The king of Turfan, K'iu Wen-t'ai, was holding his power only by walking a tightrope between the Chinese on the one hand and the T'u-kiue (Turks) on the other, and, immediately after the departure of Hiuen-Tsang, he allied himself with the latter against the former to invade Yen-k'i (Karashar).[30] The differences in political conditions that prevailed in Kucha and Turfan were clearly such as might lend credence to my view that, whereas Tocharian B was clearly the vernacular of a comparatively rich and flourishing culture, its sister dialect in the east, Tocharian A, might well have ceased to be a spoken language. The population using it was subjected continuously to the conquest of the Chinese or of the barbarians, and received sporadic infusions from the hordes of the latter, which were never given time for assimilation to the native language before a new invader appeared on the horizon.

The presence of documents in dialect B in the east, from Karashar to Turfan, does not mean that it had supplanted dialect A in that area in the period under question. Rather, its presence there is indicative of the vigor of the Buddhist culture of the west which had expanded into the monasteries of the east as a second, if not a competing, language for religious use—possibly, indeed, as the spoken language of everyday use in the monasteries alongside the traditional liturgical language of this area, dialect A.

That this was the true relationship between the two languages is not only clearly possible from the historical events that have been so hastily summarized, but it is made even extremely plausible by certain facts about the use of the languages themselves.

[29] See note 27.

[30] Fuchs, *op. cit.* 148; Lévi, *op. cit.* 18.

As we have already seen, Lévi's conclusion that dialect B was the vernacular language of Kucha has never been questioned. That it was also the monastery vernacular in the east seems to me the logical conclusion from the content of some of the manuscripts found in the region. For example, the great manuscript dealing chiefly with various kings of Kucha, especially with Suvarṇapuṣpa, comes from Murtuq (*Sprachreste B* 2, nos. 415–421), as does also a more fragmentary one in which King Kanaṣka is mentioned (*ibid.*, nos. 422–427). It is reasonable that the author would use his own vernacular language in the writing of history. Or perhaps more to the point, if dialect A had been the vernacular at this time in this region, certainly history relating the events of another region would have been composed in it. Another clear bit of evidence pointing in the same direction is that dialect B appears to have been the language for instruction in Sanskrit. Cf. B no. 550 (= T II. S 01), one side of which gives the paradigm of Skt. *anaḍvah-*, and the other of *suhaviṣ-*, with translation in Tocharian B. The signature indicates that this text was found at Sängim near Turfan.

Another bit of similar evidence, but not so clear perhaps, is to be deduced from B no. 605 (= T III. Š 75.2) from Sorčuq (region of Karashar). This complete manuscript leaf has on the recto an exercise in writing ligatures, and ends with the sentence in dialect A: *säs śäkwe-pint amok piktsi papyutäk* 'This twelfth art brought writing about (?)'. On the reverse side at the lower right-hand corner we read, also in dialect A: *cesäs amokäs toṅkitsā* [*e*]*l wäs* 'These arts Tonkitsā gave as a gift'. Subsequently[31] the empty space on the reverse side has been filled with a text in dialect B, which begins 'Since (?) Darmachandra commanded to write the "arts" in the desire (of obtaining) the dignity of a Buddha', continues with pious wishes and praise for the advantages of learning and practicing writing, and ends 'all who learn this may become Buddha'.[32]

Two Tocharian A manuscripts (*Sprachreste I A*, nos. 251 and 372) have inscriptions containing B words on the recto which is otherwise blank. No. 251*a*: [*p*]*rathama pärweṣṣe kāsu tākis sa*[*n* . . .], where B *pärweṣṣe* 'first' (translating Skt. *prathama*) is followed by A *kāsu tākiṣ* 'good may be' (I shall not attempt to complete the following word); no. 372*a*: *rweṣṣe kartse tāko*, which is entirely in dialect B and may be completed after the preceding to read (*pä*)*rweṣṣe kartse tāko*(*y*). Both

[31] "Nachträglich," so Sieg and Siegling, in prefatory remarks to B no. 605.

[32] Sieg and Siegling, *Sprachreste I A*, introd. v n. 2, cite as occurring in two other B MSS similar formulae in dialect A : *säs trit amok* and *säs pänt amok pyockäs piktsi*. These I have not been able to identify, in spite of the fact that the editors indicate that the MSS in which they occur have been arranged with the B materials for eventual publication.

inscriptions appear to be the opening phrases (the former partly, the latter perhaps entirely, in dialect B) to works in dialect A—exactly what might be expected if the prevalent written language is the former, and the latter an old "dead" language of limited use.

But possibly the most significant of all is *Sprachreste I A*, no. 394, from Sängim. The text itself is entirely in dialect A, but it has nineteen glosses in dialect B and two in Uigur. The last two glosses appear to be in a different hand from those in Tocharian B, though it is of course impossible to tell for certain from the facsimile.[33] It should be abundantly clear that we are dealing with the glossing of a Tocharian A text by a newcomer whose monastery language, at least, was dialect B, and to whom the "old" monastery language of the area was not familiar. His own native speech may have been Turkish.

The facts of language use, insofar as they can be judged, lead us then to conclude that dialect B, the native vernacular of the west, the Kucha region, was also a monastery vernacular in the east, in the region Karashar-Turfan. It was also a language of fairly recent importation, at least later than some of the extant documents in dialect A, witness the B glosses and the added B text on A manuscripts discussed above.

Other facts about the two languages themselves lend further support to the same view and, at the same time, indicate that dialect A, if not a dead language, actually was a petrified one. This is indicated by the extreme regularity of the language both in form, and, in general, in orthography, as against B. The latter shows extreme irregularities that may not be entirely attributable to orthographical variation alone or even to differences of chronology in the composition of the documents themselves, though this is in my opinion largely to blame. Professor Winter, however, believes that a considerable part of this variety of form must be attributed to dialectal differences within Tocharian B, and has attempted to show that three main dialects are to be distinguished: a western dialect, exemplified especially by the MQ (Ming-Öy Qizil) texts (near Kucha), a central dialect especially represented by Š (Šorčuq near Karashar), and an eastern dialect to which belong the S, M, D, and T texts (Sängim, Murtuq, Xočo, and Toyoq, respectively, in the Turfan area).[34] A great many of his arguments, particularly as regards phonology, are rather convincing, but those that seek to establish formal differences are less so. (There are only two of the latter: fem. pl. of gerundives in *-llona* in the west vs. *-lyana* in the east, and the substantive verb pl. 3 *skente* in the west vs. *stare* in the east). In my

[33] *Sprachreste I B (Tafeln)* 57.

[34] "A Linguistic Classification of 'Tocharian B' Texts," *JAOS* 75.216–225 (1955); "Zur Dialektgliederung von 'Tocharisch' B," *KZ* 75.233–237 (1959).

opinion there is too much chance of accidental omission of one form or the other in the manuscripts from different areas.

But in any case, irregularity of form, be it purely a scribal matter or a reflection of dialectal difference, is exactly what we would expect of a living, spoken language. Furthermore, and this is most important, the significant direction of lexical borrowing is, so far as can be determined, from B to A. Again this is what one would expect in the instance of scribes whose old liturgical language was the latter, but who have been surrounded and overwhelmed, as it were, by missionaries from the west, who not only write but speak another language whose similarities in the lexicon are just great enough to cause confusion. The morphologies of the two languages are, however, sufficiently different to keep them apart. As we all know, this is exactly what happens to the immigrants' language in America, though here to be sure it is the "invaders" who are in the minority.

Yet another point: I have spoken above about the extreme irregularity of both script and spelling in dialect B[35] as opposed to A. Professor Winter has already emphasized, within the B texts, the regularity of those from Šorčuq (in the Karashar region), to which he gives the name "Central dialect." The form of writing dominant in these texts is to be contrasted with that found especially in the west at the Ming-Öy Qizil site. Winter suggests that a special sort of ductus was developed at Šorčuq, and that the scriptorium here possessed great prestige, so that its influence was felt later back at the "home site" to the west, resulting in texts at Ming-Öy Qizil which show a mixture of both the "old" ductus native there and the "new" ductus of Šorčuq.

Let us examine the situation with regard to ascertaining if similar, though of course less striking, differences in writing and of orthography exist there in the case of A.

The greater share of the A manuscripts in *Sprachreste I* come from Šorčuq, nos. 1–383, in fact, and of these all but nine (374–383) are from one site, the so-called "Stadthöhle." The others, 384–467, come from the Turfan area: 384–393 from near Murtuq, 394–428 from Sängim, and 429–467 from Xočo.

Unfortunately, the editors of *Sprachreste I* (A texts) did not inform us about the appearance of the writing in any great detail, as they did in the instance of the B texts in *Sprachreste B*, and in the *Tafeln* part of *Sprachreste I* they chose for photography only the better preserved fragments, and of the 103 thus chosen all but seven are from Šorčuq. Of these seven, three are from Sängim and four from Murtuq.

However, the editors do make a few pertinent remarks. For example,

[35] Above, note 34.

as regards the bilingual nos. 384–386 from Murtuq, they say "Die Schrift ist ungelenk und ihr Duktus scheint einer späteren Zeit anzugehören," and "das Tocharische weist häufige Unregelmässigkeiten in der Ortographie auf." (*Sprachreste I.* 212). These pieces are fortunately among those reproduced in the *Tafeln* (pp. 60, 61, 62). Instances of misspellings are clearly *mälskes* for *pälskes* (384b1), where the preceding word is *cam* and the following *āśāwesuneyä* for *āśāwesuneyo* (? 384b1–2); *kuyolte* for *kuyalte* (384b2); *pälkāluneyā* for *pälskāluneyäṣ* (385b3); and many others of similar sort. The Sanskrit words are also quite often corrupt. This situation leads me to suggest that it is a copy of a more original manuscript by a person not adept either in using the "standard" ductus nor in the dialect he was writing. That he was not an Indian seems clear from the type of error he makes in the Sanskrit. That he was more familiar with dialect B would seem to be deduced from his use of the word *tsārwo* 'joy'. This word occurs twice here, and here only in A texts. It is clearly borrowed from B.[36]

This would seem to be true also in the case of two manuscripts from Šorčuq, nos. 219–238, and 239–242, both containing fragments of the *Maitreyāvadānavyākaraṅa.* Here we find such orthographical peculiarities as the frequent use of ṣ̱a for the more usual *śä* of A texts (cf. the editors' note 107), and also the very common writing of *ī* and *ū* for *i* and *u* where A normally prefers to write the latter, e.g., *käṣṣī* 221 b 3, 7 and often; *kākmūräṣ* 220 b 5, *lyalypūräṣ* 221 a 3, 6, *kārmetsūnentu* 221 b 4, etc. Most significant of all, however, are the spellings *lāñc* (222 a 2) for *lāñś* 'kings' and *krañc* (230 b 5 and 242 a 4) for *krañś* pl. m. of *kāsu* 'good'. These are to be compared at once with B *lāñc* and *kreñc* which are the regular forms. So far as I know these spellings occur only here.[37]

In this connection it seems possible to me that the variant spellings in B *lāś* (111 a 5 = TII. S 51.10) for *lāñc*, *kreś* (107 b 3 = TII. S 54) for *kreñc*, and other instances of the spelling *-ś* for *-ñc* or *-c*, for which I do not have exact reference, if they occur only in manuscripts of eastern (Karashar-Turfan) origin, are owing to the influence of A. Against this interpretation is, of course, the spelling of *epyac* as *epyaś* (330 b 5), where the corresponding form in dialect A also has *c* : *opyac*.

That dialect A was not a spoken language in the Turfan area seems to be deduced also from the use of extensive glossing of some B texts from the east by Tụrkish words, cf. for example *Sprachreste B* 2, nos.

[36] Cf. Winter, *JAOS* 81.274 (1961).

[37] Cf. SSS 100, 145. Winter suggests (privately) that the analogy of the obl. pl. *läñcas*, *krañcas* would easily lead to the reformation of these nom. pls., and would likewise (with P. Poucha, *Thesaurus Linguae Tocharicae Dialecti A* 62 [Prague, 1955]) complete *kra[ñc]ᵃ* at 342b4.

324 (= TIII. M 169.14), 325 (= TIII. M 146.3), 328 (= TII. S 52.3), 329 (= TII. S 38.1), and especially 330 (= TII. S 48.1) and 331 (= TII. S 57.1). So far as I know there is no extensive glossing of A texts in Turkish (cf. the A text no. 394 with nineteen B glosses and two in Uigur mentioned above), nor is there any glossing of B texts by A words. Again this supports my suspicion that, as a vernacular language of the area, A had been long since replaced by the language (or languages) of its invaders. The convert to the new Buddhist missionary effort from the west spoke in this instance Turkish, not Tocharian.

To sum up: An examination of the languages themselves, their phonology, their morphology, indicates that the two Tocharian dialects A and B have gone through a long period of independent development; how long is of course guesswork, but it might be anywhere from five hundred to a thousand years, certainly not less than five hundred. They are, in my estimation, no longer mutually intelligible.

The vocabularies, too, diverge to a certain extent, especially in Buddhist technical terms. Dialect A seems to preserve an older stratum which shows decided Iranian influence alongside a newer one of more immediate Indian origin. The Buddhist vocabulary of dialect B, on the other hand, shows less Old Iranian influence and more Indian and later Iranian.

With regard to the reciprocal influence between the two dialects in matters of vocabulary, B has been the giver, A the receiver. In matters of orthography the reverse seems true. The orthography of the B MSS is more regular at Šorčuq (near Karashar), where the influence of dialect A could be felt most strongly.[38] Indeed, farther to the east, at Sangim at least, the writers of MSS in dialect B have even gone so far as to borrow some very definite spellings from A, namely *-ś* for *-c* and *-ñc* (cf. above). Such forms as *lāś* or *kreś* are not to be considered borrowings. The instances where A texts show B orthographical characteristics (e.g., *śa* for usual *śä* and fluctuating spelling *ī/i* and *ū/u*, cf. above) are to be explained as because of the copying of an A text by a person more used to writing B than A.

Where both dialects appear in the same texts, the material in B seems clearly to be the intruder. The language of instruction, insofar as we have evidence, was clearly B. B texts are glossed by the vernacular of the region, Turkish, not Tocharian A.

So far only oblique reference has been made to the problem of the name "Tocharian." To me it is not a matter of great importance, though I

[38] Cf. Krause, *Hdb. der Orientalistik 4.3. Tocharisch* 7 (bottom); Winter, *JAOS* 75.225; both, of course, without the deduction of any orthographical influence of A on B as proposed here.

have never been convinced that the speakers of either dialect could be identified in any way with the Tocharians of classical antiquity. Most of the discussions of this isue, pro or con, have, it seems to me, argued *de parti déjà pris.* I am inclined to agree with W. B. Henning when he says: "The tendency to confuse different names with little or no regard to time and space is as prominent in recent contributions to the 'Tokharian' problem as it was in the earlier ones . . . ."[39]

The facts about the two dialects, both as regards their form and their use, and the deductions I have made from these facts, in no way support the thesis that either dialect is related to, much less a descendant of, the language of the historical Tocharians. Indeed, everything argues against it, especially against the view that dialect A represents a later migration from Tocharistan back to the area where the documents are found.[40]

Rather it had been at one time the native language of the region of Turfan, if not also of Karashar, but was no longer at the period of documentation. The vernacular was another language or other languages, one of which was Turkish. Dialect A is preserved merely in a fixed written form as the language of a conservative Buddhistic culture. But even as such its use was giving way in the monasteries to that of the vigorous missions from the west who not only wrote but spoke in dialect B.[41]

(Participants in the discussion following the conference presentation of the first version of this paper: Marku, Welmers, Collinder, Winter, Emeneau, Birnbaum.)

---

[39] *Asia Major, N. S.* 1.159 (1949–1950).

[40] So Sieg and Siegling, *Sprachreste I A*, introd. v, and supported by Pelliot in "Tokharien et koutchéen," *Journal asiatique* 224.62 ff. (1934). However, the view was later abandoned by Sieg in "Und dennoch 'Tocharisch'," *SBBAW, Phil.-hist. Kl.* No. XVII (1937), where he returned to the view that "Tocharian" A was the native language of the eastern region in particular of the realm Agni (= Chinese Yen-k'i), i.e., Karashar. To my knowledge Sieg never abandoned the opinion that Tocharian was the correct name for both dialects, and that the speakers were to be identified with the "Tokharoi."

[41] The article by Winter, "Tocharians and Turks," *UAS* 23.239–251 (1963), appeared too late for any careful evaluation for the purposes of this paper.

Dialectal Aspects of the Anatolian Branch of Indo-European

Jaan Puhvel

UNIVERSITY OF CALIFORNIA, LOS ANGELES

Anatolian dialect problems are both many faceted and multidimensional. The very position of the Anatolian group in relation to the rest of Indo-European has been at the heart of a singular controversy. The "Indo-Hittite" smokescreen had barely been dissipated in the early 1950's, and its ghost symbolically laid to rest with the passing of its protagonist, when the stage was set in earnest for a meaningful and cogent penetration of inner-Anatolian dialect problems. It is the latter that will occupy the bulk of this paper.

First, however, some disposal of the remains of "Indo-Hittite" must be undertaken and brief obsequies conducted. Despite Whatmough's laconic affirmation of implicit death and burial in connection with our Texas Conference four years ago (*Trends in European and American Linguistics 1930–1960* 81 [Utrecht, 1961]), its phantom still stalks the brains of linguists. Our assembly hardly needs further reassurances, but outside the Indo-Europeanist circle the "Indo-Hittite" issue threatens to become a revenant in the manner of the unlamented and unburied Odyssean wraith of Elpenor. Therefore, *μή τοί τι θεῶν μήνιμα γένηται*, it must be once more summoned up and exorcized. As linguistic tyros all over this country leaf through the glossary section of one of their principal introductory handbooks, called *A Course in Modern Linguistics*, Middle Irish, Modern English, Lower Sorbian, Albanian, and Marathi alike are cross-indexed by "Indo-Hittite," and the harm has to be undone post facto in at least the minds of those few who subsequently enroll for a dose of Indo-European proper, rather than acquiescing in the incidental fact that Hockett once absorbed a modicum of Sturtevant's teaching. A recent reviewer in *Lg.* (39.86 [1963]) disagrees with the expert conviction that the "Indo-Hittite" hypothesis has been proved untenable; even among those with classical training the Sturtevantian hangover has not worn off. The fortune that "Indo-Hittite" made in a whole generation of linguists is of the kind one might call "only in America." It was compounded of characteristically anomalous ingredients. On the one hand it represented a belated wave of

Stammbaumtheorie hitting our shores generations after Schleicher, much as in painting the Jackson Pollocks of the 1950's follow the Armory Show by almost half a century. On the other hand it reflected a rakish predilection for advanced styling: "Indo-Hittite" was essentially an Indo-European convertible with tail fins. It started curiously from a hunch by Emil Forrer, an idea man and facile purveyor of startling conjectures, whose most famous Hittitological sand castles crumbled rapidly at F. Sommer's hands. Forrer moved to San Salvador, not to be heard of again, but one of his more obscure suggestions was to have an important future in America. Why the "Indo-Hittite" idea never took root in Europe is a question well worth pondering by its remaining adherents. Indo-Europeanists proper may on the contrary well dispense with the obvious, ignore hollow echoes, and after this brief requiem pass along to more substantive issues.

As Anatolian philology has kept maturing, Hittite no longer stands alone or almost alone in the field of linguistic vision. Luwian has been well edited and worked over by H. Otten, B. Rosenkranz, and E. Laroche, and Palaic by A. Kammenhuber. The hieroglyphs of Hittite culture are virtually deciphered, and their language is usable with considerable confidence. Lycian and Lydian joined the ranks of Anatolian dialects in the 1930's and 1940's thanks to P. Meriggi and H. Pedersen, and have come into their own in the 1950's through the efforts of Laroche, Houwink Ten Cate, A. Heubeck, G. Neumann, R. Gusmani, O. Carruba, and others. Laroche's Luwian dictionary stands beside J. Friedrich's *Hethitisches Wörterbuch*, his work *Les hiéroglyphes hittites* promises a large measure of analogous codification, and a *Lykisches Glossar* and *Lydisches Wörterbuch* by Neumann and Gusmani respectively have been announced. In short, European scholarship will soon have created the full array of philological tools for a comparative grammar and etymological dictionary of the Anatolian languages, as far as the material allows. Its scope is liable to reveal both complexities and limitations: spatial dimensions from Paphlagonia to Syria, from the Antitaurus to the Ionian coast, a time-stretch of well over a millennium, and a grammatological range covering disparate logosyllabic cuneiform and hieroglyphs as well as alphabetic writing.

The following treatment is geared to the postulate of an Anatolian subdivision of Indo-European and to the peculiarities of Anatolia as a self-contained dialect area, with overall characteristics involving preservation as well as innovation, and with the latter implying both overall shifts and new subdivisions in the Anatolian habitat. This tenet does not signify adherence to a concept of rigid uniformity; if some detail of Luwian or Palaic is unattested in Hittite but alluringly paralleled elsewhere in Indo-European, it is quite legitimate to go over the head of Hittite, so to speak, without assuming that every item was strained through a monolithic Proto-Anatolian and hence lost in Hittite. Whether any individual démarche of this kind is otherwise necessary or plausible is a different matter. The comparison of the Luwian and Hieroglyphic passive *-ma/i-* participle (*kisamma-* 'combed' : OCS *nesomŭ* 'carried') is quite convincing (while we may never know whether or when Hittite lost *-ma-*). On the other hand, the Hittite abstract suffix *-asti-* is shared by Slavic and Germanic (*dalugasti-* : OCS *dlŭgostĭ* : OHG *angust*); since we happen to be aware of a radical paucity of inherited abstract noun suffixes in Luwian, there is little doubt about its loss in this branch of Anatolian. Watkins has recently (*IJSLP* 4.7–12 [1961]) built a very ingenious hypothesis of Indo-European denominative allomorphism on the brittle back of the Palaic hapax *malitanna-* : just as IE *-*to-* is used in ordinal numbers (Lat. *sextus*), in verbal adjectives (Lat. *rectus*), and denominatively (Lat. *honestus*), so the suffix *-*e/ono-* is claimed for Hittite ordinals (*-anna-*), Germanic and Slavic participles (Goth. *baírans*, OCS *nesenŭ*), and the denominative Palaic adjective *malitanna-* 'honied'. It is hard to see why Neumann (*Die Sprache* 7.74 [1961]) takes the stem to be *malitannu-*, because our only evidence is the dative plural in *-as*. Yet, even if we have an *-a-* stem, as is probable, the cumulative evidence of Hitt. *milittu-*, (Luwoid) *maliddu* 'sweet', the Lycian fountain *Melite* beside the Cappadocian *Melitene*, and such Anatolian women's names as *Mallidunna*, Μελιτίνη, may make one wonder about the straight supposition of an Indo-European suffix, especially since there is quite a bit of independent substratal debris in Palaic. Might we not have in *malitanna-*, *Melitene* the suffix of Gk. Πριήνη, Μυκήνη?

If we chalk up what Anatolian lacks of the common Indo-European grammatical inventory, parts of the plural paradigm of nouns, the entire dual number, the feminine gender, the aorist system, and the optative mood all come to mind. Confronted with the presence of basic noun classes, especially the *r/n* stems, the bulk of the singular cases, many basic nominal suffixes, very archaic pronominal debris, most present stems, the imperative mood, the mediopassive voice, most verbal endings, and exceedingly old-fashioned syntactic peculiarities, Proto-Anatolian rates as a very archaic Indo-European dialect indeed, despite the loose talk of its "almost modern appearance" in comparison with Old Indic and Ancient Greek. In view of the heavy substratal influences to which it was subjected it is rather surprising that its rate of grammatical disintegration was not more pronounced. In vocabulary the ratio of replacement was considerably more substantial. The seepage of indigenous elements into grammar was more insidious and gradual, yet it came to account for some of the most glaring innovations from the very beginning (absence of adjectival comparison may be one such trait, as in Armenian and Tocharian). A Hattic belt underlay Hittite proper and Palaic in north-central Anatolia, some divergent transitional idiom (which we may call Kaneshite) seems to have been submerged around the site of Kültepe, while a wide belt of pre-Luwian substratum covered large areas of the south (not to be commingled with B. Landsberger's and H. T. Bossert's problematic views concerning a third-millennium "Proto-Luwian" or *Hieroglyphenhethitisch* presence in Kizzuwatna and Arzawa). This linguistic division of the substrata is indirectly discernible in the divergent Hattic, Kaneshite, and Luwian pantheons within the hospitality of the state cults of the Hittite empire. As a trademark of the Hattic influence we might pick the suffix *-il* (Hattic *antuḫ-il* 'human') which denotes appurtenance in Hittite (*hattilis*, *luili*) and Lydian (*kaveś bakillis* 'priest of Bacchus') and is also extended to paradigmatic usage (Hittite pronominal genitive in *-el*, Lydian oblique case in -λ). Comparisons with Latin formations like *tālis*, *erīlis* continue to be made (e.g., Heubeck, *Lydiaka* 69) but have exceedingly little in their favor. Around Kanesh the suffix *-uman* (*-umna-*, *-uma-*) proliferated ever since the Old Assyrian tablets and gained some measure of entry into Hittite (*luiumna-* 'Luwian', *palaumna-* 'Palaic', *kanesumna-* 'Kaneshite', *kuenzumna-* 'cuias', *Suppiluliuma-* 'Von Lauterbrunnen'). The southern relative of this suffix seems to be the ethnic suffix Luwian *-wanni-* (*Ninuwa-wanni-*), Hieroglyphic *-wana-* (*Adana-wana-*), and Lycian *-ãñna-* (*tlãñna-*). Also in the south, an adjectival suffix *-ass(i)-* supplanted the normal genitive singular and came to provide a grammatical substitute. This suffix is present in Cilicia (*Dattassa-*, city of the Luwian storm god Dattas; *Parnassa-*, 'place of the house [*parna-*]'), in Caria, and in Greece (also sometimes in Hittite: *witassa-* 'yearly'), and its wide spread is matched by its productive use in both Luwian and Lycian. Thus Lyc. *ẽni ma:hanahi* covers a Luwian *annis massanassis* 'mother of the god' as a name of Leto, mother of Lycian Apollo (confirming a brilliant hunch of Sturtevant's back in 1928), whereas the adjective 'divine' is Luwian *massanalli-* (cf. Hitt. *attala-* 'fatherly').

Such facts bring us to the paramount achievement of Anatolian dialectology in recent years: the realization, propounded by Laroche in a famous review in 1954 (*Bibl. Or.* 11.121–124) and subsequently worked out in *BSL* 53.159–197 (1957–1958), 55.155–185 (1960), that "Hieroglyphic Hittite" is in reality a dialectal form of Luwian ("East" or "Late" Luwian) and Lycian is its latter-day West Luwian descendant. This insight, anticipated by the increasingly cogent decipherment of the hieroglyphs on the one hand, and the earlier Lycian studies of Pedersen and Tritsch on the other, is a major land-winning and marks a new stage in the maturation of Anatolian dialectology. Its results are already incorporated into Laroche's Luwian dictionary and Ten Cate's dissertation *The Luwian Population Groups* (1961), especially the chapter "Lycian as a Luwian Language" (pp. 51–86). Thus the frame of Anatolian subdivisions now appears in a new light. While in the north Hittite holds the field as a vast and static corpus of rather uniform character, with Palaic as a backwoods country cousin of limited consequence, and Lydian still resisting closer characterization hundreds of miles farther west and a millennium down in time, southern Anatolia suddenly presents an image of viable continuity, in spite of three radically diverging graphic media and many centuries of change. If Hittite itself appears monolithic by comparison, it is owing partly to the single archival source; let us recall also that Rosenkranz suggested as early as 1938 that toward the end of the Hittite imperial period it may have been on the road to becoming a scribal petrifact, and that Luwian was spreading as a vernacular of the empire. His view has been widely rejected but may contain some grain of truth. It would chime with the general evidence for widespread southern influences and the Cilician (if not outright Hurroid) affinities of the ruling dynasty. The existence of texts in localized Luwoid vernacular (e.g., the Istanuwa rituals) and of gloss words and grammatical Luwianisms in Hittite itself points in the same direction.

The sequel will explore some features of this new linguistic image of ancient Anatolia and attempt to present a summary confrontation of the relevant material. There are now significant controls for the rate of change and criteria for cogent attribution. For example, the medio-passive has disappeared from Lycian and Lydian, which is a parallel and expectable development in terms of chronology. On the other hand, Lydian has no trace of the productive *-ass(i)-* formation, which clearly disconnects it from the southern dialects. It is in general true that the Luwian type of Anatolian is in most respects less archaic than the Hittite.

In phonology the main dialectal criterium is the treatment of Proto-Anatolian *e*. In Hittite it moved toward closure (partial fusion with *i*), while in Luwian proper, Hieroglyphic, and (surprisingly and to a lesser extent) in the isolated and separately Hattic-influenced Palaic it tended to appear as *a*:

Hitt. *esdu*, Pal. *asdu*, Luw. *asdu*, Hier. *asdu* 'let him be'
Hitt. *wes-*, Luw. *was-* 'clothe'
Hitt. *iya-*, Luw. *aya-*, Hier. *aia-* 'make'

Hitt. *melit-*, Pal. *malit-*, Luw. *mallit-* 'honey'
Hitt. *meu-*, Luw. *mauwa-* 'four'
Hitt. *ed-*, Luw. *ad-* 'eat'
Hitt. *eku-*, Pal. *aḫu-*, Luw. *akuwa-* 'drink'
Hitt. *idalu-*, Luw. *adduwal(i)-*, Hier. *aduwata-* 'bad, evil'.

Most other phonological divergences (e.g., Hitt. *kimmara-* : Luw. *immara-* 'countryside'; Hitt. *kessera-* : Luw. *issari-*, Lyc. *izre-* 'hand') are in the nature of freaks (possibly ancient, like Gk. *καπρός* : Lat. *aper*) or reflect articulatory instabilities (*k* > *ḫ* in, e.g., Luw. *naḫḫuwa-*, *mannaḫuwan-*, Pal. *aḫu-* beside Hitt. *nakkes-*, *maninkuwant-*, *eku-*; Luw. *ḫisḫiyanti* beside Hitt. *isḫiyanzi*); but the merger of *e* and *a* in Southern Anatolian had serious morphophonemic implications: paradigmatic oppositions of the type Hitt. *es-/as-*, *ed-/ad-* were obliterated, and this may have triggered the overall breakdown of functional ablaut. Thus we have pinpointed a major leveling within the Luwian group, which contrasts sharply with archaic ablaut patterns such as Hitt. *kuenzi* : *kunanzi*, *ais* : gen. *issas*, *kir* : dat.-loc. *kardi* (and by extension in non-IE words like *pir* : gen. *parnas*, where Luw. and Hier. have generalized *parna-* and Lycian *prñnawa-* but Lydian *bira-* 'house'). Later in Lycian the uniformity of vocalism prevails, but the predominant timbre is *e* not only for Luwian *a* (*esu* 'let him be') but also for Hittite *a* (*erm̃me-*, Ερμα, Αρμα- for Hitt., Luw. *Arma-* 'Moon', Hier. MOON-*ma*; Ερευα- for Hitt. *arawa-* 'free'). Pedersen's view (*Lyk. u. Hitt.* 54 [1945]) that these appearances vouchsafe unique phonological conservatism for Lycian has now been easily proven untenable; after Laroche's demonstration (*Hommages à Georges Dumézil* 124–128 [1960]) that *arawa-* is connected with *ara/i-* 'communally acceptable' (*natta ara* 'nefas') and ^{LÚ}*ara-* 'kinsman, friend' (Skt. *arí-*, *aryá-*) there is no recourse but to assume a further change of vocalism during the many centuries after Luwian days. Lydian must as usual be approached with special caution; should Vetter's recent hunch (*Zu den lydischen Inschriften* 39 [1959]) be right that Lyd. *ist* means 'is', one would invoke Hitt. *eszi* and infer aloofness from the southern developments and their Palaic parallel; words like *bira-* point in the same direction.

Hittite itself has innovated in the affrication of the voiceless dental before *i* and *ē* (> *i*) (*-ti*, *-nti* > *-zi*, *-nzi*, **-tēl* > *-zil*), in contrast to the rest of Anatolian (Luw. *anniti* vs. Hitt. *aniyazi*, Pal. *atanti* vs. Hitt. *adanzi*, Hier. *aiati*, Lyc. *edi* vs. Hitt. *iyazi*; Palaic *sunnuttil(a)* vs. Hitt. *sarnikzil*). It has also assibilated *d* before *i* in *siwatt-* 'day' (vs. Luw. *Tiwat-*, Pal. *Tiyat-* 'sun god'), *siu(ni)-* 'god' (Lyd. ↑*ivs*) and *siunalis* 'divine' (Lyd. ↑*ivvalis*). Yet these are trivial phonetic matters around Hattusas and hardly deserve the publicity that Sturtevant and others accorded them in setting up the Anatolian family tree. Other trivialities concern the Luwian toleration of *-tn-* (*ḫaratna-*, vs. Hitt. *-nnas* < **-tnas*). But Laroche's adduction of *Kizzuwatna* as Luwian (*Dict. . . . louvite*, 132) is probably erroneous, if we accept Neumann's hypostatic explanation as **kez wetenas* 'cisaquinus' (*Die Sprache* 4.111–114 [1958]); it may well show Luwian phonetic overlay in the *a*, but Hittite itself tolerated *dn* very well (witness *udne*).

A salient feature of word formation is the high archaism of heteroclisis in Hittite and its disappearance (or nonattestation) in the rest of Anatolian. Kammenhuber's statement (p. 23) in her article "Zur hethitisch-luvischen Sprachgruppe" (*KZ* 76.1–26 [1959]) that Hittite had multiplied abstract nouns in *-atar* and *-essar* on the basis of scant Indo-European antecedents cannot be upheld. The infinitives of Vedic (*-tari*), Old Persian (*-tanaiy*), and Greek (*-ε[σ]εν*) provide petrified testimony of Indo-European prominence. In Luwian, thematization is one way of elimination (*ḫappisa-* with loss of *-r*, vs. Hitt. *ḫappessar* 'limb'; *ḫaratna-* vs. Hitt. *ḫaratar* 'offense'); sometimes the heteroclitic variant is lost in favor of another (*wid*[*a*]- 'water', cf. Hitt. *wid-* beside *watar*). Elsewhere, *seul le silence est grand.* The one great dialectal idiosyncrasy in the south is the immense proliferation of *-i-* stems: Luw. *anni-*, Lyc. *ẽni-* vs. Hitt. *anna-* 'mother'; Luw., Hier. *tati-*, Lyc. *tedi-* vs. Hitt. *atta-* 'father'; Luw. *nani-*, Lyc. *nẽni-* vs. Hitt. *nana-* 'brother'; Luw. *issari-*, Lyc. *izre-* vs. Hitt. *kessera-* 'hand'; Luw. *wassanti-* vs. Hitt. *wassant-* 'dressed'. To single nouns should be added the Luwian suffixes *-assi-* (adjectives of appurtenance), *-alli-* (adjectives of quality), *-talli-* (agent nouns), and the rampaging abstract suffix *-ḫi-* which has moved into the void created by the loss of Anatolian heteroclitic abstracts in *-tar* (*adduwalaḫi-* vs. Hitt. *idalawatar*, Hier. KING-*ḫi-* 'kingdom') and is gravely suspect as Hurrian in origin. In Lycian also the *-i-* stems outnumber the *-a-* stems, and detailed concordances with Luwian include the acc. sg. *-ijẽ* beside *-i*, just as in Luwian we have *tatiyan* beside *ḫarmaḫin*. Hittite, Palaic (and Lydian to all appearances) have a proper preponderance of thematic nouns, whereas *-i-* stem adjectives are prevalent in Anatolian at large, just as in Italic. Thematic nouns are otherwise by no means rare in Southern Anatolian (e.g., Luw., Hier. *pata-*, Lyc. *pede-* 'foot' beside Hitt. *pata-*; Hier. *ḫuḫa-*, Lyc. *χuga-* 'grandfather' beside Hitt. *ḫuḫḫa-*), and other stem classes (Luw. *wasu-*, *mallit-*, etc.) have been preserved, including ancient Indo-European *-i-* stems such as Luw. *ḫawi-* 'sheep' (Lat. *ouis*). However, nominal derivation is a pale shadow of its Hittite (and presumably Proto-Anatolian) self. One suffix shared in diverging shapes by Hittite, Luwian, and Hieroglyphic Luwian is the feminine formant seen in Hitt.

isḫassara- 'mistress', *suppessara-* 'virgin', Hier. *ḫasusara-* 'queen', Luw. *nanasri-* 'sister' (*nani-* 'brother'), which seems to be Anatolian in origin (Indo-Europeanized versions of the *-sar* found in the Cappadocian tablets). If it were Indo-European, possible connections might be sought with the abstract suffix Hitt. *-sar/-snas* and the thematized *-sno-/-sro-* in Lat. *trīnī*, ON *trenner* (**trisno-*) vs. Skt. *tisráh*, OIr. *teoir*; with reference to Pisani's theory about gender opposition inherent in *n* : *r* (*ukṣáṇ-* : *uxor*), one might think of *-sro-* as the Anatolian prototype of *-s(a)ra/i-*.

In noun declension the Proto-Anatolian singular case system (as seen in Hittite) was curtailed in the south, where Luwian has a nominative and accusative (agreeing with Hittite in both genus commune and neuter), a dative-locative in *-i* or *-iya*, an ablative-instrumental in *-ati* (*adduwalati issarati* vs. Hitt. *idalawit kessarit* 'with evil hand'; Hier. abl. *-(a)ti*, Lyc. abl. *-adi*, *-edi* in *esbedi medezedi* 'with Median cavalry'; cf. Hitt. instrumental *-it*, adverbial *-ta*; or Hurrian origin?), the *-assi-* replacement of the genitive (apart from rare cases like *ḫirutas* EN-*as* 'lord of the curse' beside *ḫirutassis* EME-*is* 'tongue of the curse'), and a hapax vocative *Kamrusepa*. Lycian still has the same setup, while Lydian has little to show but a nom. sg. in *-ś*, acc. sg. in *-ν*, pronominally inspired oblique in *-λ*, nom.-acc. sg. neuter in *-d*, and the *-li-* replacement of the genitive. The separate Lydian feminine once proclaimed by Meriggi and Bossert has fared badly at the hands of Neumann, Kammenhuber, and Carruba, who explain crown witnesses like *esνaν ↑iνaν* as genitives plural instead (cf. Hitt. *siunan*). It is evident that syncretism as such is not a viable tool of diachronic dialectology, while case endings are, and confirm the previous dialect picture.

The plural paradigm is skimpy everywhere and shows curious divergences. While Hittite and Palaic agree on a good Indo-European nom. pl. *-es*, Luwian has a nom. pl. genus commune *-nzi*, acc. *-nza* (and neuter nom. acc. in *-a*, as expected). This trait is not even matched by the "East Luwian" hieroglyphs where the nom.-acc. pl. ends in *-(a)i* (*atuwarai* 'the evil ones'). The rest of the Luwian plural cases are almost agglutinative in character (dat.-loc. *-nza*, abl.-instr. *-nzati*, gen. perhaps *-nzan*). The Lycian endings (nom. pl. unknown [neuter in *-a*], acc. pl. *-as*, dat.-loc. *-a* or *-e*, gen. *-ãi*) are only partly reconcilable with Luwian (acc. *-as* < *-anzi*?), while *-a* (*-e*) and *-ãi* were connected by Pedersen (*Lyk. u. Hitt.* 15–16, 36–37) with Hitt. dat. pl. *-as* and gen. pl. *-an* respectively, and no better solution is in sight. The Hieroglyphic dat.-loc. pl. in *-ī* (*arhaī*) likewise goes its own way. It seems that the Cuneiform Luwian type *tatinzi*, *patanza* is a very localized and transitory dialect phenomenon. It is highly advisable to leave both the Indo-European

-nt- collectives and the Tocharian plurals like *okonta* 'fruits' alone and to concentrate on some secondary local origin. I believe that the East Luwian *-(a)i* shows an independent extension of pronominal declension to the plural of nouns (cf. Hitt. *ape, ke*), as in Greek and Latin (cf. the similar spread of *-d* to the nom. acc. sing. neuter of nouns in Lydian, and of -λ to the oblique singular). One may then wonder whether the origin of the Luwian forms might not be a transfer to nouns (perhaps first to the genitive plural) of the pronominal ending seen in the Old Hittite gen. pl. *sumenzan* 'uestri', while *sumel* is a later formation in Hittite.

Among dialectal features in pronouns we might point out the guttural element in Hittite *ammuk* 'me, I' (matched by Germanic and Venetic) and *zik, tuk* 'thou, thee', vs. Pal. *ti, tu,* Hier. *amu,* Lyc. *ẽmu,* Lyd. *amu.* Enclitic anaphoric forms (*-as, -an,* neut. *-at*) are present in all of Anatolian, while the reflexive *-ti* sets all three Southern idioms apart from Hitt. *za.* Luw., Hier. *apa-* 'is', Lyc. *ebe-* 'hic' match Hitt. *apa-*, while Luw. *za-*, Hier. *ī-* represent individual demonstrative stems. The paradigms of pronominal declension, outside of Hittite, agree rather thoroughly with the nouns. Mutual leveling is in evidence and supports my view of a pronominal impact on noun cases not only in Lydian and Hieroglyphic but also in Central Luwian. The relative *kuis, kui(t)* (with *-t* lost in the south) is found in Hittite, Palaic, Luwian, Lycian (*ti*), and Lydian (*+is, +id*), whereas Hieroglyphic has an *-a-* stem with uncertain consonantism. The Southern indefinite pronoun Luw. *kuisḫa,* Hier. X*-s-ḫa,* Lyc. *ti-χe* sets it apart from Hitt. *kuis-ki* 'someone' and Hitt., Pal. *kuis-a* 'everyone'.

Among verb stems, Luwian, Hieroglyphic, and Lycian *-s(s)-* contrasts with the Hittite and Palaic "iterative" *-sk-*, yielding another neat dialectal isogloss. Causatival *-nu-* is found in Luwian and Hieroglyphic as well as in Hittite. Otherwise, extra-Hittite material is meager, apart from a marked Luwian tendency to intensive reduplication (*pipissa-* from *piya-* 'give', *wiwidai-*, *aruwaruwa-*, etc.; cf. Lyc. *pibijeti* vs. *pijetẽ*).

Personal forms of the verb are rather poorly attested outside of Hittite, especially in the first and second persons plural. It appears, however, that two traits characterize the Southern verb vis-à-vis Hittite: the obfuscation of paradigmatic ablaut and the apparent absence of the *-ḫi* conjugation. The latter is present in Palaic (*mūsi* 'he eats his fill' vs. *anitti* 'he performs'), but I agree with Laroche (*Dict. . . . louvite,* p. 141) that claims for Luwian and Hieroglyphic have not been substantiated (Otten's *muwai, sāi, zati* are in obscure context and need not be 3rd sg. indicative forms). This issue is a basic one for Anatolian linguistic history. The active of the *-mi* conjugation is well present everywhere (with allomorphic 1st sg. *-wi* in Luwian, *-u* in Lycian and

Lydian), and the mediopassive is well attested for Luwian (*aiari*, *aztuwari*, *wassantari*) and present in Palaic (*kitar*) and Hieroglyphic (*aiaru*). The imperative is impeccably represented in Palaic, Luwian, Hieroglyphic, and Lycian. But the preterit diverges from Hittite and is intimately tied to the problem of the *-ḫi* conjugation in the latter. The endings are:

	Palaic	*Luwian*	*Hieroglyphic*	*Lycian*
1st sg.		*-ḫa*	*-ḫa*	*-χa*
3rd sg.	*-t*	*-ta*	*-ta*	*-tẽ*
3rd pl.	*-nta*	*-nta*	*-(n)ta*	*-ntẽ*

The Hittite preterit is mainly the present with secondary endings, apart from the third plural in *-er*. Lydian has an *l*-preterit with no Anatolian correspondences (one might invoke Old Church Slavic participles like *neslŭ* and Umbrian preterits such as *ampelust* to account for its *-l*).

The Hittite and Palaic *-ḫi* conjugation, the Common Anatolian mediopassive, and the Southern Anatolian preterit are all ultimately issued from an original Proto-Indo-European aoristic middle paradigm, with singular endings first person unmarked *-Aé* (Hitt. mediopassive *es-ḫa*), dialectally marked *-Aéy* (Ved. pres. *ā́s-e*, *duh-é*, *śáy-e*), third person unmarked *-é/ó* (Hitt. *es-a*, Ved. *aduh-a*[*t*]) or *-tó* (Hom. *lú-to*, Hitt. *ki-tta*[*ri*]), dialectally marked *-é/óy* (Ved. pres. *duh-é*, *śáy-e*) or *-tóy* (Ved. pres. *ā́s-te*, *śé-te*, Gk. *hẽs-tai*, *keĩ-tai*). In addition, there is evidence for a first person (unmarked) *-Ai* (Ved. impf. *ā́s-i*, *ádviṣ-i*), third person *-i* (Ved. "aorist passive" *ákār-i*).

The Indo-European "perfect" with its intransitive, resultative, stative meaning is basically a special development of this paradigm, with *o*-grade root vocalism and a third plural ending in *-r*. The crucial first and third person singular endings were *-Ae*(*y*) and *-e*(*y*) respectively, judging by Vedic (*cakā́ra*, *cakré*; *cakā́ra*, *cakré*), Greek (*oĩda*; *oĩde*), Gothic (*wait*; *wait*), Latin (*uīdī*), and Old Church Slavic (*vědě*). Yet nothing precludes our alternatively postulating *-Ai* and *-i* as direct ancestors of the Hittite and Palaic *-ḫi* conjugation. This set, *-ḫi*, *-i*, *-er*, was revamped in two ways under the influence of the *-mi* conjugation, yielding a present *-ḫi*, *-i* (Pal. *mūsi*), *-anzi* (Pal. *musanti*) on the one hand, and a preterit *-ḫun*, *-t*(*a*), *-er* on the other. The *-er* also appears in the *-mi* conjugation (where it may well belong in its own right, as in the Vedic 3rd pl. active impf. in *-ur*, middle in *-ra* [*duhús*, *áduhra*]); but this Hittite feature is not shared by Palaic, where the middle ending *-nta* won the day instead.

The general fate of the Proto-Anatolian middle endings *-ḫa*, *-a* or *-ta*, and *-nta* was to furnish the mediopassive, marked by suffixed increments in *r* or *t*. Hittite and Luwian agree closely, even in the allomorphs

-a or *-ta* for the third singular (Luw. *ai-a-ri*, *ḫalti-tta-ri*, like Hitt. *es-a-ri*, *ki-tta-ri*). But in Southern Anatolian generally (as sporadically in Palaic), the unmarked aoristic middle *-ḫa*, *-ta*, *-nta* has otherwise gravitated toward a general preterital function (this development has some parallels in Celtic, where medial forms tended to preempt parts of certain past tenses; cf., e.g., K. H. Schmidt, *Die Sprache* 9.14–20 [1963]). There is consequently no evidence that the Indo-European *o*-grade perfect appears in Southern Anatolia, while it clearly underlies the Hittite and Palaic *-ḫi* conjugation (albeit with special endings *-ḫi*, *-i* < *-Ai*, *-i*, rather than original **-ḫa*, *-e* < *-Ae*, *-e*, changed to *-ḫi*, *-i* by analogic replacement or phonetic development [*i* < *e*]).

Of nonfinite forms, the Palaic, Luwian, and Hieroglyphic infinitive in *-una* (Luw. *aduna* 'eat', Pal. *aḫuna* 'drink', Hier. FOOT-*auna* 'walk'), and the Lycian in *-ãne* differ from Hitt. *-wanzi*, *-anna*, but their origin from the same kind of heteroclitic action nouns in *-war* or *-tar* is evident. The *-ant-* participle is found in Hittite, Palaic, and Luwian, while the south has a passive participle in *-ma/i-* (Luw. *titaimmi-* 'suckled', Lyc. *tideimi* 'son', Hier. *asīma-* 'beloved'), which is paralleled in Balto-Slavic and constitutes a remarkable instance of archaic independent survival in the South.

Space forbids a dialectological appreciation of the system of sentence particles. Hittite, the South, and Lydian alike share this noteworthy trait of Anatolian; while all show similarities of rigid structuring, the substantive material accordances in the South again compel attention.

A meaningful survey of lexical isoglosses in the Anatolian dialects is frustrated by the very uneven inventories. The rich Hittite material (which could, besides, be quite a bit richer still) is matched by some 900 entries in Laroche's Luwian dictionary, while for Palaic Kammenhuber has counted some 190 words. I do not have figures for Hieroglyphic, Lycian, and Lydian. Many stems are as yet quite impenetrable in meaning (to say nothing of etymology), and their semantic range is limited by the specificity of attested contexts. Especially Lydian lexicography is still quite desperate, and the Luwian texts are marred by the probabilities of borrowing from Hittite into Luwian.

Early in this presentation I touched on the demise of the "Indo-Hittite" hypothesis. Let us in conclusion consider briefly what alternative views prevail of late in regard to the relation of Anatolian to the rest of Indo-European.

The enlarged integration of Anatolian material is patent in the confrontation of the treatment by Porzig, whose chapter in *Die Gliederung des indogermanischen Sprachgebiets* (Heidelberg, 1954; pp. 187–192) is titled "Die Stellung des Hethitischen," with the more recent paper by

Kammenhuber, "Zur Stellung des Hethitisch-Luvischen innerhalb der indogermanischen Gemeinsprache" (*KZ* 77.31–75 [1961]). But the methods are basically the same: a confrontation of selected data, largely lexical isoglosses, combining Hittite (or Anatolian) on the one hand and other Indo-European subgroups (or combinations of subgroups) on the other. Porzig ends up holding hesitantly a motley bag of concordances which leads him to say that "ausschliessliche Übereinstimmungen ... zu den westlichen Sprachen [sind] nicht zu verzeichnen." Kammenhuber's *Blütenlese* yields a more multihued nosegay of isoglosses and the following conclusion: "Die bisherige Untersuchung hat doch wohl recht deutlich gezeigt, dass sich vieles im Idg. einfacher verstehen lässt, wenn man das Heth.-Luv. innerhalb der idg. Gemeinsprache in die Nähe der westlichen Sprachen Kelt., Germ., Illyr., Venet., Latino-Falisk., Osko-Umbr. und—Toch. lokalisiert" (p. 69). Both Porzig and Kammenhuber are well aware that there is no innovatory centum area, but merely a satem shift as a circumscribed isogloss; at the same time Gelb's and Bonfante's onetime idea of a centum : satem split through the middle of Anatolian, which still took up Kronasser's time in 1957 (*Arch. Or.* 25.513–518) and reflected a neolinguistic confusion of "satem" with "possible secondary palatalization," has been mercifully consigned to limbo. But the notion of an east-west dichotomy persists, and in the attribution of Anatolian Porzig and Kammenhuber arrive at radically diverging results. The argument is of necessity splintered into details and works via cumulative force; hence there is little point in bringing up single issues in a brief overall evaluation. If one compounds the word-geographical approach with that other dialectal division advocated by Kuryłowicz and some of his disciples, viz. a radical split into "southern" and other Indo-European, a complicated gyrocompass will soon have to become standard equipment for Indo-European dialect geographers. A separate congress might well be devoted to exactly these issues, called something like "The interrelations of ancient Indo-European subgroups." The present conference, which has the purpose of separating and shifting the individual groups in their oldest attested states, is the logical base on which further exploration might be founded. The topics treated here are mostly intentionally centrifugal—designed to delimit the divisions and gauge their self-contained inner equilibria, a matter of slicing rather than combining. The next step will be a centripetal effort of synthesis in terms of Common Indo-European, *Gemeinsprache* as well as *Grundsprache*, testing the tools of dialect geography, glottochronology, and historical reconstruction at large. Here only cursory attention to such issues has been possible, and even this spadework shows a deplorable lacuna in regard to Iranian; this omission is due to the inability of Professor W. B. Henning to be present at this conference. I would thus propose that the next conference pick up from where we leave off, and that no full olympiad should lapse before we meet again.

(Participants in the discussion following the conference presentation of the first version of this paper: Watkins, Polomé, Hoenigswald, Cowgill, Winter, Senn, Hamp, Lehmann.)

www.ingramcontent.com/pod-product-compliance
Lightning Source LLC
Chambersburg PA
CBHW021701230426
43668CB00008B/692
* 9 7 8 0 5 2 0 3 0 7 5 8 2 *